D1756349

Escape The Wealth Illusion

A Guide to Financial Liberation

L.T. Noelle

Dedication

T, I hope this book serves you well. Of all the outcomes discussed herein, you'll always be my most important. I'm proud of you my favourite little monkey.

.:------:.

L, no man has ever earned a return on investment that could rival 30 minutes waiting in the rain. It remains the single most important decision I've ever made.

Contents

ACCOMPANYING FINANCIAL PLAN TEMPLATE

A Financial Plan template in Excel format is hosted on my website:

- https://wosscapital.com/escape-the-wealth-illusion-book-financial-plan-template/
- Password: illu5ion

As we progress you'll be able to use this template to build your personal financial plan, ready to manage and execute.

FINANCIAL PLAN ACTIONS

The financial plan template contains an "A. Actions" worksheet. I'll refer to specific actions at the end of some chapters. You can use the knowledge discussed while it's fresh in memory to build this section of your financial plan. It's up to you whether you utilise the template or suggested actions, none of which should be considered financial or investment advice.

FINANCIAL ADVICE DISCLAIMER

The information provided in this book is intended for general informational and educational purposes only and does not constitute financial advice. While every effort has been made to ensure accuracy and completeness of information presented the author makes no representations or warranties of any kind, express or implied, about the completeness, accuracy, reliability, suitability or availability with regards content contained herein.

Readers should consult with qualified financial professionals where they deem appropriate before making any financial decisions. The author and publisher disclaim in perpetuity any liability for loss or risk, personal or otherwise, which may be incurred as a consequence, directly or indirectly, of the use and application of any of the contents of this book.

Financial markets are subject to volatility and risk. The value of investments can go down as well as up and past performance is not a guarantee of future results. Readers should conduct their own due diligence before implementing strategies discussed in this book and apply strong risk management to any action taken. Where required consult financial professionals and remember all actions taken and risks assumed are your own. Progressing beyond this point is deemed acceptance of personal liability on the part of the reader for any and all future financial actions taken.

Preface

MY WIFE IS A REMARKABLE woman. For starters, she's put up with me for more than twenty six years which I imagine isn't easy! She knows me better than anyone, so when she highlighted my abnormal financial practice during a financial affairs discussion it gave me pause: "you're not normal, other people don't think like you about money". What the hell does that mean?!?

In fairness, I've always known my approach to finance was in the minority. As a kid I never spent birthday or chore money, it went in a repurposed coffee jar under my bed. As an adult I never took credit cards or overdrafts despite constant societal encouragement to do so. When I need something my focus has always been on procuring the required standard for the lowest possible cost, never on income versus expenditure "affordability".

I certainly do miserly Scottish stereotypes considerable justice. Scrooge McDuck from Duck Tales, a Scottish stereotype himself, was a childhood favourite of mine! I didn't want to emulate diving into his pool of gold coins or anything quite so decadent (and likely painful!) but from a young age I had his natural proclivity for long-term accumulation over short-term consumption. This wasn't because my family had money or because I'm greedy where money's concerned, rather because I don't like to spend any I don't need to or worse, don't actually have. I avoided the symbiotic relationship with debt and consumption society often considers the route to wealth and happiness, an illusion I think is harmful. For me, money buys time, a more precious commodity than any other. Debt and consumption, in contrast, sell our time.

I'm an older Millennial who grew up with one younger sibling and two hard working parents, financially lower middle class from a rural coal mining community. Some around us had it worse but some had it better too. Our parents supported everything we did while always pushing for more, from sport to education and anything in between. We lived in a local authority consistently ranked amongst the most deprived nationally with outcome statistics set heavily against us and I think that's why our parents pushed so hard. We really couldn't have asked for a better family unit though and I consider my childhood a really happy one. We're still very close, though my mother passed a few years ago. I wish she'd been alive to see this book, I think it would've made her (as well as my father) happy. I don't believe in luck generally, so when I confess myself fortunate in the parent (and sibling) department it signifies how seriously I take the statement.

Over time my financial approach evolved from under bed coffee jars to low interest savings in a Cash ISA. Limited returns, reading multiple finance books and entering the world of finance professionally all supported my first foray into the stock market and first proper financial plan in my 20's. This new world meant lots of learning but ultimately led to the repayment of the mortgage on our family home and a debt free existence from 36. Not everyone agrees with my approach to debt, particularly the mortgage, but it's a decision I never regret. My financial decisions are built on data and mathematics, not public opinion or societal pressure.

The mental freedom alone in removing all future risk of shelter for your family is liberating. Realising you'll never have a home exist at the whim of employers (required to pay for it) is a metaphorical weight lifted off your shoulders you can literally feel.

I want to share in this book how I achieved these outcomes and help you build your personal financial plan so you might do the same. I want to explain why I think socially normalised views of wealth and happiness sold to us as achievable only through consumption and debt are illusions designed to quietly extract maximum resource from an honest but unwittingly captured populace. This Wealth Illusion, the premise for the book title, is the "normal" to my "abnormal", the construct for which I've opted out and the major reason for my wife's assertion. I think most people just want to be happy but large swathes of society have been convinced happiness looks a certain way, a carefully engineered perception measured by how much we consume. A bigger house, a newer car, a faster phone and all the other trappings of a "normal" life, fuelled increasingly by harmful debt. I contend this is actually a prison for the masses who give away their time, money and energy as part of a systematic transfer of wealth.

I know this view is unpopular as no-one likes to think they're being taken advantage of. I'll explain at length then my views on these normalised financial practices and present data I think supports the view we're essentially human cattle, to put it crudely. We're conditioned into a construct that leaves many people deeply unhappy at their outcomes, chasing an aspirational vision of "well-off" presented just within reach if we're willing to over stretch. A vision linking possessions and the constant desire for more with the happiness we crave, that promotes debt as the way to chase this vision and convinces us it's how life works.

A minority consciously challenge this illusion and find our happiness in the freedom we find outside of it. We don't feel the societal pressure to consume or to look well-off, we don't feel trapped by a debt burden and we're not imprisoned by the job we need to service the debt used to chase the lifestyle.

I want to challenge readers to think about this construct of "normal", to keep an open mind on my Consumer, Debtor, Employee triad and to question the societal norms most consider "life". None of this is criticism, most people just want to be happy and are convinced this is the way to achieve it. I simply want to provide a different perspective, one you've maybe not considered, offer an alternate vision of happy and a different pathway towards it. A place outside the herd for you and your family.

If you recognise yourself in the discussions to come, please remember my intent is simply to provoke in you a different way of thinking for your long-term benefit. It's never my intention to offend. I don't consider my way "better", I simply present it as "different", another option you perhaps didn't know available to deliver the happiness we all want in life.

Many people mistakenly assume my outcomes needed a huge salary. It's difficult for those who "don't think about money" like I do, conditioned by these societal financial norms, to see how it could be achieved otherwise. But for me going debt free was achieved with a household income right around national average most of the period. It included a year with one income as my wife studied a postgraduate diploma in teaching and a further year on maternity. Household income fluctuated between slightly above and slightly below average throughout. Not in the upper echelons of earners at that time like some assume, firmly in the lower middle class income bracket where we'd grown up. We didn't survive on noodles, but we were certainly deliberate about our expenditure. My approach is based on enforcing balance to regulate greed, an emotion within us all that needs controlled.

One of the most harmful fallacies I see permeated as financial "common knowledge" is this view that improved incomes dictate entirely improved outcomes. For many, as we'll discuss in detail, the issue is firmly on the expenditure side of the balance sheet. Improved income makes it easier but it doesn't guarantee success if it's the sole consideration. For many people I talk to with money worries their expenditure is the easier problem to rectify given the widespread levels of consumerism and debt that's normalised in today's society.

I don't advocate the need to sacrifice all spending or life experience, I certainly didn't so don't want to be misunderstood. For me it required learning, planning, prioritisation and above all discipline. One can't expect to have everything they want, whenever they want it, there's a need for balance and balance requires sacrifice. We must understand **"need"** versus **"want"** and manage "want" carefully with our future-self in mind, something natural to me because of my personality but I know many struggle with, even the idea of a distinction.

Results may vary and individual financial goals always differ, but I'm confident what I've learned over the decades could help readers make different financial and lifestyle choices. In doing so many could make their financial lives better. I use '"choices" intentionally as my results are derived from choosing a different spending pathway to most. Different is fine, life's all about choices and their consequences, positive or negative. I often wonder though how many of the financial choices people make include any consideration towards future consequences.

When my wife made her declaration then I wanted to figure out how much my approach over two plus decades was different and investigate what could perhaps help others. As I've said, people want to be happy but they're conditioned to believe the wealth illusion provides this happiness. Its normalisation demands my "tightfisted" reputation when compared against it, a humorous assertion but one carrying clear negative connotation. The inference is my financial frugality, living beneath my means and opting out of "normal" is bad. People inside the illusion perceive what they see externally as negative in the frugal minority mostly because they're unaware of the mechanics behind the scenes. When endgame is reached they invariably view those who escaped as "lucky". This is a nuanced view of social norms we'll get into in detail as I try to explain these mechanics to you, for your benefit.

I've never considered I'd anything to offer via the medium of writing but the challenge on my financial approach made me wonder. Before setting out to write this book though I wanted to be comfortable I had the credentials to offer my views. I think it's important the reader knows I've objectively succeeded by utilising the information I'll share.

I quickly found comfort within ONS (Office for National Statistics) data. I studied pension provision, savings & investment portfolios, debt and net worth and found in all of them I was, to my great surprise, multiples ahead of both the median and average for my age demographic. In fact, I was multiples ahead of **every** age demographic. What I've done via my financial plan since the mid 2000's has pushed my family quietly to just outside the top 10% wealth decile with 25+ accumulation years still ahead.

This shocked me as I don't consider myself wealthy in monetary or possession terms, the normalised vision of wealth and happiness I mentioned earlier. I don't drive luxury cars or live in a big house, don't go on five holidays per year and still have (and enjoy) a day job. I guarantee no-one looks at me and thinks "wealthy", likely the complete opposite! This realisation highlights both the ridiculous notion many have of what wealth looks like but also how wealth inequality in the UK sets the top decile bar so low people sneak up to it without realising or actually being wealthy by public perception standards. Put it this way, the top 1% is far further away still than the bottom 1%!

But at the same time my outcomes are apparently ahead of ~90% of the population. I'm demonstrably abnormal amongst my age demographic, against all age demographics actually, within the local authority (where we still live) and even at national level. My outcomes are not the normal I really thought they were. I'm happy, but I don't look anything like the wealthy, happy individual many are convinced to aspire to.

I say this only to provide credibility for what I plan to share, that it's objectively working given my demonstrable outperformance. Those I aim to help don't need another self-proclaimed expert speaking down to them and selling impossible dreams. I think my target audience benefit more from someone who started where they might be and had to figure it out, for shared perspective. Above all I want this interaction to be honest so I'm happy to clarify what I've achieved and my background so as not to project my own "illusion".

Professionally my background is in Financial Services IT and I've spent my entire adult life in this industry, approaching 25 years. I started in investments, pensions and assurance, laterally moving into banking. I promise it doesn't make me a bad person! I've never been directly involved in business operations, modern financial services are essentially large technology enterprises and technology has always been my primary skillset. It's hard not to pick up some knowledge around the mechanics of money when working in the industry though, for example learning how money is actually created. But as I've always been interested in finance, economics, markets and data it's a happy side effect.

I've been through personality profiling repeatedly in the name of "development" and always come out as introverted as is measurable, which contributes a fair degree to why I think as I do. People assume introverted means awkward socially but it's a measure of where one draws their energy and approval from, others or self, more than how they interact. I'm reserved but comfortable around people. Without whittling on about pseudo-science, in my introverted case it means a deep rooted sense of self accountability for individual outcomes and validation for what I do coming from within rather than without, succeed or fail. I acknowledge full accountability for my choices and the results derived from them, positive or negative and I don't really feel any societal pressure to look or act a certain way. I don't really care what society thinks of me nor expect anyone else to do things for me. I deal in outcomes and the buck for them stops with me.

I find this approach to personal accountability important in all aspects of life and I've yet to meet a successful individual in any field who doesn't possess the trait, including finance. I want to call this out early and we'll discuss it in detail throughout.

There are always some who struggle more than others financially and so genuinely need help. I'm under no illusion when it comes to wealth inequality, particularly given my locale, but I had assumed this a minority within the bounds of the mortgage discussion my wife and I were having that led to her declaration. I was blind to those being pulled into poverty unnecessarily, not just through uncontrollable external factors but through personal decision making blind to financial consequence and made with limited financial knowledge. This isn't an individual failing, it's a societal one in my view, so I thought I'd try to help people by sharing my story with a view to building a financial plan together that could help those people achieve better outcomes.

So, I asked others close to me how they thought about managing money, mortgage rates, debt, building wealth and planning for retirement. I looked separately at debt, mortgage, savings, investment and personal finance data available from the last two centuries, mainly UK but also a reasonable amount from the US (as the leader of global markets). I also had the opportunity to discuss directly with those who have a keener interest in finance. As a hobby I provide my views and analysis in private online groups where I'm one of a small team of analysts. We offer knowledge and experience through commentary on economics, markets, technical analysis and finance in general. This allowed me to talk to people actively working on their financial future which was hugely enlightening and gave me a fourth perspective: my own, non-financial enthusiasts, baseline data and financial enthusiasts.

I think it's a fairly rounded view of how others think and act with money in comparison to myself. As is so often the case, my wife is correct, I'm not normal. So how can I help you become abnormal too!

This isn't "how to get rich quick and easy". Enough snake oil salesmen exist and the truth is it's neither quick nor easy to clear debt, build wealth and escape the wealth illusion. For some, setting a goal of getting "rich" could seem so unattainable at the outset of their journey it discourages even trying, something society does well enough on its own! No-one ever achieved anything without starting it first so we'll be keeping things honest, sensible and practical to encourage anyone from any circumstance to stick with us, review their position and where possible think a little differently for the benefit of themselves and their families. I honestly believe everyone can make positive change in their financial lives wherever the starting point. The target need not be "wealthy", mine wasn't. I started with "free", but even "better" can make such a massive difference to people's lives. Aim for whatever seems achievable for you and build from there.

This book aims to provide first and foremost financial knowledge, through the lens by which I learned. The type not taught in schools but picked up in personal pursuits and my career in the industry. My take on personal finance, financial markets, wealth building, influence (negative and positive), fear, greed and debt with my thoughts on navigating them for a better future. I want this to be a holistic look at how people can break their own cycle so there will be more than just technical financial content. I'll share my thoughts in the context of building a financial plan together, so at the end of the book you'll have had the opportunity to build a comprehensive personal financial plan from a provided template considering short-term and long-term. And you'll have the knowledge to execute it for the benefit of you and your family.

The final thing I want to introduce here is a quote from Henry Ford, a mindset I think important when embarking upon any goal in life, including in finance:

"Whether you think you can, or you think you can't; you're right."

[Henry Ford | Founder, Ford Motor Company]

Many people consider finance a complicated arena in which they can't operate, one only for finance professionals. It's not. Yes, there'll be times during your journey you'll feel you can't change your situation. Doubt will creep in. I'd encourage you to adopt the mindset "I can and if I don't know how **yet** I'll figure it out!". The more you tell yourself you **can** do it, the more you'll become the person who **does**, the point Ford made so eloquently.

Yes you'll make mistakes along the way, we all do, but unless you quit these mistakes are just opportunities to learn. You must believe in yourself and your ability to progress, overcoming obstacles that set you back. Don't over estimate your abilities, just have enough self-confidence to improve them through learning, knowledge and skill building.

In 2024 we have access to information our grandparents could only have dreamt of, literally the worlds knowledge base in our pockets. There's little we can't figure out, few problems we can't find data to help us resolve. With strong will, self-belief, openness to learning new perspectives on money and hard work you really do have everything you need to achieve your own vision of financial freedom, whatever it is. And no-one is better placed to deliver it for you **than you**.

Thanks for reading, I appreciate your time and send you on your journey with a genuine Scots toast for future prosperity.

"Lang may yer lum reek!"

An Advanced Note on Inflation

"By a continuing process of inflation, governments can confiscate, secretly and unobserved, an important part of the wealth of their citizens."

[John Maynard Keynes | Economist]

WHILE EDITING I REALISED I had assumed existing knowledge of inflation and its adverse impact on spending power over time. This understanding is fundamental when projecting figures over long periods, something we'll do often to measure the potential impacts of our choices. It's vital one understands what those numbers mean in real terms so as not to overestimate their actual value. To ensure this I added this supplementary technical chapter to start. Inflation is a dry topic, but it's important we cover it early so you have a reference point. I'll make it as interesting as I can!

In short, you must understand a projected £1 million investment pot 40 years in the future is **not** equivalent to the spending power of £1 million today. In 40 years £1 million will have the equivalent spending power of a far lesser value in today's money because of inflation. £1 (or any currency) **can buy more** today than £1 is expected to be able to buy in future and the more time that passes the larger this delta becomes. We must account for this in our planning targets.

It can conceptually be difficult to understand so let me give a real world example. According to the Bank of England inflation calculator £10,000 in in 1978 had the same spending power as £41,905 in 2018, with an average inflation rate of 3.6% per year. The same goods and services costing £10,000 in 1978 cost £41,905 in 2018 (a factor of 4.19 times, or +319%).

To have the same standard of living in future then you'll need **more** money than it takes now to afford it, as money loses value over time. This is the essence of inflation and why we must factor it into our plans to ensure we maintain or improve our standard of living.

The 70's & 80's were an outlier period for inflation so 3.6% is arguably, pun intended, inflated. Projecting using a more normalised target of 2.5% over the next 40 years, 0.5% above the 2% central bank target in the UK and US, we arrive at £372,546. In 40 years the spending power of £1 million would be equivalent to roughly £372,546 today, at an average inflation rate of 2.5%.

I've added an inflation calculator (back and forward) to the financial plan template to let you model this yourself.

When projecting future values then you must always consider inflation, preferably with it explicitly calculated as part of the dataset. Don't make the costly mistake of assuming parity in spending power over time and risk significant shortfall when aiming for non-inflation adjusted targets. I raise this as many people do indeed make this mistake of considering future valuations in terms of today's spending power.

Now we've introduced the key consideration of real terms versus notional projections it's worth making a brief foray into inflation from an educational perspective. If you're familiar with the topic feel free to skip ahead. If not this hopefully helps a little with an overall understanding of inflation, how it's measured, how it impacts policymakers and why we need to be aware of it.

WHAT IS INFLATION?

Firstly, it's not as some suggest a "tax", not in my view anyway. Tax from an economics perspective is a mandatory levy imposed on individuals and businesses by governments to raise revenue that pays for public services. It's a "collected" payment which I think everyone understands. As the impact of inflation doesn't flow directly to public coffers, it's not collected and the levels are mostly market led I don't think it meets the criteria for a tax.

I'm not suggesting governments don't contribute to it or benefit from it, they absolutely do both as we'll cover in more detail. But these benefits are indirect and as such I think referring to inflation as a tax is technically incorrect.

John Maynard Keynes is widely regarded as the founder of modern macroeconomics and whether you agree with his outlook or not I think he was essentially saying this in the opening quote.

Governments aren't "taking" money from the public, officially and in a declared fashion like you would via tax, rather they contribute covertly to the confiscation of a portion of the value of people's money through reducing its spending power over time.

Unless an individual gains return on capital higher than inflation headwinds they're essentially becoming poorer as their spending power is decreasing. To make it relatable one could think of money in this context like an asset, say a car where rate of inflation is similar to rate of depreciation. As a new car loses value over time if traded later so does money unless any return is greater than rate of inflation. This is "Real Rate of Return", calculated as follows:

(Nominal Return on Capital - Applicable Taxation) - Rate of Inflation = Real Rate of Return (RoR)

If one had £100 and gained 4% interest in a bank account, they may think they "made" 4%. But if rate of inflation was 6% then they actually "lost" money (through spending power), silently, because their money can buy less: (4% - 0%) - 6% = -2% RoR. As with compound interest understanding inflation and real rate of return provides you opportunity to profit from it, while those who don't understand are generally left paying for it.

Goods and services inflation can be summarised as the sustained increase in prices of everyday goods and services over time, typically measured on an annual basis. It means prices are rising and the spending power (of a currency) is decreasing. Each unit of currency buys fewer goods and services than it did in the past so you need more units of currency in future simply to maintain spending power and by extension living standards. This is what people normally mean when talking about inflation, consumer based goods and services (or CPI).

Asset inflation, the ying to goods and services yang, is the rising prices of financial and tangible assets like equities, property or commodities. This occurs due to low interest rates, increased liquidity or more generally via favourable market conditions. Asset inflation contributes to wealth inequality as those who own and buy assets benefit disproportionately over those who don't.

While both involve rising prices they affect different aspects of the economy. Asset inflation primarily influences financial markets and wealth distribution where goods and services inflation directly impacts the affordability of everyday consumer items, which is why we hear about this more frequently. Together they perpetuate wealth inequality by making it harder for working people to buy appreciating assets with less expendable income while increasing the wealth of those who own assets already as their asset valuations inflate.

WHAT CAUSES INFLATION?

This could fill a book in its own right and at the end we still wouldn't agree on a definitive, single factor answer! The reality is inflation rarely has a single root cause, despite what many political commentators claim. Macroeconomics is world of finely balanced economic forces and inflation, certainly in my view from a traditional economics perspective, results from the interplay between these forces over time.

The general outcome is the same for the public, prices go up and spending power goes down. Causation though when comparing different inflationary periods can be entirely different from one to the next. Let's discuss some different types of inflation and their contributory factors.

DEMAND-PULL INFLATION occurs when there's excess demand for goods and services in an economy, caused by things including:

- **INCREASED CONSUMER SPENDING:** When consumers have more disposable income (including tax cuts, cheap credit, wage increases or stimulus payments) they increase their spending which increases demand. Increased demand impacts supply versus demand dynamics and causes inflationary pressure on prices.

- **INCREASED BUSINESS INVESTMENT:** When business investment (capital spending) increases it also leads to increased demand for goods and services. This increased demand has a similar inflationary net effect, upward pressure on prices.

- **GOVERNMENT SPENDING:** Project, infrastructure or social program spending can also increase demand for goods and services and similarly contribute to demand pull inflation. This also contributes to asset price inflation and wealth redistribution as governments take (through taxation) from low and middle classes and give to the wealthy via government contracts. The wealthy then buy assets, mostly from the middle classes, widening the wealth gap.

COST-PUSH INFLATION occurs when production costs rise and these increased costs are passed to consumers via higher prices to maintain margins. It's caused by things including:

- **RISING WAGES:** Unpopular, but when workers negotiate higher wages it adds to increased production costs leading to increases in the price of produced goods and services to cover those increased production costs. Though logical, many don't like to acknowledge this reality where rising prices are concerned.
- **HIGHER MATERIAL & COMMODITY PRICES:** Increasing raw materials and commodities prices, like oil which is widely used in production processes, can lead to higher production costs and subsequently higher prices for finished products. Higher costs are passed through the supply chain to consumers contributing to inflation.
- **SUPPLY CHAIN DISRUPTIONS:** Global events like natural disasters, pandemics or geopolitical conflict (we've seen them all recently!) disrupt supply chains and reduce the availability of finished goods or the materials required in the production process. This drives up prices as supply reduces and demand stays constant (or increases).

CENTRAL BANK MONETARY POLICY: Central banks like the Bank of England and US Federal Reserve are mandated to control inflation and maximise growth. They influence inflation through monetary policy. Expansionary monetary policy like lowering interest rates or quantitative easing increases money supply and stimulates spending, which risks demand-pull inflation. Conversely, contractionary monetary policy like raising interest rates or quantitative tightening is used to combat inflation by reducing spending and borrowing.

As a side note, I think one of the major factors leading to the generally poor state of household finances as interest rates rose in 2023 was central banks persisting with artificially low interest rate monetary policy (essentially ZIRP: Zero Interest Rate Policy) for far too long post the 2008 Global Financial Crisis. This drove demand pull asset price inflation (think property) fuelled by cheap and easily accessible liquidity in the form of debt. It also created two generations who believe low interest rates are "normal" and who now find themselves over leveraged as they discover they're not (hint: ZIRP was never normal).

The massive amount of money given by governments to the wealthy during Covid (estimates vary between £300 Billion and £700 Billion in the UK alone) and supply side issues caused by the pandemic also contributed to inflation and the increasing wealth inequality stemming from it.

UK government schemes and housebuilders intentionally restricting supply also played a large part in property price inflation. Adding demand through help to buy while supply was already low and new homebuilding remained well below the 250,000 per annum requirement outlined by the Barker Report in 2004 certainly didn't help. Remember, rarely a one factor root cause. But rates so low for so long in my view played a large part in the issues we see now: asset price inflation since 2008 moving house price to income ratios higher than they've ever been in history and widespread wealth redistribution from mostly the middle class upwards.

EXCHANGE RATES are often overlooked by the general public but fluctuation impacts the prices of imported and exported goods. Weaker domestic currency for example makes imports more expensive leading to higher prices for imported goods as increased costs are passed on.

Consider oil, used in the supply chain and priced in $'s. If the £ falls in value against the $, even if oil price remains static import costs in £ terms increase as it costs more £'s to buy the same amount of oil (or oil derived products like fuel) to import the same goods. Prices can fluctuate to account for this. This is a crude example, again pun intended, simply to make the point in an understandable way. More variables contribute to shipping cost fluctuation and timescales are far longer, but this gives an idea.

INFLATION EXPECTATION (BUILT-IN INFLATION): If consumers and businesses expect prices to rise they might adjust their behaviour accordingly, for example by raising prices or demanding higher wages to cover anticipated inflationary impacts. By doing so they actually create the inflation they feared.

This is one reason central banks "Jaw Bone" around monetary policy, releasing data but also providing commentary and forward expectations around it. They aim to avoid false expectation driving behaviours that cause those expectations to materialise. Their narrative setting attempts to influence the general public and businesses to manage risk and keep their policy agenda on track.

WAGE PRICE INFLATION is a distinct part of Built-in Inflation where workers pre-empt anticipated rising price impacts by demanding wages "keep up". As wages increase to retain and attract employees, employers pass labour cost increases onto consumers in the form of higher prices for their goods and services, making inflation self-fulfilling. In extreme circumstances this can initiate a wage-price spiral where one feeds the other in perpetuity and inflation runs out of control.

FISCAL POLICY implemented by government also impacts inflation. Tax cuts and increased spending programs stimulate demand leading to inflationary pressure on prices. Tax increases and reduced spending has the opposite effect, reducing disposable income and lowering demand thus reducing inflationary price pressure. If a government aims to stimulate growth by increasing consumer spending via reduced taxation then they risk inflation and vice versa.

Taxation is a nuanced example as there are multiple ways to raise taxes without actually "raising taxes". In the UK for example the Tory government froze tax bands till 2028 meaning as wages rise more people end up paying higher tax rates without any increase in taxation policy. This is known as "Fiscal Drift", which we'll discuss later.

REGULATORY FACTORS like sanctions, price control, tariffs or subsidies can directly impact prices and contribute to inflation. For example, when Russia invaded Ukraine and sanctions were imposed Russia cut natural gas supply impacting European countries reliant upon it.

The demand placed on reduced supply led to cost-push inflation in natural gas price. This wasn't the only contributor to rising energy prices it's simply an example of regulatory factors impacting upon a supply chain and the inflationary pressure this can bring. Oil price inflation impacting oil derived products like fuel is another example brought about by this conflict.

When discussing any of these contributory factors it's important to remember we tend to view inflation within the economy in which we operate because we see local impacts most readily. But economic events or trends in the global economy like changes in international commodity prices, supply disruptions or shifts in global demand also influence domestic inflation. In today's world the local impact of global economic variance is more acute than ever.

Not all inflation then is caused by or fully in the control of local policy makers, something you'll hear politicians try to exploit. Recall "Putin's Price Hikes" as a political strapline in early 2023 followed by the same politicians claiming "we halved inflation like we said we would" when it slowed. Interesting how politicians always claim it's not in their control when it's rising but it's in their control when they "fix it", isn't it?

Like most political spin while it's rooted in just enough truth the claim it's always someone else's fault as a default position is rarely the whole truth, as are the claims of reducing inflation as it falls. It certainly wasn't the case with the Ukraine invasion, those inflationary foundations were laid by policymakers long before (remember ZIRP, QE, Covid spending and house building failures for example). As for reducing inflation in 2023, yes politicians froze income tax bands which helped reduce disposable income and thus demand for goods and services but central bank monetary policy (interest rate rises) and the changes in utility price caps did all the heavy lifting just as the BoE forecast suggested **before** the Tory government made their "pledge".

This is standard politicking. Inflation is a useful tool for politicians (and many would argue their friends too!) and central banks, they'll just never admit to the general public they're causing it or benefitting from it. It makes us worse off and no-one votes for a politician they know is intentionally making them worse off, whatever their incentives.

There are other inflationary factors but for the purposes of this chapter it's enough of an overview to help with a baseline understanding.

THE KEY FACETS OF CPI

Now we know what inflation is, how's it tracked? For goods and services this lies in CPI (Consumer Price Index) datasets produced by policymakers on a monthly basis. This is our general indicator of consumer inflation.

Other measures exist depending on locale. PCE (Personal Consumption and Expenditure) is used by the Fed in the US as well as PPI (Producer Price Index) which is referenced by both the Fed and BoE as supplementary data. Together with CPI these provide slightly different insights, each influencing central bank policy in their own way. People are most familiar with CPI and it's the main measure used by the Bank of England for policy decisions so we'll concentrate there in this whistlestop tour.

Before we delve into numbers I must address this point: reported headline CPI tends not to be an accurate reflection of the actual inflationary impact we feel as individuals and families. Real terms inflation tends to feel higher for most than the numbers reported. There are many reasons for this. Some relate to the questionable way these metrics are reported, like permissible basket of goods substitutions, technical feature advancements or shrinkflation, where the price stays the same we just get less in a standard package. Some is within the detail where items rise and fall on a category by category basis and the overall impacts depend on how heavily we consume from each category.

An inflation print of 10% for example doesn't mean everyone sees their cost of living increase by 10%. It's generally quite subjective around individual/family spending habits as well as beholden to the choices made by policymakers within the bounds of the measurement criteria. One should always take the reported figures with a pinch of salt as a result.

It is though the measure we must track so let me explain it. CPI measures changes in average prices paid by consumers for a pre-defined basket of goods and services over time.

It begins with the selection of a **REPRESENTATIVE BASKET OF GOODS AND SERVICES** deemed to be "the average consumer". This includes items like food, housing, clothing, transport, healthcare and entertainment. It's supposed to reflect the spending habits of a typical household and is updated periodically to account for any change in consumer preference.

Basket composition leaves it open to manipulation, for example by substituting items within categories if one jumps in price more than another or utilising technical feature additions as a reason to suppress rising tech prices. Essentially more features and higher price can be recorded as no change or lower price as "per feature" price is static even though item price is rising. Even if consumers don't care about the additional features.

PRICE DATA for items in the basket is then collected regularly so the index value can be tracked and updated.

Not all items have equal importance within consumer budgets which is accounted for via a **WEIGHTED AVERAGE** system. For example, housing and food have a higher weighting than entertainment given their relative importance to the average consumer. This ensures items in the primary "needs" category like food and shelter are weighted appropriately with heavier impact on calculations than "want" based categories like entertainment.

CPI is then calculated relative to a specific base year, assigned an index value of 100. Changes in value are expressed as a percentage deviation from the **BASE YEAR INDEX**. This provides the Year on Year numbers we see reported monthly for the preceding year. The formula is:

CPI = (Cost of Current Year Basket / Cost of Base Year Basket) * 100

Primarily CPI measures consumer goods and services inflation, the rate at which general prices rise over time leading to decreased purchasing power. When CPI increases (positive value) it indicates inflation while a decrease (negative value) indicates deflation. This process runs monthly with different economies releasing their datasets as part of their calendar of economic events at different times. CPI days are considered "red news days" in markets where you'd expect price volatility across asset classes as investors react to the news. Risky trading days for sure!

In general terms markets are forward looking so "price in" inflation (and follow on base rate) expectations in advance. If data matches expectation then short-term volatility tends to even out quickly. However, if data doesn't match market expectation higher volatility across assets is more likely as market participants rush to position, seeking highest yield and lowest risk as the market reprices the unexpected news.

DISINFLATION VERSUS DEFLATION

A common mistake people make about inflation is confusing falling inflation (disinflation) with deflation. If the July print is 5.7% Year on Year followed by 4.5% in August this is **DISINFLATION**. It means prices are **still rising**, just at a slower rate than they were previously in July. 4.5% Year on Year versus 5.7% **does not**, like too many people think, mean prices are falling.

DEFLATION is when we actually see prices falling and is pretty rare in overall CPI data outside of economy wide corrective events (like recession). It's more common in individual categories between prints (like gasoline or food at home). In deflation CPI prints would be negative, for example -1.4% in August means prices are falling at 1.4% Year on Year.

This distinction is key to your understanding of inflation. If you take one thing other than RoR away from this chapter, make it this. This misunderstanding has far reaching consequences and it amazes me so many don't understand disinflation doesn't mean prices are falling or are likely to fall. Prices rarely come down much if at all post inflationary periods.

CORE VERSUS HEADLINE CPI

Another important distinction when considering CPI is Core versus Headline. Managing an economy involves making monetary policy decisions based on an array of complex factors and policy makers don't want to, if they can possibly avoid it, adversely impact on their economic targets through poor policy decisions.

Think of an economy like a tanker ship which when veering off course takes considerable time and numerous course corrections to remedy. When making those course corrections you'd want to rely on the least volatile dataset to make corrective decisions. You'd want to use the most reliable, trend following data. This is done using Core CPI rather than Headline CPI.

HEADLINE CPI includes all items in the basket, providing a comprehensive view of overall price changes. It can be influenced by volatile factors like energy and food prices making it subject to short-term fluctuations and less reliable for long-term corrective policy making decisions. **CORE CPI** removes the volatility caused by temporary variance in things like energy and food by excluding these items from calculations. It focuses on underlying inflation trends making it more stable for monetary policy analysis, which explains why it's usually the one policymakers rely on.

Why do I make this distinction? In my experience Core numbers are rarely publicised by mainstream media nor by politicians, both of whom know it's the measure by which policy decisions are likely taken. The focus is almost always on Headline numbers against central bank targets. This misleads the general public who tend not to appreciate the difference, certainly not the link to actual policy decision making. It's easy to understand why. Headline numbers are more volatile so they make for sensational headlines when going up and fantastic soundbites for politicians (who claim victory) when going down. All while Core is telling the real story. Incidentally, if you hear the term "sticky inflation" this almost always relates to Core, not Headline and describes periods where core items have levelled but don't fall over many months.

When monitoring CPI to project probabilities in central bank policy, Core is the more important metric. Those with this knowledge can find an edge in investment planning and risk based decision making by weighting it heavier than headline in their decisions. For example, if core remains stable while headline is rising this suggests overall increases are driven by volatile sectors like food and energy giving clues as to potential targets. One may decide to position short-term in energy equities. For our purposes I don't advocate messing too much with core investment accounts outside of small play fund allocations, but it's still useful to understand these wider macroeconomic levers.

A BRIEF INTRO TO PPI

I mentioned it so want to give a brief overview of PPI. The Producer Price Index (PPI) measures average changes in prices received by producers and manufacturers for their goods and services. It tracks inflationary pressure at the wholesale or producer level of the supply chain before it hits the consumer. It's generally made up of:

- COMMODITIES: Including raw materials, chemicals and agricultural goods used in production processes.
- INTERMEDIATE GOODS: Like steel, lumber and partially processed goods used in final goods production.
- FINISHED GOODS: Fully completed products.

For example, lumber prices rising can be a leading indicator of inflationary pressure on housing production costs leading to higher prices on finished homes thus housing (including rent) costs for consumers.

PPI is often utilised as a leading indicator for CPI, where changes in PPI can be used to project potential future CPI change. Central banks track it and while they don't openly make policy decisions based on PPI alone it helps their analysis of CPI and potential future trends. It can also help us because of this leading nature. For example we may position some cash for rising rates if PPI is rising, assuming rising CPI might drive change in monetary policy (base rate increase or QT).

A BRIEF INTRO TO PCE

Again, I mentioned it so want to give a brief overview of PCE. Personal Consumption and Expenditures is a uniquely US centric datapoint used by the Fed to measure consumer spending trends. Although it doesn't apply to UK Inflation directly the US market leads global markets and the $ is the Global Reserve Currency (which all commodities are priced in) so we always need to be aware of events in and around the US economy. PCE is useful for projecting US monetary policy decisions.

PCE calculates the total value of goods and services purchased by individuals and households over a specific time period, a critical component of US GDP (Gross Domestic Product). It provides insights into the health of the economy, consumer behaviour and potential downstream inflationary trends.

Like CPI it's collected in categories including housing, transport, entertainment and healthcare with these weighted based on perceived importance to the standard consumer. It's then represented as a percentage change from base year. It's used alongside CPI, PPI and others (like unemployment & NFP) in making informed policy decisions.

CENTRAL BANK MONETARY POLICY INFLUENCE

Maintaining price stability is a primary objective for central banks so monetary policy is tightly linked to performance against inflation targets. By targeting a specific inflation rate, usually around 2%, they aim to prevent excessive inflation and any deflation. CPI helps them assess if targets are being met and if not different monetary policy decisions can be made favouring reduction or increase towards target as required.

Central banks use CPI data then to make informed monetary policy decisions. If it's rising too quickly, surpassing target, they implement contractionary measures like raising rates to curb inflation. Conversely, if it's too low or negative (deflation) they implement expansionary measures like lowering rates to stimulate economic growth. Raising rates reduces disposable income for businesses and consumers by increasing credit pricing/debt service costs which reduces demand. Lowering rates has the opposite effect, increasing demand through increased disposable income, increasing inflation.

CPI also helps central banks gauge overall economic health. Rapidly rising prices indicate robust demand but it also erodes consumer purchasing power, disrupting economic stability. Consistently low inflation or deflation signals economic weakness through reduced consumer spending.

Central banks also have to manage inflation expectations, not just inflation itself. They do so by communicating targets to anchor expectations to their policies and prevent self-fulfilling inflation. "Jaw Boning", the humorous terminology used in financial circles for narrative setting through press release and presentation, is a useful tool for policymakers in preventing built-in inflation forming. It allows them to set the narrative in support of their policy decisions.

Finally, CPI is used by central banks to calculate real interest rates which adjust nominal rates for inflation. This provides a more accurate view of the cost of borrowing and real rate of return. Central banks consider real interest rates when setting nominal rates to support their economic goals.

This consideration is my primary reason for introducing the subject of inflation, anchoring your thinking in the calculation of real rate of return over nominal rate of return. I want you to be comfortable considering actual spending power of projected figures with inflation in mind, rather than thinking about those projections having the spending power of today. This is how central banks project future values and so should we.

HYPERINFLATION

No inflation overview would be complete without a note on the dangers of Hyperinflation, a risk keeping policymakers on their toes! Hyperinflation is an extreme form of inflation presenting rapidly with few, if any, mitigating measures. It's characterised by rapid, unsustainable and uncontrollable increases in general prices of goods and services. In a hyperinflationary environment prices can multiply many times in a very short period, often daily or even hourly which results in the rapid collapse of currency value rendering it essentially worthless.

It brings severe economic instability and generally leads to a breakdown of the local monetary system. Hyperinflation is typically caused by excessive money supply growth, loss of confidence in the currency, loss of confidence in the ability of a country to meet its debt obligations or some form of political turmoil and usually has devastating effects on an economy including widespread poverty, loss of savings and often social unrest.

In 2023 there are a number of national economies either suffering from or who have recently suffered from hyperinflation, including: Brazil, Argentina, Venezuela, Greece, Turkey and Iran.

THE QUANTITATIVE OPTIONS: EASING & TIGHTENING

Historically central banks would utilise interest rate adjustments to deliver their core mandate of maintaining a growing economy with high employment and controlled inflation (around 2%). In the early 2000's though, having persevered with this approach unsuccessfully over a prolonged period of deflation, the Bank of Japan (BoJ) adopted a different approach. Their attempt to find a way forward for their stagnating economy later became known as "Quantitative Easing".

Following the 2008 Global Financial Crisis policymakers around the world, having seen the approach utilised by Japan, began adopting similar policy as "extraordinary measures". The era of Quantitative Easing had begun. As I highlighted earlier I believe this contributed greatly to the inflationary period in which we find ourselves today in 2023, alongside ZIRP. Before we look at why let's define what the terms are and briefly how they work.

QUANTITATIVE EASING (QE) is a monetary policy tool employed by central banks to stimulate the economy when traditional policy measures like lowering interest rates become less effective. It grows the money supply of local currency alongside growing the central bank balance sheet, working as follows:

- **ASSET PURCHASES:** The central bank buys financial assets, typically government bonds or other securities either from market or large financial institutions.
- **INCREASE IN MONETARY BASE:** The crucial aspect of asset purchases is the central bank creating new money to pay for it. There's no "money printing", the new money doesn't exist in physical form it's simply recorded electronically as additional banking reserves in the system.
- **LOWER LONG END INTEREST RATES:** By buying government bonds the central bank drives up their price and thus lowers their yields. Lower long-term interest rates make borrowing cheaper which encourages businesses and individuals to invest and/or spend more, stimulating the economy.

QUANTITATIVE TIGHTENING (QT) is also referred to as "balance sheet normalisation" and is the reverse. It involves reducing the size of the central bank balance sheet by selling some of the assets it holds or by allowing assets to mature without replacing them. Selling is more aggressive and impacts markets while maturation is less aggressive. QT works broadly as follows:

- **ASSET SALES / MATURITY:** The central bank reduces its balance sheet by selling some of the assets (bonds/securities) it purchased during QE (aggressive with market risk) or choosing not to replace maturing assets with new purchases (less aggressive with less risk).
- **REDUCED MONETARY SUPPLY:** As assets are sold or mature the monetary base decreases, reducing money in circulation and the central bank balance sheet.
- **UPWARD PRESSURE ON INTEREST RATES:** QT puts upward pressure on long-term interest rates making borrowing more expensive and encouraging a tightening of the belt for businesses and individuals.

QE & QT are tools used by central banks to influence economic activity within their local economy via the money supply and interest rates. They're intended for periods of economic crisis or recovery to support or restrain growth and achieve policy objectives, but they've recently become more normalised. Since 2008 for example four (official) periods of QE happened in the US, where the money supply grew exponentially. Since 2019 more than 80% of all the US Dollars in existence were created through QE. 80% of all USD. Ever. Although QE can provide benefit when used well this scale of money creation in such a short timeframe has some implications! Let's talk about some of those.

The primary concern one may have when injecting huge amounts of money into the financial system and the reason I've included this content here is **RISING INFLATION**. Remember, more monetary supply aligned with low cost credit conditions means more disposable income which drives Demand Pull Inflation, both asset and goods and services. Think about what you've seen since 2008? Low rates, multiple periods of QE, asset price inflation, CPI inflation.....One can join the dots when looking at who benefits at each stage.

Speculative assets including equities, cryptocurrency and property inflate widely. QE driven price appreciation tends to create **ASSET BUBBLES** in these markets and if those bubbles burst it can herald financial instability and economic downturn. We haven't seen any burst yet and it's possible we keep kicking the can down the road with more QE, widening the wealth gap between those who have assets and those who don't, but we've certainly seen bubbles inflate in my view.

As a result of asset price inflation the major beneficiaries of QE are those who own assets and see their wealth increase with asset prices. Those without substantial assets don't benefit to the same extent. This is part of the Cantillon Effect which I'll explain in detail later. **WEALTH INEQUALITY** gets worse in this scenario.

As explained QE is often used as an alternative to raising rates leading to **ARTIFICIALLY LOW INTEREST RATES** like we saw since 2008. This negatively impacts savers, retirees and pensions but also increases disposable income through cheap debt service costs, driving inflation. It's left at least two generations thinking near zero interest rates are normal when making their financial decisions. This is incorrect. For 400 years of recorded UK rate history the long run base rate is around 5% and the period between 2008 and 2022, by any measure, is the historical outlier. The UK isn't unique here.

QE can also **DEVALUE CURRENCY**, negatively impacting international trade and leading to trade imbalances which can push inflation to hyperinflation with all the negative impacts associated.

It can also lead to **OVERRELIANCE ON MONETARY POLICY** to stimulate the economy, reducing pressure on governments and central banks to implement necessary fiscal and structural reforms. It can be viewed an "easy option" to avoid having to make tougher, more impactful but ultimately better long-term policy decisions. We know politicians in particular like easy options as their time horizons are short.

Central banks and governments understand the potential dangers of QE and know they need to carefully and prudently manage these programmes. This is where the risk presents for us, the general public. We've a single point of failure and one with no real history of successful QE program management nor any data on their adverse impacts over the long-term.

ADDITIONAL LANGUAGE

There's some additional language you may hear around inflation and the updates given by central banks and politicians about interest rate and policy decisions. It's useful to understand these.

DOVISH: When policymakers are reducing rates, loosening credit conditions, adding to the monetary supply via quantitative easing and their jaw boning is positive this is known as a "Dovish Stance". Markets, which are forward looking, tend to price this in with rising asset prices and falling currency valuations.

HAWKISH: When policymakers are increasing rates, tightening credit conditions, reducing money supply via quantitative tightening and their jaw boning is negative this is known as "Hawkish Stance". Markets, which are forward looking, tend to price this in with falling asset prices and rising currency valuations.

Markets generally function around chasing yield with asset classes traditionally acting in either a convergent (like equities and cryptocurrency) or divergent (like equities and bonds) manner. So when, for example, inflation increases market participants assume potential for liquidity tightening via rate increase so move from equities into fixed income (bonds) to benefit from these changing market conditions. The language used by policymakers gives clues as to these potential positioning changes.

AN ADVANCED APPLICATION: INFLATING AWAY DEBT

To finish I want to introduce an advanced application of inflation both Investors and central banks use to their benefit over long time horizons. It's important to financial wellbeing to understand this use case and it introduces a concept we'll discuss later: policymakers don't always act in the best interests of the electorate as the electorate generally assume, particularly the lower and middle classes who don't buy assets.

I'll explain through the Investor lens. Our protagonist, Ian Vestor utilises cheap credit to buy an investment asset for £100,000, with a 10% downpayment. The type of asset doesn't matter, could be property, an investment portfolio, a business, whatever. With rates low he secures a 20 year loan at 1.9% nominal rate on the £90,000 borrowed which he'll pay back interest only. This rate is fixed for the duration (like our US cousins long-term mortgages). Let's use the earlier long run average inflation rate of 3.6% and consider an average return on investment of 7%, below the average of S&P500 returns for the last 100 years.

Theres a lot of numbers in there, but what's the point? Well, it's threefold:

1. The notional interest rate on the debt of 1.9% is **less than** the average inflation rate. The devaluation of the currency (through inflation) is higher than the interest accruing on the debt, meaning in real terms the debt is becoming "cheaper" over time to service.
2. When Ian pays the principal back at the end of the loan period, it'll be worth significantly less than it was at the outset. At 3.6% Inflation over 20 years the actual purchasing power of the £90,000 loan would be £44,366. Less than half.
3. The value of the asset has been growing at a **higher rate** than both Inflation and the interest rate, meaning the real rate of return is positive. £100,000 at an average (compounded) 7% return over the 20 year period is (non-inflation adjusted) £386,969 at loan maturity. Inflation adjusted at 3.6% this is £190,757 (in today's money).

Over the 20 year period Ian would pay ~£34,200 in interest on the principal, but the key is he's leveraged both compound interest on a long-term investment return **and** inflation devaluing the debt to turn his £10,000 spending power today (remember, his contribution was £10,000, £90,000 was borrowed) into £129,532 spending power in the future (inflation adjusted and after debt service costs).

I know this can take a bit of getting your head around but while the value of money decreases over time due to inflation, so does the cost of fixed rate debt with lower nominal rates than inflation. I used the investor example as it's easier to understand but I'm not advocating this investment method (using credit to invest). It carries multiple risks I've not detailed (we'll discuss risk later) and macroeconomics is complex, there's no return guarantee. This example was simply introducing the premise of inflationary benefit on debt.

This benefit comes via the differing impacts of inflationary debt devaluation on borrowers and lenders, the two sides of the market. Finance is for the most part a zero sum game. Where the borrower is benefitting here as their debt is devalued over time, the lender is the counterparty making a real terms loss. If £90,000 they loaned 20 years ago is only worth £44,366 when they get it back and they only made £34,200 in interest, how's that a good deal?

Well, there's a little more to it, like how this loan money is created which we'll get to. I'll keep this example simple for now to highlight why consumer lenders prefer variable rates. What am I getting at as a wider point? Well, are governments net borrowers or lenders? The answer is borrowers. Current UK national debt is nearing £2.7 Trillion and US national debt is a staggering $34 Trillion. This borrowing happens, generally, at fixed rates through bonds linked to base rate.

Wouldn't it be in the interests of policymakers to reduce the actual value of their debt burden by running inflation higher than the interest paid on it (even for short periods)? And don't they control both ends of this deal, the lending rate and the inflationary pressure (QE and interest rates as we discussed earlier).........?

While this "Financial Repression" strategy is unusual, in fairness, it's possible and one could make an argument the inflationary periods we've seen since 1971 perhaps haven't been as hard to see coming as advertised, convenient even. While it could be a useful tool for policymakers though it has knock on impacts, including making those unaware, those who don't typically have assets, poorer. Generally the lower and middle classes.

This is a simplified overview of this complex inflation application but hopefully you get the general idea. It emphasises why I'll keep repeating we need to think differently about and better understand money to escape the system.

SUMMARY

Inflation impacts upon the spending power of our money over time. £1 million in future is not expected to have the same purchasing power as £1 million today, a mistake people often make when projecting figures over long timeframes. Financial planning should acknowledge this, explicitly including inflation adjusted projections where possible.

The Consumer Price Index (CPI) is a key economic indicator measuring changes in the average prices of a representative basket of goods and services. It serves as a crucial tool for central banks alongside metrics like PPI and PCE in formulating and implementing monetary policy. Understanding the difference between Headline (all items) and Core CPI (excluding volatile elements like energy and food) is essential for policymakers to make informed decisions about inflation targets and economic stability. We should be aware Core is the more important metric in this regard.

By closely monitoring metrics including CPI central banks aim to maintain price stability and foster a healthy economic environment. It's also true policymakers can benefit from inflation through the devaluation of their debt obligations, though it's unusual.

We monitor CPI to ensure we're making positive real rate of return, where our money is growing at a rate above inflation year on year. This is important so our spending power isn't being eroded. A return on Investment of 4% in a year where inflation is 6% is a 2% real terms **reduction** in value of our net worth. A 6% return in a year with 4% inflation is a 2% real terms **increase** in the value of our net worth.

Here, with these summary points, we conclude our supplementary introduction to Inflation. The reason for its addition should be immediately clear and hopefully it's been as enlightening as one can make the subject, explaining how inflation impacts our financial wellbeing now as well as our ability to build wealth into the future.

Let's Talk Financial Plans & Goals

"Good fortune is what happens when
opportunity meets with planning."

[Thomas Edison | Inventor]

MY GOAL IS TO HELP you build a comprehensive financial plan by the end of this book, one you can execute over time to achieve your financial goals no matter your starting point. We'll begin by defining why it's important, what such a plan looks like and how we set financial goals within it. Basically, we start at the beginning! We need a destination and directions if we want to get there.

I'll make constant reference to changing your mindset when it comes to money. I want to challenge the accepted societal norms I believe financially harmful and encourage you to operate outside of them for your benefit. Considering your personal financial goals at the start of this journey allows you to monitor how they change by the end, in many people this change can be significant.

I plan to teach my daughter all of this as she grows older so it may benefit her life as it has mine. This book will leave a written reference for her as well as helping others. I hope I'm around to do the teaching myself but if for whatever reason I'm not it's recorded in these pages for her. For the parents amongst you this should confirm how seriously I take what I'll share.

My final introductory comment is practical in nature. I realised long ago that subject matter books you don't take action after reading don't really provide any value, they're just another drain on your precious resources (time, money and energy). My ask of you then is to analyse the detail, take notes, do your due diligence as one always should and where you decide something would benefit you, action it to realise the benefit.

The aim of our interaction is to build the financial knowledge that helps you develop and implement a financial plan for your long-term benefit. To challenge your views of harmful societal norms like debt and consumption that create the illusion of happiness but leave many feeling trapped. To facilitate financial freedom over time for you and your family. These things won't happen if this book is read and put down with no action taken.

With this in mind I've included an "A. Actions" tab in the financial plan template downloadable from the contents page. I'll refer to these at the end of specific chapters to prompt you to use the knowledge we've discussed to build your plan. I've made my case on taking action now, the rest is up to you!

ARE FINANCIAL PLANS IMPORTANT?

It's certainly been a key element of my personal journey! Less subjectively, studies around the world suggest an overwhelming majority of people don't do any financial planning, but financially successful individuals do so more often than not. Who better to emulate than those successful outside of statistical norms?

At a very basic level if we don't know where we're headed, how do we get anywhere? Not having a plan makes it more likely we find ourselves standing still financially. It actually makes it more likely we're moving **backwards**, often without realising. Consider our discussion on inflation and its erosion of purchasing power over time. With no financial plan how do we manage this without unknowingly becoming poorer? How do we ensure adequate provision for retirement (we'll discuss this later)?

Finally, in finance nothing happens by accident. We need to be intentional about what we want to achieve and how we're going to achieve it, particularly as the modern world aims to extract maximum resource from us at all times. We need to know what has most value **to us** so we can prioritise our resources. If we don't plan we don't consider the long-term implications of our choices and like so many we run the risk of expending those limited resources on things with little value to us, or worse still on things that actually **hurt** our long-term financial prospects.

My CONSUMER, DEBTOR, EMPLOYEE TRIAD thesis will make clear, with examples, my view that the world is designed for us to be a source of wealth for others, not to build it for ourselves. We're financial cattle who covertly power the wealth machine. Once you accept you've been conditioned to be a consumer, employed to pay your consumer debts, you start to look at money very differently.

This mindset, right or wrong, will help you build a financial plan to deliver **your** financial goals, not someone else's.

Many people think they have a plan but only really have loose financial goals in their mind like "pay the mortgage" or "save for a holiday" or "pay the credit card". They rarely, if ever, write them down, plan how they're going to achieve them or track progress. Informality leads to failure through impulsive spending without an understanding of the full impact of those decisions. It leads to frustration at not achieving what they expected financially and in many cases financial penalty (like increased interest payments) which actually make their situation worse.

Formalised goal setting and financial planning is the first principle I want readers to take away from this book. I believe in building a house from the foundations up and I very much see this as the foundation to clearing debt, building wealth and finding true financial happiness: A financial plan with clear goals.

Having a financial plan allows us to prioritise learning and focus our time, money and energy in executing for our benefit. It allows us to track progress and adjust as required before it's too late. It makes financial success an intentional endeavour, not a casual "hope for the best" blind to the financial impacts of our immediate decisions across the vast sands of time. It's our blueprint to escape from the Consumer, Debtor, Employee prison.

WHO HAS FINANCIAL PLANS?

Most people don't have formal financial plans as I said, which may or may not surprise you. This is certainly my experience of talking to people but it's also supported by widely available data including these examples from the last ten years:

- A 2016 survey by the Certified Financial Planner Board of Standards highlighted less than 35% of US adults had documented financial plans in place outlining their goals.
- A 2018 study by Schroders showed less than 22% of investors globally had a documented financial plan outlining their goals.
- A 2022 FCA study in the UK showed only 28% of households have a financial plan in place assisting with money management and outlining their financial goals.
- In 2023 another UK study found these numbers rising to 36% and encouragingly found under 35's making plans at twice the rate of older demographics.

These research examples show fewer people have financial plans than don't and also that those who do tend to be happier with their financial situation.

Why is this, is it a knowledge issue? I think most people know how to set goals, formulate a plan and track progress. Goal setting and performance tracking has been part of business practice for decades so logic suggests people should be familiar with the process in some form via their working lives.

Is it likely the two thirds of people in the US and UK who don't plan have never been exposed to goal setting and planning? I think not, so they should have some of the knowledge required to carry out the practice for themselves. From my conversations with people I think the gap is more that people don't know they should apply the same planning and goal setting practice to their own personal finances. They don't know the benefits, don't understand those without plans are statistically unhappier with finances than those who have them or know technically how to formulate their own comprehensive financial plan, specific to them.

So I want to help you understand why you should plan and show you how to apply what you already know about planning to personal finance.

IS IT REALLY THAT IMPORTANT?

The numbers show fewer people have well formulated financial plans than don't. We also know fewer people succeed financially than don't. Correlation isn't causation though, so how can I be sure formal financial plans are really that important?

I'm a huge advocate of looking at the actions of those who succeed to understand best practice. A common saying in financial circles is "why take advice on money from those who don't have it?", those who incidentally dictate societal norms. So, given this applies to most non planners we probably shouldn't look to them as examples of sound process. Let's look at those who **do** succeed.

I want to dispel here the common myth that wealth is mainly inherited. Many studies have been conducted on this over the years including 2019 versions by Wealth-x and Fidelity Investments. They all conclude broadly the same thing, upwards of 70% of millionaires are self-made not through inheritance. These studies also show income is less important than planning and consistency. For example, teachers appear in the top five millionaire producing careers in multiple studies, above lawyers and doctors. Between 20% and 40% of self-made millionaires never earned six figure salaries at any point in their careers. These studies also show the most dangerous generations for wealth are second, who tend to protect not build and third, who do rather well at blowing the inheritance having not learned the skills we're discussing around how it was built or protected!

We can debate whether in 2023 "millionaire" still represents wealth but I'd assume most readers don't qualify (yet) so it may be their future target. The data tells us new millionaires come from people like you. They're self-made and not only can it be done, it's done more often than you might think.

For more context, I asked a friend if the many high net worth individuals he works with across his businesses have financial plans. As CEO of Crypto Caesar Capital his group helps individuals manage a combined net asset value in excess of $50 million. In line with these studies his answer was yes, in his experience HNWI's have "very well thought out plans covering most aspects of their financial lives, from investing to tax and estate planning".

What can we surmise from all this? We know most people don't have formal financial plans. We know most people don't succeed financially, many living pay cheque to pay cheque. And we know from both available studies and from someone who deals with HNWI's on financial matters regularly that wealthy individuals tend to have and follow formal and well-rounded financial plans. As I said, learn from those you want to emulate, those who've done this already even if their achievement is beyond your initial targets. People who build wealth successfully are intentional about doing so through setting financial goals, having financial plans, executing those plans and tracking progress.

I believe planning a fundamental requirement for financial success and it starts with knowing what financial success looks like as an individual. There's no one size fits all vision of it, you need to define what it looks like for you and your family and record it inside a sensible framework. This financial plan defines what success means to you and how you'll deliver it. It ensures you're covered for all financial needs and defines how to manage risk, effectively allocate resource, optimise your approach and minimise tax impact. Is it really so important? The data and my own personal experience suggests overwhelmingly **yes**.

A NON-FINANCIAL EXAMPLE

Planning seems such a simple process it can't be as important in successful outcomes as I suggest. For those still sceptical after seeing the data shared, let me offer a non-financial example most can relate to for further emphasis.

Consider two people who want to lose weight. Who do you think is more likely to be successful? **PERSON A** doesn't record the weight they start at or want to get to, doesn't plan meals and doesn't track or record what they eat on a daily basis. They exercise when they feel like it but to no set routine with no set program and have no timeframe. **PERSON B** records target weight and starting weight, tracks progress and tweaks their plans if they plateau. They plan meals and track all calories that go into each. They have a schedule for exercise they follow and a timeline set with a target date and weight they're working towards.

In the majority of cases you'd expect Person B to reach their goals and Person A to fail, right? Running this scenario through a modeller 100 times, Person B would succeed more? What's the difference between them? Clear and measurable goals, a plan to deliver them, progress tracking and adjusting as necessary. Person B has a clearly defined plan they track and execute, Person A doesn't.

In personal finance, where margins are tight, it's just as critical for long-term success. It's something we know financially successful individuals do, so why wouldn't you?

THE BENEFITS

We've discussed their importance in setting us up for success, akin to architect drawings in a house build showing target state and providing assurance during build you're getting the intended outcome. You can always tweak as new data presents during the build phase but in a controlled way based on original baseline and feedback loops you built into the process.

The main benefit in making the effort to formalise your financial plan is that it statistically improves your chances of long-term success. It shows the intent required to make meaningful change, holds you to account for delivery and provides feedback on progress to help manage positive behaviours over time. As a result it reduces financial anxiety, leaving you feeling in control of your financial destiny. They provide additional benefits too, including:

- **DIRECTION** and **FOCUS** by defining when, how and what you want to achieve with your finances.
- The ability to **IDENTIFY, ASSES & MANAGE RISK** within your finances.

- The **MOTIVATION** to make mindset and behaviour changes knowing your purpose when making them.
- The **DISCIPLINE** to enforce mindset and behaviour changes over time knowing the outcomes they can deliver.
- The ability to **PRIORITISE** day to day actions to deliver your financial goals, reducing impulsive financial decisions you "feel good" about in the short-term but hurt you long-term.
- The ability to **MEASURE** progress by knowing your targets and assessing delivery, getting **POSITIVE REINFORCEMENT** your work is having the desired results.
- The ability to **IDENTIFY EARLY AND ADJUST** when not achieving desired outcomes. You won't get to the end before realising you fell short like many potential retirees.
- The means to **REGULARLY REVIEW AND UPDATE** your plans to make sure they're in line with best practice, changing personal circumstances or emerging regulatory changes.

PLANS NEED ACTION!

I often see people trip themselves up by taking time to create amazing plans but not then taking action to deliver them. At the outset of this chapter I said reading a book without taking **action** is a waste of your resource, the same applies to financial plans.

As we know, the majority of people don't have them. But it's also true not everyone who has them will succeed in **delivering**. Remember, no silver bullets. There's a mix of people with well rounded, well thought out and clearly defined financial plans who are successful and those who have them but remain unsuccessful. Having a plan isn't the hard bit, delivering it is.

Lack of action isn't the only reason delivery can stall. Some will take action but for a multitude of reasons won't fully reach their goals. But here's the thing: You **might** fail to deliver some elements if you take action, you **definitely** fail to deliver all elements if you take none. Delivering 80% of your goals leaves you in a far better place than delivering 0%.

"Vision without action is just a dream, action without vision just passes the time, and vision with action can change the world."

[Joel Arthur Barker | Author]

Author Joel Arthur Barker describes beautifully the interplay between planning and action, highlighting how one without the other dooms a venture to failure but when we combine the two meaningfully we can change the world. In our context the world we're aiming to change is our personal financial one.

Many people put too much weight on the planning side of the scale, not enough on the action side. The imbalance should in most cases actually be reversed where planning takes less of our resource than action, the actual "doing" elements. From a financial perspective not only does this fail to move us forward but because personal finance is such a finely balanced scale it can actually move us backward. What do I mean? Let's use the financial goal of becoming debt free as our example as it's one many people have.

If clearing debt is written into financial plan goals but no action is taken to a. change spending behaviour to stop accruing additional debt **and** b. reduce debt by paying down the principal, then the debt grows through additional spending and additional interest implications. Failure to action either activity means owing more, not less. The situation in terms of clearing debt and reducing service costs hasn't improved, it's actually gotten worse. But the goal was in the plan........

This is a simple reinforcement of the point I made at the beginning. To improve your financial outlook you **must take action** to progress your financial goals, whatever those are, not just make plans. The act of formally creating a financial plan is a powerful one but you're not done there, it needs action to change your actual outcomes.

The final point I want to make on planning versus action is around the phenomenon of "analysis paralysis". I see this manifest in enough people to know it's a real issue for some. They spend inordinate amounts of time on beautiful plans detailing the perfect manner in which delivery should run. They anticipate perfectly executing this plan, which of course rarely happens, so they become paralysed when deviation occurs, unable to move forward.

I said earlier problem solving is an important skill because you'll always have problems to solve, even if you have the best plan in the history of plans. Nothing ever runs perfectly, at least the odds in my experience are pretty damn slim! The pursuit of perfect is generally the enemy of getting the job done, so adjust as required to deliver the value you want. This inflexibility also presents a secondary issue where we become tied to ideas even when in progress feedback is telling us it's the wrong idea.

It's a hard decision to stop something when it becomes clear the value you expected to achieve won't materialise. It's an issue technology organisations really struggle with, particularly over long timeframe delivery so I've seen it many times professionally. What appears the correct solution at the outset can be found to be entirely the wrong solution at any point if circumstances change, often many months later once it starts to take shape. People consider it a failure if they don't see delivery through per their original plan even knowing the value proposition has failed. They plough ahead regardless, wasting resource.

I think the opposite. Continual reflection on the value expected from your efforts and making the decision to stop something once you confirm it won't provide the expected value isn't a sign of weakness, it's a sign of strength. You should be ruthless at stopping things and moving resource to something that does deliver value in the context of your goals.

In summary then, although financial planning is important for getting out of debt and building wealth, make sure you take action to deliver your plans. Don't be paralysed by over analysis if they don't run perfectly, find a way to adapt and solve the inevitable problems so you can deliver the value you want. Getting the job done is usually more important than how you get it done when shaping your financial future.

If it becomes clear your anticipated value is not going to materialise, even after a long investment of resource, have confidence to cut losses and move future resource to other value delivering activity. If something could deliver partial value then you can make decisions on a case by case basis to continue or stop. This **does not** give you licence to start lots of things and never finish anything! It's specifically for things you're working on and confirm beyond reasonable doubt the expected value won't materialise.

FINANCIAL PLAN FRAMEWORK

We've now covered the what, why, benefits and some of the pitfalls of financial planning. With this understanding we can look at an example framework to help you to actually build a financial plan, ensuring it's actionable over time to improve your financial future.

I'll lay out the high level sections I believe a well-rounded financial plan should have and we'll spend the remainder of the book building those sections together so you end with a draft plan to refine and take forward. The framework I'll outline is unsurprisingly the one I use myself.

You may decide to include additional sections or you may feel you don't need to include everything we'll discuss. Either position is absolutely fine. This is a long-term, living plan you'll update and improve over time so you don't need to worry about "getting it wrong" at this stage. Remember, no-one ever finished anything they didn't start and this is you starting. It's a behaviour change as you formally define the financial improvements you want to make then go after them intentionally.

The individual sections warrant fully detailed chapters of their own to provide the technical detail you need to draft them. In this chapter we'll stick to the plan framework and start with the first section, **GOALS & TARGETS**. The following framework includes the key components I think you need in a comprehensive financial plan, reflected in the supplied template:

1. **GOALS & TARGETS**
   a. Long-term Goals
   b. Short-term Goals

2. **BUDGET & MONEY MAP**
   a. Assets
   b. Liabilities
   c. Money Map: Income, Expenditure (Future-Self), Expenditure (Want), Expenditure (Need)
   d. Budget based on a, b and c balanced to ensure living **beneath** means
   e. Target monthly allocation strategy for Future Self (Retirement, Debt Clearance, Investments, Asset Building, Emergency Funds, Cash Savings)
   f. A sliding scale strategy for e. ensuring "Need", "Want" and "Future-Self" are accounted for and balanced.

3. **RETIREMENT PLANNING**
   a. Target retirement duration and goals (what do you want to do in retirement and for how long)
   b. Annual drawdown requirement to cover retirement goals, inflation adjusted
   c. Projected Lump Sum requirement (if any)
   d. Required pot size based on a. b. & c. (inflation adjusted)
   e. Required Monthly contribution to get d. by a. using low, medium and high Year on Year growth models
   f. Retirement Account Details (Employer Pension, SIPP, ISA, 401k, IRA, Roth IRA etc.)

    g. Details of how b. will be comprised (from which accounts) for most efficient Tax relief.

4. **DEBT SERVICE & CLEARANCE**
   a. High Interest Short-term Debt (1 month – 2 years)
   b. High Interest Long-term Debt (2+ years)
   c. Low Interest Short-term Debt (1 month – 2 years)
   d. Low Interest Long-term Debt (2+ years)
   e. Plan to clear debt systematically in order a. b. c. d.
   f. Debt refinance or (in worst case) consolidation options for service affordability.

5. **INSURANCE REQUIREMENTS**
   a. Assessment of needs (Home, Contents, Life, Disability, Health, Car etc.)
   b. Procure requirements in a. and record
   c. Plan annual review of a. (based on policy dates) and repeat b. annually based on c.

6. **INVESTMENT STRATEGY**
   a. Investor Profile (Objectives & Risk Tolerance. Understand "you")
   b. Target allocation strategy (Markets, Geography and Asset Classes)
   c. Platforms/Brokers with consideration given to fee structure & Tax Advantaged accounts
   d. Rebalance strategy & review timeframes
   e. Regular Dollar Cost Average plans

7. **ESTATE PLANNING**
   a. Define beneficiaries
   b. Define structure of beneficiary assignment
   c. Established Power of Attorney for Financial & Health matters
   d. Trusts/other Tax Advantaged vehicle details
   e. Legally notarised Will including a. b. c. and d.

8. **TAX PLANNING**
   a. Tax Efficient accounts utilised (Pension, ISA, JISA, LISA, IRA, Roth IRA, 401k etc.)
   b. Other tools/strategies for limiting Tax Liability
   c. Accountant / Tax Advisor details
   d. Plan annual review of (local) Tax landscape
   e. Update a. and b. using advice from c. in line with d.

9. **PLAN REVIEW SCHEDULE**
   a. Review schedule for Financial Plan & Goals timescales (quarterly/bi-annually etc.)

b. Financial best practice review as part of a.
c. Update Financial Plan as required based on outputs of a. and b.

The content within each section will be specific to individual circumstances so very much personal to you. This framework though provides you a starting point, something to use to begin building your plan section by section.

PROFESSIONAL ADVICE

In some (or all) sections you may benefit from professional expertise, like tax and estate planning. Regulation changes make it challenging for us to stay within legal boundaries and best practice so advice can add value as these professionals must stay up to date so can help you operate within an often changing landscape. It can also provide a second opinion, sometimes saving you from yourself and any potentially harmful mistakes.

One should always be aware though, even if you employ professional assistance you remain wholly accountable for any actions taken, not just figuratively, legally too.

I'm generally reticent to recommend investment (including pension investment) advice due to fee structures. Often a 1-3% perpetual fee is levied on the growing value of the portfolio which can become quite significant over time. I understand our advisor community have overheads like insurance costs and many of their clients may prefer this sort of subscription model for an ongoing relationship they find value in. It's simply my observation that some people end up with one off advice, little to no ongoing relationship or value added and a lifetime of perpetual fees to pay for it at huge cost. I'd argue this money for old rope.

Ultimately if an advisor works with you regularly and adds 4% above market YoY taking 2% in fees they're adding value. If they add 0.5% YoY and take 3%, not so much. So in fairness to our investment advisors perhaps think in terms of the value they offer and if you find someone you trust who can outperform their fees then it becomes more appealing. I don't think any advisor would be offended by this view, certainly all the good ones I know thrive on being able to prove they add value. Helping people is their goal.

Tax, estate and retirement drawdown planning have a more straightforward value proposition in my view and can potentially save normal people multiple six figures over time. I think investment, budgeting, insurance and debt service decisions we can make ourselves more cost effectively with a little self-learning and limited risk. I understand this can be daunting, especially if new to you, but it's not as complicated as you may fear. Anyone can build enough knowledge to put this together and use it to make positive change. We'll walk through each of these in detail.

PLANNING TIME HORIZONS

Before moving on to the specifics of goal definition, let me do some expectation setting. For most (save for a lotto win!) clearing debt, building wealth and escaping the wealth illusion is a long-term endeavour. One needs to get comfortable thinking strategically and controlling short-term dopamine desires. As I've said there's no quick fix so we need ongoing balance, often over decades.

> *"Geology is the study of pressure and time.*
> *That's all it takes really, pressure and time...."*
> [Morgan Freeman | The Shawshank Redemption]

The Shawshank Redemption is one of my favourite movies so I'm delighted this quote fits so well as an analogy! The story is of innocent inmate Andy Dufresne and the 19 years he spent meticulously planning and executing his escape from Shawshank by tunnelling through walls with a tiny rock hammer, one chip at a time.

It's an excellent metaphor. Clearing debt and building real wealth takes time, strategic planning and execution. One little chip at a time into old habits, flawed "common knowledge" thinking, societal pressure to be "normal" and the actions in our plan. The payoff from all those chips compounded is escape from the wealth illusion, financial freedom and true happiness. For many this metaphor would be comparable to the literal freedom Andy gained from his physical prison.

Because timeframes are lengthy we need shortened feedback loops to ensure we're yielding expected results, allowing timely course corrections if not. We want to avoid the situation of UK pension savers, data showing widespread underfunding for many expecting comfortable retirement and they're mostly unaware.

We need a "one chip at a time" method for delivering larger outcomes, something to build long-term value incrementally and allowing us to ensure we're on track iteratively. Those "chips" are short-term goals, the contributory parts of long-term goals.

I build starting with long-term outcomes then identify short-term goals (or value slices) I can prioritise and deliver, building the value expected of the long-term goal in smaller chunks layered on top of each other. I suggest you follow a similar approach but ultimately the decision is yours as to how you facilitate this feedback loop.

SETTING GOALS

There are many ways to approach goal setting so if you're familiar with something you'd prefer to continue that's fine. The following methodology gives those not so familiar something to start with.

The process should be as simple as possible. Writing hugely detailed and complex goals leaves us less likely to actually deliver them or even remember why we defined them at all! The best way I've found over the years to fulfil the requirement of keeping goal definition simple and consistent is to use "What", "How Much", "By When" notation. I know, it's starting to sound corporate! But we **should** run our personal finances like a business, why wouldn't we? Businesses need to be profitable and to clear debt and build wealth so do we, not break even or run a loss!

We'll go into more detail but an example of a goal written this way to outline the method might be: *"Build a retirement savings pot comprising Pension and ISA of £1.5 million by age 55."* This example of a long-term goal should highlight the simplicity, clarity and consistency of this method and why I favour it.

LONG-TERM FINANCIAL GOALS

Long-term financial goals are generally the strategic outcome rather than a stop on the road, anything from a few months to a few decades in duration depending on the size of task and resources available to assign. If generational wealth is one of your goals the time horizon is potentially longer than a lifetime.

You'll review these regularly so can always add, remove or edit as circumstances change. You needn't worry about right or wrong at this stage, especially if this is the start of your financial planning journey. It's far more important you understand the premise of what you're doing and actually write goals down. Changing how you think and act about money comes through changing current behaviours and understanding why you're doing it. Some examples of long-term financial goals might be:

1. Become completely debt free by age 36
2. Build a retirement savings pot comprising Pension and ISA (Roth IRA in US) of £1.5 million by age 55
3. Build 3 streams of passive income totalling £3000 per month by age 45

4. Build a fund of £70,000 by the time [*insert kids name*] turns 18 to pay for Education
5. Build a business worth £1 million in revenue by 2030
6. Build an asset portfolio that returns at least £1000 per month in cash flow by age 50
7. Build a Trading Account from £5k to £50k by age 45
8. Build a Tax efficient inheritance portfolio of at least £750k by 60 to leave to [*insert kids names*]

These are simply examples of long-term financial goals, yours may differ entirely. That's completely fine, these are not defined to be copied, simply to show the practice. You'll document yours formally within your financial plan in this (or any other) consistent format so you know the outcomes you're trying to achieve. For the record, I believe 1 and 2 (with personal age targets and pension pot sizes) **should** be on everyone's list.

SHORT-TERM FINANCIAL GOALS

I regard short-term financial goals as anything within a few months to a year (or so) time horizon but there's no fixed timeframe. Ideally they deliver parts of long-term goals but they can also be items providing the balance I've spoken of in terms of living life. These might look like:

- (1) Pay off credit card A debt by August
- (1) Pay off credit card B debt by January 2024
- (1) Pay off loan C by September 2024
- (2) Build 3 months expenses emergency fund by December
- (2) Open an investment account and start adding £50 per month to it by July
- (All) Create a robust household money map by June
- (2) Increase pension contributions to 15% salary by July
- Save £1500 for a vacation by May 2024 by putting £150 per month aside
- Save £1000 for home improvements by February 2024
- Save £5000 for wedding by August 2026
- Save £2000 for a used car deposit by October 2025

Again, these are simply examples and yours may differ greatly. Those marked with numbers are short-term "enabler" or "value slice" goals contributing to the referenced long-term goal. This highlights milestone/goal linkage. As discussed these provide a shorter feedback loop to help ensure you're on target for the long-term goal and if not allows you to adjust before it's too late.

Those not marked are "non-contributor" goals, with no long-term benefit. I'll never advocate forgoing these entirely, we all need to live life. The key is not expecting everything all at once and understanding long-term financial impacts against plan for those you choose. When we understand the impact and make conscious decisions on progressing non-contributors it removes adverse and often unforeseen long-term impacts from weighting too heavily in short-term financial thinking.

I raise this for awareness because many suffer from this issue. It's one of those societal norms most people don't realise is harming their long-term outcomes. When those new to strategic financial thinking write down their long-term and short-term goals there's often a lightbulb moment, a realisation they've a long list of short-term wants contributing nothing to their future selves. Long and short-terms are completely disconnected which hasn't been a conscious choice. This is a symptom of our triad.

One of the secondary benefits of documented goal setting is it allows you see just how much of what you do benefits your future-self and how much is short-term want with little or no long-term benefit. You see warts and all the impact of financial habits on your future-self. This forms another part of our mindset change.

PRIORITISATION

Now we're clear on long-term and short-term goals and the intrinsic link between them we can discuss the next part of the goals process, prioritisation. This is one of those practices many trip themselves up with, generally through one or both of:

1. Prioritising too many things, spreading resources too thinly (same net effect as not prioritising at all).
2. Making the process of prioritisation so complex it's either impractical or prioritises the wrong things.

To mitigate these risks I employ a simple guardrail: "Pick the top 3-5 things from your backlog that give you most bang for buck at any given time."

My intent is ensuring I always identify and complete the items most beneficial to me in value order, not simply tick off a list top to bottom. For example, Credit Card A at 0% for 18 months is less beneficial to clear than Credit Card B bearing 27% interest. Overpaying the 25 year mortgage at 4% is less beneficial than overpaying the same amount on a 5 year loan at 8%. There are many examples like this, not just in debt clearance.

Alongside the overall financial impact the other variable I work with explicitly is time and it's one you should be aware of when prioritising. The overall financial benefit is important but considering lead time and whether delivering faster or slower impacts the value proposition is important too.

Again using Credit Cards A and B as examples: Credit Card A is 0% on a £2000 balance with 3 months remaining then 24%, Credit Card B is 27% on a £500 balance. For this example we're ignoring balance transfer options. Let's assume you can afford to pay £200 per month against these debts presenting 3 options:

a. Pay off Card B at £150, paying £50 minimum on Card A, then pay off Card A at £200, all monthly.

b. Pay off Card B at £150 for 3 months, paying £50 minimum on Card A, then switch amounts when Card A 0% period ends paying it off at £150, then pay off Card B at £200.

c. Pay off Card A at £150, paying £50 minimum on Card B, then pay off Card B at £200, all monthly.

When options are costed, as shown in Fig 2.1 - Fig 2.3 the optimal way to clear the debt is option a, pay Card B while making minimum payments on A, then clear A. Many assume the four times larger balance and 0% period ending makes concentrating on Card A optimal (option c). Option c though takes 15 months totalling £276.88 in interest while option a took 1 month less costing £259.13.

You're seeing here the benefit of time as a variable. Paying Card B off quickly allows payments against Card A to increase faster, reducing interest on both. This is an example of the mathematical efficiency in the "avalanche" method of paying off debts. We'll discuss this more later. The prioritisation logic here, applicable to all prioritisation not just paying off debt, is identify value in your backlog inclusive of time and prioritise based on highest value.

Prioritising based on value like this tends to operate within "biggest bang for buck" guardrails. I'm not advocating spreadsheets for all decisions, that's over complicated territory, this just shows the maths in this example. The more experience you gain the better you get at knowing where value sits without this level of detail.

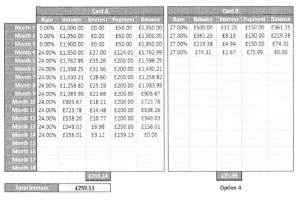

Fig 2.1 Option a table:

		Card A					Card B		
	Rate	Balance	Interest	Payment	Balance	Rate	Balance	Interest	Payment	Balance
Month 1	0.00%	£2,000.00	£0.00	£50.00	£1,950.00	27.00%	£500.00	£11.25	£150.00	£361.25
Month 2	0.00%	£1,950.00	£0.00	£50.00	£1,900.00	27.00%	£361.25	£8.13	£150.00	£219.38
Month 3	0.00%	£1,900.00	£0.00	£50.00	£1,850.00	27.00%	£219.38	£4.94	£150.00	£74.31
Month 4	24.00%	£1,850.00	£37.00	£124.01	£1,762.99	27.00%	£74.31	£1.67	£75.99	£0.00
Month 5	24.00%	£1,762.99	£35.26	£200.00	£1,598.25					
Month 6	24.00%	£1,598.25	£31.96	£200.00	£1,430.21					
Month 7	24.00%	£1,430.21	£28.60	£200.00	£1,258.82					
Month 8	24.00%	£1,258.82	£25.18	£200.00	£1,083.99					
Month 9	24.00%	£1,083.99	£21.68	£200.00	£905.67					
Month 10	24.00%	£905.67	£18.11	£200.00	£723.78					
Month 11	24.00%	£723.78	£14.48	£200.00	£538.26					
Month 12	24.00%	£538.26	£10.77	£200.00	£349.03					
Month 13	24.00%	£349.03	£6.98	£200.00	£156.01					
Month 14	24.00%	£156.01	£3.12	£159.13	£0.00					
Month 15										
Month 16										
Month 17										
Month 18										
			£233.14					£25.99		
Total Interest		£259.13				Option A				

Fig 2.1 | Option a: £259.13 interest cost over 14 months

Fig 2.2 Option b table:

		Card A					Card B		
	Rate	Balance	Interest	Payment	Balance	Rate	Balance	Interest	Payment	Balance
Month 1	0.00%	£2,000.00	£0.00	£50.00	£1,950.00	27.00%	£500.00	£11.25	£150.00	£361.25
Month 2	0.00%	£1,950.00	£0.00	£50.00	£1,900.00	27.00%	£361.25	£8.13	£150.00	£219.38
Month 3	0.00%	£1,900.00	£0.00	£50.00	£1,850.00	27.00%	£219.38	£4.94	£150.00	£74.31
Month 4	24.00%	£1,850.00	£37.00	£150.00	£1,737.00	27.00%	£74.31	£1.67	£50.00	£25.99
Month 5	24.00%	£1,737.00	£34.74	£173.43	£1,598.31	27.00%	£25.99	£0.58	£26.57	£0.00
Month 6	24.00%	£1,598.31	£31.97	£200.00	£1,430.28					
Month 7	24.00%	£1,430.28	£28.61	£200.00	£1,258.88					
Month 8	24.00%	£1,258.88	£25.18	£200.00	£1,084.06					
Month 9	24.00%	£1,084.06	£21.68	£200.00	£905.74					
Month 10	24.00%	£905.74	£18.11	£200.00	£723.86					
Month 11	24.00%	£723.86	£14.48	£200.00	£538.33					
Month 12	24.00%	£538.33	£10.77	£200.00	£349.10					
Month 13	24.00%	£349.10	£6.98	£200.00	£156.08					
Month 14	24.00%	£156.08	£3.12	£159.20	£0.00					
Month 15										
Month 16										
Month 17										
Month 18										
			£232.63					£26.57		
Total Interest		£259.20				Option B				

Fig 2.2 | Option b: £259.20 interest cost over 14 months

Fig 2.3 Option c table:

		Card A					Card B		
	Rate	Balance	Interest	Payment	Balance	Rate	Balance	Interest	Payment	Balance
Month 1	0.00%	£2,000.00	£0.00	£150.00	£1,850.00	27.00%	£500.00	£11.25	£50.00	£461.25
Month 2	0.00%	£1,850.00	£0.00	£150.00	£1,700.00	27.00%	£461.25	£10.38	£50.00	£421.63
Month 3	0.00%	£1,700.00	£0.00	£150.00	£1,550.00	27.00%	£421.63	£9.49	£50.00	£381.11
Month 4	24.00%	£1,550.00	£31.00	£150.00	£1,431.00	27.00%	£381.11	£8.58	£50.00	£339.69
Month 5	24.00%	£1,431.00	£28.62	£150.00	£1,309.62	27.00%	£339.69	£7.64	£50.00	£297.33
Month 6	24.00%	£1,309.62	£26.19	£150.00	£1,185.81	27.00%	£297.33	£6.69	£50.00	£254.02
Month 7	24.00%	£1,185.81	£23.72	£150.00	£1,059.53	27.00%	£254.02	£5.72	£50.00	£209.74
Month 8	24.00%	£1,059.53	£21.19	£150.00	£930.72	27.00%	£209.74	£4.72	£50.00	£164.46
Month 9	24.00%	£930.72	£18.61	£150.00	£799.33	27.00%	£164.46	£3.70	£50.00	£118.16
Month 10	24.00%	£799.33	£15.99	£150.00	£665.32	27.00%	£118.16	£2.66	£50.00	£70.82
Month 11	24.00%	£665.32	£13.31	£150.00	£528.63	27.00%	£70.82	£1.59	£50.00	£22.41
Month 12	24.00%	£528.63	£10.57	£150.00	£389.20	27.00%	£22.41	£0.50	£22.91	£0.00
Month 13	24.00%	£389.20	£7.78	£150.00	£246.98					
Month 14	24.00%	£246.98	£4.94	£150.00	£101.92					
Month 15	24.00%	£101.92	£2.04	£103.96	£0.00					
Month 16										
Month 17										
Month 18										
			£203.96					£72.91		
Total Interest		£276.88				Option C				

Fig 2.3 | Option c: £276.88 interest cost over 15 months

Limiting to 3-5 items concurrently stops you spreading resource (time, money and energy) too thin and risking delivery of nothing. Focussing on value means you're able to compound gains over time in the most efficient way. When completing an item start the next highest value proposition item on your backlog at that point. Rinse and repeat. Time you spend working on goals not in your 3-5, or not on your list at all, is counterproductive, an inefficient use of time, money and energy resources. So having value defined in your backlog helps with the discipline required to stick to your plan.

An additional benefit of efficient prioritisation is seeing items regularly complete, which provides strong psychological reinforcement you're making progress. This is vital for continued motivation, discipline and focus. You should endeavour to complete actions regularly so you see this positive feedback.

NO HALF BUILT BRIDGES!

Something else I observe when talking to people about their financial goals, really just goals in general, is humans have a near universal predisposition to leaving things unfinished. We're experts at taking things so far, not seeing them over the finish line then starting on the next shiny thing.

A common analogy used to describe this phenomenon is of building "incomplete bridges". The direct value in a bridge is carrying load from starting point to destination by road or rail (most freight) in the fastest time. Indirectly this may mean reduced logistics cost, faster time to market, increased throughput, higher margins and a multitude of other benefits compounding over time.

If you build 80% of a bridge you expend resource (time, money and energy) but never realise the benefit of the unusable bridge. You've derived no value from expending these resources and lost your ability to compound potential benefits over time.

The bridge analogy is of course an extreme one to make my point. There are occasions even partially delivered actions can provide benefit in financial terms, like clearing four out of five credit cards. But you don't want to get into the habit of finishing nothing unnecessarily. In my experience people get distracted easily and jump from one thing to the next for no tangible reason. Over time, it's a net negative for a number of reasons.

If your goals relate to business or involve interactions with others, not doing what you say has **REPUTATIONAL IMPACT**. You become less credible and people don't trust you. This applies to financial goals but is applicable to everything we do in life, personal and professional. You don't want people viewing you as the person who never does what they say they will.

Financial goals often build on each other towards a larger goal. Compounding effects allow us to improve our immediate situation and build wealth long-term. Non completion can have significant impact on compounding effects which is **OPPORTUNITY MISSED**.

This process requires momentum. You need to see benefit being derived from your work to maintain the motivation and discipline to avoid snapping back into old behaviours. If you never see anything complete you question "the point", reverting to type as a defence mechanism which **STALLS MOMENTUM.**

If you never see any of your goals complete you can suffer from **REDUCED SELF-BELIEF.** Think of those who give up on weight loss in February, the first time the scale doesn't show the number they wanted even if they haven't followed their diet.

These are just some knock on impacts I see this have on people, so they'll at least be risks you should consider. To mitigate them you should be a closer. When you start, finish to the standard and timeline planned and be accountable. Don't get distracted by shiny things or bored in the final stages, dig in and see it through.

I'll offer one more analogy most can relate to on the mental aspect of this. Think about what you do for physical wellbeing. Maybe the gym, walk, run or play sports, whatever you do to stay healthy. On many occasions it'd be easy to skip a session, your brain attempting to convince you it won't matter or there's a good reason (excuse) not to go. I'm sure you can relate in some fashion.

Consider how you feel when you let your devil win. You generally regret it later right? What about the times you drag yourself there, putting in the work? In my experience those days you fight yourself and win are always the ones you feel the most achievement afterwards. Beating the little devil on our shoulder provides a real sense of achievement. It's the same in all pursuits. When we finish something in spite of ourselves it's motivating because it counters any doubt about our ability or mental strength. Conversely, when we know we should've done something but the little devil wins it brings doubt and reduces self-confidence.

So be a closer, as often as you can even when it means doing it in spite of yourself. There'll be occasions where something you're working on is blocked and you can't clear it, usually when waiting for others. On these occasions it's fine to start something else from your prioritised backlog but when the blocker is cleared go back and complete as soon as you can, don't let it drift.

SUMMARY

Have a formal financial plan outlining your goals, the value they provide and when you want to deliver them. You must know where you're going to have any chance of getting there. Document long-term financial goals as a list of what you want, how much of it and by when. Slice these into smaller short-term goals using the same format then prioritise and work on delivering 3-5 iteratively. Add your short-term wants to this list so you fully understand your balance between future-self and current wants.

Documenting plans formally allows identification of issues within current financial practice. How much of what you do is contributing to future-self? How much is short-term with no long-term benefit? Many are surprised when they document and see the lack of balance, their lists skewed in favour of short-termism!

Goals provide a clear roadmap giving direction and focus. They provide motivation to make behaviour change and reinforce the discipline required to make it stick. Formally documented goals allow prioritisation in day to day life and the ability to measure progress. Progress provides positive reinforcement. Don't leave goals unfinished, be a closer. Build those bridges. Flick that little devil off your shoulder and get the job done. And don't try too much at once, 3-5 concurrently.

It's proven a clear plan and clear goals increase the potential for financial success. Millionaires have this habit for a reason. Financial security, living debt free and building wealth for the future of your family are all intentional endeavours, not accidental or lucky outcomes. Having formally documented plans puts you in the minority doing this intentionally and alongside those more likely to be successful.

I hope you understand the importance of financial plans and goals based on the data around who does this well and who doesn't. You now have a framework to start your own financial plan, so let's get to it in the remainder of this book!

ACTIONS

- Refer to tab "A. Actions" in the Financial Plan template.
- Complete actions defined in section ".: 2 :. | Financial Plans & Goals"

3

Controlling Fear & Greed

"Happy the man who learned the cause of things and put under his feet all fear, inexorable fate and the noisy strife of the hell of greed."

[Virgil | Roman Poet 70-19 BC]

I WANT TO TAKE A quick detour before the next section of your financial plan with three short chapters introducing content I believe vital to long-term success. These fit naturally in advance of budgets and money mapping, our next financial plan topic, as they'll influence your thinking about its application for you. Given my stated aim of challenging your financial views holistically, these sidebars are important psychologically and for challenging societal norms so will intertwine with technical detail throughout.

Why include content not directly related to creating your financial plan I hear you ask? I've found technical competency not to be the sole requirement for success, so while these topics don't directly input into your plan, they indirectly impact your outcomes if not managed. Finance is an endeavour where many internal and external forces act upon us. Technical proficiency provides smaller clown shoes to walk through the minefield, but without the bigger picture we're still in clown shoes, still in a minefield.

To prepare for minefield exit, clown shoe free, I must cover the human condition and the nefarious aspects of personal finance too. We start with our human predisposition to fear and greed, how they adversely impact financial decision making and how they're used by external agents against us.

EVOLUTIONARY HISTORY

These emotions helped our ancestors survive and reproduce through human history. Fear is fundamental in survival instinct, keeping us safe when navigating threats and making our ancestors cautious. The more fear they felt the more likely they were to avoid situations risking their survival or ability to pass on their genes.

Learning the concept of "threat" through fear supported the adaptation to one's surroundings in the pursuit of safety. They learned through negative consequence to avoid threatening situations in future. Think about a child touching a hot cooker, they're unlikely to repeat through fear of further injury, learned through pain (negative consequence).

Conversely, greed supported the accumulation of resources like food and shelter (and mates!). This is also rooted in the need for survival and reproduction. Scarce resources meant those more able to obtain them were more likely to be able to do both. Survival and reproduction have always had intrinsic links to human accumulation and our violent protection of resources.

These emotions have been built into our very being for over 200,000 years. With few exceptions all humans are predisposed to them now just as throughout history. Yes, we're a more advanced species than our hunter gatherer ancestors but these emotions persist within and still make us do some utterly crazy things in the present day, particularly to accumulate resources.

An odd detour for a finance book, I know. The purpose is simply to highlight fear and greed are in all of us, they always have been, always will be and their purpose is constant. They'll never go away so we must understand how they impact us and how we control them, particularly in the modern financial world.

IN THE MODERN WORLD

While fear and greed can be beneficial, modern challenges can also lead to poor individual behaviours which impact financial wellbeing. For example, in societies with abundant resource the pursuit of wealth, real or perceived, can lead to excessive consumption, debt and wealth inequality.

It may be surprising given my wealth inequality concerns that of the options available I think free market capitalism the one offering normal people a fighting chance, regardless of individual background. To borrow (and amend slightly) from Churchill: Capitalism is the worst economic system - except for all the others we've tried. My advocacy of wealth for normal people though isn't one of "excess", it's one of "enough", which hopefully comes through clearly. When talking about wealth building I **do not** mean unfiltered greed, the pursuit of excess seen too often in society and worsening the wealth inequality problem.

I don't want anyone to think our aim is the modern day obnoxious idea of "wealth" found on social media, or the corrupt reality of it we see in some institutions and politics (think 2008). This is precisely the pretence the book title takes aim at. Excess greed generally fails, it's rarely built on strong foundation. My vision for my family is invisible, "enough" to provide freedom of time and independence such we can live comfortably and no-one would know. Money buys time and having time in my view is wealthy.

This can't be realised in the modern context if we're too greedy to know where excess begins, taking too much risk or living a wealthy pretence through debt. It also can't be realised if we're too fearful to take controlled risks. Conquering fear and taking the risk to be different from societal financial norms I may suggest is your start! In the modern world if we don't work to control fear and greed then we still risk negative consequence, like becoming trapped as Consumers, Debtors and Employees. One could argue at the whim of modern day predators and rival groups, just like our ancestors.

If your vision of wealth is different, that's fine, the methodology remains. Everything we discuss applies to building enough or to excess. As you might imagine you simply stop, or don't, at enough! Either way fear and greed need to be understood and controlled in day to day financial interactions.

IN MARKETS

Financial markets are psychology driven and no quote has been used more than Warren Buffet to affirm it. He captures elegantly how fear and greed in the masses dictates price movement and being contrarian yields best results. This is important to keep in mind for our investing discussion later but also in the context of our wider mission as we aim to be contrarian to normal financial practice.

> *"Be fearful when others are greedy and greedy only when others are fearful."*
>
> *[Warren Buffet | Legendary Investor]*

This isn't a new concept. Japanese candlesticks were invented in the 18th century as a visual representation of price movement. Developed by rice trader Munehisa Homma they reflect his observations on the relationship between human psychology and price. Centuries later they remain as insightful as ever, still a primary source of analysis for technical traders around the world. Why? Human psychology doesn't change, fear and greed are constant. In markets they impact price alongside external factors like supply and demand.

Homma meticulously documented price, identifying recurring patterns in market behaviour. Through this observation he began representing patterns using symbols which evolved into modern candlestick charts. These provide a unique and intuitive way to view the psychological dynamics governing market sentiment.

Japanese candlesticks are in essence a reflection of fear and greed. Each candle comprises a solid body and wicks top and bottom: the opening, closing, high and low prices during a time period. Typically green or white represent bullish (upward) movements and red or black bearish (downward) movements.

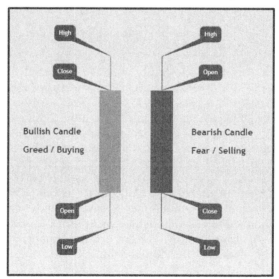

Fig 3.1 | The Anatomy of Candlesticks

BULLISH CANDLESTICKS (GREED): When market participants are driven by greed, bullish candles form. The low of candle body is "Opening Price". The high of candle body is "Closing Price". Wick low is lowest price reached and wick high is highest price reached during the time period. The longer the body the stronger the buying pressure reflecting eagerness of traders to acquire assets and potential levels of greed in the market.

BEARISH CANDLESTICKS (FEAR): Conversely, bearish candlesticks symbolise fear in the market. The high of candle body is "Opening Price" with the body low "Closing Price". The wicks signify the same, highest and lowest prices reached during the time period. The length of the body conveys intensity of selling pressure and thus potential fear in the market.

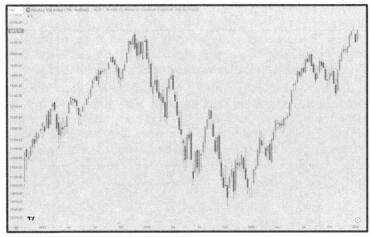

Fig 3.2 | The Modern Candlestick Chart (from TradingView)

Their visual nature, as seen in Fig 3.1 and Fig 3.2 makes them accessible to novice and experienced traders. Unlike numerical data, candles provide a quick and intuitive understanding of sentiment so traders can gauge prevailing emotions and make informed decisions. As they symbolise human psychology the principles apply to all markets, like equities, commodities, ForEx or cryptocurrency. The underlying psychology of fear and greed remains constant in them all which contributes to the enduring relevance of candlesticks across diverse financial markets hundreds of years after first implementation.

This further confirms human psychology of fear and greed is timeless, transcending cultural and technological shifts. While financial landscapes evolved over 300 years with technology advance and globalisation the fundamental emotions driving market participants remain constant. Candlesticks psychology means they continue to offer valuable insight into market sentiment even today. We even have fear and greed indexes in markets which aim to project sentiment at any given time!

IN FINANCIAL HABITS

I've made the case for fear and greed playing an important and lasting role in human history, from the early hunter gatherers through the modern world including finance and financial markets. You must be cognisant they're part of you and **don't** always serve your best interests. This is the purpose of this chapter, to highlight that a huge influence on your success will be **your** ability to control **your** fear and greed in the financial decisions **you** make.

Greed drives excessive consumption and debt accumulation, often to facilitate the projection of wealth, to attain the happiness we're convinced lives there. It's the number one self-harming thing I find in people's finances when asked for help and mostly it's invisible to them till highlighted. This isn't criticism, many people just don't realise it's societal, the expected "norm" building habitual Consumers, Debtors and Employees. Modern herd mentality is one of desire for instant gratification not of the delayed gratification provided by financial planning and long-term endeavour. We must break these habits to achieve our goals.

Fear stops us doing things differently from the herd, becoming stuck in the perceived wisdom of crowds. We follow "societal norms" blindly, finding comfort in conformity even if conformity demonstrably provides undesirable results. I guarantee others will question you when making financial changes because you're stepping out of the herd. The first time you decline an invite on financial grounds you'll likely receive friendly ridicule, might even hear "you can't take it with you". Watch for this and stay firm, focus on **your** goals and execute **your** plan.

In personal finance there are many ways these emotions manifest. Fear of loss is a deterrent from investing in potentially lucrative opportunities. Greed is a driver to engage in speculative and risky investments hoping for quick and substantial returns or consuming at levels above need. Both extremes undermine the principles of prudent financial management I'm trying to espouse, one where we must find balance somewhere in the middle.

Fear of missing out (FOMO) is a distinct example you should be aware of that drives individuals to make impulsive, wasteful financial decisions. In the age of social media, online shopping and constant connectivity FOMO is particularly prevalent and businesses use this to take advantage of you constantly for profit.

How often with items in the basket of online stores do you get a popup offering discounts "just for you" if you complete the purchase in this session? Ever got an email later saying "you left these items in your basket" or seen a website display "only 1 left in stock" when browsing? Time limited benefit, a discount that may disappear or limited supply tempting you to complete the purchase quickly or "miss out"………

This is an example of deliberate (and programmatic!) FOMO inducement to part you from your resources via impulsive decision. There are many examples of this day to day. When I say the modern world is designed to extract maximum financial resource from us, it isn't rhetoric. Make no mistake, it's a zero sum game and if you're not aware you're playing, you're the zero.

SUMMARY

This is an awareness chapter, the first in a number of non-technical discussions aimed at helping you understand technical knowledge isn't the only thing stopping us from achieving our financial goals. Other forces act upon us from individual and societal perspectives. We must be aware of and manage these too.

Psychology is a hugely important aspect of financial success. Understanding and controlling fear and greed plays a vital role alongside the technical knowledge we'll build together. I wanted to have this discussion before the budget and money mapping chapter to allow you to use the knowledge to be honest about your current expenditure. You'll likely find what we've spoken about here when you write your spending habits down.

How much is driven by consumer greed and how much is debt bearing liability? How much is driven by fear? FOMO or fear of being different to perceived "norms". How often have you decided not to do something like invest or add to a pension or take a financial opportunity because it's "too risky" without actually analysing the risk? How often have you been pressured into spending money by societal expectation or perceived loss (financial or social)? Have you ever justified spending on something with "I can't take it with me"? "I can't take it with me" is FOMO too.

I want you to think about these issues, be honest with yourself and understand we all have these voices. Those who succeed financially are better at managing them for their own benefit, not the benefit of others. The technical discussion we'll have on money mapping will provide tools to control fear and greed in our budgeting, but I want you to know what they are so you know why we're implementing these measures.

Incentives Dictate Outcomes

"Show me the incentive and I'll show you the outcome."

[*Charlie Munger | Legendary Investor*]

ECONOMICS IN ITS SIMPLEST FORM studies how incentives influence human behaviour. It assumes "rational choice", where individuals or groups make decisions based on their perception of the best outcome for **them** in any given situation. If I sat in front of a sign offering £20 to shake hands I'd likely gain a long line, but a sign asking for £20 to shake hands and I'd likely sit alone. Know the incentive, project the outcome.

The relevance in a financial context is simple, we must aim to understand the incentives of those trying to assert influence upon us and through rational choice their motive can be deduced as whatever most benefits them. For example, one of the reasons I limit debt exposure is I presume the incentive of debt issuers is to profit at my expense, not to help me. Unfortunately financial motives are seldom more complex than this.

When aiming to identify these incentives we must remember they can be positive or negative and look for both.

POSITIVE outcomes can be things like financial gain, property gain or reputational gain. For example, government programs offering financial incentive for energy efficient technology use likely increases uptake because financial incentive is stronger than environmental incentive for more people. We've seen this all over the world.

NEGATIVE outcome avoidance can be things like financial penalty, property forfeit or reputational damage. For example we're incentivised out of illegality by the threat of penalties applied. A minority find positive incentive in crime where they deem financial gain outweighs punishment risk but the majority abide by the law. Consider the recent change where some US states stopped prosecuting shoplifters below a certain theft value. Incidents increased exponentially as positive gain incentive (greed) took over from negative loss avoidance incentive (fear).

Incentives can also often be unintended, so we must look for this potential too. A simple example is standardised testing in US schools. The intent was to improve learner outcomes, financial incentive offered to achieve it, based on test results. This initiated "teaching to test" to boost scores, narrowing the curriculum and removing useful skills kids used to be taught. It led to neglect for individual needs and in multiple cases actual test score manipulation by teachers and schools to secure financial reward. Learner outcomes worsened unintentionally because financial incentive promoted counterproductive behaviour in many teachers and schools. Through proper rational choice consideration, this might have been predicted.

Incentive is the bedfellow of fear and greed, together part of human behaviour. One should aim to understand our own incentives and those behind any external interactions. Financially, failure to understand incentives often leaves us unwittingly suffering negative consequence or missing out on positive gains. People think this applies only to things like fraud and criminality but the reality is people are incentivised to exploit us in a million legal ways every day. Marketing is the literal embodiment of this as a profession. As much as capitalism provides opportunity, it comes with risk and we must remain vigilant to these risks.

We can suffer direct monetary loss (giving our resource to others) or succumb to psychological manipulation that inhibits our ability to make financial gain (not investing in ourselves). Have you ever wondered for example why media and politicians default to negativity? "If it bleeds, it leads" has been the internal guideline in mainstream news for decades and politicians constantly tell us who's holding us back, who we should be angry at (not them, obviously!). Stoking anger is an invocation of fear and fear is a pre-requisite for control. When fearful, people can be made to do almost anything but rarely anything of use to their own outcomes. Examples exist throughout human history and one need only look back to Covid for the most recent iteration .

It may seem I've turned a little Orwellian here, but let me explain what I mean. The Anglosphere regularly rates "freedom" as the most important right citizens possess. Stronger feelings for this exist in places like the US but it's fairly consistent across this demographic. Consider then how quickly the majority in these countries were made so fearful they not only willingly gave up freedom for the promise of safety, they actively sought to give it away. Those unconvinced by the narratives were held in contempt simply for asking questions or retaining rational thought.

The vitriol spewed towards those who decided the vaccine wasn't appropriate for them given their risk factors was disgusting (for clarity, I was vaccinated as it made sense for me, I'm fine with individual choice). They were banned from travelling. There were calls to criminalise them, to ban them from public services, to stop them accessing vital services like shops, hospitals and general healthcare. Some media personalities actually advocated death if they fell ill or had an accident. The rhetoric was horrible.

So I'd suggest I'm not painting western society any more Orwellian than it actually proved itself to be throughout the pandemic. Why? Incentive. The masses were convinced the best thing for their safety was everyone vaccinated, in a mask and locked indoors. Fear and outrage was stoked by policymakers and media using what we now know to be false narrative to exert control, cover their own ineptitude and quietly redistribute wealth from the masses to friends and family (estimates vary between £300 Billion and £700 Billion in the UK alone).

Orwell didn't write 1984 as a prophecy, but it nonetheless became prophetic. The "telescreens" in every home provided daily propaganda, the "party line" confirmed. Pots and pans banging at the same time every week akin to the "two minutes hate" pressure release. Anger and suspicion towards anyone with individual thought and action outside "ministry" rhetoric, set upon by the "thought police" with calls to have them all "purged". We all saw it happen.

Humans are wonderfully interesting animals to observe in these circumstances, our evolutionary psychology as we discussed last chapter is constant regardless of societal pressure or technological advancement. It means we can be relied upon to do the same things century after century if the incentives sold push the correct fear or greed buttons. Our ruling classes (the knowledgeable minority) know this and push those buttons like an 80's kid playing Daley Thompson's Decathlon! As I've said we're cattle in a far larger game.

Since we're having this sidebar, a similarly interesting and I think relevant dystopian view can be found in the concept of Moloch in US poet Allen Ginsberg's poem "Howl". Ginsberg describes Moloch as a metaphorical embodiment of societal and systemic forces demanding constant sacrifice. Derived from ancient mythology Moloch was a god presumed to demand human sacrifice in return for peace and prosperity, but Ginsberg used it as a critique of the dehumanising aspects of modern society.

He criticises the destructive forces of capitalism, conformity and societal expectation, all three critiques within my Consumer, Debtor, Employee triad. Moloch isn't a literal god demanding human sacrifice in Ginsburg's work, rather it's the representation of an all-encompassing force that consumes human creativity, individuality and freedom. It can be used broadly to discuss the demand for excessive sacrifice of personal freedoms, values or wellbeing for the naïve idea of "greater good".

I think this is relevant to our personal finance goals as this idea of individual sacrifice for the common good is sentiment I see rising since Covid and it adversely impacts on those goals. It's natural end in my view would see individual accountability for our outcomes and our agency to improve them subsumed by collective outcomes we're completely reliant on those in control to provide for us. This would make it much harder for normal people like us to drag ourselves upwards. Personal accountability and general meritocracy are values I consider vital to equality of opportunity and I'd claim the "greater good" argument has only ever been "good" for those in control, never the "greater" masses it's sold to.

Another odd detour, but relevant as I'd suggest in a financial context the Moloch in question here is my Consumer, Debtor, Employee triad. A system of conformity, herd mentality and limited creativity demanding excessive sacrifice of future-self not for individual, family or community benefit but for the benefit of those profiting from us. Agree or not, it's the metaphor I offer!

Am I cynical by nature you ask at this stage? Yes, absolutely. Is this an advantage for financial wellbeing? Also yes, absolutely!

This short chapter intends only to introduce the concept of incentives and their interplay with fear and greed. That these are used to manipulate us into conformity to our detriment and how financially being contrarian by nature, questioning the motives of all external actors, helps us escape the herd and not be taken advantage of. Alongside the technical knowledge we'll build, monitoring incentives will help you think differently about financial decision making. I want you to ask "what's in it for them?" and decide whether this fits with the outcomes you're trying to achieve.

Where Are We & How Did We Get Here?

THIS THIRD SIDEBAR CHAPTER PROVIDES some insight into the underlying problem. I want to explain my views on the harmful impacts of socially accepted financial norms, their causality and their standing as perceived routes to happiness. This'll help with your consideration of the alternate options I advocate.

This can be summarised as a pervasive lack of financial knowledge that leaves the majority of people susceptible to manipulation for financial gain by a knowledgeable minority. This minority advocate, facilitate and profit from detrimental financial practices sold as "normal" routes to happiness. Aspiring to this vision of happiness by employing these practices means many struggle with the financial aspects of their lives, unhappy and often trapped by the long-term consequences of consumerism and debt these norms are generally built around.

This isn't a criticism of the majority, simply an observation based on experience. Many people don't realise there's a choice, a different means to deliver genuine prosperity and long-term happiness without bonding oneself to the Consumer, Debtor, Employee triad. That's all I offer. Hopefully this resonates and will help you understand how I think we've gotten here as a society.

AN EXAMPLE

To bring to life this abstract summary I'll offer a short example. Store cards/accounts are one of the "normalised" practices I reference, developed by "the knowledgeable minority" who know they increase consumer spending and by extension their profits. Usage by the susceptible majority means spending more on consumer goods than those not taking similar credit options (as all study data shows) and risks entrapment in harmful debt spirals.

Even 0% interest users must service balances monthly and in doing so they're often unable to utilise cheaper suppliers for similar or same products. They become a captive audience, consuming more through the card/account that's bonded them because they can't afford to shop elsewhere while simultaneously servicing the debt. This drives more profit for the knowledgeable minority and more financial struggle for the susceptible majority who thought they were utilising "normal" means to obtain the things they "need".

This is one everyday example of a knowledgeable minority advocating, facilitating and profiting from a financial practice considered normal which often traps those with limited financial literacy. I could cite dozens of other examples, from instant at the till/cart credit (like pay in 3) to credit cards to payday loans to lease cars. All services created by a financially knowledgeable minority to maximise profits based on their understanding of money and consumer behaviour.

The cumulative effect in the daily lives of those who don't build financial literacy is rising wealth inequality, rising debt and increased dissatisfaction with their financial situation. Those who know the game profit from these products and services at the expense of those who don't, not through direct oppression or the removal of choice/free will, but rather more nefariously via the facilitation and promotion of harmful financial practice which whispers to said free will like a little devil on our shoulders.

Of course it's possible to utilise these products and services to our benefit, the concept of "useful debt" I'll discuss in detail later. The reality though, from both data and personal experience, is the majority don't utilise them beneficially. Hopefully this makes clear the practices and counterparties I'm referencing.

WHERE WE ARE

In 2023 a joint wealthify.com and Centre for Economic and Business Research (CEBR) study found only 5% of UK respondents could answer 10 simple questions about common financial topics. In a study group of over 2,200 individuals 73% fell below the 65% pass mark. This study supports my long held view on the financial literacy issue, concluding that lower levels of financial literacy are a strong predictor for the harmful financial decision making that traps people in the Wealth Illusion.

Many of these studies also show an inherent link between intelligence and positive financial decision making. I want to address this point. I know many highly intelligent individuals who implement harmful financial behaviours and I find it improbable the 73% who failed to reach pass mark don't possess the cognitive ability to succeed financially. I'm not attempting to debunk the theory, I just don't want to make this an intelligence debate as I don't believe it the root of this problem.

If we assumed everyone had the same level of financial knowledge then we might expect those of higher intelligence to outperform, yes, but in my view the assumption of shared baseline financial knowledge fails. So I view this as a **knowledge** issue, not an intelligence one as some suggest. Competence is built with knowledge and practice but "people only know what they know and never know what they don't", in the words of a respected colleague. We rarely tell people what they don't know about money, so they don't know what they don't know. I think we should start here! Let's look to upskill those who just don't know what they don't know so they might make better, more informed financial decisions.

With this in mind, let's baseline the problem statement: the National Financial Educators Council (US) describes FINANCIAL ILLITERACY as:

> *"Lacking the skills and knowledge on financial matters to confidently take effective action that best fulfils an individual's personal, family and global community goals".*

Conversely, Investopedia defines FINANCIAL LITERACY as:

> *"...the ability to manage personal finance matters in an efficient manner, and it includes the knowledge of making appropriate decisions about personal finance such as investing, insurance, real estate, paying for college, budgeting, retirement and tax planning".*

These are fair descriptions of where we are, a lack of financial literacy in the majority leaving them susceptible to manipulation for financial gain by a knowledgeable minority. Let's move to what I believe the major contributory factors.

THE IMPACT OF PEER GROUPS ON OUTCOMES

I think people generally accept what we know as a form of collective wisdom shared with those to whom we're most closely aligned. Friends, family, colleagues, teachers and so on. It's where the term "common knowledge" originates.

My colleague's quote highlights our ignorance to things we or those around us don't know, don't do or don't teach us. This creates collective knowledge gaps within social circles and we're mostly unaware of them. In finance this makes us vulnerable to those who do possess the knowledge and take advantage of it. I'm describing the herd mentality suggested previously where "perceived societal norms" originate, norms you must escape for improved chance of financial success.

Knowledge can breed fear in specialist subjects like finance. Think about people taking their car to the garage. They feel uncomfortable, often with a degree of mistrust. Most mechanics are honest though, their main incentive is to keep your business so they don't yield their knowledge as power. In finance this isn't always the case as greed, not fear, provides strong incentive in the knowledgeable minority.

"Knowledge is power" is more apt in finance. Knowing how things really work gives one an invisible power over the majority who don't and as finance ultimately underpins people's quality of life many succumb to greed and exploit their knowledge for personal gain, consciously or otherwise. My message to you then: financial knowledge gives **you** power over your own financial outcomes and reduces adverse impacts from others, so you must seek this knowledge. Consider this the notification of what you don't know, so now you do know what you don't know! Samuel Johnson, the 18th century writer said of learning:

"Knowledge always desires increase, it's like fire, which must first be kindled by some external agent, but which will afterwards propagate itself."

[Samuel Johnson | Writer]

I hope to be the external agent kindling your fire in the pursuit of financial knowledge as I firmly believe even a little can help you and your family massively.

Back to our peer groups and there's a reason successful people surround themselves with other successful people. Further, there's a reason those circles tend to be smaller. When it comes to financial proficiency, quality is better than quantity because outcomes tend to align, or certainly the probability of alignment increases within peer groups. Many studies support this.

One non-financial example is the Framingham study published in the New England Journal of Medicine in 2007 pertaining to obese and overweight adults. It found where individuals within the study group became clinically obese their immediate friend group were 57% more likely to become obese too. More surprisingly, friend of a friend probability increased by 20% through secondary association. This is only one such study as an example, there are many showing outcomes have a higher statistical chance of becoming shared with those around us than not and this applies to finance too. Our peer group has real and measurable impact on probability of success so we must choose peer groups carefully!

The concept of "social contagion" is well investigated, as confirmed in this study. Financially it's similar, people tend to adopt the same or similar financial practices as their peers through social influence. This impacts on things like spending habits, investment approaches and attitude towards debt or risk.

Consider your school friends, those closest to you on your education journey. If we're lucky our parents taught us a bit about reading or counting in advance but in general we start from similar knowledge levels. As teachers lead us through lessons we don't even know most of the curriculum exists. We don't know what we don't know, to refer to the initial quote. For example, if not taught in mathematics most of us (who don't choose to later) would never hear of Pythagoras theorem in our lives. We also wouldn't know we hadn't heard of it. Blissful ignorance of subject and subject matter, just like finance.

This point may seem like a detour but I want you to think about your personal experience in formal education and the company you kept then and keep now. I believe one contributory cause for lack of financial literacy lies here. We don't know what we don't know regarding finance and generally neither do our peers, impacting financial outcomes in our peer groups just like the Framingham study. Ever known members of your group to do similar financial things like spend on credit cards, take loans, change mortgages, cars, mobile phone contracts or go on the same expensive holidays and so on? Of course you have. In groups with limited financial expertise these things become "normalised" and the group suffer more broadly because financial action is accepted as "normal" without any question of negative consequence.

So we're not really taught about finance during our time in education where we form long-term bonds with peers who share our knowledge gap. The gap never gets filled and the group suffers longer term by association. It's certainly the case in my own formal education and later life learning experiences. None of the financial principles I've employed for more than two decades, nor the knowledge of why they're important, nor anything about how money really works was taught to me in formal education or by the social groups formed in school or university. And they're not discussed outside of my financial social group now.

How and why did we get here? It starts here, in my opinion. How much does your current peer group understand about money? How much do you discuss it? How many of you aim to make money work for you rather than you work for money? How many financial practices do you share and are they ever questioned as harmful? This first contributory factor goes hand in hand with my second observation, which I've intimated already.

LACK OF FINANCIAL EDUCATION TAUGHT IN SCHOOLS

I spent 17 years in education, graduating University at 21. Everyday components of finance like tax, mortgages, loans, debt, inflation, investing and pensions were rarely mentioned. I took Economics and Accounting electives at high school providing rudimentary overviews of some topics but most don't choose those subjects so didn't get this overview. My research suggests this has changed since my school days and we do have financial education on the curriculum in UK schools today thankfully, but coverage varies greatly. We've made steps forward, but we can do more!

Considering the useless things I was forced to learn it's quite frustrating. Money governs almost everything we do in life, like it or not, but we don't really teach our children anything about it? Cynics may surmise this isn't an accident, rather a design and as you know by now I'm a cynic by nature. Let me ask for patience as I don my tinfoil hat for a few paragraphs to further explain my CONSUMER, DEBTOR, EMPLOYEE TRIAD in this context!

*"Work hard at school, a good education gets a good job and high pay. Get a house with a mortgage, put down roots. Move to bigger houses with a bigger mortgage. Chase promotion, work harder and longer, your ambition is to climb the ladder for more money. Get a credit card, you **need** a credit card. You can't take it with you. Use credit for better credit scores, you **need** good credit scores so keep taking credit. You need this new widget, it'll help credit score using pay in 3. Don't forget a nice car, maybe two, lease is a good option to get a luxury brand. Always dress well, people won't respect you if you don't look the part..."*

This is a generalisation, not a verbatim speech we all received! We're sold a dream: if we work hard and prove ourselves we can flourish financially. The reality though is we live in a world where it's not as simple as hard work alone and where not everyone starts from an equal footing. For us normal people to have a chance we must see the system of Consumer, Debtor, Employee and build an understanding of money so we can escape it. The super wealthy you see around you don't operate in the same system.

"You'll own nothing and you'll be happy"
[Ida Auken | Politician: WEF]

These are the views I alluded to earlier, the World Economic Forum actually released this publicly. This is a selective quote, granted and they tried to clarify the intent of their 2016 paper titled "Welcome to 2030, I own nothing, have no privacy and life has never been better". Previous commentary by prominent WEF members though made it hard to convince many it wasn't prepositioning their design for our future. When considered in the context of world events over the last twenty five years it's certainly not a stretch to imagine this as a blueprint in flight. In fairness to Auken she presents the essay as an exploration of changing technological landscapes and moves towards sharing economies and access based models (like Uber and Airbnb) that if expanded could make goods and services "social", meaning no need for ownership. She theorises a better, more efficient and convenient future this way and I understand the thinking. But as Thomas Sowell famously said "there are no solutions, only trade-offs" and for many, myself included, the trade-offs in socialist visions of life are too high a price to pay. I understand the appeal and in areas like healthcare, education and wealth inequality I support shared responsibility but not at the expense of privacy, freedom or personal accountability and with the real risk of dictatorial control. History cautions us, it's never ended well and Covid gave us some insight that this lingering risk is constant.

Today, when I consider those messages received growing up, listen to the views of the political class like the WEF or observe media spin in everyday life it's hard to argue society hasn't become an infinite production line of model consumers, debtors and employees. A "cattle class" which excels at enriching others at their own expense, colonies of worker ants who don't really understand money and are convinced they're getting richer as they stay trapped in the system. This construct is my Consumer, Debtor, Employee triad. I raised some socialism risks in response to Auken's thesis so it's only fair I highlight my triad is a major capitalism risk, for balance. The difference in my mind is in capitalism we retain personal agency to do something about it. In socialism our agency is lost entirely to the state. In terms of trade-offs this retained agency is more acceptable to me, I'd rather be able to do something than have everything done to me.

It's remarkable most engage willingly inside this construct, conditioned to believe it's how life works without question. We see the minority build mind blowing wealth using the time, money and energy of the majority, who often can't reasonably survive via recompense provided but are convinced into further consumption and debt service. My favourite example of recent times is the guy in a hat worth ~£4 Billion sat on a golden throne, having just evaded millions in inheritance tax, promising us his government will "ease the cost of living crisis" for normal folks facing "great anxiety and hardship". If it weren't real you couldn't make it up. My father can't leave us his estate without the Tax Man knocking, but we're not "special". We don't play by the same rules and that's without mentioning his brother...

We must work to break free from this system so we might prosper with the agency we have, free from a society increasingly driven by consumerism and debt where we make others wealthy instead of ourselves. Where we're bombarded daily with invasive marketing intended to keep us spending, in debt and compliant. From a world encouraging us to think consumption makes us happy to stop us actually building wealth. In the 1996 novel "Fight Club" author Chuck Palahnuik described this brilliantly:

> *"We buy things we don't need, with money we don't have, to impress people we don't like."*
>
> *[Chuck Palahnuik | Writer]*

We're conditioned to be consumers, debtors and employees and lack of financial education in schools is part of this design. The majority are trapped as employees (making others money) by debt they're encouraged to take and need to pay (also makes others money) to buy things they mostly don't need (which also makes others money) thinking it makes them happy. The golden handcuffs of salary encourage effort "above and beyond" for the dangled carrot of a (negative real terms) pay rise all while living in fear of not being able to pay the debt accumulated in the name of "happiness". Round and round we go, ad infinitum.

This is what education systems are **designed** to produce, ably assisted by media, politicians and organisations like the WEF. OK, tinfoil hat safely removed, thanks for sticking with me! In all seriousness we're conditioned to believe "If I could just make a little more I'd be set" so we chase it by working harder. Data shows overwhelmingly otherwise. Lifestyle inflation is a well understood phenomenon which predicts standing still or going backwards as income increases due to a lack of financial literacy, something which should be a staple of primary and secondary curriculums. If schools educated in detail about finance, sending kids into the world with true financial competence instead of the ability to make spice racks from scrap wood things might be different. Understanding the basics for improved personal financial outcomes isn't a leap, we just don't provide the knowledge.

I've spoken about the lack of financial inclusion by design in curriculums, relevant because I think it requires remedy to break the cycle. I want to be clear though, this isn't an indictment of teachers. I know first-hand it's a thankless vocation. Teachers should be celebrated, appreciated and rewarded far more, so don't misunderstand my point. Teachers don't create curriculums, they deliver them. They're as beholden to lack of financial provision therein as everyone. Ask yourself who creates curriculums and their incentive in perpetuating an undereducated electorate. But, as much as teachers aren't at fault, lack of financial provision on curriculums is on my list of contributory factors.

THE MISREPRESENTATION OF WEALTH

Driven by politics "wealth" has become synonymous with "income". This misdiagnosis originates in easily understandable arguments made by politicians to enable them to point at "rich" oppressors and fuel division for their own ends. Higher incomes though don't indicate wealth and lower incomes don't indicate lack of it. The number of UK millionaires (2.85 million) versus number of income tax paying earners above £150k (~300k) shows this. Best case ~10% of millionaires pay top rate income tax.

Understanding lifestyle inflation means we also know those who don't manage money effectively don't benefit from increased incomes with long-term wealth. Additional income is consumed on a nicer car, a larger house, designer clothes, expensive vacations and so on. None of these indicate real wealth.

Society and in particular social media propagates "how wealth looks" myths making people think being wealthy means looking a certain way. Scores of people, many younger, project phantom wealth for likes and shares. It's all pretence, one incarnation of the Wealth Illusion. In reality most actual self-made millionaires you'd never know they were wealthy, those between £1m and £10m in net worth. To build wealth takes financial knowledge and discipline so when those people achieve it the knowledge and discipline remain. It's self-perpetuating. If interested in the trappings of looking wealthy they'd never have built wealth.

Did you know most new millionaires drive second hand cars, owned outright (never leased) and middle of the road brands like Ford? They tend to live in modest, right sized homes rarely in areas considered rich. They shop in discount stores and don't buy the expensive things we're conditioned to think look like wealth. Studies have repeatedly shown this. You'd never know stood next to them at the store. This creates an odd societal juxtaposition where many view wealth as a projected lifestyle which could never have supported actually building the wealth being projected.

Society is convinced income and status are the key metrics thus we live in an age of pretence where wealth is seen as consumption and debt driven happiness. We aspire to look like the false vision we're sold. But earning £70k with a £900k mortgage and fancy car, reliant on a job to maintain the lifestyle is **not** (in my view) wealthy. Time is not owned. A £200k home owned outright with no liabilities, £35k income and a £750k in assets with no need to work if they don't want to is more wealthy in my book. Income and status aren't the metrics for wealth. Wealth is the metric itself.

It's important you understand this as it's a fundamental mindset shift for many, especially if you're like our £70k earner and projecting wealth without building it or if you've been convinced by politicians high income equals wealth. It doesn't.

GENERATIONAL DRIFT

If I'm to convince you we exist within the Consumer, Debtor, Employee construct, cattle designed to generate wealth for others, then I must offer some explanation around why we don't notice. Generational drift is the illusion that because we get better off throughout our individual lives the system works for us. This keeps us mostly quiet but it's relative as start points are shifting downwards. Consider this example of variance in the UK:

- 2023: Average salary, £33,000. Average house price, £308,000. A 9.33 multiple.
- 1990: Average salary, £12,400. Average house price, £57,800. A 4.66 multiple.
- 1960: Average salary, £600. Average house price, £2,189. A 3.64 multiple.

In the 60's a family could afford the average house on a single income. In the 90's this was still possible but getting harder. In 2023 even two average incomes in a household sees housing less affordable than the 90's and 60's. On two salaries not one.

Generational drift is the theory that the lives of individuals and families can get better throughout their own lifetime, providing the perception of generational improvement but generational start points are shifting down meaning overall opportunity and standards of living are decreasing from generation to generation. We're moving towards the future where our children may actually "own nothing" unless **we** do something.

Plotted on a chart to make the point visual this would look like Fig 5.1 which shows individuals and families improving their living standard over time but doing so from a starting point lower than their parents. General expectation is our children will have it better than we did but as I've mentioned before from millennials forward this assumption is being massively tested if not already failed. In Fig 5.1 assume "Grandparents" as Millennials and read this as a potential path for the generations to come.

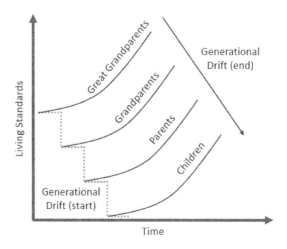

Fig 5.1 | Generational Drift

If we wish to ensure our children are better off than us we must understand this risk and build the knowledge to overcome it, both in ourselves and within them. This contributory factor applies from my generation forward and I want to ensure my daughter has the chance to escape it by leaving her a start better than my own. I fear many of her peers won't have parents with such aims.

LACK OF PERSONAL RESPONSIBILITY FOR FINANCIAL PROFICIENCY

This one is straightforward so we won't labour it. Learning doesn't stop after school and we're responsible for continually improving our skillset throughout life. Continuous learning enables success and something so important as finance should be top of everyone's skill build list. It tends not to be as it's not "sexy" despite its profound impact on our lives.

Many either don't see financial knowledge as important or if they do consider it a problem for someone else to solve. I hope by now we'd agree financial knowledge is important and hopefully we'll also agree at the end of this chapter it's definitely a problem! A problem for someone else to solve? Only if you're looking in the mirror. No-one is better placed than you to take control of your own finances and certainly no-one has the same incentive you do to improve them. Taking personal responsibility for financial knowledge regardless of age can change your mindset and skillset for the better. It's never too late, but lack of personal accountability makes this a contributory factor.

LACK OF FINANCIAL KNOWLEDGE IN OUR PARENTS

While discussing gaps in formal education I've been challenged numerous times on the role of parents in teaching their kids how to navigate the financial world. Shouldn't they do more?

This is an honest question and I think stems from the growing trend of parents considering teachers fully responsible for learning outcomes, so leaving them to it. Teachers though are there to teach approved curriculums, ensuring to the best of their ability each child attains enough competence to increase their chances of positive life outcomes. They've no responsibility for anything outside the curriculum, particularly as any class already has five or six sub classes within, different competence levels teachers must create distinct lessons for.

There aren't enough hours in the day nor £'s in school budgets for even the best teacher to deliver even the current curriculum, so anything outside of it is an unfair expectation. Parents do then need to take a more active role in learning.

As much as this challenge around parents teaching financial competence is fair on the basis just described, I have to conclude it's ultimately a failing argument. If we consider the earlier quote in this chapter: "people only know what they know and never know what they don't", we see the failure. Most parents **don't have** the financial knowledge to share. In many cases they don't even know they don't have it! Even if they want to take an active role in financial education for their children, most aren't any more equipped than teachers when it comes to subject matter.

Some develop financial proficiency independently and I'd wager, like me, they'll absolutely ensure their children learn too given the powerful advantage it provides. I've dedicated myself to writing a darn book for my daughter to ensure she's able to learn from me in the worst case scenario! For most though, if we're fair it's not a parental failing, it's more accurate to surmise they're earlier iterations of the self-perpetuating issue we're discussing. They can't share knowledge they don't have and often don't know they don't have.

So, we'd need to solve this problem before placing expectation on parents just as we would teachers. We can highlight the issue but ultimately must concede most parents, like most teachers, aren't equipped to provide the learning. Those who are will do it naturally, but lack of financial knowledge generally in parents is certainly a contributory factor in my view.

INSTANT GRATIFICATION CULTURE & NON-STRATEGIC THINKING

It's become more prominent from elder millennials forward via technology advancement and instant access to information. This isn't a criticism, these generations are simply the first to grow up fully in the information age and experience the knock on impacts. They've issues generations coming before them didn't, partly why I'm writing this book for my daughter, to help give her the tools to for example have a chance at owning a home. Earlier generations take this for granted and there's some quite ridiculous accusations levelled against youngsters today as a result.

The "Boomer v Millennial v Gen Z" arguments are humorous but there's an element of truth within the humour on both sides. Yes, rates were much higher in the 70's, but the delta between average wage and average house price was many multiples lower as we looked at earlier. These are multi variant issues not as simple as some suggest. "We had high rates and managed" isn't an argument. All variables together must be considered and solutions found regardless of generation. The financial issues of any generation shouldn't be dismissed so flippantly by any other.

Technology though has made it easier than ever for younger generations to gain instant gratification for almost anything, making effort and planning requirements near zero. This is a financial problem and a contributory factor in our wider issue.

Late millennials forward don't remember a time before having the worlds knowledge at your fingertips, before you could share every thought instantly with 8 billion people. They don't remember having to get off the internet when your mum needed the house phone and you couldn't take it with you everywhere in your pocket. I love the convenience of today, I'm a technologist after all, but I also remember the work it took to do things in my youth!

To spend your money (frivolously or otherwise) it required effort and planning. You needed transportation to a shop during opening hours, hoping to find the item you wanted in stock at an affordable price when you got there. You often needed paper money. Then you had to transport your goods to wherever you needed them. When buying something it took time and effort as well as money to earn the endorphin hit and the time and effort required was a limiting factor in overspending by itself.

By contrast, you can now fulfil your every desire via a keyword search and have it delivered to your house the next day, sometimes same day, all with 10 minutes effort. If you don't have the money you can get instant credit right there through the interface. This convenience simply wasn't possible for most of human history. Technology advance is hugely beneficial but we must acknowledge the knock on issues created by this level of convenience.

This doesn't just materialise in finance, it's in almost everything people prioritise in daily life. Seeking satisfaction in the short-term isn't inherently wrong when balanced, but excessive emphasis on instant gratification, evident particularly in Anglosphere culture, leads to long-term financial consequences:

- **IMPULSIVENESS & SHORT-TERM FOCUS:** Acting on immediate desires without considering the long-term financial consequences for your future-self.
- **LACK OF PATIENCE:** Constantly seeking immediate reward diminishes the discipline required to work towards long-term goals and their delayed rewards. Financial Wellbeing requires time, effort, planning, discipline and perseverance, all neglected in instant gratification culture.
- **DECREASED ATTENTION SPAN:** Focussing on complex, time-consuming tasks requires sustained attention and effort. Financial success is complex and time-consuming meaning it's challenging in instant gratification culture. How often do you pick up your phone mid task or when speaking to someone? It's become "normal".

- **DIMINISHED RESILIENCE:** Coping with setbacks or delayed outcomes is the foundation of building resilience. This means overcoming challenges, persevering in difficult periods and being able to lose. These skills aren't developed while hooked on instant gratification.
- **CONSUMPTION AND DEBT:** Accumulating debt through impulsive consumption and prioritising immediate "wants" rather than "future-self" impacts on financial outcomes.
- **DECLINE IN MEANINGFUL RELATIONSHIPS:** We see a rise in shallow interactions in place of meaningful relationships. Divorce rates are higher than at any time in history because people are conditioned to prioritise instant gratification. Many legitimate reasons exist for marriages ending but in 2023 some simply needed work from both parties to succeed, work our ancestors used to do. Relationships have been hard throughout human history but in current culture the habit has increasingly become get in quickly and get out as soon as either individual is unhappy in the moment, rather than do the work we used to find fruitful long-term. Divorce is bad financially for everyone other than lawyers so when frivolous on the way in or out it costs money.
- **HEALTH ISSUES:** Excessive consumption of fast food or instantly available "adult entertainment" for example has detrimental effects on physical and mental health. This has financial impact via paying for healthcare, impulsive spending or diminished capability to improve incomes.
- **REDUCED INNOVATION:** Building something new requires time, patience and effort. Favouring immediate results discourages the pursuit of more significant ideas viewed as "taking too long". This can lead to missing out on the financial benefit often found in innovative thinking.

To counter the financial impact of instant gratification we must break the mindset by developing habits promoting patience, self-discipline and long-term strategic thinking. We must adopt balanced approaches to technology and build discipline to balance instant and delayed gratification in consumer decisions. I'd never suggest cutting it out entirely, we all enjoy feeling good, but we must deliberately create and enforce balance to succeed long-term. The rising default in favour of instant gratification is certainly a contributory factor in my view.

BEING CONVINCED TO BLAME OTHERS FOR FINANCIAL ISSUES

I suspect my view on one of the more nefarious contributory factors might start contentiously for some before the explanation is complete, so I ask you stick with me to allow me to make the case fully before you dismiss it. If you disagree we can move on with the book in peace, it won't change the value in the content nor how it'll hopefully help you in your journey.

I want to spend a moment talking about the age old tactic of divide and conquer, where our wealthy political classes play arbitrary groups off against each other as a distraction. The example I'll use is the rising vilification of the non-descript group known as "the rich" who are, we're pushed to believe, our enemy based almost entirely on income as the measure. There are many examples of harmful oppressed versus oppressor narratives presented to us but as this relates to finance I'll use this one.

We've seen "anti-rich" sentiment grow in the UK and US in the last decade and it's worked very well for those pushing the "all your problems are the fault of someone else" narratives as a distraction from their own incompetence or profiteering. I don't disagree we have a wealth distribution problem as you'll have discerned from my views on wealth inequality thus far, my issue is the way those we're told to blame are framed in politics and media. It's the slow moving societal version of "Look kids, a deer" from National Lampoons. Keep the focus elsewhere so it doesn't rest where it ought to, on the actual wealthy. Incidentally they're often the people spinning us these narratives!

Before moving on I'll make an important linguistic distinction. "Rich" and "Wealthy" are distinct terms but in political and social discussion the two are intentionally conflated. For this example I'll use them interchangeably but you should know the difference as this conflation is key to my point. "Wealthy" generally means sustainable long-term abundance tied to assets, investments and financial security. It's substantial net worth with income usually coming via assets not through the exchange of time for money. "Rich" typically means outwardly projected affluence often based on high incomes which usually come from the exchange of time for money but may lack the stability and longevity associated with actual wealth. Wealth operates outside of the system, rich is doing varying degrees better than others still inside of it alongside them.

And let me clarify again I'm not playing down wealth inequality here nor making light of the huge disparity in outcomes between haves and have nots. I support the aspiration of resolving the wealth distribution issue, particularly given my locale and lived experience. My view though is nothing gets resolved through dishonesty, misdirection or creating false division amongst people and I think politically driven narratives like this propagate with the intent to stoke division for votes and/or financial gain in the narrative spinners, not create meaningful solutions.

I personally favour wealth taxation on **actual wealth** above certain net worth value, not taxation increase linked to income which only really moves wealth from middle classes to the already wealthy. Income taxation pulls normal people who are trying to escape the system down, it doesn't raise anyone up. I understand it'd be difficult to implement a wealth tax as those with true wealth are capable of parking it in different jurisdictions for tax purposes. They're financially mobile and already do this perfectly legally. Nonetheless I think it's the aspirational taxation change most likely to benefit the wealth disparity problem, certainly more than income based policies which adversely impact the lower and middle classes not the wealthy targets usually claimed. Income based policies though are generally the focus of public discourse and this vilification of "the rich". Another example of the illusion.

This manifests regularly in "the rich should pay more". We saw the furore when the Conservative government proposed scrapping the 50p tax rate (minimal impact given how few earn above the level, ~300k people). It was used by the opposition to whip people into a frenzy about "tax breaks for the rich". We heard meaningless soundbites like "those with the broadest shoulders should carry more responsibility" from political leaders. Sounds sensible when politicians, enabled by complicit media, repeat these soundbites unchallenged. Grandiose even. Nodding heads and all round agreement "the rich", a vague, unspecified group are the problem and should "pay their share". Complete misdirection. Lies even, in my view.

So what's my issue? Firstly, It's entirely a perception argument leaving it up to those receiving the soundbite to translate what "the rich" means to them. It's deliberately left unquantified, inevitably leading to people believing "the rich" being referenced are the same "rich" in their own subjective heads, living in mansions and driving Lamborghini's. The literal vision of Richie Rich. Even when this isn't the vision people tend to think anyone a little better off than them is "rich" which while understandable (it's all relative) is counterproductive in the wealth inequality debate as "rich" is the wrong target.

Have you seen the Spiderman meme where multiple versions of Spidey point at each other claiming they're the real Spiderman and the others imposters? That's the situation created here, intentionally, in a nutshell. It's disingenuous but achieves the intended result, divide and conquer. The reality is income tax rises in all of human history have generally impacted two groups most, the lower and the middle classes. The actual "wealthy" the average person envisions being discussed sit back and laugh at this argument because they understand how money works knowing income tax rises wont impact them **AT ALL**.

Given the content of the last few paragraphs I should clarify political affiliation: I've none. I don't trust any politician or political party to do anything outside of their own self-interest. I've known local and national politicians personally and wouldn't trust them to run a bath. Harsh? Maybe, but my lived experience nonetheless. I wasn't defending Tories earlier. I'm Scottish and grew up in the 80's so a strong dislike of all things Tory is genetic and though I should be their target demographic I'll never tick "Conservative & Unionist" in any box. Not many Scots of my generation could ever trust a Tory.

In fairness I feel no differently for any party. The rosette colour changes, the self-interest remains. I don't think anyone else is coming to save us so their soundbites are just noise where our own personal progress is concerned. I try to work with an even hand when it comes to politics but given my distaste for the practice this generally falls on the negative side! Take this for what it is.

Back to taxation: Income Tax was implemented initially for "the rich" (by definition at the time) and politicians convinced poor and middle classes to adopt it as it wouldn't impact them. Once adopted the powers were eventually used to tax everyone but by then those initially targeted had found ways around it leaving those in the lower and middle classes most adversely impacted. History rarely repeats exactly but it often rhymes. In the entirety of human history you can find few if any examples of benevolent rulers who gained power and ever gave it back to the people or didn't use it in ways not initially declared.

Humans are strange creatures when it comes to power, driven as discussed by fear and greed. What they say they'll do rarely matters over time, only what they **can** do and their ongoing incentive to utilise it. This was summarised by Lord Acton in his 1887 letters:

"Power tends to corrupt and absolute power corrupts absolutely. Great men are almost always bad men, even when they exercise influence and not authority; still more when you add the certainty of corruption by authority."

[Lord Acton | Philosopher]

As true today as in 1887, the Covid Pandemic showed politicians of all parties in this light. Lock down Christmas party, tested positive but got the train home, canoodling in commons with their secretary or 200 mile drives to test their eyes are working while we're all locked indoors. Again, we don't play by the same rules.

Anyway, "the rich" and "pay more income tax" question. Let's look at the numbers to see who would actually be impacted to further my income tax case. Before we do I want you to have a number in your head you think represents the top 25% of earners in the UK in 2023. Top 25% earners must be rich by definition, right? They're in the top quartile of all income earners, the right side of the curve, so must be who the "tax the rich" proposals are aimed at. That's my perception of "rich" anyway (see what I did there!). Here we go. 2023 ONS data:

- **£26,340** before tax to be top 50% UK earner
- **£40,920** before tax to be top 25% UK earner
- **£62,160** before tax to be top 10% UK earner
- **£84,660** before tax to be top 5% UK earner
- **£175,416** before tax to be top 1% UK earner

How close were you with £40,920 gross (£31,848 net)? Did you think earning ~£32k net before pension contribution was notionally "rich" in the UK by income standards? Top quartile earners include teachers, nurses, civil servants, police officers and fire services among others.

There's my issue with this politically fuelled argument, the way it's presented allowing everyone to imagine what "rich" means. It conditions people, intentionally in my view, to blame someone else for their problems because blaming someone stops you being energised to improve the situation yourself. You stay a good consumer, a good debtor and good employee like you're meant to.

Further, it pits people unknowingly against friends, neighbours and family members statistically "rich" based on income. In a society of such wealth disparity none of these people feel rich. Why? As we discussed earlier, income doesn't reflect wealth. Earning £x with liabilities totalling £x + £20 is a deficit. Liabilities greater than income mean reliance on income to service debts but you notionally own nothing and must exchange your time for money to sustain your lifestyle. This isn't wealth.

The average UK house price according to ONS is £308k at time of writing. A 25 year term with 10% deposit means monthly payments at 5% (long-term mean) are ~£1,621. On £40.9k (top quartile salary) with 12% pension contribution, take home is ~£2,375. 68% of take home pay for a top quartile earner, someone considered rich, required for an average priced home? Not a lot of wiggle room for being wealthy in there?

This divisive political rhetoric steals people's hope, motivation and incentive to work at improving their situation by convincing them solutions aren't within their own gift. It replaces motivation to find those solutions with a sense of injustice towards vague, non-quantified oppressors for whom channelling their energy in the form of anger serves no benefit. It certainly doesn't help the way personal accountability, hard work, determination and skill building would in improving probabilities of positive financial outcomes.

To be clear I'm not suggesting the equally politically fuelled and disingenuous nonsense of "people just need to work harder" or "get a second job" as the answer to all societal problems. This also annoys me. All I'm saying is no-one ever finished anything without starting and political language is designed to break people's will to start helping themselves. It removes motivation by making the outcome seem impossible without political help so few make the effort. Convince people they're held back by invisible hands only politicians and political parties can free them from, break societal will so the masses believe it's futile to expend any energy other than anger towards invisible hands. It's a mass psychological winding up of a spinning toy, pressing the button and walking away.

> *"The World breaks everyone, and afterward,*
> *some are strong at the broken places."*
>
> *[Ernest Hemmingway | Author]*

Those who fight, not accepting the fate they're told is inevitable, are the minority. Those who build knowledge come back stronger at the broken places. These few are those who win out in the end, those who escape our Moloch of Consumer, Debtor and Employee. This is the minority we should strive to be and mindful of this we should understand it takes cynicism around the messages we're fed. The incentive for spinning these narratives is rarely, if ever, to our advantage.

Back to the subject at hand, the reality is the wealthy, the actual "rich" most people imagine when left to their own perception are rarely if ever included in these earnings numbers as they **don't** earn income like the lower and middle classes. Their money comes mainly from assets which are taxed very differently. They don't work for money like us, their money works for them.

To hammer this point home I'll again use this example. The UK has 2,849,000 registered millionaires in 2023. 2.85 million and a little over 300,000 people earning a salary over £150k per annum. Only around 500,000 earn in excess of £110,000. You do the maths on whether you think income tax changes would impact the wealthy, or whether this is a disingenuous argument led by our political class ultimately ending up in lower and middle classes being worse off.

I'm reminded of the old joke "how do you tell if a politician is lying? Their lips are moving".

When politicians stoke the masses with "tax the rich, they're your enemy" rhetoric, the outcome is the same as it's been in every major civilisation in human history. The low and middle class get squeezed, the wealthy get wealthier and the powerful retain power. It becomes a race to the bottom for everyday people and wealth inequality gets worse because we don't tackle actual wealth redistribution. Tackling wealth redistribution would be my preference.

How else does this manifest? Let's have a look at housing. Unbelievably, wealth disparity and poor financial habits mean most top 5% earners in the UK are comfortably in the middle class, they're not wealthy when their liabilities are accounted for. Better off than most in income terms, no argument, but not in the wealthy class from an economics perspective. After tax and NI (no pension) ~£58k net which is 5.3 times lower than average home price (£308,000). In the existing tax system they're already working more than 4 months per year for the government. 4 months of their gross salary goes directly to HMRC without passing go every year. This applies to most in the top 25% of earners, not just top 5%. How many more months should we make middle class earners work for free to "tax the rich" when they can barely afford their homes, their food and their heat? We're already at one third of a year working for the failing services the state provides. How much more before we have a serious conversation on wealth taxation to fund those services and the profligacy of government spending?

Put a different way, the top 5% still need a chunky deposit for a mortgage on average UK homes. Needing mortgages at all on average houses doesn't sound very "wealthy", struggling to get approved for one without large downpayments certainly wouldn't qualify, surely. And that's the top 5% of earners.

Let's look at another metric: according to UK Parliament figures 60% of income tax comes from the top 10% of earners with around 500k earners above £110k. If only 500k people pay tax on incomes over £110k then best case 2,249,000 (83% of) UK millionaires pay tax on incomes below £110k. In reality most of the 60% comes from middle class earners. Top 1% earners pay more now than ever (28.5%) but we can see they mostly aren't the wealthy people picture in their minds. Top 50%-99% earners pay 62% of all income tax with bottom 50% earners 9.5%.

Squeezing middle class earners in a race to the bottom while they celebrate "the rich" being taxed more is beyond parody. More importantly, it doesn't help anyone, it lies to them, making middle down worse off and angry. As I've said, I'm in favour of progressive taxation but given the actual wealthy don't earn their money through income, income tax changes don't impact them they impact everyone else.

People should pay their fair share, I always have like most middle earners. How you define "fair" is the question. Is 10% paying 60% unfair, or 50% paying 90.5%? Politicians don't think so, they want **more** from everyone in the middle class without really touching the wealthy. My frustration therefore is with this narrative focussing on income not wealth. It's used intentionally to "divide and conquer" with outcomes overwhelmingly negative for those it claims to help. It makes wealth inequality worse and silently makes harder the upwards mobility I advocate.

As I work on editing later chapters the Scottish Government have announced their 2023 budget, ably demonstrating what I've talked about here. They've gone after "wealth" by increasing tax on higher middle class incomes. I posted about it on X (Twitter) and the first response? "Piss off then". Intentionally misrepresent wealth as income? Check. Impact only the middle classes not the wealthy? Check. Stoke division among those you claim falsely to help? Check. Check. Check.

I've given more detail than required in this example and I'll still be labelled a "Tory" by some hard of thinking in the political space (like I was in said X interaction!). So be it, all I ask is you think through the argument I've presented around wealth not being equal to income and my preference being the taxation of actual wealth to help remedy wealth inequality. Unfortunately I'm not hopeful on this happening, the world isn't and never will be fair despite noble aims. But we can't operate on how we think the world should be, we must operate on how the world **is**. There's no other way to improve as many people's situation as possible.

Allowing ourselves to be convinced someone else is holding us down, stoking useless anger in place of useful determination is not operating in reality. Don't let rhetoric derail you from your goals. Understand wealth disparity has existed for all of human history and the same divisive tactics have been employed to stop the masses trying to escape it. You have agency, there's a multitude of things within your control. Channel your energy here. If you truly think someone is holding you back, look in a mirror, you'll likely find them there.

BEING SUSCEPTIBLE TO SUGGESTIONS OF HOPELESSNESS

This was intertwined with the last point but warrants its own discussion to cover specifics. It's another method of reducing any drive people have to improve their situation through a form of psychological torture. I'll use mainstream media examples here but it exists in politics and society in general. The crux of it is people are convinced there's no hope, so freely give up their agency by not even trying. This is a major contributory factor to people not learning how to improve their financial situation.

 I've observed in my interactions with those who do better financially there's little interest in mainstream media. Most of them aren't and haven't been for some time interested in news, finance related or otherwise. We're generally taught to stay updated with current events via print and broadcast media, so why do these folks, myself included, pay no attention? The negative impact of modern media reduces drive and determination.

TIME IS PARAMOUNT FOR PRODUCTIVITY and mainstream news covers many topics, most totally pointless. I couldn't give less of a crap who got kicked off what island for what reason. Waste of my time. It's more efficient to find relevant information on topics of interest, leading into the second point.

Someone else's interpretation isn't required. Being fed a narrative coloured by reporter or publication bias or network affiliation serves limited use. I don't like being told what to think, so I'll interpret the detail and **RESEARCH MYSELF APPLYING CRITICAL THOUGHT** to make my own conclusions based on evidence. No longer do "reporters" simply relay facts, they want to set narrative and I'm certainly not buying what most outlets sell.

Mainstream **NEGATIVITY BIAS** has existed my entire lifetime. Negative events capture attention and increase revenue but sucks hope from the audience, impacting their drive and determination to take action within their gift. Constant exposure isn't conducive to the focus and determination required to deliver positive outcomes. Why expose myself to "If it bleeds it leads"?

Sponsors, advertisers, political affiliations, funding sources and a dozen other considerations make media inherently **BIASED**. Tribal, with little if any attempt to hide it. **SOUNDBITES** and **SENSATIONALISM** is the formula for their primary goal: making money. It's no different to YouTube clickbait. Everyone knows how to drive views and revenue these days so I don't trust what media tells me because I think it's rooted in agendas using sensationalism to promote fear. I'd rather investigate myself.

Too many are susceptible to suggestion from outside sources including media and politics. Negative suggestion with inherent bias convinces them they've no control, no agency to do anything. Sensationalising horrible, uncontrollable things using fringe examples to stoke fear promotes hopelessness which inhibits focus and determination to work on things we **can** control. Removing negative influence is a powerful productivity tool, promoting focus and drive towards resolving the issues within our control, including building financial proficiency. However, ensure you don't replace one echo chamber with another. Differing perspectives shouldn't be viewed negatively by default, honest and factual good faith debate is useful so don't dismiss those too easily.

Personal information sources should be accurate, unbiased and where possible peer reviewed. We don't want to drag ourselves away from all opposing views or any debate into confirmation bias. This leads me to the final contributory factor.

THE RISE OF ECHO CHAMBERS AND SOCIAL POLARISATION

Earlier we discussed the influence of social groups in promoting harmful societal norms. This topic presents an opposing view of that argument. Our previous discussion focussed on the negative aspects of perpetuated norms and social regulation within the groups, this promotes a potential benefit of that same social regulation. No solutions, only trade-offs, to quote Sowell again.

Historically, social groups were local, working on a pseudo social consensus mechanism. Members received the same news and information from journalists and ideas viewed as radical within the group were regulated. This helped somewhat to prevent echo chambers and any rise in "extremist" belief. If someone in a local social group put forth an idea not welcome by the group then rational (mostly!) debate could change their view.

This wasn't all positive, clearly. I'd out historic attitudes to race, sexuality and gender for example, which were negatively perpetuated within these groups for a long time. As someone who cares not about meaningless group attributes, only individual character and competence, I consider this a huge improvement.

Nonetheless, breakdown of social group regulation has some negative consequence. It's never been easier for individuals to find echo chambers (often online) and social media algorithms are designed this way, actively escalating news stories to fit the biases they've identified we have from previous views. Two people can have news feeds reporting the polar opposite as "truth" at the same time. This evolution means the positive regulation that once happened within social groups is diminishing and proponents of outlying views thus rarely forced to debate. This leads to rising polarisation of views, intolerance of opposing viewpoints and most worryingly the inability to debate genuinely with or even respect as peers those who think differently on any subject. We've become too tribal, us and them, and I think this another contributory factor. It inhibits critical thought, which is absolutely required to operate differently from the crowd financially.

The globalisation of social ideas has undoubtedly had positive impact for previously marginalised groups and I think this a good thing. Highlighting these trade-offs doesn't mean I don't support those benefits, it's simply a comment on the trade-off: a societal shift away from critical thought where debate and discussion on opposing views is discouraged, violently. A more polarised society of "us and them" than I've ever known, of opposing "tribes" who can't respect opposing points of view under any circumstance and who apply the most extreme position to anyone who dare think differently. "You think tax harms the lower and middle class, you're just a rich person who wants to kill poor people" for example. This is falsely applied position, entirely disingenuous: the two do not equate or even logically flow together, yet it's a lazy link people make. I think this rise in tribalism, of polarisation, is a form of "de-evolution" and certainly a contributory factor in our financial literacy problem worthy of mention.

SUMMARY

There are many contributory factors, more than I've covered, but I want to specifically raise awareness of:

A. The impact of peer groups on outcomes.
B. Lack of financial education taught in schools.
C. The misrepresentation of wealth.
D. Generational drift.
E. Lack of personal responsibility for financial proficiency.
F. Lack of financial knowledge in our parents.
G. Instant gratification culture & non-strategic thinking.
H. Being convinced to blame others for financial issues.
I. Being susceptible to suggestions of hopelessness.
J. The rise of Echo Chambers and Social Polarisation

And within these, two ideas permeate across all:

K. People are unaware they don't really know how money works.
L. The CONSUMER, DEBTOR, EMPLOYEE TRIAD convinces society it's "normal" to work to service the debt used to consume needlessly.

These are the main contributory factors of financial illiteracy, our root problem, as I see them. Hopefully you recognise them and understand the arguments made about why they're important to overcome to be successful. The good news is we **can** overcome, with a little knowledge and some simple changes in financial practice. I know, I've done it! This chapter is about awareness of external factors and nefarious actors influencing our decisions, making sure you recognise them in your daily lives and consider them alongside fear, greed and incentives. These three sidebars highlight technical proficiency alone isn't enough, these and many other societal factors also need careful consideration.

The takeaway, aside from understanding the problem and it's contributors: take control of your own destiny. Don't let anyone convince you you're powerless. Make the things you want to happen, happen.

"Be the person getting things done, not the person convinced things are getting done to them."

[L.T. Noelle | Writer]

Budget & Money Map: Living Beneath Your Means

"It isn't what you earn but how you spend it that fixes your class."

[Sinclair Lewis | Author and Playwright]

TURNING ATTENTION BACK TO THE technical aspects of our financial plan, let's look at understanding your individual money map so you can identify efficiencies. This is the second section I think everyone should actively manage in their formal financial plan, encompassing short-term financial wellbeing and long-term financial security.

I'm intentional in distinguishing between short and long-term because it's clear from both data and my own experience we're generally a lot better at the former, even though both can be optimised. We don't do a good job of giving our future-self the same consideration in budget and planning terms as our current self, then wonder why our future-self is broke when we get there!

By the end of this chapter you should understand the importance of a budget managing short-term needs and wants together with long-term financial security. You should have enough knowledge to create your personal money map and know how to balance present and future self within it. And you should understand the common budgeting problems negatively impacting people's ability to effectively build wealth long-term. The goal from then becomes managing and sticking to your plan!

Looking briefly at data for some perspective: a 2018 study conducted by the UK Money Advice Service showed current financial wellbeing score higher than long-term financial security by a factor of 6.8 to 4.7 (out of 10). A delta of 2.1 points, or 44.6%, reinforcing my point we're better at short-term budgeting than planning for long-term financial security. Or at least we think so.

This isn't an unexpected finding. Short timeframes are easier to visualise and the endorphin return is instant. Longer timeframes are more abstract, not so easy to visualise in terms of outcome and the payoff is delayed. There's an element of common sense in this result but in the context of our discussion so far I think there are some interesting observations can be made around causality and improvement, so let's look at four such points.

Firstly, if two thirds don't have financial plans as we found earlier, it stands to reason long-term financial security would score lower. Building wealth is an intentional endeavour and in this context 4.7 out of 10 actually seems higher than we may expect based on less than 33% of adults actually doing any long-term planning. My question becomes: how much would the gap close if we increased the number of formal planners?

Secondly, society in 2023 generally suffers from short-term thinking as previously discussed (instant gratification culture). Those who consider financial timeframes beyond their next birthday are in the minority but when it comes to legacy, generational financial planning beyond one's own existence, the numbers are smaller still. Most think about it only in their twilight years, so how do we make this thinking happen earlier?

Thirdly, cultural reinforcement of my Consumer, Debtor, Employee triad has negative impact on long-term thinking. Consumerism is short-term by definition and society has been conditioned to consume, aided by freely available debt and encouraged by increasingly digital culture. Long-term planning including wealth building means breaking one's conditioning to operate inside the triad. How do we reprogram these behaviours?

Finally, pretence: The Wealth Illusion. The pursuit of appearing (a false vision of) wealthy is short-term thinking, it reduces capability to build real wealth long-term. Striving for a glamourous Instagram persona today consumes excessive resource leaving nothing to build for tomorrow. The outcome is pretending in perpetuity. It's expensive to fake a false vision of wealth! How do we educate people about this, especially young people?

This is all inferred by Sinclair Lewis in the opening quote, his sentiment something I certainly see adversely impact many with ample opportunity to improve their financial circumstances. They're stuck in the cycle. They struggle with income versus spending in the short-term which leaves no resource to assign to future building, to their future selves.

It's an epiphany inducing moment for some when I ask "*you know your income isn't a spending target right? You know your money has no expiry date (yet!)?*". Blank stares greet me often. People are conditioned to spend to their income and beyond (credit) and they can't rationally answer why. Yes, this is where my disdain for "you can't take it with you" comes from, it's not a rational answer to any spending question!

Changing this thinking in people is hard, taking effort and commitment on their part. Those based in short-term thinking who begin long-term planning can find it really difficult to give up having all things they want like they've been used to. We often see regression quickly to old habits. Retraining your brain away from consumerism and "now, now, gimme" attitudes isn't easy. Take this as a friendly note of encouragement to stick with it.

To the point Lewis made, income is only one side of the scale and while obviously having higher income increases one's potential ability to build wealth long-term, opportunity can only be realised at any income level if expenditure is intentionally and purposefully controlled.

For many, those who could do better over longer timeframes, this isn't the norm. Additional income is immediately consumed through ingrained monetary behaviour where people consider income a target for expenditure. An "I can afford" mindset we're going to help you remedy. This proved infinitely powerful for me over the years in allowing me to actually benefit from increased income by stopping it being immediately consumed.

CAN EVERYONE BUILD WEALTH WITH REDUCED EXPENDITURE?

No, I don't claim wealth lies in reduced expenditure for everyone. There are, generally speaking, 3 distinct categories people fall into (individual circumstances always vary within):

- **INCOME ISSUES:** Expenditure is fully managed with no over consumption but cost of living consumes everything. The only solution is increasing income.
- **EXPENDITURE ISSUES:** Income could support long-term wealth building but expenditure shows uncontrolled consumption and debt. Income fully consumed short-term.
- **BOTH:** Income is consumed mostly by cost of living but could reduce short-term expenditure and increase income.

For all three groups increasing income and reducing expenditure obviously helps to some degree. But for those living in poverty or on very low incomes the benefit of increasing income usually outweighs the benefit of reducing expenditure, particularly the first group where it's often already cut to the bone. Reduction in expenditure where it is possible though helps to:

- Reduce over consumption, freeing resource to better assign to long-term planning.
- Increase discipline in individual spending habits helping manage increased income when achieved. This reduces the risk of lifestyle inflation where increased income is consumed immediately with no net benefit.

For those whose income could support wealth building but who live a lifestyle of consumption, reducing the expenditure alone can have amazing long-term benefit. For some there's work to do on both sides where income is low but there's still some opportunity through controlled expenditure. Each individual situation will be different, but the principles remain the same.

I'm not blind to inequality though. I'd never suggest those living in real poverty struggling to put food on the table just need to spend less to build wealth. That's clearly a stupid position (despite many politicians adopting it!). I don't subscribe to the notion those living in poverty just need to work harder to drag themselves out, I think this another incarnation of divide and conquer, those considered "poor" conditioned to vilify those considered "rich" and vice versa. Neither position, lacking in any nuance, serves useful purpose. I imagine living hand to mouth on welfare offering £84.80 maximum unemployment benefit per week, or £101.75 for disability isn't by choice or living a lavish lifestyle.

Unfortunately in 2023 those living in poverty extends far beyond those on benefits anyway. This angered me when I started investigating. According to the Joseph Rowntree Foundation (in 2020/21) roughly 1 in 5 people in the UK lived in poverty, some 13.4 million people. 7.9 million working age adults, 3.9 million children and 1.7 million pensioners.

Numbers have increased for 2022/23 with cost of living challenges and when compared to unemployment claimant numbers, 1.55 million in June, we can extrapolate in work and in pension poverty, as well as child poverty, make up a large proportion. In 2023 only around 12% of those officially living in poverty are claiming unemployment benefit by those numbers, which admittedly seem low. Further, the UK has 12.7 million children according to ONS meaning ~31% of children, 1 in 3 rounded, is living in poverty. Appalling for a G7 nation.

These statistics would anger any right minded individual, but we must be realistic about possible actions. I'm not selling false promises so although expenditure is wholly within our control and will be the focus of our discussion, it may offer limited options if income is your issue. You should still be aware of and work to control expenditure for the benefits mentioned previously, but you may need to focus on income.

The primary option for income improvement is skill building. Identify something you can do or could learn to do better than others and build proficiency there to provide better income opportunities. Organisations like The Open University even offer free part time courses for those on low incomes so research these kinds of options. "Upskill" sounds ridiculously simple I know and it's not intended to be condescending. You'd be amazed how many don't realise competence and expertise are the primary factors in income and they're both **entirely in our control**. So look to control the controllable. It's not easy, but it's the place to start and as I keep saying, no-one ever finished anything without starting.

If you identify you need to focus on income you can still review expenditure to understand long-term implications rather than just short-term monthly or weekly budget implications. You may find areas of opportunity you didn't realise existed. Either way don't be disheartened, whichever side of the scale you need to address opportunities exist, some we'll discuss in this chapter, some later.

OPPORTUNITY COST: IDENTIFICATION AND CALCULATION

Whichever group you think yourself in your money map will show reality. It surprises some who think their issue income that when written down it's apparent it's actually expenditure. This is true particularly of those beginning to build their understanding of finance and unaware previously of their consumer conditioning.

Before we look at money mapping I want to talk about calculating long-term impacts of short-term financial decisions. Few factor this into decision making at all. I'm talking about "Opportunity Cost", a term you'll find cropping up in our discussion and you've probably heard before. For those to whom the concept is new it's the term used to describe the cost of potential lost profit when forgoing one potential option in favour of another. What is your potential loss in making choice A over (best alternate) choice B?

It's widely used in finance to assess implications and/or sacrifices in a set of options to make sure they're considered in the decision making process. It doesn't provide a framework for making binary decisions in my view, I certainly wouldn't do the calculation and always select the option providing best long-term outcome on a balance sheet. I like a holistic view of finance so it isn't always about long-term bottom line. It's fine sometimes to make conscious decisions foregoing long-term benefit to enjoy short-term happiness. As I've said I believe in a balance between now and future not an existence free of luxuries. The key word though is "conscious" which opportunity cost provides for. Faced with a choice between two or more alternatives it helps evaluate what we're giving up by choosing one option over another. It's about understanding the implications of each choice.

For example: If you have £3,000 in savings adding £200 each month earning 4.5% interest and you plan to use it as a home deposit at £10,000, but you want to go on holiday too. This may present 3 options:

1. Take all money and go on holiday
2. Take some money and go on holiday
3. Leave all money in savings and plan to save extra each month for a holiday next year

Pretty self-explanatory so far. Most people think if they select option 1 or 2 then their "Opportunity Cost" amounts to the total removed from savings. If option 2 is favoured and £1,500 is removed for example they consider £1,500 the cost of their choice. But adding £200 every month to £1,500 could take 3 years 3 months to reach £10,000 (at 4.5% YoY) and adding £200 every month to £3,000 could take 2 years 6 months. Would you trade 9 months additional time to meet your deposit goal for a holiday? What if you did it every year? Would you be willing to wait over 2 additional years to meet your deposit goal for a 1 week holiday every year?

People don't think about long-term impacts of short-term choices this way. This method measures in years rather than traditional £'s (or your local currency) to give perspective. You could look in terms of £'s too, over say 10 years. At 4.5% YoY £1,500 plus £200 per month is £33,148.28, but the same £200 per month with a £3,000 balance is £35,477.74. Would you be willing to pay an additional £2,329.46 over 10 years for a £1,500 holiday, £3,829.46 in total? And remember, that's just for one holiday, not one per year! Opportunity cost (OC) formula for completeness is:

OC = Return of (best) forgone option - Return on chosen option

Practically this analysis helps the consumers, those who conflate "need" with "want" as society intends for us. The expenditure side of their scale is overweight short-term "want" liabilities they think they can afford without calculating or even considering the impact long-term.

A practical example I see a lot is continually trading up mobile phones because suppliers offer it near contract end. A want for the new iPhone at £47 per month (current UK average) rather than sticking with a perfectly useable phone and dropping to cheaper airtime only contracts. In this scenario our hypothetical consumer decides they can afford the upgrade, but let me lay out the opportunity cost for someone starting at twenty and employing this approach for 10 years. We'll model against a cheaper airtime only option at £15 per month.

£47 - £15 = £32 per month potential saving. £32 per month is £384 per year. At 5% (half the average S&P 500 return) that's £5,071.41 after 10 years in gross profit (not £3,840 as many calculate without compound interest) upgrading every time your contract allows. Expenses are £5,640 (£47 x 120 months) versus £1,800 (£15 x 120). Total difference after 10 years is: £3,271.41 (£5,071.41 return - £1,800 costs) profit on the cheaper phone versus £5,640 loss on the iPhone, for the same £47 capital expenditure. Opportunity cost of £8,911.41 over 10 years.

What if the same individual left the money invested from 30 till 60, a further 30 years at the same 5% projection? £21,918.34 at age 60. What if we used the average S&P500 return of 10%? £88,493.07 at 60. How much do phones potentially cost you? Still think it a good use of resources?

Most people don't think about money this way. They look at £47 per month and think "I can afford that now". They don't look at opportunity cost over time. If invested via ISA and achieved even 6% return tax free, after 30 years it could make a huge difference to their future self. From saving £32 per month between 20 and 30 and leaving it to grow.

Imagine the same person kept adding £32 per month to an investment ISA for 40 years instead of 10. A projected £107,435.92, tax free at 8% annualised return, or £186,951.10 at the S&P average of 10%, for investing £32 per month saved on a mobile phone between 20 and 60. What if they found more than £32? What if reducing other contracts and consumer spending found £100 per month for 40 years? £196,857.22 at 6%, £335,737.25 at 8% and £584,222.17 at 10%. Even a lower target of 6% is around £200k and 10% is over half a million. For £100 per month, consistently, over 40 years (remember, these are not inflation adjusted, I'm testing you!).

This is how the wealth game is played. Slow, consistent, methodical.

It's how I paid my mortgage at 36. Investing small amounts and increasing when able. This is why self-made millionaires drive second hand cars, live in right sized houses and buy clothes at discount outlets. Where do you think my monthly mortgage payment went once cleared? I didn't increase my expenditure to live lavishly, it's invested because every £ you reduce from expenditure and put to work in assets is a £ working for you. An employee who doesn't get tired, doesn't sleep, doesn't eat and doesn't complain. They just beaver away in the background making you more money.

I project on 4.5%-8% annualised returns. I'd rather under project than over. The examples here are all 4.5% to 10% falling within long run S&P average. Alternate assets exist one can invest in (like businesses or property), I'm giving market examples through experience as I've personally benefitted from investing this way. The general point is reducing expenditure linked liabilities to invest in income or capital growth assets is how long-term wealth and financial security is achieved.

Knowing the long-term impacts of financial decisions is fundamental so I want you to know how to calculate them. In every financial decision you should be asking yourself "what's the opportunity cost?". You can still make conscious decisions for short-term benefit, but at least you know the impact and made the decision in an informed manner. Changing mindsets to think about financial decisions in these terms means natural reversion to balanced financial planning, where short and long-term are more evenly represented than in most people's current budgets which are almost universally short-term heavy. This is one of the key mindset shifts I've spoken about.

WHAT IS CASH FLOW & HOW DO I USE IT?

This is a standard financial term describing how cash flows through your personal balance sheet. Understanding it is another key part of budgeting and from a bigger picture perspective is vital for clearing debt and building wealth. Mapping shows you how money flows through your possession and can also act as your monthly budget. I certainly use mine this way.

Managing money works similarly for personal finance as for business, which is apt as like I've said you should run your personal finances like a business anyway. You should be aiming to make profit you can reinvest in growing your business (you), not aiming to spend it all. Your money map is recorded in a ledger showing how and where your money moves in and out, what you own, liabilities and net worth. It should cover the 4 key elements of your personal finances:

- **INCOME:** From salary, asset yield, or combination of both.
- **ASSETS:** Things you own **generating more money**, either through regular payment (like rental property or dividends from equities) or value growth over time (like property, investments, pensions).
- **EXPENDITURE:** Your committed monthly outgoings, things you have to pay to other people including servicing debt and taxation.
- **LIABILITIES:** Things you (notionally) own **costing you money** through ongoing payment (mortgaged home, mobile phone, financed car for example).

Note: If you live in a jurisdiction subject to property taxes even on mortgage free properties, you'd likely record them as liabilities because they cost money on an ongoing basis. In the UK, fully paid off property is more of an asset as we're not subject to ongoing property taxes (at present). Our homes, once paid, do not have the tax liability our US cousins do. You should look at your asset and liabilities columns in light of local regulations which may impact how you choose to record personal details.

The purpose of the mapping exercise is to show where your money goes and if it's working adequately **for** you. As with the mobile phone example, identifying even small changes in liabilities can divert to building assets with significant impact on long-term financial security. The aim should be a better balance of long-term building and short-term consumption, serving both current and future selves. Small amounts regularly make a huge difference.

Most people don't record liabilities alongside assets to know how overweight they are. As with overall planning, formally documenting this within your financial plan allows you to see exactly how cash flows through "You inc.", facilitating conscious adjustments not just short-term "can afford" decisions.

There are many ways to do this, from pen and paper to Excel or Google sheets. Below is a straightforward example (what I use) with fictional data included to show what a completed money map looks like. This is included in the financial plan template should you choose to use it.

Fig 6.1 | Example Money Map from Financial Plan Template

- **ASSETS:** Things you own that make you money, listed alongside actual value (or equity value in some cases).
- **INCOME:** Where your (gross, pre-tax and deductions) income comes from monthly. This may be salary, asset yield or a mix of both.
- **ASSET BUILDING (FUTURE SELF):** Assigned post income and intentionally recorded above expenditure needs and wants as a psychological trigger that we should consider our future-self first. Most look at bills first, themselves last if anything left. Consumerism demands this. You should **always** be first. Many people advocate this, including Warren Buffet for example. To clear debt, build wealth and have long-term financial security, your financial goals can't

be an afterthought they must be robotic, consistent and prioritised, so assign to them (to you) first.

- **OTHER EXPENDITURE & SAVINGS (WANT):** Expenditure not "Needs". Things like holidays, a new car or a new kitchen. You'll have identified these in your goals section of your plan. Non-contributory type goals.
- **GENERAL EXPENDITURE (NEEDS):** Items you pay in full or in part (shared). Actual outgoings on a monthly basis that generally constitute "Needs" and thing's you're obligated to pay (including taxes).
- **LIABILITIES:** Things you own that cost you money, linked to expenditure line item ("Want" or "Need"). Outstanding liability listed, not perceived value. How much you actually owe, including interest, what you'll **actually** pay back.
- **TOTALS:** The value of your Assets minus your Liabilities is your notional Net Worth.

Fig 6.1 is an example money map showing where money comes from, where it goes and how much is assigned to building your future versus how much goes towards liabilities (someone else's future). It lists all expenses to help identify those you could potentially trim and tracks net worth over time. Critically, it highlights how much of your available time, money and energy is actually delivering the goals you previously defined. Many people find little, if anything, assigned to those goals and the lightbulb illuminates: "This is why I'm not where I want to be financially!".

The example shows an **individual** money map. To convert to a **household** money map with multiple contributors simply create individual tabs per person and an overview tab to consolidate using Excel references. I use this as our household budget, all I need to manage our finances is contained here.

ASSETS & LIABILITIES: WHAT'S THE DIFFERENCE?

Assets make you money, for example regular income (like a rental property) or capital accumulation (like investment accounts or owned outright property). They may incur expenses (like account management fees or maintenance costs) but they're lower than the amount returned annually in income or capital growth meaning RoR is positive.

Liabilities take money from you through ongoing costs, payments or debt service with capital appreciation or income (if any) lower than these costs. For example a mortgaged house appreciating at £5k per year with mortgage, maintenance and tax overheads of £10k per year. Or a mobile phone per previous conversation.

My intent isn't to vilify liabilities, they're necessary through life both in utility and enjoyment. The key is, you guessed it, understanding the difference and maintaining balance! The Consumer and Debtor pillars of our dark triad encourage society to favour liabilities over assets without balance, without thought. Budgets considering no more than short-term income versus current liabilities perpetuate this. We're encouraged to collect liabilities because it inhibits our ability to build assets, the route to wealth and infinitely better for long-term financial security.

"I want a new car, my current income is x, I've y left per month and the car is less than y, so I can afford it. The advert was snazzy and the salesman is a good guy". This common thought process is many people's "budget", entirely framed in affordability today with no consideration of opportunity cost tomorrow.

Some readers will question whether the majority really make financial decisions based on short-term dopamine pursuit as I suggest. What supporting evidence exists outside of my subjective conversations with people from all walks of life about finance? Let's look at UK Pension data as a broad example to highlight how many actively plan, or don't, for the future.

If you have a final salary (Defined Benefit) pension then congratulations, those schemes are generally closed outside public sector roles due to cost and risk, so most younger employees can't access them. These assets have huge advantages for non-planners through a guaranteed benefit in place of pot building requirement. Defined Contribution pensions are also assets but in the form of investment accounts one contributes to regularly from salary, expecting growth over time to fund retirement. We must build the pot to a value that sustains our retirement. In DC schemes, trouble is brewing. In May 2023 average pots in the UK by age range were:

- **25 - 34:** £9,300
- **35 - 44:** £30,000
- **45 - 54:** £75,000
- **55 - 64:** £107,000

Those are averages, meaning a small number well above bring the average up and there are more people below, the median will be lower. So, the disparity is worse than average numbers suggest in my view, which isn't a uniquely UK centric problem. For example, I've 10 times my demographic average having planned for two decades. To provide context, the 2023 Pensions and

Lifetime Savings Association modelling of annual income requirements are split into 3 living standards per today's figures (non-inflation adjusted and at time of writing):

- **MINIMUM:** £12,800
- **MODERATE:** £23,300
- **COMFORTABLE:** £37,300

£12,800 per year sounds pretty grim, I have to say, but what pension pot value is required at retirement to achieve this? Using a £4,715 per £100,000 annuity product (today's prices) as an illustration, to achieve these values **after tax** and **non-inflation adjusted** you need (not including state pension):

- **MINIMUM:** £273,700
- **MODERATE:** £534,337
- **COMFORTABLE:** £883,647

Let's recap the problem. The average pension pot for those reaching minimum retirement age is £107,000. One fifth of moderate pot size, less than half the £12,800 minimum. Younger ranges are markedly lower. We're approaching the first majority DC over DB pension retiree generation and it's likely to be rough for many, even if using drawdown in place of annuity.

We'll explore these numbers and the difference in annuity versus drawdown later, I highlight here simply in support of my view the majority manage finance short-term. Pension provision, a long-term financial security and one of the best wealth building measures available to normal working people, shows we don't consider long-term outcomes against short-term wants. Another example would be the unfortunate reality that only 7% of UK adults contribute to a Stocks & Shares ISA. The Pension and Lifetime Savings Association website contains a wealth of information on retirement savings and though we'll discuss pensions later it's still worth signposting here: www.plsa.co.uk.

ASSETS & LIABILITIES: WHAT CAN YOU DO?

I won't advocate a joyless existence to enable all resource going towards future you, I favour conscious balance as I've said throughout. Adopting a decision making process that considers current versus future-self where asset versus liability distinctions and opportunity cost become important is where to start.

Review your current money map and honestly assess whether you're living too much now and not assigning enough to future. As the mobile phone example showed and as I'll keep repeating, even small changes early enough can yield excellent results without impacting quality of life. Be intentional about monthly income being assigned to building assets for the future. Ensure this contribution happens **first**, before anything else, not as an afterthought if there's any left over. Embrace paying yourself before anyone else.

The assets chosen are personal preference. I like investment portfolios and a small trading account. I'll describe these in detail later including their differences (and they are very different!) but you may prefer property, or building businesses or investing in skills to create services (like a website for example) to yield income. Whatever works for you. I do think everyone should have an investment account they contribute to regularly and leave for retirement, even if not their primary means of asset building.

To build wealth you must balance allocations, increasing your allocation of resource towards assets for future-self and reducing it towards liabilities, particularly those you don't need. You must change how money flows through "You Inc." to ensure adequate investment in future you. This is another mindset shift, a different way to think about money to set you apart from the crowd.

4.23% of the UK population are millionaires and as discussed previously those should be the example. We want our money working like theirs: balanced and building assets for our future. We shouldn't emulate the 95.77% who exchange time for money to pay for liabilities making them feel good short-term. This cycle traps people because they don't know any better, it's what we're conditioned to believe life is. Consumer. Debtor. Employee.

NEED VERSUS WANT: KNOW THE DIFFERENCE!

I'd wager you've seen this section coming, I've said it often enough already! Society conflates entirely need with want. Many either don't know, pretend not to know or don't care for the difference. How often have you said "I need a new [blank]"? Did you really, or did you "want" one?

> *"Just because you feel good, doesn't make you right."*
>
> *[Skunk Anansie | Rock Band]*

Mass marketing, product placement, social media, influencers, our own psychology and social perspectives are just some of the things that convince us we "need" things we actually "want". Constant reinforcement of consumerism and debt, of living beyond your means, often for image. It drives me insane. There's a massive difference between need and want which must be understood and managed if we're to prosper long-term. The cosmetics industry, for example. It's fine to want to use these products to feel good about oneself, but many are convinced they **need** to spend huge sums on creams for every body part despite humans surviving for millennia without them. Say Hyaluronic acid one more time. I dare you. I double dare you (in a stern Samuel L. Jackson voice in your head)!

I use this example intentionally as I'm aware it's not wholly financial, the psychological and societal influences I've referenced weigh heavily here. Cosmetic spending growth links directly to intrasexual competition psychology, where women (the primary cosmetic consumers) feel internal pressure to "keep up" with perceived beauty standards. Technical advancement in cosmetics changes these standards, perpetuating a fear in many consumers of the impact of not meeting them. Intrasexual competition effects are well studied from a psychological perspective and cosmetic companies exploit their impact as a self-perpetuating marketing campaign. For perspective, the seemingly limitless profit on offer means more advance in cosmetic technology in the last fifty years than the jet engine, climate change or cancer cure. Incentives!

Given my mantra of dealing with how the world is, not how one wants it to be, I accept societal reality here with a degree of empathy for those incurring the financial overhead. It's an example of how we're conditioned to consume, how it's reinforced socially and how financial incentives for promoters drive technological advance. This still constitutes "want" not "need" though so my finance point stands alongside the psychology point.

A less controversial example is tech gadgets or mobile phones. Or replacing cars every 3 years with luxury models over functional cheaper alternatives. Or designer clothes over regular clothes. Let me define precisely:

- **FINANCIAL NEED:** Necessities or essential requirements individuals and households fundamentally need for overall well-being. Maintains a reasonable standard of living without over spending on unnecessarily expensive versions. Typically essential for survival, safety, utility and health.
- **FINANCIAL WANT:** Desire for non-essential items, additional goods or services beyond basic needs or unnecessarily expensive choices (like designer clothing or

luxury cars). A preference for luxury items or discretionary spend not essential for survival, safety, utility or well-being.

I realise this likely an unpopular topic, it always is when talking to people individually as it's such an ingrained behaviour, reinforced essentially from birth. The "You can't take it with you" approach as justification for overspending on wants now at the expense of long-term financial security. Be honest with yourself. Nothing we discuss is criticism if you see yourself in these observations, you're conditioned to do this, we all are, this is simply about making you think consciously about it to understand long-term implications. Some examples of **needs** include:

- **FOOD AND WATER:** Nutritious food and clean water to sustain yourself and your family.
- **HOUSING:** Mortgage or Rent payments to secure safe, right sized accommodation.
- **UTILITIES:** Electricity, water, heat and other essential services like phone & internet.
- **HEALTHCARE:** Medical expenses and health insurance.
- **EDUCATION:** Educational opportunities for oneself or dependents. Investing in you.
- **TRANSPORTATION:** Necessary and appropriate.
- **CLOTHING:** Appropriate clothing, functional over branded

Some examples of **wants** include:

- **ENTERTAINMENT AND RECREATION:** Movies, sporting events, hobbies, nights out and leisure activities.
- **TRAVEL:** Vacations to explore new places.
- **FASHION AND LUXURY GOODS:** Purchasing designer clothing, high-end accessories or luxury items.
- **TECHNOLOGY AND GADGETS:** Buying the latest smartphones, computers or other electronic devices.
- **DINING OUT:** Enjoying meals out, including at expensive or gourmet establishments or takeaway/home delivery.
- **HOUSING:** Larger than required or moving to new houses when not required/too often.
- **TRANSPORTATION:** Changing car too often, leasing vehicles or acquiring luxury cars.

It's completely fine to spend money on wants, understanding the difference from a financial perspective simply helps prioritise how you expend your resource. It helps you make informed financial decisions based on the reality of circumstance, in line with your goals and values and with fear, greed and incentives accounted for. Most of all it helps you balance short-term financial wellbeing with long-term financial security, current-self with future-self.

I'm advocating, again, finding balance, this time between spending money on things you need and thing you want. Be honest with regards why you're allocating resource. Is it a need or a want? If it's a want then understand long-term implications, your opportunity cost and make the choice consciously with the knowledge of what you're actually giving up long-term. You can still make want based decisions, you're just thinking differently, in a way naturally providing balance in financial decision making. Your future-self will thank you for it!

FUTURE-SELF FIRST!

It's been mentioned multiple times but it's important to explain that the order one should pay their creditors is future-self first, then everyone else after. This popular tactic is how you budget without leaving you waiting to see what's left before building for your own future. You build first then budget on what you have left. We've generally been conditioned backwards in this regard!

It may not be familiar to you but this popular financial principle, one I've followed for over two decades, emphasises the importance of prioritising your own financial goals before anyone else's if you've any hope of delivering them. Whatever goals defined earlier, allocating a portion of income to those as soon as you receive it, before paying anyone else, ensures you're always chipping away. Remember, we aim to move forwards one little chip at a time like Dufresne. The benefits in this approach include:

- **ESTABLISHING FINANCIAL DISCIPLINE:** It cultivates responsible financial behaviour by encouraging you to treat building for your own future as a non-negotiable expense, required before any other expenditure. It helps you develop healthy money management habits long-term which fight lifestyle inflation as incomes rise.
- **ENCOURAGING PROACTIVE FINANCIAL PLANNING:** It prompts you to be proactive in financial planning which is one of the outcomes we seek from this book. It motivates you to create a budget including present **and** future you, track your expenses and make conscious choices about your spending habits. By prioritising your future financial security you become mindful of current financial decisions and you're engaged in managing your money effectively.

- **LONG-TERM WEALTH ACCUMULATION:** Investing in yourself early by accounting for future you allows your money to benefit from compound interest and long-term growth. Creating the means of consistently contributing to investment accounts or other assets builds compounded wealth and improves your financial future. We showed in our phone example the power of small amounts over time.
- **PRIORITISING YOUR GOALS AND VALUES:** It allows you to align your spending with your short **and** long-term goals, as defined in your financial plan, always prioritising the funding of these first not just "if there's anything left". By allocating money towards your documented financial goals you ensure your resources are supporting what truly matters to you, not simply paying other people.
- **REDUCING FINANCIAL STRESS:** Being intentional about clearing debt and building wealth provides a sense of financial security, a peace of mind. It reduces stress about unexpected financial challenges and reduces anxiety about funding retirement and paying for shelter for your family. The mental impact of putting your future-self first from a financial perspective cannot be underestimated.

This doesn't mean neglecting your financial obligations or any responsibilities to others. It's about making the delivery of your own financial goals a priority and ensuring you allocate a suitable portion of your income to benefit your future-self, unlike the majority. It reduces the risk of using your income like a target, depleting to zero through consumption of immediate wants without delivering any long-term benefit for your future-self.

> *"Do not save what is left after spending, but spend what is left after saving."*
>
> *[Warren Buffet | Multi $Billion Investor]*

By consciously making your future-self your primary creditor as Buffet advocates here too, you increase the probability of a secure and fulfilling financial future with the opportunity to break free from our Consumer, Debtor, Employee triad.

LIVE BENEATH YOUR MEANS

How can we ensure we invest in ourselves first and still meet our obligations, what are the mechanics of this? Nothing ground-breaking, we must simply live beneath our means as unpopular as the suggestion is in modern society. I won't labour this point, it's very simple: for those we discussed earlier with incomes capable of wealth building, living beneath your means is **how** you support yourself being primary creditor and how you build wealth over time. You stop considering income as a spending target you try to hit with expenditure! Be this mobile phones, luxury cars, luxury holidays, designer brands or any of the other popular consumer habits eating our resource for no long-term benefit.

This is more applicable to those in our second and third groups, where expenditure is the issue or it's a little bit of both. Those who have income that could support improved long-term outcomes but consume it without due consideration for their future-self. For those in our first group who have a genuine income issue, living beneath one's means comes as part of a longer term plan after income is successfully increased, to help fight lifestyle inflation and improve long-term outcomes.

I've said before, self-made millionaires tend to live in modest homes, drive modest cars and shop at discount stores and this really should be all the guide one needs. If those who can afford otherwise are doing what I advocate, where's the rest of their money going? That's right, they're paying their future selves by living beneath their means and investing in their long-term goals.

LIFESTYLE INFLATION: "IF I COULD JUST EARN A LITTLE MORE"

I've referenced lifestyle inflation a few times so let's discuss what it is and why it silently kills better outcomes for our future selves than our present day selves.

Lifestyle inflation refers to the tendency of increasing one's expenditure in line with increases in income. While it's natural to want to enjoy the benefits of increased income, lifestyle inflation if not controlled makes you worse off than you were before the income increase. Unfortunately most people don't know what it is, never mind try to keep it in check so it's something I want you to be conscious of going forward.

It often leads to **DEBT ACCUMULATION** with associated debt service costs. A higher mortgage from a new home purchase after an increase in income is a common reason. Or a new car or vacation. As expenses rise and increased income is consumed entirely people turn to credit cards or loans, resulting in a cycle of debt. Interest payments eat more into income than before which keeps you trapped on the wheel needing more income to support your lifestyle. Round the loop again you go when more income is secured in future and you never feel any better off in terms of true wealth, freedom of time.

When expenses increase in proportion to or exceeding income growth, which is more common than you'd think, there's **LITTLE ROOM LEFT FOR INVESTING FOR YOUR FUTURE-SELF** as they become an afterthought not the primary creditor they should be. You may struggle to allocate money towards emergency funds, retirement planning or building long-term wealth in general. Without consistent investing in assets as we've discussed at length it becomes challenging to escape the triad. One shouldn't think about working for money as the end of the transaction, one should think about working for money to buy assets that eventually mean they don't have to work for money anymore, when those assets can support them. This is how one achieves freedom of time as early as possible.

By prioritising consumption and short-term gratification over debt clearance and long-term wealth building, lifestyle inflation means you **MISS VALUABLE INVESTMENT OPPORTUNITIES**. Investing consistently is essential for maximising compound returns, allowing your investments to grow as much as possible over time. If income is primarily allocated towards liabilities to maintain inflated lifestyles you miss opportunities to generate substantial returns in future and free your time.

RELYING ON HIGH INCOME to sustain inflated lifestyles is risky. Job loss or unexpected financial challenges can significantly impact your ability to maintain the wealth pretence long-term. If you haven't built solid financial foundations you'll find it difficult to adjust during periods of financial instability like increased cost of living and rising interest rates. In 2023 this is a problem many families are wrestling with having lived at or above their means for a considerable period. Again, I understand wealth inequality, I'm talking about those who genuinely had other options here!

Inflated lifestyles also **LIMIT FINANCIAL FLEXIBILITY**, reducing your ability to adapt to changing circumstances or take new opportunities. This is apparent in 2023 with cost of living and interest rate rises too. It may become difficult to learn new skills, change careers, start a business or take investing risks because your expenses require high income to sustain them. Clearing debt and building wealth requires the flexibility to make strategic financial decisions as opportunities arise and this needs liquidity not found in negative income versus expenditure ratios, weighted in favour of short-term liabilities over assets.

To mitigate the impact then and increase the probability of meeting your goals it's critical to strike a balance between enjoying income and maintaining a disciplined approach to investing in assets for your future-self. By living beneath your means, consciously managing your expenses, avoiding excessive debt and consistently allocating funds towards long-term goals you can create solid financial foundations that increase your chances of achieving financial independence and long-term wealth.

Allowing expenditure to grow in line with or above income is lifestyle inflation. It's amazingly common and falling foul of this, like so many do, is at the expense of future you. Making better decisions, understanding opportunity cost and managing income increase with balance in mind serves you better now and in future. "If I could just earn a little more" doesn't work if expenditure is unmanaged.

EMERGENCY FUND: SHOULD I HAVE ONE?

The emergency fund debate can be a heated one. My view is it's dictated by individual circumstance, not universal. Cookie cutter approaches are commonly proposed including the popular 6 months' worth of expenses emergency fund, but this lacks nuance in my view and can have longer term implications in terms of opportunity cost, especially if people build this in cash (or cash equivalents) and leave it idle over years.

Many universal emergency fund advocates are US based, operating in very different regulatory environments to other countries, UK included. Location based variables contribute to my view of funding emergencies based on individual circumstance but to be clear, I do think everyone should have a plan for how they'll pay for emergencies. I don't advocate the head in the sand approach to risk, ignoring potential financial implications and hoping the risk doesn't materialise. Having a clear plan helps to avoid being forced into additional debt by unforeseen life events, by extension helping control the debtor aspect of the triad which is clearly important in my view.

There's also a useful psychological benefit of knowing you've made this provision. Knowing how you'll cover "life coming at you fast" from a financial perspective helps remove anxiety about things like a car breakdown or a fridge replacement for example. This gives you confidence the capital you've assigned to long-term goals, or even balanced short-term wants, isn't at risk in case of emergency.

EMERGENCY FUND: HOW MUCH?

This can only be answered by reviewing the variables specific to you as an individual. like local regulation, contractual situation, the level of your monthly expenses, other earners in the household and the methods available to store (and continue to grow) an emergency fund.

Given these variables are numerous I completely understand why the 6 months of expenses view is popular. It's simple so people can easily understand it, especially in a soundbite. But there's a cost for this simplicity not often made clear. Think back to our inflation discussion and RoR and you'll realise keeping high levels of capital in a location losing against inflation is costing you money through reduction in spending power over time. And as expenses inflate you'd need to keep growing this losing allocation over time to meet the static monthly guideline.

Just as there's risk in not having an emergency fund at all, there's also risk in having one larger than actually required. So how does one refine the requirement to create something both fit for purpose and lowest possible opportunity cost? Let's start with the goal of your emergency fund, what's it there to cover? There are generally two requirements people consider:

- Covering lost earnings if you find yourself out of work, allowing you to meet monthly expenses for a set period while you find new work.
- Covering large one off expenses like medical bills, a car repair or boiler replacement should something unforeseen occur in your life.

It's definitely of benefit for everyone to keep a fund that can cover the latter requirement, things falling into the "need" bracket. But this requirement is usually significantly smaller than 6 months expenses, right (depending on locale)? So why measure requirement based on expenses if you don't require protection from lost income?

The answer I think lies in the origin of this idea. The assumption both of these requirements always exist is where the 6 month guideline was born and is one I see put forward by our US cousins most often. The thinking is 6 months is enough time to find a new job, the fund enabling you to survive and pay your bills. It's a catch all safety net covering both requirements and this makes sense in a US locale (for most).

But in the UK salaried roles usually have more employee protection than our US counterparts enjoy. Salaried UK employees generally have between 4 and 12 weeks' notice periods, they don't get a box and asked to leave same day (I'm 12 weeks for example). Further, we generally have better severance provision under redundancy protections (even in statutory terms) than the US, with many employers offering enhanced terms as a benefit over and above. Again, in my own case as an example I earn 3 weeks redundancy (severance) pay for every completed year of employment over and above 12 week notice period.

If you contractually have 12 weeks' notice and another 12 in redundancy/severance (up to £30k tax free) through 4 years' service, you already have 6 months "unemployment" funds fulfilled by an employer as a contractual obligation. We can argue the case of an insolvency situation and obligations not being met, but in the UK the government does have a Redundancy Payments Service (RPS) offering some protection and managing risk is probability based, not possibility. Insolvency probability is low so we can generally accept within tolerance and knowing that although not ideal we would still have investments or assets to fall back on in a worst case scenario.

This redundancy scenario isn't uncommon. I took voluntary redundancy in a restructuring event in a previous role with severance of 24 weeks plus 12 weeks' notice. My father did similar in his career and many of my colleagues and acquaintances have done too. We found work within notice period meaning no break in employment and thus no need for a fund to cover lost earnings. This isn't everyone's experience, I'm aware, my point is we had more than 6 months provision as redundancy obligation without the inflation risk and opportunity cost of keeping our own. Our contract covered 6 months income replacement as a soft "asset".

Someone with £1,500 per month expenses and these sorts of contractual protections in place pays a high opportunity cost for maintaining a separate fund of £9,000. A higher risk, arguably. This is one example where blanket advice may not be suitable and why you must take your individual circumstances into account.

Discounting wage replacement requirement and looking only at potential one off expenses might be more suitable. Setting aside £3,000 for car repairs, boiler replacement or other household emergencies may be more optimal. This represents a 66.7% or £6,000 delta between 6 month guideline and actual requirement, capital better utilised delivering long-term financial goals. Over 30 years at 7% compounding it's £45,673, so £39,673 opportunity cost, £18,914 inflation adjusted (2.5% average). A high price for your future-self to pay for something they perhaps don't need?

This is one example showing how the amount you keep in your emergency fund should be dictated by your own personal circumstances. There are others, for example where you live in a household that can cover all expenses from one income of two or perhaps if you live in a locale where medical expenses aren't state funded and are expensive. The general point I'm trying to convey is while 6 months expenses may be a simple soundbite most can understand and follow, don't follow blindly without considering the implications for you. Think it through and refine what you set aside in light of your own situation. If you do decide you like the simplicity, to my previous point, at least it's a decision you're making consciously with an understanding of the opportunity cost implications, reinforcing positive behaviours.

To wrap up, let's quickly have a look at some questions you may ask yourself when considering an emergency fund. This list is by no means exhaustive, it's simply a high level set of questions to give you an idea of what you may consider:

- What are your monthly expenses and potential largest one-off costs (Car, Boiler etc)?
- Do you need to cover shelter (rent/mortgage)?
- What's your local employee protection regulation (redundancy terms and conditions)?
- What's the contractual notice period in your job?
- Do you need to cover employment loss or just unforeseen emergencies?
- How does it affect your mental state (how much would make you stop worrying about an emergency)?
- What access do you have to hold the fund (bank v high interest saving v Money Market for example)?
- How much can you sensibly put towards it each month?
- How quickly do you want to have this fund accrued?
- Do you need it to pay any vital insurance (health, home, car etc.)?
- Are medical expenses state funded or personally funded?

Thinking about these kinds of things should help you to define the purpose, size and location of your emergency fund, as well as allow you to plan how quickly you can build it and what you need to allocate monthly, for how long, to do so.

EMERGENCY FUND: WHERE SHOULD I KEEP IT?

Emergency funds should be both liquid and easily accessible. Those are the two primary considerations. Cash accounts fulfil both requirements but other assets (like art or property) take longer to sell into cash (illiquid) or are potentially time limited (like Bonds subject to duration risk) would not. You wouldn't want to find yourself in a situation where you needed to pay for a boiler repair in winter but it took two weeks to sell an asset to cover the cost. That's not a very practical emergency fund. Potential emergency fund vehicles then and the main risks associated are:

- **CASH (INFLATION RISK):** Plain old Cash, either in bills themselves in a jar (not recommended!) or a standard cash account in a bank. Generally standard accounts pay low interest so your primary risk is inflation eroding the value of the fund. This is though the most liquid and most easily accessible which is both good and bad: if it's too easy you may be tempted to use it for non-emergencies!

- **HIGH INTEREST SAVINGS ACCOUNT (INFLATION RISK & POTENTIAL DURATION RISK):** A better cash option, current interest rates make it easy to find 4-6% yielding accounts. Inflation risk remains but it's generally lower due to the higher interest rate. The other risk to be aware of is duration risk as some high interest savings accounts are locked for a period. For emergency funds I'd prefer not using fixed term variants, I'd favour either easy access or a max withdrawals per year versions. The latter often offer up to 3 withdrawals before losing higher rates providing an incentive **not** to withdraw frivolously.

- **MONEY MARKET FUND (INFLATION RISK & MARKET RISK):** The final option I want to highlight (and where I keep my fund) is a Money Market Fund. This is a cash equivalent instrument generally tracking a target return in line with something like the overnight lending rate (linked to central bank rate). They carry some market risk over cash or savings accounts and are a little more illiquid (settles next day for me) but they're lower risk than equities and more liquid investment instruments than bonds (like a UK Gilt or US Treasury). I prefer this to high interest savings as I can leverage these instruments inside of my ISA, meaning no tax obligation on any gains and I'm not eating into my tax free allowance for cash accounts. It strikes the right balance for me between liquidity, access, risk and cost but I don't advocate for everyone.

Note: Be aware of tax allowances on savings interest in your locale. This is £1,000 for basic rate and £500 for higher rate tax payers at present in the UK. Anything above these per year across all accounts outside of ISA's is liable for income tax (through self-assessment) on the additional amount.

You should also consider location can easily change over time, it isn't fixed. I started in a current account and moved to Money Market later, so moving is always possible. Locate where it best suits you having considered the options, benefits and risks. Where it absolutely should be is separated from regular accounts to ensure it remains untouched for genuine emergencies! The "you" risk! Discipline will always be a requirement.

ALLOCATION STRATEGY: A GUIDE TO SLIDING SCALE ALLOCATION

We've discussed the importance of balanced decisions to benefit both present and future-self. I've outlined what I believe the key considerations individuals must make when doing so, particularly in relation to need versus want and understanding opportunity cost. The final topic I want to cover concerns how one builds an allocation strategy to achieve this balance. This is what I've been building towards. I'm referencing specifically how you split your Income across the three broad categories of expenditure to deliver your financial goals. There's nothing in reality you can't fit into one of these categories and very little ambiguity about where:

1. Expenditure: Future-Self
2. Expenditure: Needs
3. Expenditure: Wants

You review target allocation as part of ongoing financial planning to ensure it remains fit for purpose. I hope I've convinced you financial planning isn't fire and forget, it's something we build on and refine throughout our lives to ensure we can deliver our goals. What differs amongst financiers isn't so much these categories, rather how they should be optimally balanced against one's income. My view and the one implemented throughout my life is percentage based sliding scales, not fixed £/$ targets. This best accounts for the general financial path most experience, the risks inherent within and future scaling with growing income.

This "normal" financial path looks a little like: initially income is low so "needs" are a higher proportion. We default then to "wants" as the next largest income slice and "future-self" is often an afterthought, if at all. As we get older and experience grows income tends to grow as well. As "needs" grow at a slower rate than income, the habits formed early persist and we increase "want" based expenditure, acting like income is a target we must always zero (cars, clothes, homes, holidays and so on). This leaves "future-self" still under represented or out in the cold all together.

I'm sure most readers, if honest, recognise this in themselves, their parents or those around them. It's a problem likely coming to a head in the next few generations where a majority no longer benefit from DB pensions and the insulation they provide from the long-term consequences of these choices. Many will realise they didn't commit enough to their DC pension (future-self) to afford the retirement they assumed. Working for longer through necessity is going to shock a lot of people, I think.

A scaling method like I've used for decades manages this risk and allows for appropriate balance, following just a few simple principles. As with any good scaling strategy it means working in percentages rather than absolute figures. This allows process and risk management to remain consistent even when the £/$ figures behind the %'s grow with income. It's scalable. You build good habits early and persist over time. How does this work in practice?

- Start with income.
- Sum the costs of current "needs".
- Calculate how large a proportion of income "needs" is in % terms (let's say 60% in this example).
- Whatever % remains (40%), assign roughly 65% to your future-self.
- This leaves the remaining 35% as disposable income for your "wants" category.

These %'s can obviously be tweaked as you see fit to suit your own circumstances. 65%/35% of after needs income is the personal scale I started with and I honestly think a reasonable starting point for most. Needs % is likely to change over time as income grows and debt disappears so this is a dual level sliding scale. We'll see this in practice in some examples in a moment to make it clearer. As always, the implementation is yours, so it's up to you what you deem appropriate.

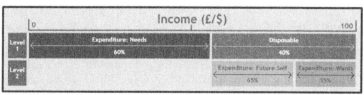

Fig 6.2 | Income versus Expenditure Dual Sliding Scale Example

"Future-self" and "wants" should already be defined in your financial plan goals. Things like paying off debt, paying a mortgage, building a retirement fund or an emergency fund are "future-self" where going on holiday, getting a new car or a new phone are "wants". You can fit your goals neatly into the three categories of expenditure by design. These complement long-term, short-term enabler and short-term non enabler goals avoiding any duplicated effort.

Over time we should aim to **decrease** needs % as income grows, achieved simply by keeping it as static as possible in £/$ terms. This is why self-made millionaires drive second hand cars and live in right sized houses even after they grow wealth. Buffet still stays in the house he bought in 1958! Keeping needs stable in £/$ terms reduces its proportion against income as income grows, meaning the future-self column grows in % terms as wants stays the same in % terms but still grows in £/$ terms (as the same % of a larger amount). This is the balance and flexibility I've discussed, provided by the scaling method. These principles support key behaviours for building wealth over time:

- We consciously aim to keep needs as consistent in £/$ terms as possible so the % stays the same or reduces over time with rising income. This fights lifestyle inflation and reinforces the habit of intentional endeavour required for financial security.
- We aim to keep wants static in % terms but allow ourselves to enjoy more as the £/$ figure goes up with increasing disposable income. We can still live life and experience the things we choose but also fight lifestyle inflation with the benefit of rising income balance built in intentionally.
- The % of needs versus income reduces as income rises, so % of income to future-self increases on the sliding scale. This makes sure we have the resource needed to deliver the long-term goals we have, intentionally and methodically.

I'm aware this can read more complicated than it actually is, so let's look at some working example case studies to hopefully remove any confusion.

SCALING CASE STUDY 1: IVY STRONGPLAN

Ivy, 23, is a Graduate Software Engineer earning £37,000. She rents a flat with a friend while saving a deposit for her own place. Rent costs £1,500 per month split 2 ways. She likes to vacation once per year and spends roughly £2000 in total for 2 weeks. Ivy drives a car on hire purchase, nearly new costing £210 per month for 4 years, with a monthly insurance payment of £79 through a parent. She uses her car to commute.

Other financial "needs" include food/utilities/mobile and total £415 per month. She's no student loan debt as she's Scottish and tertiary education here is fully funded. Ivy is a member of her employers workplace pension scheme contributing 15% gross salary (a tax benefit) and has a 0% for 18 months credit card she's paying down every month at £80. She'll clear the debt in 8 months without paying any interest. She doesn't have an emergency fund at present but wants to start one targeting £1,500 at £75 for 20 months.

INCOME: £37,000 equals monthly gross: ~£3,083.33

EXPENDITURE (NEEDS): £2,095.97 (67.9% of her gross income):

- Tax (PAYE): £317.67
- National Insurance (PAYE): £244.30
- Rent: £750
- Car Payment: £210
- Car Insurance: £79
- Food/Utilities/Mobile: £415
- Credit Card: £80

This leaves Ivy with 32.1% of her income, or £987.36 in her sliding scale.

EXPENDITURE (FUTURE SELF): £462.50 (15% of gross salary) already goes to pension and she's benefitting from tax saving on this amount, not insignificant over time. This equates to 46.8% of her future-self plan. Her target is 65% (£612.16). Her emergency fund takes £75 and the remaining £74.66 she'll put into a Global Index Fund inside a tax efficient ISA:

- Pension Contribution: £462.50 (15% of earnings)
- Emergency Fund Building: £75 for 20 months (if unused)
- Investments: £74.66

EXPENDITURE (WANTS): This leaves Ivy £375.20 per month, 35% of her post needs income. We know her goal is to go on vacation once per year and her £2,000 all-inclusive requires she save £166.67 per month:

- Holiday savings: £166.67 (£2000 after 12 months)

She's covered all needs, she's invested in her future-self first via pension, emergency fund building and her ISA. She's made plans for holiday as a want and she's clearing down her debt in the form of the credit card repayment. Ivy has a balance of future-self versus current wants at 65% / 35% of post needs income and a further £208.53 disposable for any more wants.

To address the elephant in this particular room: I know £208.53 isn't a lot for fuel, socialising, makeup, haircuts, clothes and so on but remember when I said it wasn't quick or easy building for future-self, it takes both sacrifice and balance? This is what sacrifice and balance looks like in this case.

In her growth career Ivy could decide 15% into pension is ample for now and she could slide her scale to move a % equivalent to £74.66 into "want" until the credit card is paid before starting her ISA investment portfolio. This would mean £283.19 disposable income for 8 months, rising to £288.53 once the credit card is paid in month 9. Over 40 years at 6% opportunity cost is £6,143, £2,288 inflation adjusted at 2.5% for an extra £597 over 9 months in the present. So Ivy has options still leaving her with a balanced budget that delivers her goals, she can flex these scales in multiple ways.

Unfortunately, I see more often than not the future-self column being diverted to current want without considering long-term impacts this way. Let's have a little look at those long-term impacts in this scenario to join the dots on everything we've been talking about. Ivy is 23, if **_nothing changed_** (income and expenditure remained flat: unlikely, but for modelling purposes):

- Projected pension pot at retirement (68), at 6% growth YoY over 45 years could be: £1,281,019.
- Her ISA pot over the same 45 years at the same 6% YoY could grow to: £206,514

If Ivy didn't have a balanced future-self column these are the outcomes she'd potentially be giving up, her opportunity cost to have more of what she wanted right now without contributing to her goals. Note: timing, YoY return and drawdown severity during the period may impact performance in both cases, these are projections not guarantees.

Clearly things will change though. Salary is likely to increase meaning pension contribution and ISA contribution increase. There's market risk to factor in as we'd expect some drawdown periods over her time horizon and inflation risk also exists on both expenditure and the buying power of her investments. But the general point is by ensuring her future-self was taken into account first (and early), by assigning a portion to assets (in this scenario pension, emergency fund and investments) and by being intentional about this as part of her financial plan, Ivy could potentially amass close to £1.5million by her retirement at 68.

People generally earn more against their expenses as they age if avoiding lifestyle inflation. Arguably things can only get **better** for Ivy from here if she stays consistent and continues to refine and execute her plan. Other things will change over 45 years. Ivy wants to buy her own home, either herself or with a family, rather than pay half rent forever. She won't keep the same car for 45 years or the same job with the same income or go on the same holidays. But these variables are **not** a reason to skip this planning, they're a reason to do more! They're things we must manage consciously to ensure we understand their impact and make good, well informed choices along the way. The need for balance is constant.

As a potential choice later what if Ivy kept her car, still in good condition, for 6 years post her 4 year loan ending, diverting monthly payments to her ISA for 6 years before the need for a new car arises? She'd keep her car for 10 years rather than replace after paid off in 4 (this is incidentally the approach I've taken my entire life)?

£74.66 per month for 4 years, £284.66 for 6 years at projected 6% YoY could be £30,531.70 after 10 years. Not a bad start on a house deposit for her long-term goal. It involved no other change than fighting the temptation to buy a new car once her current car is paid off, diverting saved payments to her ISA until a new car may actually be needed. This is the same principal as the mobile phone dilemma we discussed earlier with a larger capital outlay. But people are conditioned to replace as soon as it's convenient for the seller, not the buyer. A study of European consumers by CarVertical found the average time people replace their cars in the UK was 1-3 years compared to 4-6 years in the wider EU. Fewer than 10% of UK consumers waited 7-10 years.

I'm clearly not suggesting nothing ever changes or things always run smoothly. Quite the contrary, things will always come up and projections will never be exact. But, those things would come up whether we prepare or not. Personally, I'd rather prepare for a higher probability of better outcomes than forego even the possibility of them through fear and failing to prepare.

The example of Ivy Strongplan (sorry, it made me giggle!) hopefully makes clear the sliding scale allocation strategy I'm a proponent of and you see how it might benefit you not only now but over time. For anyone still not quite clear, I want to look at a second case study as it's an important technical aspect of your financial plan.

James, 32, is a retail worker earning minimum wage, £19,760. He lives with his wife and 2 children in their 3 bedroom end terrace just the right size for them. Mortgage payments are £1,100 which he splits, like all bills, 50/50 with his wife who also works in retail. As homeowners they have insurance payments to cover too.

The family vacation at home most years for £1,000 in total, but every 4 years like to go abroad to give the kids new experiences. They budget £4,000 for this holiday. They have one family car which costs £236 per month plus £420 per year in insurance which they save during the year and pay upfront to save money.

Food/Utilities/Mobile/Home Insurance costs £750 per month for the household and they budget £50 per child for new clothes and other expenses. James has a credit card with a small balance he's paying £50 towards clearing every month. He expects to clear this in 18 months. He's been allocating 10% of his wage to his pension and has built an emergency fund of £500 at £50 per month. His target is £3,300, to cover 3 months mortgage payment if there were issues in the retail sector where both earners work (concentration risk), so he'll be building this for some time.

INCOME: £19,760 equals monthly gross: ~£1,646.67

EXPENDITURE (NEEDS): £1,319.30 (80.1% of his gross Income):

- Tax (PAYE): £86.90
- National Insurance (PAYE): £71.90
- Mortgage: £550 (£1,100 / 2)
- Car Payment: £118 (£236 / 2)
- Car Insurance: £17.50 ((£420 / 12) / 2)
- Food/Utilities/Mobile/Home Insurance: £375 (£750/2)
- Kids Fund: £50 (£100 / 2)
- Credit Card: £50

This leaves James with 19.9% of his income, or £327.37 in his sliding scale.

EXPENDITURE (FUTURE SELF): Pension contribution is £164.67 (10% of gross salary) benefitting from tax saving. This equates to (£164.67 / £327.37) 50% of remaining income after needs, but his target is 65% (£212.79). He puts £50 into an emergency fund meaning £214.67, 65.6%.

- Pension Contribution: £164.67 (10% of earnings)

- Emergency Fund Building: £50 for approximately 56 months (if unused)

EXPENDITURE (WANTS): This leaves James £112.70 per month for wants, around 34.4% of his post needs income. We already know the family wants to go on vacation once per year at an average over 4 years of £7,000 (3 x £1,000 and 1 x £4,000). This equates to £1,750 saved per year, James covering half at £875:

- Holiday savings: £72.92 (£875 after 12 months)

This leaves James £39.78 expendable income. He needs to rethink his expenditure and consider the holiday abroad for now, or find cheaper alternatives. Again, this is just an example and individual circumstances will vary, the idea here is to highlight how two different people with different circumstances could budget around a similar sliding scale framework to cover their immediate requirements but also take care of their future selves and financial goals. The numbers don't really matter in these examples so don't fixate on them, the process is what matters. A few important notes on James case I've intentionally included to highlight:

- He's underfunding his pension for a comfortable retirement, one of the people I've been cautioning about since introducing pension statistics. Assuming his current pot is the average of his age bracket (£9,300) then at 6% YoY his projected pot is £332,572 at 68, non-inflation adjusted. He can't do much realistically on current income, adding more to his pension helps less than improving earning potential over time.
- They might consider postponing the family holiday for a year or two to pursue qualifications or gain expertise to increase their earning potential. This would be a future-self goal. As I mentioned at the start of this chapter some can find enough in the expenditure (like Ivy) but for some (like James) an investment in competence and skillset aiming to improve income is more useful. If James is successful in retraining for a growth career he could potentially increase his income significantly over time which because we're working in % allocation rather than set £/$ figures will scale within his plan following identical processes.
- I intentionally included family vacations to show it fit into this process. We need to live now as well as plan for future. This could clearly be removed from James's budget, even just one holiday abroad. It can always be added later when appropriate. This is included to highlight wants **always**

make way first if required. Too many keep the holiday and drop future learning and/or emergency fund building. Short-term thinking. You can replace a holiday multiple times by investing in future earning potential.

ALLOCATION STRATEGY: SCALING OVER TIME

I hope these examples make the process clear. To finish I want to quickly explain scaling over time and how the approach outlined supports consistent balance, actively managing against the risk of lifestyle inflation as part of the process. Scale levels one and two likely fluctuate: if income rises but expenditure doesn't then "needs" allocation reduces in % terms against income and disposable income increases. In this scenario sticking to our second level scale of "future-self" at 65% and "Wants" at 35% means these allocations **both** grow in monetary terms, ensuring we maintain balance between enjoying the fruits of increased income now and still allocating to future goals.

Similarly, if "needs" increases but income doesn't then disposable income gets smaller. Perhaps moving from a flat into a family home in Ivy's case is an example of increasing "needs". Keeping the second level consistent at 65%/35% has the same outcome as above, future-self is still accounted for but reduces in monetary terms while we must reduce wants to fit 35%. We of course have the option to slide this layer 2 scale if we choose for the short-term, but it's better over the long-term if we don't so we should understand the implications, as we've discussed.

	Income	Needs	Future 65%	Want 35%
Baseline	£2,500.00	£1,300.00	£780.00	£420.00
+ Income	£3,000.00	£1,300.00	£1,105.00	£595.00
+ Needs	£2,500.00	£1,800.00	£455.00	£245.00
+ Both	£3,250.00	£1,800.00	£942.50	£507.50

Fig 6.3 | Sliding Scale In Numbers: An Example

Fig 6.3 shows an example of this in practice for the 3 scenarios, rising income, rising needs and both. Note how future and want change automatically as part of the % based scale regulating balance consistently and allowing proper budgeting outside of simply what we think we can "afford".

Level 2 on this sliding scale can be tweaked through time if required too, as long as it's conscious and with the impact understood. For example, younger readers early in their careers with lower incomes may prefer 45%/55% or some such. Fine if appropriate for personal circumstances and consciously considered. As income grows one can slide more towards a balance favouring future-self. The caution I'd give as we discussed earlier is the sooner you start planning for future self the less you actually have to assign because of compounding over long time horizons.

Similarly, as you get older and income grows you may decide 35% is too large in monetary terms for "wants" so you weight heavier future-self, 80%/20% or some such. Think of those with cleared mortgage and kids left home, their largest lifetime expenses are paid and lifestyle inflation is controlled. "Needs" have dropped significantly, meaning disposable income has grown, so it's easier to both enjoy life and build legacy for their family because of the work done earlier.

The key is a framework like this provides flexibility whatever stage of life you're in, but it enforces balance, discipline and conscious decision making that factors both current and future you. It's not easy until practiced, but as I said the money game isn't easy and if it were everyone would win. The maths though is absolutely solid. This is my blueprint for living beneath my means, how I was able to clear all debt and pay down the mortgage and how I constantly build for the future while enjoying the present. This sort of framework is applicable to **everyone**, with a little time and effort.

SUMMARY

Having defined financial goals in the first section of our financial plan we need to ensure the resource required to deliver them is consistently assigned. We must understand how money currently passes through our possession, review it and make conscious choices to build a new budget to live beneath our means for the benefit of our future-self. This includes understanding the implications of our financial choices over time and factoring them into the decision making process. "Affordability" is about more than income versus expenditure at this point in time, we must consider how it impacts our future-selves too.

This requires some technical knowledge as described in this chapter, but also the psychological learning and behaviour changes detailed throughout the book. I emphasise constantly society being geared towards keeping us trapped inside the Consumer, Debtor, Employee triad with the examples we see daily of how this is achieved and how people perpetuate it on themselves with their financial decisions. Budgeting appropriately with future-self considered, maintaining a money map and living beneath your means are the technical tools we use to escape.

I've argued with data and examples that the vast majority of people budget based on what they can afford right now, conflating want with need and oblivious to opportunity cost for their future selves in those choices. It's often a heavy cost to pay. My challenge to you is to be honest about your expenditure. How much goes to needs, how much are wants, how much is for future you to make your life better? How much have you let lifestyle inflation impact your future-self when income has increased, whether knowingly or the far more common unknowingly? Do you suffer the same issues as most?

If we want to rescue time for our future selves we must break free from the Consumer, Debtor, Employee triad and the habits of the masses trapped within. We must change **our** habits, thinking and plans so we're **not** doing the same as everyone else. To outperform we must operate differently. It's not easy. It requires thought, intention, discipline and above all consistency. But it's absolutely achievable and can be made mechanical through systematic frameworks like the sliding scale of resource allocation which regulates your resource utilisation over time.

Understanding the difference between need and want, learning how to consider opportunity cost in your choices and making those choices consciously, with balance in mind, removes you from the herd. Knowing the difference between assets and liabilities and consciously assigning resources to building for future you increases the probability future you will prosper. Understanding lifestyle inflation and guarding against it will allow you to build over longer timeframes. Thinking a little differently and doing all of these things intentionally means the difference for your future-self can be phenomenal.

<u>ACTIONS</u>

- Refer to tab "A. Actions" in the Financial Plan template.
- Complete the actions defined in section ".: 6 :. | Budget & Money Map: Living Beneath Your Means"

Keeping Down with the Joneses

"The Wealthy stay so by living like they're poor. The poor stay so by living like they're wealthy"

[Uncredited | The Internet]

ANOTHER BRIEF FORAY INTO PSYCHOLOGY, this time reflecting on those who sell their future wealth and happiness in return for the perception of wealth and happiness in the present. My intent is to provoke thought in those unconsciously living this harmful social norm so they might make a different choice consciously. There's no judgement toward those consciously choosing this life.

In this spirit, my opening quote isn't wholly accurate. Clearly some wealthy individuals spend without restraint and others are so impacted by wealth inequality there's no pretence keeping them poor. These two groups exist outside normal distribution, the latter far larger than the former. Our discussion here doesn't include either, its focus rests upon those who believe happiness is found in society's false vision of wealth, those who could build sustainable wealth and happiness long-term but choose unsustainable happiness short-term. This is often driven by a tendency for instant gratification, those who weight sliding scales heavy on wants with limited consideration towards future-self.

Separating this group from comfortable financial futures is a mindset instilled in youth, another tentacle of Consumer, Debtor, Employee: comparing ourselves to others and feeling not only a need to "keep up" (fear) but an entitlement to (greed). In reality, it's financial self-harm to think this way, trapping us in the cycle with limited ability to build better individual futures.

This old Scottish phrase would be used in a derogatory context normally but I want to use it differently, as a metaphor describing the issue. I think it's pretty succinct here and also fairly humorous for a rather dry finance book. The Joneses are "all fur coat and nae knickers". In our context it means outwardly projecting wealth with possessions, lifestyle and attitude but underneath the expensive exterior they're selling their future time and energy, potentially retirement. Their wealth is an illusion. They aren't really wealthy and they're making themselves **poorer** long-term, often **unhappy** too by pretending.

For some this is unconscious human nature mixed with social conformity and those are the people I wish to challenge to make different choices. Those who think if their neighbour can seemingly afford a luxury car and two week cruise they should be able to afford them too. They live next door so can't be so different? So they "keep down" with the Joneses, short-term happiness eventually replaced with the feeling they can't quite get ahead, or they "just need to earn a little more" as we discussed earlier. And as I'll discuss later, a potential realisation they sold their retirement.

For others though, appearing wealthy has actually become more important than being wealthy. Social media, marketing, technology, sports, entertainment, politics and mainstream media all contribute in their own ways. The individual financial impact, as should be obvious from our money mapping exercise is the inability to actually build wealth because of debt fuelled over consumption. It enforces Consumer, Debtor, Employee behaviour by conditioning people to believe looking wealthy while making other people actually wealthy is desirable. This is the modern majority, unfortunately.

> *"only when the tide goes out do you learn who has been swimming naked"*
>
> *[Warren Buffet | Multi $Billion Investor]*

He has too many good quotes, so I make no apology for referencing him again. I interpret this one with some nuance, the tide in his quip in my mind is the proliferation of cheap debt. In 2023 this tide is receding, fur coats are moth eaten and whichever metaphor you prefer we're starting to see undergarments, or not!

WHAT'S THE WEALTH ILLUSION AND HOW DOES IT WORK?

The what is simple: the projection of wealth either consciously or unconsciously through external perception. People see new cars, new houses, luxury holidays, designer clothes and all the other

Instagram ready "fur coats" and presume wealth based on societal misconceptions around how wealth looks.

An old boss said often of my refusal to promote personal brand that "perception is reality". I hated it. Not because he was wrong, he's a smart guy who I admired as a colleague, it annoyed me because he's right. Narrative is almost always more impactful than truth as we see in media and politics daily. This doesn't sit well with me but as an observation on almost every facet of daily life it's unfortunately true. For the majority of people, perception is indeed considered reality. This perception is our Wealth Illusion.

How is also simple in my view: the explosion in consumer debt. Since 1990 personal debt in western civilisation has spiralled out of control. The numbers are a little insane. In the UK for example, prior to 1990 household debt was high but relatively manageable, remaining lower than household gross disposable income. At the turn of the century it became easier to obtain and more accepted as a societal norm. Household debt began to exceed disposable household income in 2001 and the UK, like many countries, never looked back. In 2013 outstanding debt sat around 131% of household disposable income having peaked above 150% in 2008.

Overall it rose from below £400 Billion in 1990 to £1.5 Trillion by 2013. In 2021 it was £1.7 Trillion and in 2023 it stands at a whopping £2 Trillion. Consumer debt, not national. For context, according to the BoE inflation calculator £400 Billion in 1990 is ~£945.3 Billion in 2023 based on real inflation data. Personal debt growth has more than trebled inflationary effect.

In 2021 the ONS figure of £1.7 Trillion equated to £33,410 for each UK adult, 107% average UK salary at the time. In 2023 it rose to £34,716, on par with rising average wages (£34,963 in December).

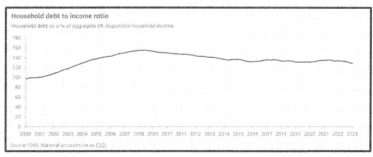

Fig 7.1 | UK Household Debt to Income Ratio

By the end of 2024 the OBR (Office for Budgetary Responsibility) projects household debt to income ratio will rise above 150% again, around where it peaked prior to the 2008 GFC. This isn't dissimilar in trend to other western economies. Remember those WEF targets from earlier? "You'll own nothing and you'll be happy". This is how we eventually get there, by trapping the population in debt servitude. The continued inflation of asset markets combined with static wage growth, increasing taxation and spiralling debt service costs in populations the world over eventually leads to working people having the means to own nothing. Many of our younger generations would contest we're already there. It also drives us towards a situation where the middle class, the last bastion of working people who still buy assets to some degree (in dwindling number) having this ability removed, forced into a position where they have to sell those assets to the wealthy, furthering wealth inequality.

How do so many Jones families maintain the pretence then? Debt funds the illusion and their debt service costs keep them trapped as Consumers, Debtors and Employees like they're meant to be, oblivious to the opportunity costs tomorrow of the choices made today. **FAST MONEY, SLOW PROBLEMS.** They're oblivious to their debt captivity or to potential future impacts of, for example, aging populations with increasing debt burdens and declining birth rates. These together may force those unprepared into working longer in life to fund fiscal issues at both ends.

With aging populations come higher state pension and social care burdens. An increasingly elderly populace reduces tax income as less tax is generally paid once retired. Population decline also means fewer young people joining the system, reducing tax income on the long end. It means higher social costs for an increasingly elderly populace and lower tax income from a reducing working age populace to fund it. World leaders know social care systems are pseudo Ponzi schemes with funding predicated upon population and demographic stability, generations of younger taxpayers paying for elderly retirees. Theres no UK "pension fund", the system needs new tax paying employees as older employees retire in relatively stable number.

To explain this point, population stability requires a birthrate of ~2.1 live births per female over time (without immigration). It's where the phrase "2.1 children" originates. Below 2.1 and a population is officially in decline, above 2.1 means population growth, notionally. Western countries have been below 2.1 for some time, meaning a potential for mass population decline over the next 100 years and elderly citizens with extending life expectancy growing as a proportion of the overall populace.

The UK is currently 1.6, US 1.7 and Germany 1.5 for example. South Korea has the lowest replacement rates in the world at 0.7, meaning every 100 citizens produce ~24 (0.7^4 x 100) great grandchildren. Their death rate of 0.728% equates to population decline of 2.8% per year. Using exponential decay formula we can more accurately project (P(100)=100×(1−0.028): 25.1) an extinction rate of ~75% (every 100 people now becomes 25 later). Covid, for context, was ~2% and closed the world for 2 years. Why then little coverage of the replacement rate problems?

Well, I'd suggest western societies **need** immigration from growing populations (like sub Saharan Africa for example) and immigration is a touchy political subject so it's somewhat repressed as a talking point. Secondly, if the populace is aware of the potential individual financial impact of aging populations it's harder to trap people forever in the Consumer, Debtor, Employee cycle. The promise of state supplied pensions and reasonable retirements is a strong incentive to keep working without digging too deeply. A tangential point sure, but one in this context worth making for awareness. Replacement rate issues are fascinating with wide reaching impact in socio-economic terms so well worth deeper investigation personally than we have space for here.

Back to the Joneses and people are conditioned to be "normal". Take credit to pay for things we want because instant gratification is how the world works. Dopamine is arguably a form of currency. We accept how everyone else does it as the way it must be done. Psychologically this is known as "status quo bias" or "tradition bias", a cognitive bias describing the tendency to adhere to familiar practice and established routine for no other reason than historical or perceived norm. "Societal norms" like credit and consumption are tradition bias encouraging individuals through fear of being different to resist change, even when more effective alternatives like those I describe demonstrably exist.

This stubbornness frustrates me when talking with people about finance. I've no "Morpheus complex", I'm nowhere near as cool for starters, but I do wish I had metaphorical pills to offer to help people see the system for what it really is. They've been conditioned, it's not entirely their fault. Keeping down with the Joneses is to make other people money through credit based consumption of things we want to keep down with all the other versions of ourselves making other people money. We're back to Spiderman memes again!

My plea to you is simple: if you're this way inclined but you truly want to improve your long-term outlook, stop it. Look at your money map and be honest with yourself. Are "needs" oversized for your family? Are you prioritising future-self? Are you making financial decisions solely in the now because you think you should be able to afford what you see in society? Is your budget process "I can afford it"? These and many more things indicate you're keeping down with the Joneses and by doing so future you is losing ground, having to work another year beyond your expected retirement. And another. And another.

This may be difficult to hear, but hopefully having read this far you understand the need to raise it. So stop. Stop keeping down with the Joneses, unconsciously or otherwise. The reality is most Joneses are broke and making themselves generationally poorer by propagating the illusion of wealth built on spiralling levels of debt. Eventually, they will "own nothing", but they won't be happy. If you truly want to change financial outlooks over time, truly want to live a life free from debt and filled with opportunity of time then you must be willing for people to think you're poor and not care. There's no-one who looks at me and thinks I have what I have. And I couldn't give a singly shiny......penny, let's say penny.

A SOCIAL EXPERIMENT

Many have offered versions of this hypothesis and I wholeheartedly agree through my own experience: if we reset money to zero and gave everyone £100,000 to do with as they pleased then in 10 years' time those struggling now would be again and those wealthy now would have all the money again.

I truly believe this because knowing how to build wealth, how to make and keep money and how to get out of the Consumer, Debtor, Employee triad is a pursuit of knowledge, time and consistency. Wealthy people (first generation) had to figure this out. The people who couldn't figure it out before, who spent everything they had and wondered why they were broke, don't know how, have never done it before and thus would be most likely to repeat past mistakes. There's a reason many prominent self-made millionaires lost it all and were able to gain it back. It's not luck, it's knowledge. There's also a reason second and third generation wealth is at most risk and lottery winners often end up broke.

Trader me thinks I'd have an edge (statistical advantage) and I'd trade heavily in the direction of the same people collecting all the money again. How about an example, one nearly making me crash my car so angry was I no-one challenged the answer? A large radio station here runs a competition where randomly picked entrants win large amounts tax free. I listen on my commute and happened to catch this winning call. It started in a heartfelt way, a single mother, newly divorced and raising two kids, in tears as the presenter confirmed she'd won a figure well in excess of twice the national average salary, tax free. They asked "what does this mean to you?" and she fought through her tears to explain things have been really tough with cost of living increases, she's struggling to make house payments and feed the children, things have been horrible and this'll change their lives.

I was, initially at least, delighted for her. Someone genuinely needing a break and the universe provides an opportunity to make a huge difference for children clearly living in poverty, some of the 33% I highlighted earlier. Nice to hear. The presenter then asks "so what will you do with the money?" and without pause for thought, having just explained their dire circumstances the winner answers "I'm taking the kids to Disney World in Florida for a holiday". What. The actual. F*ck!

I remind myself people don't know any better, it's not their fault. They've been conditioned to consume like this without thinking so it shouldn't surprise me. But still, I wanted to help her. I wanted to explain how she might better secure her kids future and while not the instant gratification of a trip to Florida the kids would remember for a lifetime actually securing their lifetime and a chance to break the cycle was maybe a better idea. But I couldn't.

It's one example of the phenomena I've described and why I believe resetting money would result in the same haves and have nots. It's a knowledge, psychology and execution problem, which is why we've so many Joneses. This isn't an easy change as its entirely in the mind and goes against societal norms, against peer group(s). You must though stop thinking and acting like the 90% if you want to break free from them. Acting the same and wondering why you share their outcomes is like having a 0.7% birthrate and wondering why populations disappear in 300 years.

As I said earlier, humans struggle today to think in those timeframes, they're too abstract. We **must** force ourselves to operate outside of the short-term, instant gratification world of pretence in which all of our Joneses are trapped. Or put more firmly: F*ck the Joneses, they're broke! Draw a line in the sand and stop trying to keep down with them. In reality that's choosing to remain trapped inside the Consumer, Debtor, Employee triad, regardless of external factors impacting our finances.

On Track for Retirement?

"You can be young without money, but you can't be old without it."

[*Tennessee Williams | Playwright*]

LET'S TURN ATTENTION BACK TO long-term and the retirement provision within your financial plan. Most people want to retire early enough to enjoy it but many are unwittingly under prepared. We must ensure this doesn't include us! Pensions and retirement planning are fairly complex financial subtopics so it's little surprise people struggle with them. The aim of this chapter is to explain some of the key concepts to help with your own planning.

If you're working you should be contributing to some form of retirement account. If you're not then you should remedy this as part of the actions in this chapter. Even if you're below minimum auto enrolment age in the UK you can request enrolment or open a SIPP, the earlier you start the better. Let's look briefly at retirement account options.

PENSIONS & RETIREMENT ACCOUNTS

The most common types of pension and retirement accounts in the UK and US include:

- State Pension (referred to as Social Security in the US).
- (UK) Employer / Occupational Pension (Defined Benefit or Defined Contribution, Includes Auto Enrolment).
- (UK) SIPP (Self Invested Personal Pension).
- (UK) ISA (Individual Savings Account. Not specifically for retirement but a useful option).
- (US) IRA (Individual Retirement Account. Roth & Regular).
- (US) 401(k).

There are regulatory differences between UK and US equivalents, mainly in allowances and tax benefit, but they're broadly similar in actual operation. The same applies in most jurisdictions, there are generally functional equivalents of listed accounts so check availability in your locale. UK DC Pensions are (relatively) equivalent to US 401(k). UK SIPPs are similar to US IRA's. The UK also has access to ISA's which aren't pension accounts specifically so not tied to statutory retirement age, one can withdraw from most ISA's at any time. They're investment accounts so don't benefit from income tax relief on the way in like pensions but some use them as part of retirement provision (myself included) so certainly warrant mention. They do benefit from tax savings on any capital growth, similar to US Roth IRA versions, which makes them appealing for drawdown planning.

A rough cheat sheet for UK readers: pensions are income tax efficient on the way in, taxed as income on the way out and only accessible 10 years (maximum) before statutory retirement age (currently 66 but rising). For ISA's income has already been taxed pre deposit so all capital gains are completely tax free on withdrawal, at any age. Both are investment accounts making long term investments in markets, compounding over time.

PENSION TYPES: STATE PENSION

State pensions are provisioned by government through taxation and available to eligible citizens. The UK requires 30 years full National Insurance contributions for eligibility. The US also has a state pension, referred to as "Social Security" but neither are particularly stellar compared to other countries. For example:

- A 2022 report showed the UK had one of the worst performing pensions in Europe with 15.5% of pensioners living in poverty compared to Germany: 9.2%, France: 4.4%, Denmark: 3.6%, Italy: 11.3% and Holland: 5.2%.
- The same report showed the US at 23% pensioner poverty rate, worse than Europe but comparable with Australia: 25% and Japan: 20%

UK state pension is payable at age 66, rising to 67 by 2028 and at time of writing provides a maximum of £203.85 per week, equivalent to £10,600 annually if you have full 30 year National Insurance contributions. This regularly rises with inflation. In the US the average monthly payment is $1701.62 (2023) and is payable from age 67. The long-term viability of such schemes is open for debate, but they currently support many retirees globally.

The Mercer CFA Institute Global Pension Index compares pension provision across various nations and though it could be argued subjective is a useful place to review how your local provision compares. In 2023 the Netherlands led the way, topping the table with a score of 85 from Iceland in second place and Denmark in third. The UK placed 10th. The system compares pension adequacy, sustainability and integrity with strengths and weaknesses reviewed and areas for improvement highlighted. It's a useful resource for pension comparison.

PENSION TYPES: (UK) EMPLOYER / OCCUPATIONAL PENSION

Sponsored by employers who pay into a scheme on behalf of the employee, these generally include both employer and employee payments through either salary sacrifice or an additional benefit package. They fall into 2 categories:

DEFINED BENEFIT, often referred to as "final" or "average" salary and sees retirees receive regular predetermined payments based on factors like salary history and length of service. This is calculated by specific formulas within individual schemes. Once the default and enjoyed by many current UK retirees they're mostly closed to new entrants outside some public sector roles. They became too expensive for employers who assume all of the risk as they're obligated to meet agreed benefit levels regardless of market environment.

DEFINED CONTRIBUTION including Auto Enrolment (AE) in the UK is where both employee and employer contribute an amount based on salary and/or benefit package. The minimum monthly AE amount is currently 8% (3% employer minimum) unless opted out. Essentially these are investment accounts expected to grow over time with retirees able to buy an annuity or drawdown from the fund in retirement. In defined contribution schemes all risk is assumed by individuals: market risk (their pot falling in value) and longevity risk (outliving their accrued pot).

PENSION TYPES: (UK) SIPP (SELF INVESTED PERSONAL PENSION)

SIPP's operate like general investment accounts but benefit from the tax advantages of employer pensions. Two major differences are that the individual manages investments themselves rather than a pension manager and higher rate tax relief must be claimed manually through tax return.

As deposits have generally been income taxed via PAYE, SIPP providers top up the additional % to cover basic rate tax. Higher rate tax payers (and extra Scottish bands) claim higher tax benefit via self-service tax return. As they're more like general investment accounts they offer more diverse investment opportunities over (typically) narrow employer pension equivalents which offer fewer instruments. Fees also tend to be lower, both platform and fund which can both be high in employer schemes.

PENSION TYPES: (US) IRA (INDIVIDUAL RETIREMENT ACCOUNTS)

Individual Retirement Accounts (IRAs) are personal retirement accounts individuals can set up and contribute to individually, like a SIPP. They offer tax advantages on the maximum annual contribution of $7,000 (2024 under 50) or $7,500 (2024 over 50) and come in two main types:

- **REGULAR IRA:** Contributions typically tax-deductible and earnings grow tax-deferred until withdrawals made in retirement when they're taxed as regular income. Closer to a UK SIPP in terms of operation and tax status.
- **ROTH IRA:** Contributions are made with after-tax money but qualified withdrawals in retirement are tax-free, including capital gains. Closer to a UK ISA in terms of operation and tax status, but with a 59½ age requirement.

There are other considerations and regulations linked to IRA's like qualifying income ranges for tax deductible status so make sure you understand what these are, employing the skills of a qualified financial planner if required. The IRS website details these very well including the 2024 changes.

PENSION TYPES: (US) 401(K)

Employer sponsored retirement savings plans similar to UK DC schemes. Employees contribute a portion of salary with some employers offering matched contributions. These are invested in market instruments like equities, commodities, property and fixed income aiming to grow over time to support retirement drawdown, just like the UK versions.

These can be either traditional (tax-deferred contributions) or Roth (after-tax contributions). Again, the IRS website does a good job of detailing the regulations linked to 401(k) accounts, like the $23,000 annual allowance, so be sure to check these out so you understand your entitlements and obligations if US based.

PENSION TYPES: ANNUITIES

Not strictly a pension type but I've mentioned them previously so want to explain a little. Annuities are financial products one purchasers providing guaranteed income during retirement. Individuals invest lump sums or make regular payments to insurance companies and in return the insurer provides payments for a specified period (usually life in retirement).

There are multiple variations like fixed, index linked or variable and they can be single or joint, to leave a benefit for surviving dependents or not. They can be used in part alongside drawdown or fully for retirement provision.

PENSION ALLOWANCES

Annual allowances apply for all UK pension types. For earners this is currently £60,000 per annum or 100% of income, whichever is lesser. For non-earners it's £3,600 per year, £2,880 to receive the 20% top up to get there. Most countries have set limits ($23,000 US 401(k) at time of writing) so make sure you're aware of your local rules. There are also lifetime contribution allowances in some jurisdictions. The UK was £1,073,100 but in the 2023 spring statement the government announced a pause in 23/24 and plans to scrap entirely in 24/25. Again, check your local rules.

THE HIDDEN PENSION PROBLEM

The overall situation has improved since the 2012 introduction of Auto Enrolment (AE) in the UK, on the surface a positive change forcing both employers and employees to make some provision for retirement. Many wouldn't have done otherwise.

In 2012 only 41% were enrolled into private pensions. The issue is similar in the US where a 2022 SCF (Survey of Consumer Finances) survey found less than 50% of people had retirement provision outside of social security. Post AE in the UK this rose to 81% in 2021, a positive change politicians can (and we know love to!) pat themselves on the back for initiating. But the reality when digging deeper is it's an issue improved, but still appears problematic with most potentially impacted having no idea. In AE they see a lifeboat but much like the Titanic they don't realise capacity might not be enough for everyone to get out safely.

Why? The minimum at 8% is low and people using this with AE over long periods are potentially underfunding. Many assume 8% is adequate so stick with it for too long and many won't be aware it's an issue until looking to retire because they don't have the knowledge to calculate return and don't track their progress. Can we quantify this? Yes, In May 2023 average pension pots per age range in the UK were, as we saw earlier:

- **25 - 34:** £9,300
- **35 - 44:** £30,000
- **45 - 54:** £75,000
- **55 - 64:** £107,000

Those are averages, meaning a small number above bring the average up. The disparity is worse in my view. For example, I've 10 times my demographic average having planned for two decades and because I track it. I currently commit in excess of 24%, 3 times minimum, to meet projected goals and started in my 20's at 18%.

To reiterate the context discussed previously, 2023 Pensions and Lifetime Savings Association modelling of annual income requirements is split into 3 living standards per today's figures (non-inflation adjusted):

- **MINIMUM:** £12,800
- **MODERATE:** £23,300
- **COMFORTABLE:** £37,300

The average UK salary (Dec 2023) is £34,963. Both minimum and moderate calculations fall well below this and though it's close to 'Comfortable' most on the average salary would contest the comfortable description with today's cost of living challenges! Yes it's assumed housing costs are gone by retirement, kids too, most people's largest expenses, but still, comfort is a stretch!

UK state pension is currently £10,600, below minimum living standard. This is paid fully in addition to private pension if one has 30 fully paid National Insurance qualifying years. If not it's partially paid based on contributions. My view, shared by a few, is that those under 45 in 2023 shouldn't count on state pension being paid. The UK, like most western countries excluding Norway, has worsening fiscal problems (we highlighted one with birthrates). If I'm worrying unnecessarily and state pension exists when I retire, great, but I'm not including in my projections. I'd rather over fund retirement than underfund it by trusting someone else, politicians no less, to deliver it for me.

£12,800 sounds pretty grim, I have to say. What pot value is required to achieve this? Using a £4,715 per £100,000 annuity product (prices today) to achieve these values **after tax** and **non-inflation adjusted** you need (not including state pension):

- **MINIMUM:** £273,700

- **MODERATE:** £534,337
- **COMFORTABLE:** £883,647

Let's recap so you understand problem scale. Average pension pots for those reaching minimum retirement age are £107,000. One fifth of moderate pot size, less than half the £12,800 minimum. Younger ranges are markedly lower still. We're approaching the first majority DC over DB pension retirees and it might be rough for many, even if using drawdown in place of annuity. There are some of caveats here, for clarity:

- These figures are for individuals, not couples.
- AE only started in 2012 so we haven't seen full impact over time for those starting from age 22.
- These figures **DON'T** include housing costs.
- These figures **DON'T** include State Pension.
- These figures **DON'T** account for taking tax free lump sum.
- These figures are based on annuity costs today: joint 50% benefit rising by 3% policy.

Problem scale may not be as I fear and a lot can change both financially and politically, but I'm not one to rely on hope nor am I the only one concerned. The Pensions Policy Institute conducts ongoing studies on pension adequacy and their report "The Future of Retirement" highlighted similar issues related to increased life expectancy requiring larger pots to mitigate longevity risk.

My message is simply: plan as early as possible, figure out what you need and figure out how to deliver it. Depending on age it may be a difficult realisation but remember you can make positive difference by starting now. Whatever you do from here is a potential improvement. Better to plan and track than get a surprise when you think you can retire and find out you can't.

THE HIDDEN PENSION PROBLEM: COUPLE VERSUS INDIVIDUAL

The numbers presented so far are for individuals and many will reach their golden years alongside a partner. Two incomes covering two living costs impacts calculations, but doesn't "double up". The same categories for a couple in the UK, according to the Pensions and Lifetime Savings Association 2023 modelling are:

- **MINIMUM:** £19,900 (additional 55%)
- **MODERATE:** £34,000 (additional 46%)
- **COMFORTABLE:** £54,500 (additional 46%)

Rising 46%-55% for a couple, there's certainly benefit to provisioning and living retirement together. **Note:** Always ensure beneficiary declarations are updated with pension providers. Providers don't have to follow them, legally, but it makes your wishes clear in the event of your untimely death.

THE HIDDEN PENSION PROBLEM: AUTO ENROLMENT IMPACT

In 2012 the UK government tried to relieve some burden on the state by enforcing measures to remedy widespread lack of retirement planning via Auto Enrolment. This reform meant workers older than 22 earning above the threshold of £10,000 (2023) were entitled to workplace pensions contributed to by employee (minimum 5%) and employer (minimum 3%). AE is a Defined Contribution (DC) pension scheme.

We have limited data currently on impact over time, specifically those starting age 22. The situation should improve in theory: 8% (min.) of current UK average wage is £2,797. Over 46 years (22 to 68) at 4.5% YoY return (low projection) potential returns are: £427,025. Between "Minimum" and "Moderate" levels before state pension. Around £15,728 after (current) tax at 4% drawdown.

As I said I intentionally exclude State Pension from my calculations as I'm unconvinced it'll still be around. I'd rather be over funded if it is than underfunded if it's not. I'm managing risk.

Cynical me also thinks AE may be a long-term political move to remove state pension burden entirely. As above, current projection at 4.5% for 8% of UK average wage is around £17,081 before tax (£15,728 after), higher than current state pension. 8% of UK minimum wage (£19,760 at time of writing) at 4.5% over 46 years is: £241,344.90 so £9,653 per annum at 4% drawdown. These numbers are too conveniently close for me not to be suspicious of this being a long-term replacement strategy, either removing for everyone or by excluding those with private provision above a threshold. I should add inflation adjusted the state pension in 46 years (at 2.5%) should rise to £33,007 and above calculations aren't inflation adjusted (again, testing you)!

THE HIDDEN PENSION PROBLEM: HOUSING COSTS NOTE

ALL calculations presented, including minimum to comfortable retirement levels and required pots to achieve them assume nil housing cost. Base assumption in most retirement conversations is retirees have no housing overhead. If reaching retirement with costs like rent or mortgage you'll require **more** than outlined.

Given the housing crisis (affordability and stock) in the UK, this is likely to add to this issue over time, not help it!

THE HIDDEN PENSION PROBLEM: TAX FREE LUMP SUM NOTE

UK pensions allow for 25% as a tax free lump sum. These pot size calculations assume this **isn't** taken. If you require the tax free lump sum, perhaps to pay off a mortgage, it means pot size to maintain the listed income levels increases. It should also be noted lump sums can be taken over time in drawdown pensions, you don't need to take 25% of the value upfront. If buying an annuity or using a Defined Benefit pension you do need to take upfront. For those instruments it generally makes sense for tax efficiency.

This benefit isn't enjoyed everywhere outside of the UK so check your local regulations to see if it applies to you. It should also be noted that living abroad can impact the tax you pay on your pension, depending on resident status. If you plan to live outside of your home country in retirement, make sure you check the tax implications to avoid double paying or impacting on your drawdown plan via higher than modelled tax burden.

THE HIDDEN PENSION PROBLEM: ANNUITY OR DRAWDOWN

Some of these figures assume purchase of an annuity, an insurance product guaranteeing fixed income for life. Example rates today for a Joint life 50%, 3% increasing annuity from 65 is £100,000 per £4,715 benefit payment. This increases by 3% per year and continues to pay 50% to your beneficiary should you die.

Single life products are available but only pay benefit until the holder dies with no beneficiary payment. Many have no annual increase. Single life, no increase policies for a 65 year old today are £100,000 per £7,264 benefit payment. You can mix and match in retirement, purchasing an annuity for an amount but leaving the remainder invested for drawdown as something of a hedge.

I haven't used annuities in these models to suggest them the best option, it's very much a personal decision based on individual circumstances. I just wanted to use both annuity and drawdown to avoid favouring one. Annuities are used by many advisors for illustration purposes given straightforward calculations.

Post UK pension changes in 1995 retirees can opt to utilise Flexi Access Drawdown as well as annuities. I've used a couple of drawdown examples at 4% too. Drawdown is where one removes the desired amount annually like a salary, leaving the remainder invested aiming for continued growth. You may have heard this practice referred to as something like "the 4% rule", one of many drawdown strategies people commonly employ. There are pros and cons to both options, summarised below.

ANNUITIES PROS:

- **RISK MANAGEMENT:** Eliminates the risk of outliving savings (longevity risk) and protects you from market volatility (market risk). They're static insurance products rather than market fluctuating investment products like drawdown pensions.

- **GUARANTEED INCOME:** Provides guaranteed income for life, or a specific period, regardless of how long you live or market fluctuations. If purchasing a joint annuity rather than single life your beneficiary is entitled to a portion for the remainder of their lives in the event of your death, generally 50%. You can purchase increasing annuities if you want to factor in the price of inflation. These are generally more expensive.

- **NO INVESTMENT DECISIONS:** Once you buy an annuity there's no concern about managing investments or making any complex financial decisions. There's no account to manage, simply an insurance that pays out at the purchased level until death/expiry of annuity.

- **SIMPLE AND PREDICTABLE:** They're straightforward instruments. You know exactly how much you'll receive regularly making budgeting easier.

ANNUITIES CONS:

- **POTENTIALLY LOWER RETURNS:** Compared to drawdown annuities generally offer lower returns, particularly if you don't live as long as expected. This is the price you pay for removing market risk and longevity risk.

- **LACK OF FLEXIBILITY:** Once purchased you generally can't access a lump sum investment or cancel/transfer (after the cooling off period). This limits your ability to adjust financial plans if circumstances change later in life.

- **NO INHERITANCE:** Unless you have a joint annuity or a guarantee period, payments typically cease upon death providing no inheritance. If your plan allows a proportion of benefits to be left it's generally to a spouse or partner, but it can include (adult) children in some cases. This is rare and rules vary so check product details. Professional advice may help, but one thing's certain, if you're allowed to leave a portion to (adult) children but don't define them in your beneficiary statement providers won't go hunting for them!

DRAWDOWN PENSIONS (FLEXI-ACCESS DRAWDOWN) PROS:

- **POTENTIAL FOR GROWTH:** Investments stay invested in the market so favourable market conditions could see account growth even during retirement when drawing down from it.
- **FLEXIBLE WITHDRAWALS:** You control how much you withdraw each year providing flexibility to adapt to changing financial needs. You may hear about strategies Like "the 4% rule" or, my preference, "Dynamic Withdrawal Strategy". You have more ability to adjust than annuities.
- **INVESTMENT CONTROL:** You retain freedom to choose how to invest, potentially leading to higher returns if investments are performing well. This is tempered by market risk though, which you must be mindful of (a con).
- **INHERITANCE POTENTIAL:** Any remaining funds after death can be passed to beneficiaries as an asset, subject to inheritance tax, providing legacy annuities don't offer in the event of an early death for example.

DRAWDOWN PENSIONS (FLEXI-ACCESS DRAWDOWN) CONS:

- **LONGEVITY RISK:** No guaranteed income for life, so you have a risk of outliving your pension pot if drawing too much or market conditions turn unfavourable. Dynamic allocation strategies aim to mitigate this to some degree but the risk persists throughout needing careful management.
- **MARKET RISK:** Fund value can fluctuate depending on market conditions, potentially leading to lower income or running out of money if investments perform poorly.
- **COMPLEXITY:** Managing investments and calculating withdrawal rates can be complicated. Inexperienced retirees can make suboptimal decisions, taking too much too early when the pot seems large for example.
- **INCOME UNCERTAINTY:** No stable, predictable income like annuities making budgeting more challenging, particularly in periods of market fluctuation.

Each has pros and cons so the right choice will depend on individual circumstances, risk tolerance and financial goals during retirement. A combination of both can help, enjoying the benefit of guaranteed income alongside the flexibility and growth potential of drawdown. Before making a decision you may wish to consult with a financial professional to assess which options align best with your retirement objectives. They'll also be able to advise on tax efficient retirement, as overpaying tax is a risk in both.

THE HIDDEN PENSION PROBLEM: STATE PENSION BENEFIT

As discussed, previous figures don't account for state pension benefit. If this is paid then pot size requirements reduce. Including state pension, overall pot requirements for the income levels described previously are:

- MINIMUM: £48,038 (£12,865 gross for £12,800 net, including £10,600 state pension)
- MODERATE: £336,246 (£26,454 gross for £23,300 net, including £10,600 state pension)
- COMFORTABLE: £720,487 (£44,571 gross for £37,300 net, including £10,600 state pension)

Other locales offer different levels of state pension, for example the (current) US average monthly payment is $1701.62 for $20,419.44 per annum. Check the provision in your locale if you'd like to model these in your projections.

THE HIDDEN PENSION PROBLEM: SUMMARY

Pension provision across the UK population, the primary lifelong financial security and wealth building measure, highlights a lack of long-term planning. Auto Enrolment will help some but not all and not any time soon, even though it's a long-term step in the right direction. I hope the numbers discussed show why you must take control of your retirement provision and as early in life as possible. I'm personally in favour of state pension reform, moving towards investment structure, but it's an emotive political subject.

RETIREMENT ACCOUNTS: OTHER OPTIONS

Let's quickly discuss some additional accounts you may consider from a retirement planning perspective, specifically the humble ISA in the UK (Roth IRA closest US equivalent) and general investment accounts. Many countries have some version of these so you can refer to your local regulations to identify how (and by how much) you can leverage them or their equivalents.

GENERAL INVESTMENT ACCOUNTS are held with a broker and one uses them to buy and sell market instruments like equities, commodities and ETF's. Cryptocurrency accounts are also considered general investment for tax purposes. These accounts provide access to markets with capital gains due on profit above personal allowance. Depending on trade frequency and success, potentially income taxable as well (though more unusual). Capital Gains allowance is reducing to £3,000 in the UK in 2024 but some countries (like Germany) enjoy tax breaks for any instrument held longer than 12 months. Generally these should be utilised after ISA (or tax advantaged accounts in your locale) and pension allowances are exhausted for this tax inefficiency reason.

ISA'S are tax efficient accounts and UK readers enjoy a £20,000 annual allowance. The main types are Cash, Stocks & Shares and if under 40 Lifetime ISA (LISA). We also have an additional £9,000 allowance for a Junior ISA in a child's name.

CASH ISA'S are either easy access or locked (generally 1-3 years) cash accounts paying interest on deposits tax free. Unlike pensions you can withdraw any time penalty and tax free.

STOCKS & SHARES ISA'S are investment accounts where one can invest in the different instruments available in markets, for example individual equities, commodities and ETF's. We'll cover these later in detail. Capital growth, dividend and interest is tax free inside the account and on withdrawal. They're similar to DC pension accounts but with tax advantages on the way out, not the way in. Again, withdraw any time penalty and tax free.

LIFETIME ISA'S are specifically for under 40's and only for either the purchase of first homes or retirement. £4,000 per year is the allowance from our overall £20,000 but for every £4 deposited the government will add £1. So, deposit £4,000 and you'll receive £1,000 more, an instant 25% return. Funds are invested in market instruments like the Stocks & Shares ISA, seeking capital growth. All return is tax free but if used for any purpose other than defined you pay a 25% withdrawal charge.

JUNIOR ISA'S are opened in the name of a child, similar to a trust fund. Anyone can deposit cash (like parents or family members) and the parent manages the investments. Withdrawals are locked until 18 where ownership of the fund passes to the child. It's a good way to teach kids about investing and markets.

Historically only one ISA account of each type could be funded per year but changes in April 2024 will mean we can fund multiple accounts per year up to the standard £20,000 limit. This will be useful for keeping core and play portfolios separate and trying new providers. In the US there's a withdrawal age limit on the Roth IRA of 59 and a half and the allowance is only $7,000, so we definitely have a good deal in the UK at present. It baffles me then that only ~7% of the UK populace contributes to a stocks and shares ISA annually (last ONS data from 21/22 tax year).

Tax benefit on money paid into a pension, particularly for higher rate tax payers, means pensions generally return better yield over the long-term. 20%-45% more in deposits compounds over time. There's no suggestion you should forgo a pension in favour of an ISA, however if you're able to adequately fund a pension and can afford to utilise some or all of your ISA allowance annually then it presents useful options later.

Pensions are age limited, generally statutory age minus 10 years so they're inaccessible in real terms until 56/57. If you know your "number", the income you want in retirement, every multiple of it you build in an ISA gives you **THE OPTION TO RETIRE EARLY**. For example if £30k is your number and your ISA reaches £90k by statutory age -13 (standard 10 plus the 3x£30k saved) you can retire early without needing the pension (if those 3 years missed contributions don't upset pension goals of course).

Also, pensions are taxable on the way out, efficient on the way in, ISA's are the opposite. If you wanted £55k per year in retirement then the portion over £43,663 in Scotland, £50,271 in the rest of the UK (as Scotland pays more tax) is liable to higher rate tax. Every £ you pay in tax from your pension is one less in your pocket. You could, though, utilise your ISA which is tax free. Taking maximum for basic rate tax from pension then the remainder from the ISA **SAVES 40%-46% TAX ON THE ADDITIONAL AMOUNT** until the ISA depletes. Small figures add up and from a drawdown perspective mitigating longevity risk so your money outlives you means every £ is vital.

Not a necessity by any means but an ISA does provide the benefit of flexibility if you can build alongside your pension. Retirement planning should prioritise building a pension due to working life income tax advantages in my view, but I also utilise the benefits of ISA's for a multitude of reasons (it's the vehicle I used to pay my mortgage at 36 for example).

EMPLOYER SALARY MATCH NOTE

A quick interlude to highlight employer salary match. This is where employers match up to a certain level (often 6%) any employee pension contributions. This is free, tax efficient money. When considering compounding effects over long periods an employer match can be hugely advantageous to long-term wealth building. If you have this option: Max it out. As much as you can as early as you can. I'll say again, it's free money!

L.T. Noelle

MAKING YOUR PLAN

Conventional financial planning would ask something like "what age do you want to retire", starting calculations from there. Before we do similar though I want to explain age as a planning number only, trying to break your link between retirement and a fixed age.

Most people think they can't retire before a certain age or worse they only need to make it to a certain age to retire. The former run the risk of working longer than they have to and the latter, as previously discussed, risk reaching their desired age and realising they can't afford to retire. In my view retirement isn't an age, it's a number in a retirement portfolio (pension and other assets) supported by debt clearance. The sooner debt is cleared and your account built, the sooner you have options. Strong retirement planning and execution of those plans **buys you time**.

I don't think you should view retirement as a static age like many do, other than for these planning purposes, where we need to project over a time period. Retirement should be the number allowing you to live the lifestyle you want with high probability of your money outliving you. For example, if your retirement account number is £900,000 by 65 and you want £35,000 (in today's money), then if £900,000 is built by 62, with an additional ISA pot of £105,000, you have the ***option*** to retire at 62.

Waiting for 67 because "target age" may see you work longer than required, when you had the funds needed to retire earlier. Remember, for me wealth is about gaining **time**. I'm not saying blindly take the option, you may enjoy work and decide a few extra years for more retirement capital, retaining the ISA, is optimal. All I advocate is knowing your numbers so you know when you have the ***option***. As my father has always said:

"Better to have it and not need it, than need it and not have it".

[L.T. Noelle Senior | Wise Father]

MAKING YOUR PLAN: WHAT TO CONSIDER

If you've a Defined Benefit (DB) pension, many of these considerations will be moot as you'll be limited by the terms and conditions of your scheme. These do in general offer better retirement provision than Defined Contribution (DC) though. If a Defined Contribution (DC) scheme member, including AE and SIPP, then calculating pension requirement involves some personal considerations. Everyone has different needs depending on expected retirement age, desired lifestyle and life expectancy among other things. It's useful to have a modeller to view the impact of these together over time, so one has been provided in the financial plan template. The variables within are mostly self-explanatory, but include the following, worthy of explanation:

ESTIMATED REQUIRED INCOME: Estimate how much income you'll need to cover anticipated annual expenses in retirement. This includes housing costs (if any), general living expenses like food and utilities, travel, hobbies, healthcare (if required) and any other expenses you think you'll have. Be realistic, it doesn't help to underestimate. Expenses should inform you fairly well what kind of retirement income you need. Consider additional sources of income you may have like rental property, part time work or a business. General guidelines suggest around two-thirds of pre-retirement salary as a yardstick, though this depends on each individual too. I currently invest more than 50% of income and won't need to keep that up, for example. I prefer to look at current expenses then and estimate a figure for things like holidays, hobbies and socialising. Define a number you're happy with that allows you to play with calculations.

ESTIMATED LIFESPAN: Estimate, as best as anyone can, life expectancy. Clearly no-one can predict with any real accuracy their lifespan but an approximate age based on family history and health helps to plan how long you might need money to last. If struggling to put a number on it, use standard government numbers for your country as a guide. In the UK this is 81 for males, 83.6 for females in 2023.

YoY RATE OF INVESTMENT RETURN: Again, difficult to project, especially if you've little financial experience, but you must estimate an average rate of return over your investment horizon. I personally use 3 figures and built the modeller such. These provide low, mid and high ranges. I'd rather over fund than under so I use 4.5% Low, 6% mid and 8% high. I plan on 4.5%. You also need to factor you're not likely to be taking as much risk in retirement, so there may be "pre" retirement (average) RoR and a post-retirement average RoR as funds move towards less risky assets like bonds or money markets. The modeller allows you to tweak all of these and model on low, mid and high outcomes.

ANNUAL CONTRIBUTIONS: How much will you contribute to your pension as a % of income while saving. Full contribution, including employer match if applicable.

CURRENT PENSION POT SIZE: How much you've currently saved, for projecting potential size at retirement using YoY return in line with additional contributions between now and then.

DESIRED RETIREMENT AGE: What age would you ideally like to retire and start drawdown from your pension. You can play with this number to see the impact on overall plans but for now just pick the age you'd like to stop working.

LUMP SUM REQUIREMENT: Will you need a lump sum on retirement to clear any outstanding debt like a mortgage. Generally, it's permissible to take up to 25% tax free.

INFLATION MODIFIER: Inflation (CPI) causes the price of goods and services to rise over time, impacting our spending power, so we take this into account for pot projections. You can't know the level inflation is going to be, but calculating on an average range of 2%-4% is reasonable.

You can see and play with the full set of variables in the modeller. Playing with different values will allow you to visualise their impact over time and help you make plans you think have the best chance to deliver your retirement goals.

MAKING YOUR PLAN: WOSS FORECASTING TOOL CASE STUDY

Theo Doretire is a 36 year old long haul driver making £42,345 with a pension pot around current average for his age, £34,567. He's getting serious about planning for retirement and knows he needs to invest more, so plans to increase to 14% (£494) per month towards pension going forward. This goes into an employer scheme meaning he saves tax on his income.

Theo wants to project on the lower bound of returns to be safer, knowing they're not guaranteed anyway. He'll be using 4.5% pre-retirement and 3% post as he moves investments into less risky assets. Theo expects to work till 68 and have the state pension, aiming to get close to £25,000 net in his drawdown to match the £28,000 net his wife has in her provision. Above the "comfortable" level for a couple. He's happy to accept the risk of state pension being reduced, removed or eligible age increasing. The couple have no other savings provision for retirement.

He'll project based on average life expectancy for a man in the UK, 81, plus 2 years. So he expects to need his money to last until age 83. He plans to pay his mortgage and be debt free by 68 so won't take a tax free lump sum. Let's feed all of this data into the modeller.

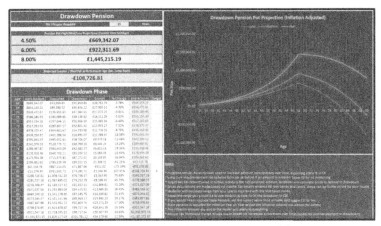

Fig 8.1 | *Theo is short his plans in our Modeller*

Inflation adjusted and accounting for tax Theo is projected to run out of money 2 years short of his 83 target, contributing £494 per month. Around £108,726 short. He's able to calculate at 4.5% projected return he could hit target by increasing monthly payment from £494 to £565 (14% to 16%). £71 per month is potentially all that stands between Theo and his retirement goals, which he spotted early so can do something about.

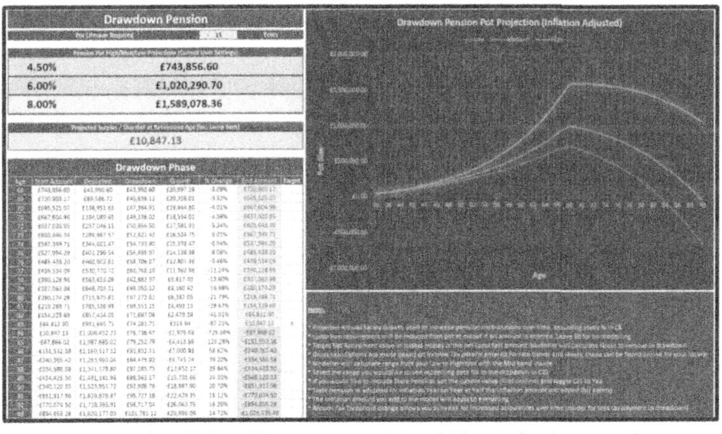

Fig 8.2 | *A slight adjustment to 16% and Theo is back on track*

You can play with these numbers in the modeller provided. This illustrates why having a calculated target and tracking against it is so important. If you do this early enough even small amounts can have a huge impact over time due to the wonders of compounding. I think you can probably guess already what the actions are going to be at the end of this chapter!

Additionally, modelling on lower end return projections mitigates somewhat the risk of under preparing. As you can see in the modeller and image, the mid return would last beyond 90 and the high figure leaves legacy. These would be a bonus if they came, but shouldn't be projected on in my view.

There are many different pension calculators out there doing similar jobs to the WoSS template. This is mine and you're free to use it for modelling purposes. If you'd rather use different tools it's absolutely fine, the message is to do the calculations, know your details and track you're on course to achieve what you want. Most calculators give slightly different answers depending on configuration, they should all be roughly in the same ballpark though. Given these minor differences having something convenient and easy for you to track with then sticking with it so as not to mix data sets is optimal.

Retirement planning can also benefit from professional retirement planning advisors who can discuss individual circumstances. If nothing else, it's good to get a second set of eyes on your plan, they may spot a mistake and mitigate its impact over time or offer an alternate option to your benefit. This is a detailed calculator to get you started either way.

OTHER CONSIDERATIONS: TAX AND ALTERNATE INSTRUMENTS

Having a tax efficient plan for retirement allows you to maximise the longevity of your savings and mitigate longevity risk. Every £ (or unit of local currency) you pay in tax is one less £ paying for your retirement or continuing to grow your estate. We should then consider other instruments in our drawdown planning.

ISA's, offshore bonds, general investment accounts and cash accounts are among the other instruments we can utilise. Each has their own distinct tax allowances (or zero rate bands) helping to make a difference to drawdown planning from two perspectives:

1. Tax Efficiency: Legally making our money last longer during retirement by minimising taxation.
2. Legacy: Legally maximising how much is left for your beneficiary inheritance.

For example, efficient planning of when and where a couple should draw £54,500 per year in retirement income (comfortable couple number) could save hundreds of thousands in tax payments through retirement. Utilising the tax allowances they already enjoy like income tax nil rate, starter rate for savings, personal savings allowance, dividend tax allowance and capital gains tax allowance lets the couple build income streams paying notionally no tax and achieving around their desired income:

- £12,570 income each from pensions (max individual tax free allowance) at 0% tax = £25,140
- £5,000 allowance each in interest payments (from perhaps an offshore bond) = £10,000
- £7,000 each from ISA's at 0% = £14,000
- £1,000 allowance each from high interest savings accounts (for ~£20,000 capital at the moment) = £2,000

£51,140 for the couple paying no tax. Zero. Legally utilising the allowances we already have. If they drew entirely from the pension of one person then tax would make their income £38,919.40, a £12,580.60 delta for every year of pension drawdown. Either they must live on less or drawdown more to achieve the same living income. These are indicative numbers highlighting tax free allowances rather than an exact illustration, simply to support the point. As you can imagine over a full retirement this has a huge impact to your savings and the potential legacy you leave behind.

Tax and drawdown advice is one of those specialities worth paying for. Getting it wrong can be costly and it's a complicated area of regulation within most jurisdictions (intentionally!) the services of someone who deals in this world daily are invaluable. This overview is to get you thinking about tax and to highlight for those unaware there are numerous legal ways to minimise the tax burden in retirement to make the most of your savings.

There are other instruments one can utilise to provide income during retirement. Property features for many as a supplementary income source for example. There are additional overheads to this approach, as you have more responsibilities as a landlord than an investor, but it's still a useful option if you have the initial capital requirement to cover startup costs.

Whatever method you decide best suits you, have a plan for both the building and drawdown phases, track against this plan and adjust as necessary. Don't leave it too late and put yourself in the position there's little you can do. Over long time horizons small, fixable problems can become large issues quickly.

DRAWDOWN TIMING: PUTTING IT ALL TOGETHER

Our example in the previous section focussed on linear drawdown, utilising all accounts/instruments from the date you retire through to end of life. There's another consideration I want to introduce as part of this chapter: non-linear phased drawdown. This sounds complicated but let me try to explain via an example. I'll stick to 5 separate instruments but you can build this sort of timeline from as many as is required.

Willa (53) and Benjamin (54) are a married couple approaching retirement. They'd like to retire next year while Willa is 54 and Benjamin 55. They've built an ISA worth £320,000, Benjamin has a Defined Contribution Pension worth £800,000 and Willa, a school teacher by trade, has an average salary Defined Benefit pension. There's a hefty penalty for taking this DB pension early, but at 68 it provides £42,000 per annum.

The couple also have an investment property, a small flat providing £500 per month (£6000 per year) in rental income, mortgage fully paid. For the purposes of this example we'll assume they've an emergency fund set aside already for repairs/work required on this property. They'd like to earn £54,000 during retirement.

At 55 and 54, they're not able to draw from pensions so in phase 1 they must rely on other income. Between now and Benjamin turning 57 they utilise rental income and ISA, which is completely tax efficient:

- £6,000 from rental income in Willa's name (tax free)
- £48,000 from ISA (tax free)

The couple do this for 2 years, earning £54,000. This leaves £224k in ISA and pension continued to grow at 3% (lowered risk) making it £848,000. When Benjamin reaches 57 phase 2 begins and he starts drawdown from pension. He can do this via Tax Free lump sum, a maximum of 25% in as many smaller increments up to 25% as required. With £6,000 income from the rental property, the couple can cover their income requirements as follows:

- £6,000 from rental income in Willa's name (tax free)
- £12,570 in pension income from Benjamin's fund (zero tax utilising income allowance)
- £32,250 (3.80%) tax free lump sum from Benjamin's fund (zero tax)

ISA and Pension continue to grow during drawdown and the couple pay, legally, no income tax. They continue to fund retirement through Benjamin's pension, adjusting each year for inflation until tax free allowance is depleted, taking ~6 years, Benjamin 63 and Willa 62. From here phase 3 begins and they take the maximum zero tax income from pension and top up using the ISA, which has grown to £267k. £32,500 for 4 years until Benjamin is eligible for state pension. This depletes the ISA to ~£130k. The couple still haven't paid any income tax.

Once Benjamin starts state pension the requirement from ISA reduces by ~£8000 (accounting for tax, without inflation adjusting state pension to show worst case). Benjamin pays ~£4k in income tax now, the first in 10 years. This happens for 2 years until Willa is eligible for state pension and her Defined Benefit pension.

Phase 4 begins with Willa taking maximum 25% lump sum and putting it in a general investment account, ~£120k. This means her pension drops to ~£31.5k, plus her state pension benefit of £10,600 for a total of £42.1k. Their rental income still provides £6,000 making £48.1k per annum. This will all be income tax liable at this point, leaving Willa's after tax income as £36,730.40.

Benjamin is eligible for £10,600 state pension benefit too and can take the remaining income tax free allowance from his pension (up to £12,570 total) so a further £1,930. The couple now earn ~£49,230 and can draw the further £5k tax free from their ISA if required. This continues until the ISA depletes, at which point they draw from the £120k tax free that Willa has been earning return on in her GIA (tax will be paid on capital gains at 10%), then all from Benjamin's pension post GIA depletion. They could also have chosen to feed £20k per annum from this GIA into their ISA, but for this example we'll assume not.

This is obviously a high level example with a lot of moving parts I haven't mentioned, the idea is simply to introduce the concept of building retirement income in the most efficient way and phasing those decisions optimally into specific time periods to best suit you and your goals. Typically you wouldn't define this so precisely while saving, you'd identify the first phase or 2 then refine as you know more over time. Given the outlook this is definitely something an expert planner could help with.

To put this into perspective, if the couple had a single pension, Benjamin's £800,000, achieving their £54,000 net income means £67,500 gross. This adds £11,197 income tax year one (England). Increasing drawdown by inflationary 2% every year with growth at 3%, Benjamin pays £136,934.67 in income tax over 10 years, those same years they paid nothing in the previous breakdown. His pot would reduce to £223,081.27 and they'd run out of money in a further 3 years.

					Tax Free £12,571	Band 1 £50,270			
Start	DD	Growth %	After DD	Growth	Taxable	20%	40%	Tax	Outcome
1	£800,000.00	£65,700.00	3%	£734,300.00	£22,029.00	£53,129.00	£10,054.00	£1,143.60	£11,197.60	£54,502.40
2	£756,329.00	£67,014.00	3%	£689,315.00	£20,679.45	£54,443.00	£10,054.00	£1,669.20	£11,723.20	£55,290.80
3	£709,994.45	£68,354.28	3%	£641,640.17	£19,249.21	£55,783.28	£10,054.00	£2,205.31	£12,259.31	£56,094.97
4	£660,889.38	£69,721.37	3%	£591,168.01	£17,735.04	£57,150.37	£10,054.00	£2,752.15	£12,806.15	£56,915.22
5	£608,903.05	£71,115.79	3%	£537,787.26	£16,133.62	£58,544.79	£10,054.00	£3,309.92	£13,363.92	£57,751.88
6	£553,920.87	£72,538.11	3%	£481,382.77	£14,441.48	£59,967.11	£10,054.00	£3,878.84	£13,932.84	£58,605.27
7	£495,824.25	£73,988.87	3%	£421,835.38	£12,655.06	£61,417.87	£10,054.00	£4,459.15	£14,513.15	£59,475.72
8	£434,490.44	£75,468.65	3%	£359,021.79	£10,770.65	£62,897.65	£10,054.00	£5,051.06	£15,105.06	£60,363.59
9	£369,792.44	£76,978.02	3%	£292,814.42	£8,784.43	£64,407.02	£10,054.00	£5,654.81	£15,708.81	£61,269.21
10	£301,598.86	£78,517.58	3%	£223,081.27	£6,692.44	£65,946.58	£10,054.00	£6,270.63	£16,324.63	£62,192.95
								£136,934.67	

Fig 8.3 | Single Pension Drawdown Depletion. Tax Inefficient

Hopefully this gives at least some insight into how retirement drawdown plans are built and how complex finding the optimal drawdown plan can be. Don't be too fixated on these numbers, they're just to make the example case, look more at the process, the idea of optimal drawdown utilising tax allowances. For couples who want to retire early and leave as much of a legacy as possible this planning can save hundreds of thousands in tax overhead in retirement, money they've earned they can pass to their children or live on themselves rather than pass to the state to squander.

UK STATE PENSION UPDATE: FEBRUARY 2024

I considered updating this entire chapter in light of a report released by the International Longevity Centre on February 5th 2024, during my final edit. I decided though this supplementary section was best. The report findings support the scepticism I've shared throughout around the future of UK state pensions and confirms the approach of **not** planning for one as appropriate.

> *"The UK and other ageing populations will have to increase their state pension age to 71 by 2050 to maintain the number of workers per retiree."*
>
> *[ILC Report | UK Think Tank, Feb 5th 2024]*

At a high level it suggests the same ageing population issue I raised earlier. Based on the Old Age Dependency Ratio (OADR), an ageing population with declining replacement rates increases the social security burden and younger employees might pay the price for the current pension Ponzi long term. The ILC agree with my musings, suggesting in this report the UK retirement age will have to rise to 71 by 2050 to maintain the UK state pension.

This means those born after April 1970 wouldn't receive state pension before age 71 and raises a number of questions around private pensions and time served careers. If it came to pass, politicians would be telling our young people, those who already can't afford many things the generations coming before them take for granted (like a home) that they must now work 6 years longer (65 to 71) to pay for the early retirement of older generations as well. This is unlikely to be received positively and nor should it be.

There are other options and this emerging detail should generate adult discussion around the state pension. We could end the triple lock for starters (where pensions increase annually by whichever of inflation, average wage growth or 2.5% is highest). Or, as has been suggested many times we could overhaul the state pension system entirely so it's front loaded, rather than a rear ended Ponzi. But political incentive, with pensioners a growing voter base and pensions always a hot political potato, means we likely see increased retirement age considered the "easiest" thing to do politically, even though it doesn't fix the problem.

This is just think tank output at this stage so doesn't change the detail we've discussed. What we'll need to consider is the potential impact on private pensions and 10 year withdrawal rules. If state pension moves to 71 by the time I hit 56, I don't want to have to wait 5 years longer if I hit my number. So, we may need to monitor how this progresses and review how we balance investments between instruments like ISA's and our pensions themselves, to provide the flexibility I spoke of before this report was issued.

SUMMARY

The retirement planning section of our financial plan aims to provision comfortable retirement while leaving some legacy if possible for our children. In the wealth building equation this is one of the longest endeavours one can progress and for normal people the one which historically creates most wealth.

Retirement provision in many countries, including the UK, is light and many people don't realise or have time to resolve their shortfall. With people generally living longer, many will likely find themselves working for longer than anticipated or running out of funds during retirement. Defined Benefit pensions help for those who have them but for those in Defined Contribution schemes like Auto Enrolment there's a widespread lack of knowledge about how they work and how to use them to adequately plan for retirement. The majority of people don't realise how much they need to save, but you now know how to model this for different potential outcomes for yourself.

You hopefully also now have a high level understanding of the available retirement instruments and the benefits each provides to help you build your plan. You also know how important efficient tax planning is during drawdown to mitigate longevity risk, the risk of you outliving your money.

Prioritising future-self should be at the forefront of our thinking now and the provision for retirement through pension and other investment vehicles or assets is a key component of it. Your retirement plan has two elements, the accumulation phase where you plan and build what you need and the drawdown phase where you plan the most efficient way to cover your needs for as long as possible while minimising tax exposure.

Do as much building as you can as early as you can for maximum benefit. If you have employer salary match use it! If you are eligible for a LISA and the 25% government free money top up, use it! Our main advantage in building retirement funds is the time horizon available, its long length making small compounding amounts very powerful over time.

This is an important part of your financial plan, one you should spend time learning, documenting, executing and reviewing. This, more than any other endeavour in your lifetime (save a lotto win!) has the potential to deliver your financial goals.

As a supplementary note, it was revealed recently that between two thirds and three quarters of higher rate taxpayers and between one third and half of additional rate taxpayers in the UK aren't claiming the additional tax relief on their pension via self-service tax return. This is quite staggering, but I'd suggest it's simply lack of knowledge, as we've been discussing. If your pension contribution happens via salary sacrifice you're probably fine, but please check, regardless of pension type that you've had the full relief. If not, you can claim up to 4 full tax years historically. Do this as soon as possible if you've missed out.

ACTIONS

- Refer to tab "A. Actions" in the Financial Plan template.
- Complete the actions defined in section ".: 8 :. | On Track for Retirement?"

Quit Making Excuses

"He that is good for making excuses is seldom good for anything else."

[Benjamin Franklin | Scientist & US Founding Father]

ANOTHER SHORT PSYCHOLOGICAL INTERLUDE AS we discuss the widespread human mastery of excuse making. As Franklin famously said, the ability to make excuses is rarely found in those who succeed, so it's important we don't fall into this trap in our financial quest. It undermines our mantra of accountability.

Those who default to making excuses think they adequately justify why they can't (or didn't) achieve a desired outcome, this faux justification absolving them of accountability. This exists in all human pursuits like going to the gym, losing weight, getting a new job, improving one's finances or even writing a book. Anything humans can do has multiple excuses created by those who don't to rationalise why it couldn't be done.

This proclivity for self-sabotage impacts individual financial outcomes, particularly in those deeply convinced of their excuse and more so still where convinced its rooted in nefarious action of others. This has become more common, the oppressor fallacy. I'm not suggesting oppression doesn't exist, that we live in a utopian world where there aren't hurdles to overcome. Those of us coming from "normal" backgrounds and joining financial circles know we don't have the advantages of many whose parents come from this world, for example. Life isn't fair and to express a view otherwise would be as foolish as pretending it should be. I'm simply stating many who believe themselves oppressed today are demonstrably not, it's just a convenient substitute for accountability.

Many who are convinced they're being financially oppressed, held back from achieving their financial goals by some invisible hand, are in reality and by any sensible measure being held back by their own choices. I've some sympathy as my Consumer, Debtor, Employee construct makes clear I think these beliefs are cultivated intentionally within us as a means of control. We're encouraged to think in terms of division. But I'd suggest that even where this encouraging influence exists we still retain free will to make choices in spite of it. If we succumb to any baseless suggestion, then who's really at fault? My clear view on accountability should answer this question.

It's a sensitive subject and I've no wish to offend in broaching it, but in the context of financial improvement it's an important obstacle for us to overcome. To build solid foundations for a secure financial life you must operate in reality. Improved outcomes are within your gift and your mind remains free, your decisions your own. Franklin is blunt but he's ultimately correct. A penchant for making excuses is seldom a trait of the successful individual. You won't find many who accidentally woke up with money after making excuses about why they couldn't get it, they get there because they tend toward accountable behaviours, not victim behaviours.

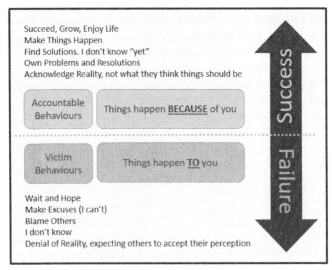

Fig 9.1 | Accountability Matrix

The Accountability Matrix is a simple representation of the dichotomy between these behaviours and their correlation to success and failure. A graphical view of Franklin's sentiment. Convincing swathes of society to imprison themselves as victims is Consumer, Debtor, Employee by design. Things happen to you, not because of you, so why bother? If you're convinced you can't succeed because it's not in your power to do so, it's in the hands of a shadow oppressor, then you invariably give up the fight as hopeless before you even start. You're convinced you've no agency, so you give it up willingly, securing the same outcome as making any other excuse. This is such a shame when observed in highly competent people.

We all have agency, what differs between individuals is how we use it. This is what separates success from failure among similar individuals with similar challenges. Think about it this way, even if you think me crazy have you more chance of succeeding when you force yourself to try, or when you convince yourself not to? Achieving 50% of something is better than achieving 100% of nothing. Using your agency to try, even if you don't fully succeed, is usually still more fruitful than making excuses not to try.

The intent of this chapter isn't to provoke anger, rather to implore you to assess your situation honestly and not to give your agency away because someone else said you had none. Retain accountability for you, find solutions, own problems and in general make things happen for you and your family. Doing it in spite of societal pressures and the disadvantages you may have is how you win. Be the person things happen because of, not the one things happen to. Excuses are easy, success is not.

BASE RESOURCE: TIME, MONEY & ENERGY

My position is clear, we each have agency and I'll argue it comes in the form of the base resources we can all exchange to improve our outcomes. These resources are Time, Money and Energy, your individual "capital". A job exchanges Time and (sometimes!) Energy for Money. When getting fit and losing a few lbs you exchange Time and Energy to achieve that goal. When you sign up for a course or buy a book to learn a new skill you exchange Money and Time to gain Knowledge. So on and so forth. Everything we can do to make our lives better can be broken down into an exchange of Time, Money, Energy, or a combination of all three.

They're also, coincidentally, the three most common excuses people make that stop them from achieving their financial goals:

- I don't have enough TIME to learn how to manage money, lets watch Netflix.
- I can't AFFORD to save or invest, I have a luxury car, a holiday and large house to pay for.

- I don't have TIME or ENERGY to go to the make a financial plan, let's play video games.

These are relatable examples used specifically to make the point: humans love excuses and this applies to financial improvement as much as every other facet of human life, like going to the gym! A distinct difference though between top 10% and bottom 90% is they take the course, or read the book instead of watching Netflix. They invest in assets before consuming liabilities. When they're tired they drag their asses to the gym. They. Don't. Make. Excuses.

To give all of your Time, Money and Energy to others before thinking about yourself is noble in many cases (like a parent or carer for example). But it also doesn't help your situation, you need to find balance so you can move forward as an individual for the benefit of all those around you. One of the few things in your life that's truly 100% in your control and absolutely subject to change is how **you** assign **your** resource.

If you've time to watch two hours of YouTube, the latest famous family, who got voted off whatever island or whatever your mind numbing show of choice is, you've **TIME** to invest in yourself. **You're** choosing not to. If you've money to pay for fancy gadgets, gourmet coffee, brunch every day, takeaways every week, luxury cars or whatever else consumer sentiment dictates, you've **MONEY** to invest in yourself. **You're** choosing not to. If you've the energy to go out on a Friday night after work, play golf on a Sunday, go to the pub to watch football, play 4 hours of video games or whatever else you do to pass time, you have **ENERGY** to invest in yourself. **You're** choosing not to.

Did you know, as an example, the accumulated wealth of the poorest 20% in the UK is almost exclusively found in consumer discretionary products like cars, phones, tech gadgets and so on. Basically "stuff" with a depreciating value, often paid for by credit. At the opposite end of the spectrum, wealth in the richest decile is made up of assets and financial products accumulating in value over time. This is a reflection of the differing levels of expendable income, sure, but at the same time it's a reflection of different choices and I'd argue these practices wouldn't change in these groups if we levelled the expendable income variable. We'd see the same people use all of their income on consumer discretionary products at higher income levels (the well understood lifestyle inflation problem) and the same people find a way to buy assets to generate more wealth at lower income levels. I made this argument previously and it stands here too. Wealth inequality is a societal problem, one I'd like to improve, but I think a massive contributor to it is financial knowledge. Those who build wealth have it, those struggling tend not to. As well as structural change to things like wealth taxation (again, on actual wealth not income), we should fix this too for societal benefit.

Ultimately you, no-one else, makes your financial choices. No faceless oppressor, no glass ceiling, no invisible hand holding you down. These are **your** choices and these choices are where wealth (or any other goal you have) is won or lost. Changing the way we invest our Time, Money and Energy is free and small changes prioritised well start a snowball effect. Unfortunately many people choose not to improve their own long-term circumstances for gratification now, then make excuses that rarely stand up to even the lightest scrutiny. Do you recognise any of this in yourself? Most people do if they're honest. So let's go about changing it!

Again, to confirm, I'm not talking about all people here, I'm aware wealth inequality exists. Don't use the existence of exceptions as an excuse (see what I did there!), you know who I'm addressing and who I'm not with this chapter. This is for the consumers who have the capability but are unaware, mainly, of the impacts of their consumer choices over time. Those who make excuses rather than review their part in their outcomes.

SUMMARY

A short interlude, but an important one, especially at this stage in our journey where some may be starting to think "this is too complicated for me". It's not, keep going, you've come this far! The message here applies to life in general and by extension finding financial security. Quit. Making. Excuses. Not "I can't do it", make it "I can't do it **yet**".

Take accountability for yourself, figure out what you need to figure out and prioritise the spending of your base resources on improving **your** potential outcomes. Stop making excuses for things you think you can't do and start prioritising your resource to find ways you can do them. Build good habits and accountable behaviours. It's what sets successful people apart from the crowd.

ACTIONS

- Refer to tab "A. Actions" in the Financial Plan template.
- Complete the actions defined in section ".: 9 :. | Quit Making Excuses?"

Let's Talk About Debts Baby!

"Debt is the slavery of the free."

[Publilius Syrus | Writer & Roman Slave, 1st Century BC]

THE SEQUENCE OF CHAPTERS PLACING excuse making directly before this debt conversation isn't coincidence! The next topic of financial planning discussion is our relationship with, attitude towards and general lack of suspicion around debt. In my experience it's an area where excuses are plentiful, the majority collapsing under minor examination.

I'll clarify in advance: not all debt is to be vilified. A good friend from my financial circle would never forgive me if I didn't say there's a huge difference between useful debt that works for people and useless consumer debt that works against. This is absolutely true, he and I discuss often the issue being one of knowing the difference. I think it's fair to say most people do **not**, thus suffer the burden of useless consumer debt. This useless and harmful consumer debt is the focus of our discussion here.

The intro quote comes from Syrian writer Publilius Syrus who was taken to Italy as a Roman slave in the 1st century BC. He won over his master with his intellect and was set free to build legacy as a writer and philosopher. Many of Syrus' maxims are still commonly used today, like "the ends justify the means", "ignorance is bliss" and "honour among thieves". This lesser known example is perfect for the coming debt discussion.

Obviously a lot has changed since this was penned by Syrus over 2000 years ago. Then, debt slavery (or servitude, bondage or peonage) was utilised to create obligation between the working class and wealthy landowners or merchant employers. It restricted autonomy in the former and provided the wealthy asset and capital owning latter with cheap, obligated labour to help them accumulate more wealth via the <u>time</u> and <u>energy</u> of others.

Hmm. Kinda sounds like the Consumer, Debtor, Employee triad I've been describing to you actually, doesn't it? Just a different incarnation, in a different time. Sing it with me: "tale as old as time......". OK, the fairytale references end here, you get my point. The idea of debt for service is nothing new, methodology changes and technology allows for more efficient ways to implement the general theory, not to mention levels of debt now are far in excess of any number our ancient Roman ancestors could fathom, but the premise remains as deliberate now as ever.

The major difference I'd hypothesise is that throughout the overwhelming majority of human civilisation we, the plebians, knew the game. It was generally understood debt was a form of bondage and taking debt was seen as a last resort, utilised mainly for the purpose of staying alive. In times of natural disaster for example where food supply became scarce many common folk, where risk of death outweighed their risk from debt servitude, accepted the crutch for their own or their family's survival.

In 2024 though we actively seek a life of debt servitude for what often amounts to shiny buttons. Moreover, we've been convinced it's normal, everyone does it and there's nothing of concern at all in the ever more creative ways third parties invent to entice us into useless debt. It's forced into our eyes and ears on a daily basis, invoking this mass debt delusion: we think it's normal, good even.

"The greatest trick the Devil ever pulled was convincing the world he didn't exist"

[Charles Baudelaire | 19ᵗʰ Century Poet]

"The second greatest trick the Devil ever pulled was convincing the world he's the good guy"

[Ken Ammi | 21ˢᵗ Century Author]

I couldn't decide which of these I liked best in this context but decided together they encapsulate the message I'm trying to convey. They also show the timeframe over which these things remain relevant given the 200 year gap in history between these individuals. Society is so hypnotized by debt they never question motive, no-one ever asks "why do these people want to give me money to buy meaningless stuff? Why does my bank text message me so often **offering** debt I don't ask for? Why are credit scores higher when I'm in debt than when I've none?". Do people think credit providers push their debt so hard because they're the good guys? Have they perfected the pursuit of convincing the world debt servitude doesn't exist?

Useless consumer debt is a huge contributor to increasing wealth inequality in my view, as the profit made on said debt generally goes from the working class to the wealthy. It's used to accumulate more wealth from the "passive income" generated by the assets the wealthy own, just like in ancient Rome. But "passive income" is a misnomer, the reality is this income is being worked for by someone else who is exchanging their time and energy for it. For example, if you use a loan to buy a car you're working to earn income to pay the interest to the issuer who's using your time and energy to gain yield for themselves. The income is only passive for the creditor who utilises your time and energy to make money, it's very much active for you! The same can be said of rent, credit card debt and just borrowing in general.

Too many people don't understand this dynamic, that accruing debt is trading your future time and energy resource, often for meaningless trinkets, so a third party can earn yield from you. You're one of the bodies in those pods in the Matrix movie.

FRACTIONAL RESERVE BANKING & MONEY CREATION

Let's look at money creation basics so you understand a little more about how the banking part of the debt game is rigged. In simple terms, banks lend money into existence, literally create it from thin air through new loans. A magic banking licence money tree. Many, even those who work in banks, don't understand this process. Why do banks market debt heavily? Because they profit through charging interest on money they're allowed to create, often with your actual assets as collateral. I'll let this sink in while I quickly explain how fractional reserve banking worked in tandem with money creation.

Fractional reserve was a pretty fundamental aspect of modern finance, shaping the way banks operated to generate profit. The fraction requirements were actually removed in most Anglosphere countries in the last decade, meaning banks need retain none of the deposits (though in practice they still do and the money creation process remains). Central banks defined recommended amounts commercial banks within their jurisdiction should retain in reserve to cover customer deposits. This was the "fraction". In the UK it was 12%, US 10%. In practical terms this meant when you deposited £1000 into your bank account they were recommended to retain £120 (UK) in reserve, the other £880 to be used by the bank to generate their own profits, including the writing of loans. The theory is this simultaneously served the needs of depositors while facilitating economic growth (through lending and asset purchases).

The "magic money tree" introduced earlier is the ability banks have to create new money through this process. Even though fractional reserve is a thing of the past, the money creation aspect remains. Consider our previous example where you deposit £1000. The bank may decide to retain 12% (£120) in reserve. Another customer takes a loan for £880 (conveniently, for the purpose of this explanation!) so the bank credits their account with £880. You still have £1000 shown as a balance in your account, and the other customer shows £880 as a balance in theirs, but £880 of this £1880 total is accounted for twice, your original deposit and the new loan written against it. From an accounting perspective the bank has corresponding assets and liabilities on their balance sheet to cover the loan, but the £880 borrowed is essentially new money added to the money supply that didn't exist before, subject to "money multiplier effect".

Our borrower above uses this money for its intended purpose, to buy a laptop paying £880 to Amazon. Amazon now have that £880 deposit in their bank. The first bank created the money based on the original £1000 deposit and the second bank now face a similar situation: keep however little they see fit in and profit based on the rest. They write another customer loan for £774.40 (to stay consistent in this example at 12%), creating more new money based on the money created by the first loan. This process repeats, effectively creating new money with each round of lending, money created based on money another bank already created earlier. Money multiplier effect means single deposits can lead to large amounts of money creation through successive rounds of lending and depositing.

Now, I've simplified this example to one of single customers to keep this understandable, but this process operates at scale across total deposits from all customers. As an example, Lloyds Banking Group had a deposit total (across retail and commercial) of £471.4 Billion in 2023 according to statista.com. They're permitted (within wider lending regulation) to duplicate (create) new money from this for profit. This isn't highlighting Lloyds negatively, simply as an example of the process in action.

Banks profit from this in several ways. Primarily they charge interest on loans. The interest rate is our cost of borrowing and the difference between interest earned on all loans and interest paid on all deposits is net interest margin. People complain when rates rise and banks are quick to update loans and mortgages but not deposit accounts: this is why, higher lending rates equate to more profit on the money created and a wider spread between credit and deposit rates means more profit still. Also, if you default on secured loans they take your collateral to cover the "loss". Read that again, it often takes a second time to get suitably annoyed.

Banks also charge fees for services like account maintenance or overdrafts and engage in financial market activity with reserve funds like investing in government securities or participating in interbank lending markets. These generate additional income but present more risk. With risk in mind, you may have heard the term "run on the bank". It happened to Northern Rock in 2008 and more recently to Silicon Valley Bank in 2023. In 2008 it was huge lines outside branches, people trying to withdraw their money, but in 2023 three button clicks through phone apps gets the job done.

Technology advance means the speed the risk can materialise today can be devastating. If customers simultaneously try to withdraw more than the bank have liquid access to they're in shortfall and must begin liquidating assets to cover withdrawal obligations. If asset selling incurs a loss then they lose money.

This was the problem with Silicon Valley Bank. The assets reportedly held (long-term US Treasuries and Mortgage Backed Securities) are some of the safest investment instruments available and generally fine long-term. SVB had been silly with the duration risk (too much long term maturity) but had more than enough in asset value to cover customer deposits. Social media fuelled concern though led to masses of depositors trying to take money out, forcing SVB to sell some of these instruments to cover withdrawals, at a large loss. These losses spooked more depositors and a death spiral began. An electronic "Run on the Bank" brought the fastest and largest bank run in US history.

This risk is accepted because ultimately it's very profitable for banks. For us, our risk is generally low of bank failure but worth noting. If holding more than compensation scheme amounts in any one banking group (£85,000 per person per banking group in the UK) the risk is anything over this amount should the bank fail. Most countries have similar compensation schemes so check your jurisdictional rights and where possible, if you have more than covered try to spread it around for risk management purposes.

In summary, fractional reserve banking was a cornerstone of the financial system and many of its practices remain after the fraction became zero more recently. These enable banks to leverage deposits to create "new" money through lending and profit from the interest. This supports economic growth and financial intermediation but also exposes banks and customers to risk, requiring appropriate management and regulatory oversight. It highlights the intricate relationship between commercial banks, new money creation and the economy in general and highlights why these organisations "market" debt so heavily to us: it's extremely profitable.

DEBT SERVITUDE: POINT OF CLARIFICATION

I've drawn parallels between past and present and the relationship we in the west have with consumer debt. Unfortunately, even in 2023 the forced labour implementation of Syrus' ancient Rome impacts an estimated 8.1 million people in (mainly) developing nations. I do **not** conflate these two things. The horrors of physical slavery past and present are clearly incomparable to issues we face as cheap labour trapped by debt. Cheap, physically free labour is not the same as forced, physically restrained labour and I'd never claim so nor minimise the impact of the latter.

There's no amount of financial planning nor taking control of one's own destiny can help with physical forms of slavery and I make no such suggestion.

My thesis is simply that debt servitude in the west evolved into a form of mind control, not physical control. Minds can be educated and practices changed because we retain physical agency. It's important to draw this distinction so this conversation isn't construed as minimising the evils slavery. Physical slavery was, is and will always be abhorrent. I hope you understand the distinction and this clears up any misunderstanding.

CAN DEBT BE USEFUL: DEVIL'S ADVOCATE

There's a difference between harmful debt and useful debt, it's not quite so binary as "all debt is bad". I'm happy to leverage debt where it's useful, but this isn't the way most people think of debt.

For example, I'm replacing our kitchen after 13 years and taking the 5 years interest free credit on offer. I could pay upfront, I have the capital, but with 5% easy access savings accounts and nil cost of credit why would I? Over 5 years the spread provides a ~17% compounded benefit for me by drip feeding monthly and the risk is low because I have the money to pay it in a worst case scenario. This is an example of "useful" debt. I earn a yield above inflation, a large discount on a purchase I was already making and the inflationary impact on the debt reduces real terms cost of the kitchen further over the period. It's a win, win (win) for me.

I want to concentrate then on this "useful" distinction instead of the more common "good" or "bad". It's a more accurate definition in my view. Debt can be "useful" in certain circumstances, where people both understand it and have the discipline to manage it. In my experience the societal debt issue stems from a lack of these attributes rather than debt itself.

My kitchen example is one of nil cost useful debt. Generally life purchases where large capital expenditure is required would also qualify, capital most don't have in liquid cash. Like mortgages for home purchasing or car loans if "right sized" for the individual. These can represent useful debt as they enable us to attain assets or services we otherwise couldn't for long-term benefit or to cover genuine need. You can see in these examples nil cost is not my yardstick for "useful", as mortgages and car loans incur interest. This is sometimes necessary. The use case though is different from say high interest credit card debt for a luxury holiday or larger than required loans for luxury cars. These are "harmful" debt.

Debt can also be useful in a business context, something like buying rental properties where yield covers monthly mortgage and taxes, building long-term asset value for the debt holder. Or using debt to purchase a solid business through something like a business loan or even seller financed purchase. Cashback credit cards you repay fully every month are another popular utilisation of useful debt. They're higher risk, if you miss your payment. It's too much work and too low reward for me, but I know many who do it successfully (including my father).

Employing useful debt to their advantage is something wealthy individuals tend to do well, using debt responsibly with strategic outcomes in mind rather than as a way to facilitate impatience and greed. There's certainly a case to be made for using debt then, within specific guardrails. I raise this point because people don't always use it responsibly, they over leverage and often impulsively to finance expensive liabilities they don't need. They often ignore interest rates or take credit for introductory discounts which cost them more in the long run. There are many examples of harmful societal debt habits and I'll make some warnings on these later.

Debt often comes up when I talk to people about their finances, clearly trapping them as Consumers, Debtors and Employees. I'd be surprised if most readers couldn't find examples of harmful debt in their own finances and I'd be even more surprised if the realisation didn't come with a "but....", so at this point I'll remind you why this chapter follows our discussion on making excuses!

> *"You drown not by falling into a river, but by staying submerged in it."*
>
> *[Paulo Coelho | Brazilian Novelist]*

If this induced an epiphany that makes you concerned at your current debt exposure I want to offer this relevant non-finance quote as reassurance it can be escaped. Let your epiphany be the metaphorical grabbing of the lifebuoy, you now just need to pull yourself out the river, you don't need to drown in it.

THE DEBT RIVER: NUMBERS

Let's look in more detail at the UK consumer debt river. This will help you understand why it's such a concern and how it impacts so much on personal finance. The UK is not unique so serves as a useful example for most western consumer bases. I want you to read this with previous thesis in mind: if we want to break free from the herd, we must **not** do what the rest of the herd is doing.

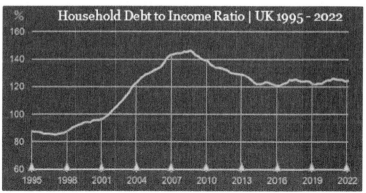

Fig 10.1 | UK Household Debt to Income Ratio

Fig 10.1 data from the ONS and Bank of England shows "Debt to Income" ratios for UK households from 1995 to 2022. I want to concentrate on this period as it's when we surpassed 100% for the first time and it dovetails nicely with the average house price to average earnings ratio we'll discuss shortly.

Though it sits outside of this time period I also want to highlight 1971 and the end of the Bretton-Woods agreement of fixed exchange rates instigated by US President Richard Nixon. Public and private debt has grown exponentially since around the globe and we should acknowledge this event as a contributory factor. For example, in the US from 1900 to 1971 national debt stayed below $0.33 Trillion, the main spike upwards was World War II. From 1971 to 2023 it jumped to $34.1 trillion. A 100 times increase inside 52 years post Bretton-Woods, US debt acting like a degenerate cryptocurrency!

In parallel the Economic Policy Institute shows that from records beginning in 1948 to 1971 productivity and compensation rose in a near 1:1 relationship. Since 1971 compensation has been effectively flat in real terms as productivity grew 246%. Workers are producing more in return for less, contributing to the rise in debt usage (to fill the gaps) and the rise in wealth inequality. We've already looked at how unaffordable housing has become with average income to average house price ratios near trebled since the 1960's, where an average home was affordable with a single earner in the household. In 2023 even with two average earners housing is still less affordable than on one 60's salary.

The rise in public and private debt then has been parabolic over just four generations: Gen-X, Millennials, Gen-Z & Gen-Alpha. One could surmise in these generations dangerous levels of debt have been "normalised", people not able to remember a time before debt in much the same way many within them can't remember a time before TV could be paused. In the context of "own nothing and be happy" current generational attitudes towards normalised and I would argue reckless debt are rather stark, particularly for Gen-Z and Gen-Alpha.

Looking at the chart, 1995 to 1998 was a little over 80% debt to income. It reached 100% during the dotcom bubble rising again into the 2008 Global Financial Crisis (GFC) where the UK peaked around 150%. An increase of 75% (+60/80) in 13 years. It dropped post GFC to ~125% (2022) but OBR research projects a rise back above 150%, creating new all-time highs, by the end of 2024.

Why does the rising ratio and the general societal attitude towards debt concern me? Inside four generations we've accepted as normal a massive change in the personal economic landscape. One where we accept expending more of our time and energy resource for less money in return and where people see debt servitude not only as a last resort for survival like our ancestors but as a normal part of everyday life. If, like me, you believe we're designed to operate inside the Consumer, Debtor, Employee triad, owning nothing and being (un)happy then this is the way most people get trapped there. To build wealth and escape the system we need to live beneath our means, unburdened by expensive and useless debt and able to invest in our own futures, not someone else's. This becomes harder to do and less understood with each generation. Stagnant income, asset price inflation, rising debt burdens and generational drift have us racing toward WEF 2030.

If I can return to housing as an example, growing up most people aspire to own their own home, to put down roots in a community where they can raise children. We're social beings and from at least the start of the 20th century the ability to build a family in homes our children hopefully inherit has become an important part of a successful, functioning society. This is becoming an aspiration many from Gen-Z forward feel either out of reach completely or worth taking on larger and larger debt burdens to achieve. This creates either a house of cards built on a mountain of over leveraged debt or general social unrest (through a lack of being able to put down roots).

Limited (suppressed) housing supply combined with 15 years of near nil cost credit, long-term wage stagnation and the societal normalisation of increased debt has contributed to the rise in house prices which ultimately makes the issue worse for each generation. It's part of the generational drift equation. Most people who got on the ladder in earlier generations celebrate as they believe their house price going up is a good thing. It is for them and we're conditioned to think this way, but they don't look at the effect this has on their children and grandchildren as real terms wages remain stagnant and prices keep going up. 2008 should have been a warning but appears to have been nought but a blip, prices continue to rise at a faster pace than wages.

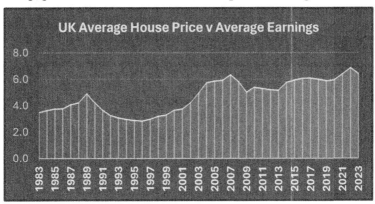

Fig 10.2 | UK Average House Price v Average Earnings Ratio

Fig 10.2 shows average house price to average income ratios from 1983 to 2023. In 1995, like debt to income, average house price started climbing from ~3.0x income towards new all-time highs at ~6.5x, just before the 2008 GFC. The 2008 housing bubble of inflated prices was built on over leveraged cheap debt and poor lending practice, reliant on "prices always go up". Reckless consumer lending practice played a large part but the actual crash stemmed from a greed driven debt game played by financial institutions via CDO's. These aimed to make money on the debt multiple times over (at a high level).

Collateralized Debt Obligations were basically large collections of graded debt wrapped as single instruments and traded on the open market. They contained some risky loans (you may have heard referred to as "sub-prime") alongside other debt assumed to be "safer" due to incorrect ratings. The CDO's were incorrectly rated and sold (some would argue fraudulently) worldwide as mostly AAA rated debt instruments due to the perceived makeup of the debt within, marketed generally as a mix of AAA to BB. The incorrectly rated debt within (ratings agencies absolutely complicit) meant these were far from AAA instruments, so when defaults breached a fairly low threshold at around 7%-8% it started a systemic collapse.

So yes, financial institutions got greedy and that was the final straw for the 2008 crash. And yes, ratings agencies got greedy too, exacerbating the sub-prime issue by incorrectly rating the debt for profit. You'll get no argument from me there. But let's be clear, as much as banks, credit houses and ratings agencies facilitated widespread recklessness around borrowing, some would argue criminally, they still needed reckless borrowers pressing the buttons. They still needed the normalised societal attitude towards over leveraged debt I'm cautioning. I said at the outset personal accountability is a key aspect of my personality and I expect the same from others. I feel for those impacted by 2008 but in the spirit of education we must acknowledge it couldn't have happened without the levels of reckless personal debt taken by private homebuyers, often on multiple homes! Even though bank and ratings agency behaviour was abhorrent and absolutely outside of our control, taking the reckless debt on was **not,** this was greed driven personal choice at an individual level and one we should, but it seems didn't as a society, have learned from.

So should we be concerned in 2022 we surpassed pre GFC highs in terms of income versus house price ratio, this metric hitting 7.0x? I'd suggest rates returning to mean and inflation running high is probably going to make non fixed term deals fairly expensive for those already maxed out on debt pretty soon. If the economy goes into recession in 2024 or early 2025 (which I think is higher probability than not, personally, based on the indicators I track) then people are going to struggle to service their debt. I hope I'm wrong, but I'm positioning to be right, managing risk.

I don't think we'll see a house price crash. The massive transfer of wealth from the working and middle class to the wealthy during Covid is likely parked in cash at the moment given higher risk free available yield but when rates start falling, asset purchases will be back on the table. Housing is generally a target asset for rental yield so this will likely fuel house prices continuing to rise as the wealthy utilise cash on hand to buy them up from those who can't afford them anymore, the wealth inequality spiral in a nutshell.

Some who over leveraged were likely badly advised or didn't realise what they were getting into, but ultimately rates are returning to normal long term levels which shouldn't be a surprise. Zero Interest Rate Policy went on so long though we now have multiple generations of borrowers who consider it normal and are pinning their hopes on rates returning to zero levels. Add the acceleration in house price away from income and owning nothing while being unhappy is becoming reality. I think we might see continued house price increase, continued real terms wage stagnation and the 40 or even 50 year mortgages being floated becoming normalised. "Work till you die" mortgages I'd suggest.

With rising life expectancy it'd certainly be a perfect way to extract more from the plebs, a way to keep us trapped in the Consumer, Debtor, Employee cycle for life by abusing our desire to own a family home. An entire lifetime in work, cheap labour to pay for a home costing multiple times the purchase price. A £350,000 home over 40 years at 5% pays back ~£1,689 per month for a total repayment of ~£810,497. That's an awfully big opportunity cost. It would alleviate somewhat the pension/social security issues we discussed around aging populations by shifting drawdown to the right and keeping older people working longer, or worse with rent in retirement as homeownership reduces.

I don't believe managing our debt is a capability issue, I think it's a psychological one. Some of the most capable people I've ever known don't understand the problem or the discipline required to solve it. It's never laid out for them. This list of just some of the numbers highlights, along with the mortgage and house price numbers prior, how debt driven we've become:

- In Feb 2021 according to the ONS, UK Consumer (personal) debt stood at £1.7 Trillion (now above £2 Trillion in 2023).
- This equates (2021) to a figure for an average adult of £33,410, 107% the average UK salary at the time.
- By 2024 OBR research shows the household debt to income ratio will likely rise to at least 150%.
- In 2022 median household savings in the UK were £2,160. That's 7% of the average UK salary.
- Average savings were £5,403 per household, nearly double median, showing disparity between rich and poor families.
- Low income families saved on average £95 per year or less.

As with everything we discuss, correlation doesn't always indicate causation. But I think the case compelling that increasing debt and psychological indifference to it drives normal people, over generational timeframes, to being unable to ever escape our Consumer, Debtor, Employee Moloch. It's pushing them towards owning nothing, working longer, having little in the way of legacy for their children and it contributes to generational drift.

THE DEBT SPIRAL: HOW DEBT DESTROYS WEALTH

In our budget and money map discussion we looked at the long-term impact of paying for expensive mobile phone contracts versus a cheaper, equally functional handset. Let's recap quickly.

	Monthly	Invested	10Y @ 5%	40Y @ 5% No Adds	40Y @ 5%
New iPhone	£47.00	-	-£5,640.00	-£22,560.00	-£22,560.00
Alternative	£15.00	£32.00	£3,271.41	£21,918.34	£88,493.07
Opportunity Cost	-	-	£8,911.41	£44,478.34	£111,053.07

Fig 10.3 | Wealth Impact of £47pcm mobile v £15pcm alternate

Fig 10.3 shows the potential outcomes of two options. We're conditioned to consume, as I keep reinforcing so most take option one. The practice of continually upgrading perfectly functional products to newer versions. People are tricked by small increments into thinking this doesn't cost "much more" or "it's interest free" debt for the handset portion. I want to use this example as it allows me to make the point interest free debt variants aren't always "useful".

"It's only £2 more per month" is a mathematical failing. The difference isn't between current outgoing and new, it's between outgoings at the point of materiality, when the existing contract ends and new cost begins. Airtime contracts are a fraction of the overall contract. If it costs £15 airtime only versus £45 current and £47 upgrade then the delta is £32, not £2. This is one of those excuses I warned about, people know how numbers work but this is a convenient way to justify wanting new shiny things. Confirmation bias. The difference, as one can see in the "Opportunity Cost" row over 10 and 40 years is significant.

Airtime only, cancel anytime contracts are available for as little as £5 p.c.m. You can find handset deals for as little as £15. Why do you think most operators allow you to "upgrade early as a VIP"? Maybe their data shows once you see lower monthly payments you're less likely to upgrade? So they make you feel special to commit to new 24 month subscriptions, maximising their profits before you see the real cost impact. Remember, always ask what's their incentive. In any event, this is debt, you "borrow" the device and pay it back over time.

This example is for mobile phones but it applies to all consumer spending. Take Car notes as a second example, cleared after 3-5 years then automatically replaced with a new car and new note. Or worse still the perpetual subscription of lease cars where you never own anything. Think about mortgages when moving home multiple times, absorbing market price change and resetting inflationary debt benefits. This is lifestyle inflation, not only absorbing new income but further stressing existing income for no long-term benefit. The debt spiral so many enter through consumer spending habits is why I say many have opportunity in their expense column without increasing income, they just don't know it.

We'll discuss later paying my mortgage at 36, but this is **how** I did it. Super simple. I sweated assets and invested the delta. Whether you agree they're assets or not is irrelevant, the maths is the same. The best part is no-one realised. Whispers about my old phone or beat up old grandad car mattered zero to me, I knew the plan and I'd done the maths. I could still call, text and surf and I still got from where I was to where I needed to be. The function was the same as everyone else, I just did it much, much cheaper and made the saving work for me in the markets.

People think it luck or high income. The uncomfortable truth is they could have done it too by long-term planning, sacrificing some wants and limiting debt overhead. It's a debate I have often, always asking the same question: How many cars have you had in the last 20 years, I've had 3, all 2-3 years old when VAT and early depreciation paid? You've had 7 from new? We found our delta.

When I explain the maths on cars, or phone handsets, or my proclivity for spending hours in discount outlets, or why I've moved house once in 20 years, it's an epiphany moment. People are just conditioned to consume via debt without thinking.

Debt is like a snowball pushed down a hill getting bigger and bigger. Many have no idea the impact it has on their long-term wealth with every revolution. As it grows, debt service costs rise and before they know what's happening it consumes income with nothing left to build for future you. Every £ you can put to work for you is a £ making more £'s. Every £ you give to someone else is a £ less working for you. You're a business and the £'s are your employees, why the hell would you want all your employees working for someone else instead of you?

Consumer, Debtor & Employee

20% Avg Mtg	Avg Car Loan	Avg Mobile	Inflation
£884.40	£350.00	£47.00	2%

Year	Housing	Car	Phone	Invest	RoR	Wealth
1	£10,612.80	£4,200.00	£564.00	£0.00	5%	£0.00
2	£10,612.80	£4,284.00	£575.28	£0.00	5%	£0.00
3	£10,612.80	£4,369.68	£586.79	£0.00	5%	£0.00
4	£10,612.80	£4,457.07	£598.52	£0.00	5%	£0.00
5	£10,612.80	£4,546.22	£610.49	£0.00	5%	£0.00
6	£10,612.80	£4,637.14	£622.70	£0.00	5%	£0.00
7	£10,612.80	£4,729.88	£635.16	£0.00	5%	£0.00
8	£10,612.80	£4,824.48	£647.86	£0.00	5%	£0.00
9	£10,612.80	£4,920.97	£660.82	£0.00	5%	£0.00
10	£10,612.80	£5,019.39	£674.03	£0.00	5%	£0.00
11	£10,612.80	£5,119.78	£687.51	£0.00	5%	£0.00
12	£10,612.80	£5,222.17	£701.26	£0.00	5%	£0.00
13	£10,612.80	£5,326.62	£715.29	£0.00	5%	£0.00
14	£10,612.80	£5,433.15	£729.59	£0.00	5%	£0.00
15	£10,612.80	£5,541.81	£744.19	£0.00	5%	£0.00
16	£10,612.80	£5,652.65	£759.07	£0.00	5%	£0.00
17	£10,612.80	£5,765.70	£774.25	£0.00	5%	£0.00
18	£10,612.80	£5,881.01	£789.74	£0.00	5%	£0.00
19	£10,612.80	£5,998.63	£805.53	£0.00	5%	£0.00
20	£10,612.80	£6,118.61	£821.64	£0.00	5%	£0.00
21	£10,612.80	£6,240.98	£838.07	£0.00	5%	£0.00
22	£10,612.80	£6,365.80	£854.84	£0.00	5%	£0.00
23	£10,612.80	£6,493.11	£871.93	£0.00	5%	£0.00
24	£10,612.80	£6,622.98	£889.37	£0.00	5%	£0.00
25	£10,612.80	£6,755.44	£907.16	£0.00	5%	£0.00
26	£10,612.80	£6,890.55	£925.30	£0.00	5%	£0.00
27	£10,612.80	£7,028.36	£943.81	£0.00	5%	£0.00
28	£10,612.80	£7,168.92	£962.68	£0.00	5%	£0.00
29	£10,612.80	£7,312.30	£981.94	£0.00	5%	£0.00
30	£10,612.80	£7,458.55	£1,001.58	£0.00	5%	£0.00
31		£7,607.72	£1,021.61	£0.00	5%	£0.00
32		£7,759.87	£1,042.04	£0.00	5%	£0.00
33		£7,915.07	£1,062.88	£0.00	5%	£0.00
34		£8,073.37	£1,084.14	£0.00	5%	£0.00
35		£8,234.84	£1,105.82	£0.00	5%	£0.00
36		£8,399.54	£1,127.94	£0.00	5%	£0.00
37		£8,567.53	£1,150.50	£0.00	5%	£0.00
38		£8,738.88	£1,173.51	£0.00	5%	£0.00
39		£8,913.65	£1,196.98	£0.00	5%	£0.00
40		£9,091.93	£1,220.92	£0.00	5%	£0.00
	£318,384.00	£253,688.33	£34,066.72	£0.00		

-£606,139.05	£0.00

Breaking the Cycle

20% Avg Mtg	Avg Car Loan	Cheap Mobile	Inflation
£884.40	£350.00	£18.00	2%

Year	Housing	Car	Phone	Invest	RoR	Wealth
1	£10,612.80	£4,200.00	£216.00	£348.00	5%	£365.40
2	£10,612.80	£4,284.00	£220.32	£354.96	5%	£756.38
3	£10,612.80	£4,369.68	£224.73	£362.06	5%	£1,174.36
4	£10,612.80	£4,457.07	£229.22	£369.30	5%	£1,620.84
5	£10,612.80	0	£233.81	£4,922.90	5%	£6,870.93
6	£10,612.80	0	£238.48	£5,021.36	5%	£12,486.91
7	£10,612.80	0	£243.25	£5,121.79	5%	£18,489.13
8	£10,612.80	0	£248.12	£5,224.22	5%	£24,899.02
9	£10,612.80	0	£253.08	£5,328.71	5%	£31,739.11
10	£10,612.80	0	£258.14	£5,435.28	5%	£39,033.11
11	£10,612.80	£5,119.78	£263.30	£424.21	5%	£41,430.19
12	£10,612.80	£5,222.17	£268.57	£432.69	5%	£43,956.02
13	£10,612.80	£5,326.62	£273.94	£441.35	5%	£46,617.24
14	£10,612.80	£5,433.15	£279.42	£450.18	5%	£49,420.79
15	£10,612.80	£0.00	£285.01	£6,000.99	5%	£58,192.86
16	£10,612.80	£0.00	£290.71	£6,121.01	5%	£67,529.57
17	£10,612.80	£0.00	£296.52	£6,243.43	5%	£77,461.65
18	£10,612.80	£0.00	£302.45	£6,368.30	5%	£0.00
19	£0.00	£0.00	£308.50	£17,108.46	5%	£17,963.89
20	£0.00	£0.00	£314.67	£17,238.38	5%	£36,962.38
21	£0.00	£6,240.98	£320.96	£11,129.91	5%	£50,496.90
22	£0.00	£6,365.80	£327.38	£11,140.25	5%	£64,719.01
23	£0.00	£6,493.11	£333.93	£11,150.80	5%	£79,843.00
24	£0.00	£6,622.98	£340.61	£11,161.56	5%	£95,366.11
25	£0.00	£0.00	£347.42	£17,927.97	5%	£118,958.78
26	£0.00	£0.00	£354.37	£18,074.28	5%	£143,884.71
27	£0.00	£0.00	£361.46	£18,223.51	5%	£170,213.63
28	£0.00	£0.00	£368.69	£18,375.72	5%	£198,018.82
29	£0.00	£0.00	£376.06	£18,530.98	5%	£227,377.28
30	£0.00	£0.00	£383.58	£18,689.34	5%	£258,369.96
31	£0.00	£7,607.72	£391.25	£630.35	5%	£271,950.33
32	£0.00	£7,759.87	£399.08	£642.96	5%	£286,222.95
33	£0.00	£7,915.07	£407.06	£655.82	5%	£301,222.71
34	£0.00	£8,073.37	£415.20	£668.94	5%	£316,986.23
35	£0.00	£0.00	£423.51	£8,917.15	5%	£342,198.55
36	£0.00	£0.00	£431.98	£9,095.50	5%	£368,858.75
37	£0.00	£0.00	£440.62	£9,277.41	5%	£397,042.97
38	£0.00	£0.00	£449.43	£9,462.96	5%	£426,831.22
39	£0.00	£0.00	£458.42	£9,652.21	5%	£458,307.61
40	£0.00	£0.00	£467.58	£9,845.26	5%	£491,560.51
	£191,030.40	£95,491.37	£13,046.83	£306,570.45		

-£299,568.60	£491,560.51

Fig 10.4 | Example 40 Year Opportunity Cost: Phone, Car and House

Here's a quick example to reiterate the point. Starting with only a cheaper mobile phone, keeping a car for 10 years with a 4 year loan and investing the delta till you can pay the mortgage completely, then reinvest the full amount (no lifestyle inflation). Base assumptions to make this understandable as follows:

- 30 Year mortgage on 120% the average (current) UK monthly payment.
- Average (current) UK car payment (£350pcm)
- £47pcm in line with prices for high end phone versus £18 for midrange phone deal identified
- Mortgage payments remain the same for term (no interest rate rises)
- Car and Phone payments increase by inflation which is assumed the 2% annual BoE target
- YoY growth of 5% (half the S&P 500 average)

On the left is the average Consumer, Debtor, Employee who pays their mortgage per 30 year term, has a constant car loan replacing regularly and high mobile costs through replacing when upgrades are available. They reduce nothing from these 3 expenses over 40 years, meaning consumption of £606,139 (including interest costs).

On the right is me. Year one investing mobile saving then in year five rolling completed car payment in too. In year 10 a new car is required and the process starts again. The mobile and car savings invested clear the mortgage after 18 years, 12 years early saving ~£49,891 in interest. I then roll mortgage payments into investing too for the remainder of the 40 years. I've consumed ~£299,569 including interest, half my consumer counterpart. Investments have grown to ~£491,560.51 versus £0.00. I'm wealthier by £798,130.96 ((£491,560.51 - £299,568.60) + £606,139.05) just by sweating cars and mobile phones. We both had the same means here as the same assets are "affordable" and we both had the same functional benefits throughout.

This was my mortgage payment playbook. Reduce expenditure, sweat assets, invest. When investments grow to settlement figure pay mortgage. Start again rolling mortgage payments into investment cycle. Many could achieve some version of this even as interest rates and cost of living rise only time horizons potentially increase, with reduced capital investment.

DANGEROUS DEBT: CREDIT/STORE CARDS & PAYDAY LOANS

I want to turn attention to some of the more dangerous instruments of consumer debt: credit cards (including store cards/accounts) and short-term cash advance loans, also known as payday loans. I doubt there's any surprise these make my naughty list but let's look at why, starting with the latter.

Payday loans have been a concern of mine for some time. I'm not alone in my distain for these products or those offering them, consumer advocacy groups advise against because they're never a solution to the underlying problem that makes people use them. In many cases they actually exacerbate financial issues in those who are, in requiring to take these measures at all, clearly in a financially vulnerable position.

I consider these to be debt factories and predatory by nature. They often prey on the most vulnerable who either don't know any better or can't access more appropriate financial products because of poor credit histories which these often make worse. The UK Government at least legislated maximum fees and charges, but even with those caps the practice itself as far as I'm concerned is comparable to legalised loan sharking.

If you utilise these products because you feel you've no other choice, you have my concern. In your place I'd investigate local community banks and/or credit unions or any local debt advice groups. Unfortunately there are some concerns here as well, in options like debt consolidation and trust deeds (Scotland). These can have adverse long-term impacts too but if you're having to avail yourself of payday loan services just to get by then you really are into lesser of two evils territory. Advice from a reputable financial or debt advisor local to you really could be invaluable.

If however you utilise these services as a convenience, to get things you want in between paydays because of impatience, greed and impulsive spending, then we've some work to do around your financial literacy and consumer psychology. You're committing financial self-harm by chasing those dopamine hits.

Short-term payday loans are quick, easy access loans with huge (and I mean huge) APR's. They usually don't require credit checks or any financial knowledge to enter into and offer quick cash for the real risk of financial hardship. Risks include:

- **MASSIVELY HIGH INTEREST RATES:** Typically APR (Annual Percentage Rates) from several hundred to 1500%. These exorbitant rates can trap borrowers in a debt spiral.
- **SHORT REPAYMENT OUTLOOK:** Often require borrowers to repay the full amount plus fees and interest within two to four weeks. Tight timeframes can be challenging for those already facing financial difficulties, leading to rollovers and extensions which incur additional fees.
- **HIGH FEES AND CHARGES:** Typically very, very high fees. The UK cap means 30 day loans have maximum fees (and

charges) of £24 per £100 borrowed. If borrowers default then £15 plus interest on the borrowed amount is the maximum fee. The overall fee cap also means the maximum you can pay back on any of these loans is 200% of the borrowed amount.

- **AGGRESSIVE DEBT COLLECTION:** Some lenders use aggressive tactics to ensure repayment, from constant phone chasing to the threat of court judgement. Some have even been known to threaten they'll contact employers or family members which for those already vulnerable causes unacceptable anxiety and stress.

- **DEBT SPIRAL:** Many who can't afford to repay the initial loan on time decide to roll over the debt into a new loan, with associated additional fees. Given fees are already ludicrous in comparison to the borrowed amount this spiral can continue indefinitely, trapping people in a situation they simply can't escape.

- **ADVERSE CREDIT SCORE:** I don't like credit scores but we live in a reality where they're used to define credit risk thus a reasonable score is required for access to reasonably priced credit. Many who utilise payday loans already have poor scores but defaulting on these loans has further adverse impact making it challenging to secure credit in future thus perpetuating the debt spiral. Some cynics may call this a repeat custom benefit for these lenders.

I genuinely believe these products are one of the worst examples of a financially knowledgeable minority exploiting a majority lacking in financial knowledge for their own gain. And in this case it's often exploiting those in the worst financial situations at the cost of making those situations worse. They're unscrupulously marketed during the working day and don't, in my view, meet the requirement of "responsible lending". I really, really don't like this exploitative practice, if you can't tell.

To wrap this rant up, these instruments should be avoided whenever and wherever possible. The vulnerable members of society they target are less likely to be reading this book unfortunately, so this warning likely doesn't land. For those I think my audience though, this is a hard "stop it" from me. The habit of utilising short-term, payday loans is the most expensive debt river you can drown yourself in. Don't do it!

To credit cards, store cards and store accounts: these are generally the next highest cost debt utilised by the masses. They're better as an option than payday loans with typical APR around

22%-24% (if not paid in full). For short-term needs they're certainly better than 1500% APR! But they also play a huge part in the needs versus wants aspect of the problem we've discussed, feeding into the Consumer, Debtor Employee cycle by facilitating over spending on wants.

Store accounts/cards can be particularly dangerous in this regard. Retailers who utilise credit accounts for online orders delivered to your door next day, returns at no additional cost (other than travel to store) for example. This introduces convenience risk, where account holders overspend due to the perceived convenience benefit. It removes price competition as they buy more expensive items on account rather than from cheaper competitors. This makes it easy to run up large debts trapping users in a similar debt spiral to payday loans. Servicing account debt means they can't afford to utilise cheaper, settle upfront competitors so they continue buying more expensive products on account, enlarging the debt and debt service costs.

These are to be avoided in my view. The level of discipline required to leverage the convenience without runaway debt is demonstrably beyond most people and the consumer debt numbers show this clearly. I include those even with no debt service fee in this warning. Studies have consistently shown credit instruments result in higher overall spending on consumer products than cash equivalents. It's why they've become more common, stores and lenders see these as a method for increasing profit at consumer expense. Incentives! One such study, to show my working, is that of Dun & Bradstreet who found people using credit cards spent on average 12%-18% more on similar transactions than those utilising cash.

There are those who can be disciplined with credit cards and store accounts, using them only to buy items they would have anyway at no additional cost. They tend to always have the cash available but choose the card/account for the benefits, always clearing the debt before it costs **any** money and enforcing on themselves no impulsive spending guardrails. This is useful for those with the discipline, but most don't have it which is how these companies make money. My rules for credit cards and store accounts are simple:

1. It must be something you would buy anyway (not impulsive) and the cheapest available alternative.
2. There must be tangible benefit in using the card/account (cashback, miles, discount etc.).

3. You **must** have cash available to pay for the item already and be planning to use it to generate higher yield than the credit.

Number 3 is the most important to me. If you don't already have the cash to buy the item, you can't afford it, put the credit card/store account down! The more you spend in consumption or interest, the less you can assign future-self so the more you miss out on the powers of compound interest. Useless debt is a wealth killer and the higher the cost the bigger the problem. Largely, issues with credit cards and store accounts are similar to those of payday loans, scale the main difference:

- **HIGH INTEREST RATES:** Typically 22%-24% if you carry a balance. This can lead to rapid debt accumulation and a debt spiral where it becomes challenging to pay balances.

- **PSYCHOLOGICAL DISCONNECT:** Studies like that of Dun & Bradstreet show a tendency to spend more compared to cash. The disconnect between consumption and tangible cash leads to an increase in impulsive spending habits.

- **DEBT SPIRAL:** Ease of use leads some into a debt spiral where they spend more than they can afford. This cycle of accruing interest on top of interest is difficult to break.

- **FEES/CHARGES:** Potential for annual fees, late payment fees and cash advance fees for example, which accumulate.

- **CREDIT SCORE IMPACT:** Missing payments or maxing out credit limits can negatively impact credit score leading to difficulties obtaining loans or higher credit costs in future.

- **TEMPTATION:** The Jones hypothesis. These instruments create a false sense of wealth by allowing people to fund a lifestyle beyond their means. Convenience makes it easy to ignore budgetary constraints and our aim in wealth building is to live beneath not above our means. The dual impact of overspending and paying interest to service overspending debt is another wealth building killer.

These instruments have a place where users are disciplined, using them only to their advantage. Unfortunately this isn't the majority as debt levels confirm: $986 Billion in the US in 2023 and £66.4 Billion in the UK. Many people utilise this useless debt to fund consumer lifestyles they simply can't afford. Interestingly these numbers show a marked increase of 50% in the US but a decrease of ~8% from the UK peak of £72.4 Billion over the same four year period since 2019. This is an interesting delta. Perhaps reduced use to pay for foreign travel during Covid in the UK? It doesn't matter, it's simply an interesting divergence.

If you're caught in this socially accepted debt cycle, successfully marketed the convenience of credit like the masses, I implore you to ask one more time: Is doing what the majority are doing how I break the cycle and make my family situation better?

PAYING THE MORTGAGE AT 36: WHY?

Let's focus on long-term debt for a moment and talk about paying the mortgage at 36. It's a regular occurrence for people to openly question my sanity around this decision but it may be an aspiration of yours so it warrants exploration. Questions usually come from two distinct groups: those within finance querying from a financial benefit perspective and those outside finance who question how such a thing was even possible.

For context we live in a modest 4 bed, 2.5 bath on a corner lot in a small rural town. An older home built in the 70's and right sized for us, nothing too flashy. It's in the locale we grew up in, still considered one of the most deprived local authorities.

When sketching the outline for the book I knew I'd have to explain my rationale, show that I carefully considered the implications including opportunity cost. I'm always happy to discuss the reasons behind my choice as I'm completely comfortable with it, but still, it gets tiresome defending against the views of those who haven't done this, no matter which group they belong to. In the immortal words of Cardinal Ximenez:

"Nobody expects the Spanish Inquisition!"
[Cardinal Ximenez | Monty Python]

My financial inquisitors usually assume this purely a financial decision and argue on that basis. A projection of their own priorities means I must not understand the cost of my choice. This incorrect assumption, the choice being made purely on financial grounds, is where their argument fails. The financial aspect over the long-term was certainly one of the factors considered but I prioritise value differently from many of these folks based on my life experience. Time is more important to me than money.

This is a message I've tried to reinforce throughout: Only you can define your financial goals and make informed decisions to deliver them. Further, you're entirely accountable for those decisions, no-one else, so you should never feel beholden to anyone other than you and your family (and the law, obviously!). Decide what's best for you and go about delivering to the best of your ability. An informed decision where you're aware of all the angles isn't something you need justify to anyone.

My goals involve managing risk and money appropriately over the long-term to provide my family time and to build legacy for our daughter. My plan ensures wealth can grow and my wife and I are comfortable as early as possible. More importantly it aims to leave both capital and financial education for our daughter so she's never beholden to the Moloch of my triad. If she's the one who reaps full benefit of our efforts when we're gone then I'm perfectly fine with that. French theologian Hyacinthe Loyson described this thinking in his 1866 Parisian sermon:

"These trees which he plants, and under whose shade he shall never sit, he loves them for themselves, and for the sake of his children and his children's children, who are to sit beneath the shadow of their spreading boughs."

[Hyacinthe Loyson | Theologian]

I've always been a long-term thinker, from my coffee jar under the bed to today. It's the very premise of this book, to help you break the short-term cycle and develop strategic plans beyond even your own life. If my only achievement is ensuring my daughter can sit in the shade of the trees I plant, so what. She's more important to me than I am, I'm willing to pay that price, any price, for her benefit.

The criticism I generally receive from a financial perspective is that utilising market profits to clear the debt early rather than stay invested gave up potentially larger gains on capital than the interest costs on the mortgage over the same period, mortgages being relatively cheap debt. Further, inflation impact makes the initial debt and its ongoing service costs lesser over time, as we discussed earlier. The longer it's left the cheaper it becomes to service and pay back in real terms.

Hypothetically, this is a sound argument. It's a basic yield spread calculation with added inflationary impact on debt service factored in. In simple terms their theory is making 7% on money is better than using the same money to service debt costing 2.5%. It's not, though, as impactful over the long-term as these inquisitors generally think. Why? They always forget the principal payment and where it goes after debt clearance! We'll look at this maths in a bit.

Were any factors outside this hypothetical loss considered in my decision? Yes, so let me start by explaining the origins of paying the mortgage asap in my financial goals. In 2007 I'd been dabbling in markets for a few years, happy to put money into a stocks and shares ISA every month via direct debit before I ever saw it. I did this Dollar Cost Average (DCA) in search of modest real rate of return (RoR). I'd started after a round of redundancies early in my career brought the realisation I'd nothing in terms of safety net. Real rate of return, as a reminder, is the amount any investment returns annually over and above inflation.

DCA, by way of quick explanation, is the act of drip feeding small amounts of capital into the market on a regular basis. One buys the same instrument(s) for the same £ amount at regular intervals regardless of price. This helps in smoothing price volatility over long timeframes and mitigates market timing risk. It's a solid strategy, likely to outperform trying to time the market for most people and something we're going to discuss later when we get to investing proper.

My investing was done through my Stocks and Shares ISA, as discussed earlier a tax efficient vehicle with no age limit on withdrawals. We're limited to deposits of £20,000 per annum but profit is tax free, capital gains or income. ISA investing was in addition to my pension, where I contributed the maximum allowable to earn the employer salary match (tax efficient and free money) and I invested less than half my ISA allowance these years.

In Financial Services IT the next restructure is always just around the corner, redundancy risk constant. I'd been through a few rounds unscathed already but wanted to make sure if I was ever impacted properly it was to my advantage, not my detriment. This is where the plan to pay the mortgage by 40 was born.

A year later we had an event you may have heard of: the Global Financial Crisis (GFC)! Banks, including the one I'd just moved my mortgage from, Northern Rock, collapsed. Job security in Financial Services was tenuous, so it was quite a worrying time.

I continued to deploy capital before when markets were essentially on sale. RoR grew alongside my portfolio as markets recovered and as the job situation settled my wife and I wanted to start our family, so we bought a family home with the intention of never moving again. Part of our plan to go debt free asap was one move only from our two bed flat (apartment for my US cousins!). We started a new mortgage in 2012 with rates at near zero picking up a good fixed rate 5 year deal to ensure security of ongoing costs.

I was increasing my financial knowledge pre 2008, but post the crash my curiosity went into overdrive. I started investigating as what happened, who was involved and what other opportunities existed. This meant discovering growing levels of debt, finding it around 150% of income as we discussed earlier when interest rates moved to ZIRP (Zero Interest Rate Policy) around the globe.

This, quite frankly, scared me from a risk perspective. I'd learned that success in finance demanded risk management as a key skillset, a mantra I still advocate today in the coaching I provide to market enthusiasts:

"We're risk managers first, everything else after. We can't make money if we don't protect capital, so capital protection is our primary goal."

[WoSS Capital | Investor & Trader]

In late 2012 I hypothesised another potential issue brewing. The growth in cheap debt was great for my investment portfolio and my new property valuation, but it concerned me from a long-term perspective. ZIRP is supposed to be a temporary measure to alleviate short-term financial stress in an economy, not a long-term policy according to every economics and policy book I read. But it seemed to be benefitting those with money most of all, as they were buying assets on sale with cheap debt at the start of one of the largest bull runs (we now know) in history. I don't doubt this included policymakers themselves and their friends. I inadvertently benefitted because of my financial plan, but I still feared that by the time our 5 year fix was up interest rates might rise towards long-term mean, impacting my ability to invest and pushing up our mortgage cost significantly at refinance.

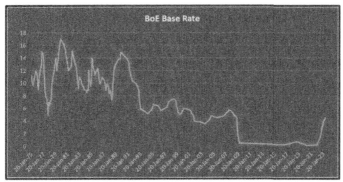

Fig 10.5 | Bank of England Base Rate 1975 to 2023

Fig 10.5 shows my concern graphically: the Bank of England (BoE) base rate between 1975 and 2023 (nearly 50 years). For those unaware, the BoE base rate is used to define UK mortgage rates (in simple terms the calculation for mortgage providers is base rate plus a bit). A cursory glance at the decade from 2009 to 2022 shows you the problem I feared. In 2012 I spotted the exceptional lows of the period we were in and surmised by 2020 we'd likely be returning to mean. It couldn't go on at ZIRP forever? I was early as this held till 2022, but it's what drove my mortgage repayment goals. I didn't want to be debt heavy in a return to mean (rising) rate environment, I wanted to be cash heavy to take advantage, so make hay while the sun shines.

The mean of the entire period is 9.88%. 1975 to 2008 GFC was 10.06%. These both include the 1970s and early 80's where inflation was spiralling out of control though, including the "winter of discontent", so we can normalise somewhat by using the 20 year period between 1988 and 2008, prior to GFC. The mean was 5.94% these 20 years. In fact, if we look back through the entirety of recorded history, back to the 1700's, the mean UK base rate range is 4%-6%. This is historic "normal". US rates are broadly similar, though the range tops a fraction higher than 6%.

We've multiple generations of Debtors though, as I said earlier in this chapter, who think super low interest rates are the norm because of recency bias. Because central banks left them too low for too long it's all some people remember. This hugely benefitted investors as markets like liquidity, but for those who don't know money, don't invest and consume via debt it's a ticking time bomb. Recency bias, incidentally, is a cognitive bias where individuals give greater importance to recent events or information, assuming more significance than past data. It leads to distorted decision making as people overemphasise recent trends or events and overlook historical patterns. You can see from the chart in fig 10.5 how this happened post 2008.

Leaving ZIRP in place too long meant rapidly increasing asset prices at the same time as stagnant wage growth, meaning average house price to average income ratio doubling. Below 3.0 x salary in 1995 to 7.0 x salary in 2023. We were already in a situation where younger buyers felt it impossible, but rates returning to mean results in those already in homes struggling to afford them too. They were unknowingly overleveraged in a low rate, high liquidity, "up only" market.

So why did I pay the mortgage early? You've probably joined these dots based on the detail. I projected mortgage rates would double, possibly treble, meaning higher interest burden and reducing my ability to invest for our future. Further, from a risk management perspective I wanted to de-risk shelter provision for my family should we see another 70's and 80's cost of living crisis. To remove any risk of ever losing our home in the event of turmoil in my industry which left us unable to pay for it. I wanted to break the shackles of "having" to have a job, especially if I was right about the potential impact on interest rates in future.

I don't wish to be alarmist here, quite the opposite, it's simply a risk management play for me. Do I want to be holding a liability (house) costing me twice as much in debt service if I'm right or do I want to render debt service calculations moot, removing interest rate risk entirely even if I'm wrong. What gives me higher long-term probability of fully escaping Consumer, Debtor, Employee? I decided I was happy to pay any opportunity cost premium for being wrong before I even did the calculations. In trading terms, this was my invalidation condition and I was willing to take the stop loss. But I did the calculations anyway!

So here's the numbers (indicative to keep this anonymous) to make clear the premium I paid, my "opportunity cost" for paying the mortgage early. Keep in mind my fixed rate ended in late 2017 when we'd still have ~20 years left on the mortgage.

- Outstanding Mortgage: £150,000 / 20 Years @ 2.5%. £790 per month for total repayment of £190,780. £40,780 in interest (if rates stay low).
- If rates revert to mean: £150,000 / 20 years @ 5.94%. £1,070 per month for total repayment of £256,580. £106,580 in interest (using the mean rate of 20 years prior to 2008, not mean rate plus a bit from a lender).

Interest rate risk on expiry of our fixed rate was stark from a wealth perspective. It would mean the inability to keep contributing to my ISA at the same levels due to the increased monthly mortgage payment which would cost ~£66k in additional interest payments for the same home. Quite frankly at a 5.94% we were, like so many are now, over leveraged.

By 2018 I'd built a little over £110k in my ISA through investing first and being disciplined in spending. We still lived our lives, it was just balanced. I was on track to have enough to pay the mortgage off within 4 years, just past 40. Then, a restructure was announced in my workplace and I had the opportunity to opt for voluntary redundancy. Redundancy terms were favourable due to length of service (16 years), a little over £60k to leave.

This is what I'd been planning for. This decision was now on my terms, with no worry at all about "paying the bills". I could take the package and use it, along with my ISA, to pay off the mortgage and it mattered not if I got another job quickly as our house was safe and we could cover all other bills from my wife's salary, a more secure role as a teacher. The question was simple: am I willing to pay the risk premium involved in liquidating my ISA to completely de-risk my family's future requirement for shelter? It's still a source of some humour for those colleagues I had at the time who tell me I didn't even let them finish the announcement before I was jumping up and down with my hand up shouting "me, me, I'll go!".

Let's look at the numbers on this decision in any case to see what I lost financially. I used a 6% projection figure but actual percentage return would be the same either way so this modelling figure is only to allow for comparison:

- £110,000 ISA with £3,996 invested each year (£333 per month) at 6% projected growth over the 19.5 years (remaining) life of the mortgage. Return: £491,968.73.

This is the number "opportunity cost" advocates point towards. The cost of liquidating the investments to pay off the mortgage, my missed growth potential. Even if rates had reverted to mean, £105,780 in saved interest over 19.5 remaining years is still significantly less than £491,968.73 earned by retaining the ISA and adding ~£3,996 as normal per year. Adding nothing and just leaving the ~£110,000 if I could afford no further deposits projects £342,654.99, three times the potentially higher interest payment.

It's not a valid argument though and let me explain why. Per earlier: **people always forget the principal**!

I've explained that my strategy is to invest whatever I save, not inflate my lifestyle, so as soon as the mortgage is paid the mortgage payment rolls into the ISA alongside the £3,996. With the mortgage payment still required I could afford to put £333 a month into my ISA but I'd still have been paying £790 per month into the mortgage. Clearing the mortgage meant I could pay the full £1,123 (£790 + £333) into investments. We count the principle payment in opportunity cost per my methodology:

- £15,000 ISA balance (I started a new job immediately so invested some of the remaining payoff) with £13,476 additional invested each year (£1,123 per month) at 6% projected growth over 19.5 remaining years. Return: £550,267.22.

But wait, this is higher return over the same period than leaving the £110k in the ISA and paying down the mortgage as normal, before even considering the impact of increased interest payments, even with the positive spread? Correct.

- Opportunity cost proponents: £451,188.73 (£491,968.73 in ISA less £40,780 in paid interest).
- Me: £591,047.22 (£550,267.22 in ISA plus £40,780 in saved interest).

So, an opportunity cost of potentially +£139,858.49 in my methodology, versus the one so often proposed, forgetting the principal. Over the remaining 19.5 year life of the mortgage, paying in full and diverting the monthly payment to the ISA is projected net positive. The negative opportunity cost is actually found in **not** paying the mortgage and getting to the higher regular investment figure sooner. This is **without** rates returning to mean, where I'd have to divert ~£280 from current ISA investment to the mortgage to cover the increase. The delta there would've been greater. And rates did go up, albeit 6 years later, to **more** than 5.94%.

This is an example of poorly used opportunity cost argument in my view. Yes, mortgage rates were cheap and markets returned higher yield, the spread was in favour of investing over paying the mortgage. Those facts are absolutely true. But there's a couple of other facts also absolutely true:

- When using spread to your advantage by building an investment portfolio instead of overpaying the mortgage debt itself (the assumption yield spread arguments are always based on) you can save **HALF** the damn portfolio in debt service costs straight away, more if rates rise.
- When using investment return to pay off the mortgage so early and diverting full principal plus original ISA payment into new investments, your capital payment increases by nearly **4 TIMES** per year, 19.5 years early, earning higher yield sooner on one end while reducing debt service fees significantly on the other. All by capitalising the interim portfolio to pay down the loan.

Furthermore, I de-risk shelter forever for my family and going forward I'm more relaxed about my career, working because I "want" to , not because I "need" to. As it turned out I got a new role before I even left the first. I put myself in a position, with my long-term plan, to put my hand up and be paid to leave. They paid roughly a third of my mortgage to get me to go quietly, shaving ~4 years off my timeline and I walked into a better role on the Monday after my notice period. I still would have paid the mortgage by 40 without this opportunity, because that was the plan, it simply saved some time.

Had I not made the plan in the early 2000's and built the portfolio in the first place, I'd **never** have put my hand up for redundancy, like I'd never done in previous opportunities and probably still be there earning less than the new role. Having a long-term outlook when others didn't, sticking to it and sacrificing things no-one noticed gave me the opportunity to use the situation to my advantage. I was able to buy time and options through planning, discipline and execution. And it was quiet, just the way I like it.

Now I'm an employee not through necessity to pay my debt, but because I want to be. I enjoy what I do and those I work with and it allows me to add to my asset column where my money is put into instruments to make my family more money we can use to buy time. My employer is funding my goals in return for my time and energy, I'm not selling it for someone else's. I'm exchanging my time now while my daughter's in school anyway for **more time** later. This is all on my terms.

A quick note on inflation and the mortgage debt: while it's true over the 19.5 years it would've made the debt cheaper in terms of real terms servicing costs, as the return is higher overall in my method it's a moot point. Yes, inflation would have eaten into the debt over 19.5 years, but the alternate would've eaten into the lower return number too, so it doesn't matter so much here as I was impacted on both sides roughly equally.

Hopefully this explains how and why I did it. The truth is I'd do it again just for the mental freedom even if the numbers didn't make so much sense. I'd pay the opportunity cost for the freedom provided. There's no big secret or get rich quick scheme here. Slow, methodical and disciplined adherence to a long-term plan. If there's a secret the majority don't know, it's perhaps this:

- Putting ~£146 per month into an Index Fund tracking the S&P 500 between 20 and 65 would make you a millionaire at 65 during **any** 45 year period in the last century.

This is what debt stops you from being able to do. For many people, £146 per month is significantly less than their debt servicing fees on debt they don't really need, so isn't obscene. Debt used to live beyond their means rather than build their future.

CLEARING DEBT: HOW & IN WHAT ORDER

Excessive debt without consideration of long-term impact is a silent dream killer. Even small numbers over a long enough time horizon can impact hugely on your ability to build wealth. Compound Interest works both ways, either for you or against you.

"Compound interest is the eighth wonder of the world. He who understands it, earns it. He who doesn't, pays it."

[Albert Einstein | Physicist]

There are many ways to tackle your debt, but two popular approaches are known in rather wintry language as the **DEBT SNOWBALL** and the **DEBT AVALANCHE**. In the debt snowball one focusses on paying off the smallest debt first while making minimum payments on all others. Once the smallest debt is clear you roll the amount you were paying into the next smallest debt. Rinse and repeat. The idea is the momentum from paying off small debts quickly motivates you to tackle larger ones. In the debt avalanche one focusses on paying off debts highest interest rate first while making minimum payments on all others. Once the highest interest debt is clear you roll the payments into the next highest. This minimises interest paid over time saving you money.

These are both perfectly useable methods depending on your goals and discipline. Personally I favour a hybrid model which provides benefits from both, paying off debt as follows:

1. **HIGH INTEREST SHORT-TERM DEBT** like credit cards, store cards or accounts and payday loans.
2. **LOW INTEREST SHORT-TERM DEBT** like personal loans.
3. **HIGH INTEREST MEDIUM TO LONG-TERM DEBT** like car loans, homeowner loans and some student loans.
4. **LOW INTEREST MEDIUM TO LONG-TERM DEBT** like a mortgage, business loans, some student loans and some personal loans, with low rates, over longer periods.

The idea is to focus immediately on high cost short term debt and pay only the minimum towards the others, then work forward from there. Generally this runs in 1-4 order. Don't spread yourself too thin trying to pay them all at the same time. The methodology I explained earlier, always rolling the principal forward, applies to debt servicing too, not just investing. I've used it as you can see in my car loan into investment into mortgage approach. Clearing debt from highest to lowest cost is mathematically the most logical way to compound debt clearing effects in your favour, the slight tweak in my 1-4 method is clearing all short term debt for the mental benefit and to build discipline before tackling the longer term debts.

On longer term, lower cost debts like mortgages you may consider utilising the investment approach described earlier instead of paying to them directly. Where market return is potentially higher than debt service costs you can reduce payment timeframe by investing and clearing the debt with investments once valuations meet. This approach carries more risk, investments can go down in value as well as up, but over longer periods it can help, as it did me, clear debt down faster with more efficient wealth impact overall. This will be your decision based on suitability for your circumstances.

This is the general blueprint, no secret sauce as with most of what we've covered. Reduce expenses, find however much you can, attack the first debt, go from there.

REFINANCE & CONSOLIDATION

If your debt is genuinely unmanageable then refinancing or debt consolidation may be an option to consider. This consolidates your debt into a single payment to one provider, where said provider pays outstanding debts with a new loan and you owe them in isolation. Sometimes this involves writing off an amount of current overall debt as well. It needs to be weighed carefully though as it can have adverse impacts on your long-term finances through either negative credit scoring or even bankruptcy.

Some methods, if not implemented properly and with due consideration, can leave people in a worse position than before. For example the growing in popularity Trust Deeds (Scotland), Individual Voluntary Arrangements (IVA) or debt consolidation loans have led to several reports of people having issues. I'm in no way an expert in these instruments and detail is fairly light on issues faced so it'd be worth utilising the services of a reputable local financial advisor to help with options specific to you.

These options should be last resort. I don't believe in rewarding poor decisions when it's possible to work through them. It reinforces bad habits as there's no "fear" of consequence through learned experience. But in situations where it really isn't possible to get out of the debt river on your own, these can be an option of last resort to stop you from drowning. I certainly don't want that!

CONSIDER POTENTIAL CHARGES

When clearing down debt, particularly loan and mortgage debt, be sure you understand your terms and conditions. Many mortgages only allow a certain level of annual overpayment for example and some have an early repayment charge if within a lock-in period. Some Loans have similar early clearance fees. So just a short note to remind you to check your paperwork, ensure there's no hidden fees and if there are, factor those into calculations. In most cases the cost/benefit of clearing the debt still outweighs these, they simply impact calculations a little. But you should always know the cost and make decisions based on the full picture.

EMERGENCY CASH FUNDS

We discussed in budget and money mapping that a small cash fund is useful for everyone for breakdowns of home appliances, cars and similar. If you've significant levels of debt this cash fund to cover these sorts of unforeseen repairs is a necessity when you start to pay it off.

Why? If you've worked super hard for 6 months to clear a chunk of debt but don't have a backup fund, then come home one day to a puddle on the kitchen floor from a broken fridge freezer, what will your only course of action be (as you need a fridge)? Credit Card? Potentially undoing the hard work you've done and making you wonder "what's the point?". Psychological strength is a key part of getting this done so having this fund can help manage the risk.

Before you start going after debt then, have this fund available or be starting to build it alongside debt repayment. Better to have it and not need it than need it and not have it!

SUMMARY

Of the people I try to help with their financial worries it's this topic more than any other I find holds them down, financially and mentally. We've been conditioned to believe it's cost of living, rising asset prices, politicians or the rich, all of which is true to an extent, but fixing those aren't in our gift. Debt utilisation is. For many, their own personal choices when it comes to debt keeps them submerged in the river as much as anyone else.

It's become so normalised and the long-term impact is invisible, rarely featuring on people's list of reasons for their financial situation. There's usually an excuse for why the debt had to be taken but the reasoning behind it rarely includes an honest reflection on the personal choice made, often want not need based.

I never have this conversation with the intent of shaming anyone because I genuinely believe people just don't know any better. The reality behind the "Debtor" portion of my Consumer, Debtor, Employee triad is simply a knowledge gap, one I'm trying hard to close for you in this chapter. I often get pushback during this full and frank debate with people, so I point out, according to details of the conversation, things like:

- "You've had 4 cars on finance in the time I've had the one I currently drive".
- "You always buy luxury cars larger than you need and more expensive to finance and run".
- "You've a private number plate on a credit card: you know you get a number plate free with the car right?".
- "You've replaced your mobile every 18 months at £45 on a loan contract, I've had mine for 5 years at £12 max".
- "You've moved house 5 times in the past 15 years, each time starting a new 25 year mortgage, I've moved once in 20 years and the single mortgage is gone".
- "You've 3 spare bedrooms in your new house, do you think it's right sized for you now or in future?".
- "You spend £250 every week on credit cards socialising and eating out, you know that's £13,000 a year? Could you half it and invest £6,500? Or even third it and invest £8,666? You're 35 now, if you did you could have £726,225.34 at 65 at 6% YoY, more if you put into a SIPP for the 20%-40% bonus".

These conversations always have some variation of these or similar points because I find most people have similar habits, to greater or lesser degrees. They have the same misunderstandings and the same blind spots when it comes to consumerism and debt. This is, as I've hypothesised, what we're conditioned to be. These many conversations have supported this chapter, given the issues are so common from person to person. The optimal way forward is to limit debt to what's useful, like:

- Interest free loans on things we'd have bought anyway, where we already have the cash we can utilise to gain higher yield elsewhere in the same time.
- Credit card purchases where we have the cash, would have bought the items anyway and there's some benefit like

cashback to using the card, paying it off in full before interest is accrued.

- Using loans to buy right sized larger assets that we need (like home and car) and sweating them for as long as possible post debt clearance, investing the principal.
- Sweating smaller consumer gadgets to keep monthly costs low, like mobile phones and tech. Invest the principal.

We should always look to reduce exposure to useless debt, particularly high interest variations. It bonds us to the creditor and sells our future time and energy to service. For items we don't need, we want, we should be honest about the categorisation, avoiding debt through impulse and instant gratification. We should **always** avoid payday loans and other short-term, super high interest debt. We should work towards clearing current debt in sequential order, usually highest cost to lowest.

We should also have an emergency fund while going after debt, making sure enough is set aside we don't suffer setback through an emergency repair.

Most of all, start thinking about your debt, questioning the incentives of those who offer it and building your understanding of what it means for you long-term. Understand what's useful and what's useless then stop taking on useless debt!

Stop thinking about debt purely as a monetary cost, start thinking about how much of your time and energy it takes to generate the money to pay it back. Think about my assertion earlier that we're utilised as human cattle for the benefit of others and realise your debt is someone else yield farming you! Someone else using your time and energy to make themselves money in service of your debt.

See debt for what it is and regulate how you use it to your benefit. Make it "useful" for you, don't be cattle generating yield for someone else in exchange for shiny buttons.

ACTIONS

- Refer to tab "A. Actions" in the Financial Plan template.
- Complete the actions defined in section ".: 10 :. | Let's Talk About Debts Baby!"

The Loyalty Lie: You're Just a Number

"Loyalty to a job is as illogical as loyalty to a stock paying below market. You lose money and when things go sideways you're exit liquidity."

[WoSS | Bought the Corporate T-Shirt]

ANOTHER SHORT DEVIATION FOR A controversial issue that impacts long-term financial wellbeing in many people. I'm going to have fun here, potentially upsetting those who love their job and mistakenly think their job loves them! In this chapter we'll break from expenditure to look at income, but through a very specific lens: loyalty and its opportunity cost over time. It's a facet of income generation many don't consider, don't know to consider or make excuses not to consider.

YOUR JOB DOESN'T CARE ABOUT YOU

Strong start! Let me explain this statement fully though: "job" doesn't equal "colleagues" or "boss". I wouldn't be so absolute about the intricacies of interpersonal relationships and my experience tells me it's possible to work with and for people who do actually care.

In the early days of my career I worked for genuinely decent people who recognised and rewarded competence to the best of their ability, people I learned from and was able to progress under. Laterally, I've had the freedom to be selective around roles to ensure this is maintained. With enough experience to tick boxes at interview and no pressure of needing the job I can treat them as opportunities to interview prospective bosses. When I accept roles now it's because I choose the boss. I've turned down roles with better packages because the prospective boss didn't pass **my** interview. This is one of the liberating aspects of being debt free.

So, within any organisation there <u>will</u> be individuals who genuinely care about you. This isn't our focus here though, I want to discuss the parameters those people must operate within at organisational level regardless of personal feeling. Specifically, the powers they have, or rather don't have, to impact our finances. I also want to outline some of the social engineering prominent in workplace culture that's used by most organisations to mitigate retention risk and control real terms resource costs.

I'm UK based so my experience is from the UK market. This experience tells me operating methods are broadly similar regards pay and reward, public and private sector:

- There generally exist organisation wide salary scales based on role level or grade.
- Starting salaries for new hires are generally negotiable within this range (normally around the median).
- Annual reviews are generally non-negotiable, performance based, organisation wide scales (based on collective bargaining, often done by Trade Unions).
- These annual reviews rarely keep up with inflation or the market, particularly for those higher in their salary scale.

Hopefully these sound familiar, I'm sure they will for most. So what's the problem? Simply put, the market sets your value and it's linked to supply and demand, your competence and wider economic measures like inflation. But when you're loyal to a job you've taken yourself off the market, undervaluing yourself against it from the first annual pay review onwards. The longer you stay, the further you get from your potential market value. Most people I speak to accept this year on year, thinking "I'm getting paid more" without realising:

- They're getting paid below their current market value.
- Their below inflation pay rise was actually a **pay cut.**

I want to be very clear on this point because it's become super clear to me through years of financial discussion there exist too many who don't join these dots:

If your annual pay rise is less than inflation, you didn't get a pay rise, you got a real terms pay cut. You're now doing the same job for less money. It costs the organisation less in real-terms to pay you.

This can be a difficult concept to explain as most people view fiat money (your £, or $ or € for example) as fixed value. £1 is always worth £1 right? "If I got a 2% pay rise then every £1 I got last year is now worth £1.02". That's how people generally think. As you know from our inflation introduction though this is completely **wrong**. If CPI is 10% (as it is when writing), your 2% pay rise actually means your previous £1 is "worth" 92p (notionally to make the point). This is usually where I lose people in discussion!

For now, just understand your employer knows this. Their accountants know it. Those who make decisions on annual pay scales know it. They knowingly, willingly and intentionally make you and your family poorer on an annual basis because it makes their resource cost, you, **cheaper** in real terms. They just get your boss to tell you the number, a boss who has minimal if any control over those numbers so whether they like you or not is irrelevant. In large enterprise they can only operate within the parameters dictated by the organisation which are generally strict. In smaller organisations there's more flexibility but still not a huge amount.

This isn't an attack on organisations or those who run them, their costs go up year on year through inflation as well so it's their job to control them in whatever way they can to remain profitable. Otherwise they couldn't provide the jobs in the first place. My aim here is to highlight how many employees don't understand the mechanics of the cost of loyalty, because it can be a detriment to our financial outcomes and that's what we aim to improve.

MONETARY VALUE: VARIABLE VIA INFLATION & DEBASEMENT

I want to explore further the concept of variable fiat currency value. Bretton-Woods, an international agreement implemented in 1944 by allied nations, aimed to control international financial market stability as World War II ended. High level, it agreed international currencies like the £ and F (French Franc) would peg to the $ at a fixed exchange rate, the $ pegged to Gold at a fixed rate per ounce.

The "Gold Standard" as it's sometimes known gave stability to international markets, established the $ as de facto World Reserve Currency (WRC) and notionally gave fiat some intrinsic value through the Gold peg, a fixed supply commodity. In 1971, mass $ accumulation outside of the US and the ongoing expense of the Vietnam war led President Nixon to bring Bretton Woods to an end. This initiated modern floating exchange rate markets. Fiat money was no longer linked to a fixed commodity so central banks could print and issue as much fiat as they desired. The age of inflation (and rising debt) began. Fig 11.1 shows US currency in circulation 1917 - 2023. I've marked 1971 vertically, making clear at a glance something certainly changed with the supply of USD ($) post Bretton-Woods. You can also see the increase since 2019, the Covid period, where the chart goes near vertical.

The cumulative effect of this Covid period, according to the Bureau of Labor and Statistics (BLS), is that $1 of goods and services in 2019 needs $1.19 today (19.34% currency debasement). Or $1 earned is notionally worth ~81c today in comparison. The UK is worse. £1 in 2019 would buy the same as £1.28 in 2023. A 27.86% currency debasement. Every £1 earned then notionally worth ~72p today. These are based on official government figures so it's fair to assume this the "best case". These figures simply make my point around spending power versus fiat value.

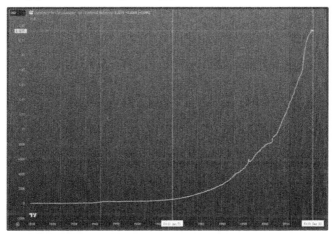

Fig 11.1 | US Monetary Supply 1917 – 2023 (From TradingView)

If you've ever wondered why your income increases year on year by 0.5%-2.0% but you feel poorer, this is your answer. Money is conceptual and its value changes in terms of spending power over time based on wider economic factors like inflation, QE, tax changes and monetary debasement. We aren't educated on mass to measure currency in terms of what it can buy, so most people default to the denomination and this assumes £1 always equals £1. This thought process is encouraged, another facet of the triad designed to keep us compliant.

When people view money as fixed value they only consider whether their salary number "goes up" year on year thus missing the bigger picture. Income change should be measured by whether spending power increases or decreases, not simply by the number itself going up. If spending power decreases, which it does year on year for the majority of loyal employees, you aren't getting a pay raise my friend, you're getting a pay cut while being expected to provide the same level of output. Over a 40 year career this loyalty, accepting below inflation pay increases where "number go up" while staying loyal to a job can cost **millions**. This isn't hyperbole.

Historically there was a trade-off where organisations offered Defined Benefit (Final or Average Salary) pensions as default benefits. The organisation bore the pension risk and this pension could, in some ways at least, counteract the negative impact of employee loyalty on income by funding retirement fully. Those who still have them can certainly still look to this as a trade-off. In the modern age though, where employers have removed this benefit and expect the employee to assume all pension risk via Defined Contribution pensions, themselves linked to income, employers benefit disproportionately from your loyalty.

YOUR ANNUAL PAY CUT: THOUGHT EXPERIMENT

You're sceptical of "millions" lost through monetary debasement and the stealth annual pay cuts from loyalty to a job. I know you're sceptical because most are when I have this conversation. So, let's do a quick experiment.

We'll use actual YoY inflation figures from the UK (IMF Data) from 1983. We'll use these to project a potential path for CPI 40 years into the future, a full 40 year career. We don't expect this exactly, but it allows us to project the actual impact of the past 40 years inflation post Bretton-Woods using numbers relatable to today. We'll use current average UK Salary of £33,000 (at time of writing). This is an indicative salary but the thesis is the same for any higher or lower number so as a start point it doesn't matter.

We'll calculate a standard 2% raise even though I know from experience 2% is far from standard, many companies offer much lower. We'll calculate the actual amount salary would need to rise each year to simply **maintain** spending power (i.e. for the salary to remain static real terms against inflation). We'll calculate the delta between 2% and maintenance, then assume we'll invest at 6% YoY. This will tell us 2 things:

1. How much of a pay rise or pay cut we'd be seeing year on year (and cumulatively).
2. Opportunity cost had you invested it for an average return.

Year	UK CPI	2% wage increase	CPI Wage Increase	Delta	6% investing Cumulative Delta
1983	4.61%	£33,660.00	£34,521.30	£861.30	£912.98
1984	4.96%	£34,333.20	£36,233.56	£1,900.36	£2,982.13
1985	6.07%	£35,019.86	£38,432.93	£3,413.07	£6,778.92
1986	3.43%	£35,720.26	£39,751.18	£4,030.92	£11,458.43
1987	4.15%	£36,434.67	£41,400.86	£4,966.19	£17,410.10
1988	4.16%	£37,163.36	£43,123.13	£5,959.77	£24,772.06
1989	5.76%	£37,906.63	£45,607.03	£7,700.40	£34,420.81
1990	8.06%	£38,664.76	£49,282.95	£10,618.19	£47,741.34
1991	7.46%	£39,438.05	£52,959.46	£13,521.40	£64,938.51
1992	4.59%	£40,226.82	£55,390.30	£15,163.48	£84,908.11
1993	2.56%	£41,031.35	£56,808.29	£15,776.94	£106,726.15
1994	2.22%	£41,851.98	£58,069.43	£16,217.46	£130,320.22
1995	2.70%	£42,689.02	£59,637.31	£16,948.29	£156,104.62
1996	2.85%	£43,542.80	£61,336.97	£17,794.17	£184,332.72
1997	2.20%	£44,413.66	£62,686.39	£18,272.73	£214,761.78
1998	1.82%	£45,301.93	£63,827.28	£18,525.35	£247,284.36
1999	1.75%	£46,207.97	£64,944.26	£18,736.29	£281,981.89
2000	1.18%	£47,132.13	£65,710.60	£18,578.47	£318,593.98
2001	1.53%	£48,074.77	£66,715.97	£18,641.20	£357,469.29
2002	1.52%	£49,036.26	£67,730.05	£18,693.79	£398,732.87
2003	1.38%	£50,016.99	£68,664.73	£18,647.74	£442,423.44
2004	1.39%	£51,017.33	£69,619.17	£18,601.84	£488,686.80
2005	2.09%	£52,037.68	£71,074.21	£19,036.53	£538,186.73
2006	2.46%	£53,078.43	£72,822.63	£19,744.20	£591,406.79
2007	2.39%	£54,140.00	£74,563.09	£20,423.10	£648,539.68
2008	3.52%	£55,222.80	£77,187.71	£21,964.92	£710,734.87
2009	1.96%	£56,327.25	£78,700.59	£22,373.34	£777,094.70
2010	2.49%	£57,453.80	£80,660.24	£23,206.44	£848,319.21
2011	3.86%	£58,602.87	£83,773.72	£25,170.85	£925,899.46
2012	2.57%	£59,774.93	£85,926.71	£26,151.78	£1,009,174.32
2013	2.29%	£60,970.43	£87,894.43	£26,924.00	£1,098,264.21
2014	1.45%	£62,189.84	£89,168.90	£26,979.06	£1,192,757.87
2015	0.37%	£63,433.64	£89,498.82	£26,065.19	£1,291,952.44
2016	1.01%	£64,702.31	£90,402.76	£25,700.45	£1,396,712.07
2017	2.56%	£65,996.36	£92,717.07	£26,720.72	£1,508,838.76
2018	2.29%	£67,316.28	£94,840.29	£27,524.01	£1,628,544.53
2019	1.74%	£68,662.61	£96,490.52	£27,827.91	£1,755,754.79
2020	0.99%	£70,035.86	£97,445.77	£27,409.91	£1,890,154.58
2021	2.52%	£71,436.58	£99,901.41	£28,464.83	£2,033,736.57
2022	7.92%	£72,865.31	£107,813.60	£34,948.29	£2,192,805.95

Fig 11.2 | 40 Year UK Inflation Impact on Spending Power

In this example, over a 40 year career the final delta is £34,948.20 **per year** reduction in salary value as a measure of spending power. The cumulative total over these 40 years is £740,248.88. Had you invested the delta year on year the return at the end of 40 years projects ~£2.1 million at 6% average. This is simply an indicative projection on how much you could lose through loyalty, these numbers aren't absolutes but illustrate the potential issue.

When I say loyalty to a job can cost you millions, they know this and they **don't care**, I have my reasons!

KNOW YOUR MARKET VALUE & DON'T BUY THE CULTURE HYPE

Now we know the potential impact of long-term loyalty to a job, what can we do about it? The answer lies in knowing your market value, continually improving skills to increase it and not being afraid to test the market regularly for new roles.

Negotiating is a key skill for building wealth. It can be uncomfortable as it's often made to seem "wrong" and it can be confusing as it's another tangible skill seldom taught in schools. It can though make a difference in significant missed earnings and wealth building potential over time.

It doesn't have to be awkward and it's not as difficult as many fear. My approach is simply to apply for roles every few years which initiates conversation with recruiters allowing me to gauge market rate for my skills and experience. If offers are forthcoming the power dynamic from a negotiating perspective shifts. For current employer I can have the conversation armed with market rate, one actually being offered, along with detail collected annually on how much of a real terms pay cut I've accepted already. If we provide value, which we should all strive to do, then this generates conversation and often better offers from both.

We can and should treat everyone involved from both organisations respectfully, but ultimately neither employer would feel guilty about making us redundant in future if it suited their business model so I refuse to feel guilty about ever making decisions to best suit mine. You shouldn't either.

Some frown upon my transactional attitude towards employer relationships because they're conditioned to be an Employee, the third tenet of my triad. Ever wondered why companies put such effort into "culture"? Into knowing the "vision" and being part of delivering it? On "employee wellbeing", being a "great place to work" where you can "bring the best of yourself" and all that other bullshit? This is designed to build loyalty from employee to employer, to get you bought into the company, to believe you're part of the family so you go above and beyond in helping to deliver their goals. Why? Because loyal employees deliver more for less, stick around for real terms pay cuts every year and reduce real terms RevEx spend. Loyal employees accept moving further from their true market value with each appraisal like a good worker ant.

Per our example, you pay a heavy price for this loyalty or as my brother eloquently puts it "munching the corporate biscuit". But most don't realise the impact or don't understand when someone raises it. I'll give a couple of humorous examples. In my previous role there were mandatory induction sessions for new employees to welcome them. The facilitator was a lovely woman, proud she'd been there over 25 years and had "seen everything". Once she gave her intro she posed an "icebreaker" question: "What makes you get out of bed and come to work in the morning, what do you love? And it can't be the money". I absolutely refuse to play this game and explaining so was like speaking Klingon. The reality is I'm there because we made a deal, the organisation pay me the market value we agreed upon for my services. They want my skillset, I want their money, let's not complicate this any further! This wasn't received well, because it's not the answer they usually get, one about how people "enjoy the challenge" or "love the work". These always make me laugh. Let's deposit £10 million in these folks bank accounts and see if they turn up at 8am the next day, through a 2 hour commute, because they "love the work"!

I've had similar conversations with recruiters. "The role is x just now and the package is y, but with the potential to grow into [insert fancy role title here] within a year and a package closer to what you're looking for". My response: that's great, come back to me in a year once the role materialises and we can talk. Silence and confusion. The reality is the fancy role title with the better terms in future is a unicorn. It doesn't now and will never exist. The conversation alone tells me they expect me to do the role now for below market value without the fancy title (meaningless anyway) and I don't want to work for a company looking to take advantage of me from the off. I've seen it so many times, people enticed by the promise of jam tomorrow which never comes.

So know your worth and if an employer doesn't, if they want to treat you poorly, then you absolutely need to review the terms of the transaction. Those beanbags in the fancy office with a wellbeing day once per quarter can cost you, as I've shown, significantly in terms of time (or the money to buy it) over a career. Corporate culture and the building of loyalty is a one way benefit not in favour of employees. I hark back to a common mantra: what are the majority doing and if you want a different outcome are you going to achieve it doing the same things as the majority?

GONE WHEN IT SUITS

I've inferred this but let me say it explicitly. In times of trouble, or even in times of change, when it's no longer cost effective to underpay you against the market, when it becomes cheaper to do business in a different locale or outsource some of the company, or move into a different market not requiring your skillset, your status as nothing but a number on a spreadsheet will be very quickly confirmed.

Your "loyalty", all those extra hours, what you did over and above, all the nights and weekends you worked for free because you bought into the culture, your consistent above average performance reviews...........**none of it will mean anything**. Not a single thing. I've seen it from both sides many times. When it's of more benefit to the company for you to leave, say your goodbyes, it's done. It still amazes me so many people are shocked by this reality.

I still do a good job, delivering to the best of my ability because I take pride in my own performance. I'm 100% accountable for what I do. I'm not advocating we ever provide poor service as that helps no-one, we always need to provide value or we don't deserve to be there regardless. All I'm saying is you can provide value by doing the job you're contractually paid to do and do it well **within** the parameters in which you're paid to do it **without** becoming attached to the job or the company and **without** accepting you must do it year after year to your detriment.

We're discussing in this book how to find financial security, clear debt and build wealth. You impact those goals negatively if you don't know your own value and allow yourself to be given pay cuts year after year. It's even worse if you do this through the one way street which is corporate loyalty. You'll always be a number on a spreadsheet when it suits the business need, so you must take care of your own needs.

MOVING TIMEFRAMES

I think we've adequately covered why making positive change on the income side of your balance sheet, to help with your long-term financial goals, means you need to assess your relationship with your job and ensure you're not being taken for granted through year on year pay cuts. The last thing I'll offer before moving on to multiple income streams is some data, as is my style.

In the UK, ONS data highlights those who change jobs every year have consistently higher pay than those who stay. This makes a bigger difference in younger workers, aged 16-24 according to the study but applies across all age demographics. In the US the BLS did a study of around 20 million people and found in 2021 those who moved job earned up to 12% more year on year than those who stayed "loyal".

This certainly resonates with me and those I've spoken to around the world. I spoke to a young man recently who I had the pleasure of managing for 3 years. He moved role for a 30%+ rise only 3 years after coming through an apprenticeship programme in Software Engineering. Two years later he applied for and was offered a role back with his old employer at over 100% previous salary, which his new employer eventually matched to keep him. Had he stayed at the original company for those two years he'd likely have less than 10% wage growth, 90% worse off, but he'd still be just as good, with the same skills, doing just as good a job. His case is not an isolated one, this is a supply versus demand world and his skillset, the one he consciously reskilled into in his mid-20's from a retail role, is in demand. He's an example of everything this book advocates and it was an absolute privilege to be a tiny part of his journey.

One caution I'd offer though as a hiring manager is around these timeframes from the ONS study and moving jobs every year. You must be careful about the perception of moving too often and the potential impact on your ability to get your foot in the door for interview. You don't want to stand out in a negative way from the crowd. My sweet spot tends to be 2-3 years in an organisation and review where I'm at versus inflation and the market. The first year I've negotiated market value (and never accept the first offer!), the second is an opportunity to see how wages keep up with inflation and the third is a confirmation year where I can decide on course of action. If I'm ahead and happy, I'll stay, if not, I'll discuss with my manager and look externally.

Hiring managers rarely look negatively on 3 year outlooks (certainly I don't, I find it reasonable) and it allows you to reset market value, if you want to, absorbing only a few years of pay cuts. You can generally make this up in the 3 year cycle through negotiating back to market value.

BUILDING MULTIPLE INCOME STREAMS

Now we've spoken about the impact of loyalty to your job, let's chat briefly about the habit the majority of people have where said job is their only income stream and they often work extra hours in it for free. This societal norm sees most equate a job to income in a 1:1 relationship. Those who successfully build wealth though rarely have just one income stream.

According to a 2023 article written by Kimberly Olsen (Millionaire, TEDx Speaker and Coach) the average millionaire has 7 sources of income. They don't, like the majority of people, rely on one job. I wasn't overly surprised by this given the financial circles I travel in where "grinding" on multiple different fronts is very much the norm amongst the most successful people I know. My anecdotal experience supports the article conclusion.

Remember, again, it's what the masses are **not** doing that sets financially successful people apart.

We've spoken a lot about how people can find savings in their expenditure by thinking differently and often this alone can bring the long-term financial success they crave. Well, the same is true of income, anyone can add additional income streams it just takes a little effort and creative thinking. What are you good at, what are you interested in and what skills or knowledge do you have others may benefit from? These are the types of questions to ask yourself. Some common additional income streams with varied barriers to entry include:

- Rental Property (AirBNB, long-term residential, holiday).
- Royalties (Authors, Artists, Musicians and Video Creators).
- Affiliate Marketing.
- Peer to Peer Lending.
- Dropshipping.
- Content Creation (Courses, Videos, Newsletters).
- Starting a Side Business related to an interest.
- Dividend Investing.
- Trading.
- Buying a Business (Self or Seller Financed).
- Websites offering services.

Obviously there are many options, these are just examples. Suitability will differ person to person. The key message is that having a job doesn't mean you need to rely on it alone for income, most people have some skills or knowledge allowing them to at least try to generate additional income streams. You lose nothing if unsuccessful, provided you don't enter into one with high capital entry costs and this presents an opportunity to learn new skills that potentially make you more marketable in your day job.

It takes time and energy (and commitment), so you may need to step away from Netflix, but as we discussed in the making excuses chapter the majority of people would rather define the reasons they can't do something than actually try! Consider your options when it comes to income streams and don't be afraid to give something a try. I may not make significant sums from this book, it wasn't my primary goal anyway, but I've learned so much about writing in the 14 months it's taken me (so far!). This learning will be with me forever.

SUMMARY

Hopefully this hasn't been too controversial for those who love their job and truly believe it loves them! If nothing else it should make you think, whether you agree or not. Distilling the messages into key point summary:

The value of money is variable, not fixed. £1 isn't always worth £1 as it's impacted by inflation, debasement, tax changes and QE. What matters is the spending power of £1 at any given time, year on year. Know, test regularly and track your market value and understand your compensation against this value. Salary going up doesn't mean a pay rise if spending power is shrinking. Understand inflation, how it's calculated and why it matters to your spending power. Track your salary versus inflation as a baseline, not versus itself to ensure it's actually a pay rise and not a real terms pay cut.

Your loyalty means nothing unless it remains convenient for the business. Corporate culture exists to keep you loyal as it's cheaper to develop culture than to pay market value across a workforce. The optimal timeframe for moving to stay on market value and not impact perception is 2-3 years.

You're not limited to one income stream, millionaires average around 7. Understand the only thing stopping you from building additional streams of income is you. Find something you're interested in and give it a go, worst case you gain some skills and experience potentially beneficial to earning potential in your day job.

There's a lot in this brief summary but hopefully you identify with what I've explained and understand why I think it's important. Most people can use this information to make a positive difference in their financial life.

ACTIONS

- Refer to tab "A. Actions" in the Financial Plan template.
- Complete the actions defined in section ".: 11 :. | The Loyalty Lie: You're Just a Number"

12

Are You Sure About Insurance

BACK TO OUR FINANCIAL PLAN and it's time to look at your insurance requirements. These are specific to individual personal circumstance, so while I can detail some products you might wish to consider, you must review alongside your personal situation to ensure you provision appropriate cover for you and your family.

For example, if you live in the US you may need to consider health insurance where those in the UK or Canada who enjoy health services free at the point of use may not. Or, if you're the main household earner you may want to consider income on death policies to ensure your family has defined income replacement in a worst case scenario. A single person living alone is unlikely to need such a policy.

These two examples show how differing circumstances can change individual decisions. Others include homeowner status, longstanding health conditions and number of dependents. Variance of personal situation means it's impossible to offer a one size fits all plan for insurance, so we'll concentrate on defining the common types along with the benefits they provide. This should help with your personal decision making. A local, reputable financial planner will be able to assist further with personalised insurance provision if you deem this necessary.

Comparison sites like moneysupermarket or gocompare are also reasonable places to review insurance products. They offer most that we'll discuss and their standard input forms help identify questions to ask yourself to define personal need.

LIFE INSURANCE

This product provides financial protection to named beneficiaries in the event of you and/or your partners death. When an insured person passes away during policy term the beneficiaries named in the policy receive a predetermined sum, known as the death benefit, from the insurer. In the UK there are different types of life insurance designed to cater to differing needs and circumstances. These include (but aren't limited to):

- **TERM LIFE INSURANCE:** Sometimes known as "Decreasing Term", this provides cover for a set period, generally 5 to 30 years. If the insured dies during term the predetermined benefit is paid to named beneficiaries. If the policyholder outlives term the policy expires and no payout is made. Term life insurance is generally more affordable than other types of life insurance and people often use it to cover, for example, clearing the mortgage if one earner passes away.
- **WHOLE LIFE INSURANCE:** Also known as permanent or perpetual life insurance this provides cover for the entire life of the insured as long as the monthly/annual premiums are paid. If the insured dies during term the predetermined benefit is paid to their named beneficiaries.
- **OVER-50S LIFE INSURANCE:** Designed for those aged 50 and older who can find it difficult to qualify for traditional life insurance due to medical history and/or existing health conditions. It usually offers guaranteed acceptance without medical examination. The predetermined death benefit is paid to the named beneficiaries upon policyholder death and premiums are typically fixed for the life of the policy.
- **FAMILY INCOME BENEFIT:** A type of term life insurance paying regular income to named beneficiaries instead of a lump sum on death. Payments continue for the remaining policy term post insured death. This type of life insurance intends to replace a level of income to help with ongoing expenses for the family.
- **FUNERAL INSURANCE:** Also known as final expense insurance, it's a cheaper version of whole life insurance aiming only to cover different levels of funeral/burial costs. As such the benefit is far smaller than other life insurance policies and usually no medical history is required.

These are the main types of life insurance policies available in the UK but broadly similar products are offered in most countries. Life insurance is one of the options everyone should seriously consider and the first on my list of insurance provision. I want to ensure my family have both lump sum benefit and regular income to cover bills in the event of my death so I utilise both options. At the very least I wouldn't want my family to incur funeral expense at such a difficult (I think!) time.

As an illustration, £7.40 provides a joint life, first death (M/F in their 40's, non-smokers) decreasing term policy with a lump sum of £110k, along with £9.60 for an income policy on my life alone providing my family ~£1000 every month for term (19 years remaining). So £17 per month to cover what we've defined as required. Remember, there are many factors impacting on price, like lump sum amount, so always confirm coverage meets your needs and the premium is in line with other, similar providers.

There are a few other considerations I want to mention, to give you a full picture and help avoid any nasty surprises later.

Life Insurance policies, including those described already, also offer **JOINT COVERAGE** options for couples through a single policy, rather than two separate. This usually reduces monthly/annual premium costs. You should be cognisant of the different versions though as it could adversely impact you in the event of a death if you choose the wrong one:

- **JOINT LIFE, FIRST DEATH:** These are more common, providing either lump sum or ongoing regular income (as defined in the policy) on **first death** in the couple, the beneficiary is usually the other named policyholder. It's intended to help the surviving partner.

- **JOINT LIFE, SECOND DEATH:** These, however, are payable on **second death** when both policyholders pass. The beneficiary is usually a child or family member as defined in the policy. The surviving partner is entitled to **no** benefit post first death, the policy benefit realised after second.

If you want to leave the benefit to the surviving partner, choose first death, if the surviving partner is not the target beneficiary you may opt for second to leave to children or to cover funeral costs.

DEATH IN SERVICE is an employee benefit offered by some employers, usually as a salary sacrifice. It provisions a payout in the chosen multiple of annual salary for the named beneficiaries in the policy. Many companies offer cost effective cover at higher levels too, so it's worth considering. Often people don't know they have this benefit if it's applied automatically and comes off gross salary, so check your benefits to confirm. Also, **ensure your beneficiaries are kept up to date.**

Life Insurance is an important part of insurance provision and one, in my view, that should be universal. Identify what you need and use comparison sites for quotes, checking policy details meet your needs. For joint policies, make sure you sign up for the one you want, first death or second, to avoid a costly future mistake.

CRITICAL ILLNESS COVER

Often included under life insurance, but I prefer critical illness as its own distinct product. It provides a predefined lump-sum to the holder if diagnosed with an illness covered by the policy during term. Lump sum requirement is generally how they're priced, higher benefits meaning higher premiums. Individual factors like age and pre-existing medical conditions also impact premiums.

Illnesses covered by these policies vary, but typically include severe and life-threatening conditions like cancer, stroke, heart attack, organ failure, some major surgery and sometimes specific disabilities. It's another insurance often offered by employers as part of elective benefit schemes so check if this is something you already qualify for. My provision for this, a lump sum of £50k for both myself and my wife, comes through salary sacrifice costing in the region of £15 per month (£7.50 each). You also have the option to add this as a bolt on (or rider) to some life insurance policies rather than take standalone versions. As a bolt-on it generally offers the same cover as the standalone version in addition to the death benefits already defined. It may even be cheaper together.

If diagnosed with a critical illness included in coverage during the policy term, the insurance company pays out the lump sum benefit defined. This can be used as policyholder deems necessary, for things like covering medical expenses, clearing debt or simply to provide financial support to allow for time in recovery without worrying about the financial strain of not being able to work.

Different policies cover different illnesses so check the list in your plan of choice to ensure it meets your needs. There are also policy requirements holders must meet for successful claims, a common one being "survival periods" post diagnosis, often 14 days or more. One must review the schedule of cover for any policy to understand these requirements alongside what's covered and any exclusions.

Critical illness requirement will depend entirely on personal circumstances. Many see this as an optional addition to life insurance or something they might add later in life. The likelihood of contracting a critical illness and the potential cost overhead in countries where health cover is public is lower in younger years for example, so this makes some sense. I do use this one though.

If you decide it's needed then it's important to carefully review and compare policies from different providers to ensure you choose one suited to your needs, covering any illnesses that concern you (perhaps based on family history).

HEALTH INSURANCE

In the UK our health service is nationalised (currently) meaning everyone has access to medical care free at the point of use. The NHS, though it has issues, is very much a national treasure so political attempts to privatise are widely (and rightly) met with distain. Leaving the politics aside, if you live in the UK (or any country with social healthcare) the requirement for health insurance is reduced to essentially nil. Some employers offer discounted policies as part of benefits packages which may be a reasonable option, but ultimately it's personal choice in these jurisdictions.

However, if based in private healthcare jurisdictions like the US, well rounded health coverage for your family is a necessity, from both a health and financial perspective. It isn't uncommon for people in these locales to be bankrupted by the desire to stay alive if they're unfortunate enough to contract an illness requiring expensive treatment. I've first-hand experience of this. I once broke ribs in Colorado while snowboarding and had to attend the local hospital. Thankfully I had travel insurance who approved the visit. I met with a nurse, a doctor, had an X-Ray to confirm broken ribs, a couple of other tests, got some advice on aftercare (nothing can really be done for ribs) and a prescription for pain medication.

In and out: 90 minutes. The bill was over $7,000. I nearly fell of my chair when it came by mail at home in the UK, but my travel insurance covered it. So, our US cousins would likely see the requirement for health insurance as far more of a priority than we do. Again, many employers offer insurance (with or without dental) as part of their benefits package which can help, so do check employee options. If not, a private policy would be required.

As with all insurance it's key to make sure the policy you adopt covers your needs. Check inclusions/exclusions and limits, plus any excess requirements (voluntary and compulsory). You certainly don't want to discover you have a large bill after receiving some treatment because some or all of it wasn't covered.

You should also ensure you follow any process required by your provider because stepping outside process can see some or all of the claim declined. This applies to UK private policies as well. For example, receiving treatment for non-urgent issues without prior approval or when the care carried out by the provider exceeds pre-approval by the insurer. An example of this would be receiving approval for an ultrasound for a gastrointestinal issue but the consultant on the day deciding an MRI was also required. If the

MRI was not pre-approved, the insurance provider may decline the claim for it, leaving you to cover the whole cost.

So, know what you need, know what you have access to through public services and your employer, read the policy details carefully to ensure you're covered for everything you want, for everyone you need covered and when you need to make a claim against the health insurance make sure you follow the required process, limiting treatment to only what's pre-approved.

DISABILITY COVER

Offers income replacement if you're unable to work due to disability, either contracted through illness or an accident. It helps maintain standard of living and covers expenses during the period defined in the policy. The types of disability and levels of cover, like all insurance, will be outlined in the policy schedule.

Some employers insist upon this so offer it through benefits packages for a small salary sacrifice, so check if it's something you already pay for at work. The decision on need for this protection will depend on personal circumstances. Most don't need it, some choose to have it or like me must take it through their employer.

A decent rule of thumb would be to look at your expenditure versus any lump sum or social security payments you'd receive in the case of disability. If there's a shortfall in your ability to cover expenses (particularly shelter) should you be unable to work, this may be an insurance you'd consider. If not, it's maybe not needed.

This is sometimes referred to as Long-term Care Cover and these versions can include issues related to aging and illness as well as physical disability through injury. Long-term Care policies with extended coverage are rarely utilised by younger, healthy individuals, becoming more popular with age. As with all life or illness related insurance, premiums tend to rise as one gets older.

PERSONAL ACCIDENT INSURANCE

This is another commonly used policy or bolt on (in disability or life cover). It's generally pretty cheap, a few £'s per month and pays holders or named beneficiaries the lump sum benefit defined in the schedule for accidental injury (or death).

These policies have some pretty strict exclusions, for example anything connected to pre-existing conditions, any self-inflicted injuries and any injury sustained while pursuing extreme activity or sports (like skiing, snowboarding or climbing) if not explicitly added to the policy in advance. If this coverage interests you, be sure to understand the schedule and pay particular attention to the exclusions and conditions based on "how" injury is sustained.

CAR/AUTO INSURANCE

If you own a motor vehicle and drive on public roads it's a legal requirement (certainly in the UK) to have insurance. Varying options exist with premiums reflecting level of cover and driver experience. In the UK the main types are as follows:

- **THIRD-PARTY:** Minimum level required by law, it covers liability for injury to other people and damage to their property caused by you. **Does not** cover any damage to your own car or injury to yourself.
- **THIRD-PARTY FIRE & THEFT:** Same as Third-Party but additionally provides protection against fire damage to and theft of your vehicle.
- **(FULLY) COMPREHENSIVE:** The most extensive option, it covers damage to your own vehicle and any third-party liability. It includes cover for accidents, theft, fire, vandalism and other misfortunes.
- **BLACK BOX:** A black box device is installed in your car to monitor driving behaviour and based on its data insurers offer personalised premiums encouraging safer driving.
- **TEMPORARY:** Short duration cover typically one day to a few weeks. Useful when borrowing or sharing a car for brief periods like with a housemate, sibling or from a parent.
- **MULTI-CAR:** Insures multiple cars in the same household, for example spouses and children, under a single policy. Insurers discount this policy over individual policies to gain and retain business.

My preference is Fully Comprehensive with protected no claims bonus. No claims bonus counts how many years of no claims a policyholder built up to show insurers they're a safer driver. It's something like a credit score but for car insurance. The better your no claims bonus the larger the discount on your policy for being, notionally, a safer customer. Protected no claims requires a small additional premium to stop your counter being reset to zero in the event of a single claim. Any claim will still be taken into account in premium pricing but the years of no claims discount built up will still apply. Different insurers have different conditions for no claims protection, mine allows two claims in a five year period for example.

One other specialist option in the UK is **CLASSIC CAR COVER**, designed to provide specialised cover for vintage and classic car owners. It's unlikely most readers, indeed most people (me included) would ever need this but for completeness I've listed it.

The US has slightly different options, though broadly aligned to the UK:

- **LIABILITY INSURANCE:** Mandatory in most states it covers legal liability for bodily injury and property damage caused to others in an "at fault" accident. It's typically expressed with multiple coverage limits: bodily injury liability per person, bodily injury liability per accident and property damage liability. Some states, like Florida have a "no fault" policy meaning both parties are held equally liable no matter who's actually at fault.

- **COLLISION INSURANCE:** Covers cost of repairs or replacement for your own vehicle regardless of fault.

- **COMPREHENSIVE:** Broadly the same as the UK variant, often referred to as "full coverage".

- **UNINSURED/UNDERINSURED MOTORIST COVERAGE (UM/UIM):** Protects you if involved in an accident with someone who has insufficient or no insurance. Helps cover medical expenses and property damage. Under/Uninsured drivers are a bigger issue in the US than the UK.

- **PERSONAL INJURY PROTECTION (PIP):** Pays for medical expenses of the policyholder and any passengers injured in an accident regardless of fault. PIP is mandatory in some no fault states.

Other options are available like legal cover, towing and labour cover or rental reimbursement (which covers the cost of a rental car while yours is under repair). These are generally considered addons. Most should be able to find the coverage they need within main plans but some addons can also be useful, so check availability.

Wherever you're located, owning a car comes with the responsibility of ensuring you're adequately insured to protect you and others in an accident. You should consider the various options carefully and select the policy providing the coverage you need. It can save you undue financial hardship in the long-term.

You should note: some policies require **both** voluntary and compulsory excess, the total excess the sum of these figures. This can confuse people. For example, if your policy has voluntary excess of £150 and compulsory excess of £250, in the event of a claim you're liable for the first £250 + £150 = £400 before the insurer pays any higher balance. If the overall repair is less than this, it's to your detriment (from a renewal and claims perspective) to involve the insurer at all.

It's also worth noting most UK fully comprehensive policies include minor windscreen repair (chips) without impacting no claims or incurring an excess charge. If your policy has this it's always better to utilise chip repair before cold weather makes them cracks, at which point it becomes chargeable and won't pass an MOT. Prevention is better than cure here financially.

BUILDINGS & CONTENTS (HOME) INSURANCE

While not mandatory legally, this is generally a requirement for mortgage lenders in the UK and US. Once a mortgage is paid the obligation no longer exists but it's still a good idea to retain this insurance given the importance of your home and possessions. There are generally two major components to UK policies:

- **BUILDINGS:** Covers the physical structure of the property including walls, roof, floors, windows and permanent fixtures like fitted kitchens or bathrooms. Protects from damage caused by things like fire, storm, flood, subsidence and vandalism covering cost of repair or full rebuild of the insured property.
- **CONTENTS:** Covers belongings and personal possessions inside your home like furniture, appliances, electronics, clothing and other items. Most insurers advise you think of this in terms of "if you picked up your home and shook it, everything that falls out". It provides protection against loss or damage from theft, fire, flood and optionally accident, helping compensate for cost of replacement or repair for your belongings.

Each component has their own level of cover so ensure this meets your requirements. Many contents policies now list "unlimited" but some still refer to actual £ amounts. Buildings is more generally £ amount where policyholders pick what it would cost to rebuild (not home sale value, rebuild value). There are also additional add-ons you can include with UK policies:

- **ACCIDENTAL DAMAGE:** Covers accidental damage to buildings and contents like those caused by DIY.
- **PERSONAL POSSESSIONS:** Extends coverage to valuable items you take outside the home like jewellery, laptops and electronics. Normally these must be declared individually

with their valuations so if you have this cover ensure you've detailed the individual items and have appraisals where required.

- **LEGAL EXPENSES:** Covers legal costs if you need to take legal action related to buildings or contents.
- **HOME EMERGENCY:** Provides coverage for unexpected emergencies like a broken boiler or flooded room due to burst pipes.
- **OUTBUILDING & BICYCLE:** Provides cover for any belongings located in buildings on your grounds, outside of the main building. These aren't usually covered by default. Some policies include bicycles, others require separate bicycle cover as an add-on.

Buildings and Contents policies can seem daunting given differing levels of cover, but they function in the same way as all other insurance policies. Check fully the details of the policy schedule for things like no claims discounts and voluntary or compulsory excess amounts. Also check for any exclusions like flood damage if located in a flood plain. Then select the policy meeting your requirements with acceptable cost and conditions.

Also be sure to check your policy requirements for personal possessions. If they need declared and itemised make sure you do this to avoid disappointment. Worth noting many policies have a limit on things like how much cash is covered in the home for theft claims (often ~£1,500) and any single item limits (normally anything valued over £5,000 requires explicit declaration). Make sure you know and declare these if required.

US versions are broadly similar, with some notable distinctions and additional options:

- **DWELLINGS COVER:** Equivalent to UK buildings cover.
- **PERSONAL PROPERTY:** Equivalent to UK contents cover.
- **LIABILITY COVERAGE:** Covers injury to others or damage to their property while on your property, if you're found responsible. Helps with legal costs and any liability judgment up to policy limits.
- **ADDITIONAL LIVING EXPENSES:** Assists with living expenses like temporary accommodation if your home becomes uninhabitable due to events covered in the policy.
- **MEDICAL PAYMENTS TO OTHERS:** Pays medical expenses if a guest is injured on your property, regardless of fault. Designed to provide quick resolution for small claims, helping prevent lawsuits.

- **PERSONAL LIABILITY UMBRELLA POLICY:** Additional coverage for higher value items above policy levels.
- **SCHEDULED PERSONAL PROPERTY:** Equivalent to Personal Possessions cover in the UK.
- **FLOOD INSURANCE:** Standard US policies rarely cover flood damage. If you're in a flood-prone area you may need to purchase separate insurance through the national program (NFIP) or a private insurer.
- **EARTHQUAKE INSURANCE:** Also typically not included in standard policies, so If you live in an earthquake prone region you may need additional earthquake insurance.

These cover the main considerations. Most of these policies are available globally with differing local options and names. As always, ensure chosen policies meet your requirements, know any exclusions and how the claims process works. Also, be aware of applicable excess payments should you make a claim: if the value of the claim is less than the excess amount there's little benefit in going via your insurer, it'll push your premium up for no benefit if you have to cover the full cost out of pocket anyway.

TRAVEL INSURANCE

Designed to protect travellers against unexpected events before or during international travel, generally providing financial and medical protection. Cover and premiums vary between providers, typically including:

- **CANCELLATION OR INTERRUPTION:** Covers non-refundable expenses if the trip is cancelled or curtailed for reasons covered in the schedule. These can include illness, injury, death, natural disaster or other unforeseen events. Non-refundable means any costs both **incurred** (i.e. you paid them) and **not refunded** by the service provider. You can't claim things you didn't pay or already had returned.
- **EMERGENCY MEDICAL EXPENSES:** Covers costs of medical treatment if policyholders become ill or injured during a qualifying trip. Can include evacuation if transport is required to a (nearest) suitable hospital or medical facility.
- **BAGGAGE AND PERSONAL BELONGINGS:** Compensates policyholders for lost, stolen or damaged baggage and personal belongings during any qualifying trip.
- **DELAY:** Covers policyholders against substantial delays during travel, for example due to flight cancellations. May also reimburse for additional expenses incurred, like

overnight stays as a result of delay (if not covered by provider already, the airline in "delay" example).

- **PERSONAL LIABILITY:** Provides cover if policyholders become legally liable for causing injury or property damage to a third party during any qualifying trip.

- **DISRUPTION:** Covers additional expenses and transport costs if policyholders trips are disrupted or delayed due to unforeseen events.

- **LEGAL ASSISTANCE:** Provides legal assistance or advice in case policyholders encounter legal issues during any qualifying trip.

Other inclusions and exclusions apply to specific policies so ensure to read the schedule carefully to confirm it meets the level of cover required. Cover limits and excess levels also vary so be sure to check these too. There are a few other items of note when it comes to Travel Insurance:

- **EHIC & GHIC:** Some providers require you possess the EHIC (European Health Insurance Card) or GHIC (Global Health Insurance Card), freely available via the UK Government Gateway. If your insurer has this stipulation and you don't have this provision they could refuse to cover medical expenses should you make a claim, even if premiums are fully paid. Check policy requirements, but given they're free they're worth getting in any event.

- **WORLDWIDE, WORLDWIDE INCLUDING US OR EUROPE:** All policies stipulate where geographically the policy is valid, cover being invalid for all other locations. These requirements increase the cost of the policy, with worldwide including US generally most expensive. Ensure your policy covers the areas you plan to travel to.

- **ANNUAL OR SINGLE TRIP:** If you travel once per year, Single Trip for a specified date range is generally the cheaper option. Any more than once and Annual Multi Trip can be the more cost effective. If annual multi trip is the better option be sure to check the stipulations on maximum number of days per travel year and max length of stay per single trip so not caught out.

- **WINTER SPORTS COVER:** In most policies winter sports cover isn't included but is available as an optional addon. This can be expensive but if going on a ski or snowboard trip for example you need to add this. Ensure you check the cover as not all winter sports addons are created equally. For example many specify "on-piste" cover only, meaning if injured between runs or in the backcountry you could have problems. Many also don't cover terrain parks, if you're a freestyle skier or rider. I've seen people in Europe dragging friends with broken bones back between the ropes to get "on-piste" before calling Ski Patrol. It never looks pleasant!

- **SPORTS COVER:** Some sports aren't covered as standard, listed as exclusions in policy schedules. Winter sports, sky diving or white water kayaking for example. If you plan to partake in sports during your trip be sure to engage your provider to add to policy in advance, don't assume coverage.
- **PRE-EXISTING MEDICAL CONDITIONS:** Most policies stipulate costs associated with pre-existing medical conditions are **not** covered, so any condition you've already been diagnosed with needs an additional conversation. Most insurers will be happy to add coverage for an additional premium up to certain expense levels, but you need to have this agreed and added to the policy in advance.
- **INDIVIDUAL OR FAMILY:** A single policy to cover the whole family is generally more cost effective than multiple individual policies. If you're travelling as a family you should investigate this option.

When travelling internationally it's really important you have adequate insurance to cover unforeseen events. I've been thankful for this cover more than once. As a final note: travel insurance is sometimes offered with bank accounts via small monthly fees. You should check to see what provision, if any, your account offers and confirm if it meets your needs before taking any further cover.

As with all insurance, sounding like a broken record, ensure the cover you purchase meets your requirements and make sure you're aware of any exclusions and excesses or any processes you must follow (like EHIC/GHIC) for the policy to remain valid. If you travel at all, this really does need to be one of your insurance provision considerations.

NICHE CONSIDERATIONS

We've covered the insurance types I consider "mainstream", those applicable to most people to some degree. There are more niche considerations worth mention as they'll apply to some individuals and families. The same rules apply, check policy schedules, know inclusions and exclusions and ensure the cover you need/want is provisioned. These include:

- **LANDLORD INSURANCE:** if you're a landlord with rental property, either residential or commercial, you'll require landlord insurance to cover the specific concerns of this venture. This can include property damage, missed payments and legal costs for example.
- **BUSINESS INSURANCE:** If you run a business you likely need business insurance. This covers things like general liability, property insurance and professional liability.
- **UMBRELLA INSURANCE:** Provides additional coverage beyond the limits of other policies, protecting against large lawsuits and useful for those with substantial assets.
- **PET INSURANCE:** For those beloved furry (or slimy!) members of the family. This insurance provides essentially health insurance for your pet, ensuring any qualifying vet bills are covered so you don't need to worry about how you'll pay if your furry family fall ill or have an accident.
- **GADGET INSURANCE:** Some people like to cover their gadgets specifically against loss or damage, things like mobile phones, laptops and EarPods. Companies like Protect Your Bubble offer this sort of cover as do some Bank accounts in the same way they offer Travel Insurance.
- **BREAKDOWN COVER:** This insurance provides various levels of cover for vehicle breakdown at or away from home if you're a driver or passenger. Another that can be part of premium bank account offerings, so check your provider.

There are others, but those with those sorts of considerations likely already seek help from professional services (Financial Advisors and Accountants) so we won't go into any further detail. I mention these only for completeness.

PAYING ANNUALLY VERSUS MONTHLY

Some products offer pay monthly or pay annually options. Annual payment usually includes a discount so it's optimal to pay this way where one can. It's also useful to then stagger the policy start dates to avoid all annual policies being due at one time.

My preferred method is to project all annual premiums then calculate how much I need to save per month through the year in advance to cover them. I divert this amount into an interest accruing account monthly then when a premium comes due I use this account to pay for it. It requires a little more organisation to gain the benefit of annual pricing and the accrued interest on the amount of all premiums over the year, but it's not a burden.

Many people I speak to tell me they pay monthly because they can't afford the annual price, the reality is they've just not been organised enough to facilitate it over the previous year so if this is you (and I refer to excuses again) try and figure out how you can remedy this, even if just for one or two policies at first to gain the benefits.

Using this approach we benefit from the annual payment but keep our budget on a monthly basis. We pay ourselves monthly, into a separate account to gain the interest then pay the provider annually. I benefit from (now 4.5%) interest on the principal and the annual cost saving as well. There's obviously a level of discipline required so you don't dip into this money and we need to be mindful of tax allowances on interest but the benefits are tangible for minimal effort.

AUTOMATIC RENEWALS

Premium costs are variable year on year but you should **never** accept current provider renewals without checking against the market. It's habitual for providers to artificially increase renewal fees in the hope people just roll it forward. Compared against the market you can usually find cheaper options for comparable cover.

This applies to all annually renewing cover. Longer term cover like life policies are usually fixed with inflationary rises agreed within schedule. It takes work on your part, but comparing annual renewal quotes against market and at least challenging current providers to match quotes you find if you want to stay with them can save hundreds annually.

Recent UK legislation aims to make this less of a problem as new customers can't be offered introductory deals significantly lower than existing. But I suspect this simply makes everything more expensive for everyone! One of those economics unintended consequences of incentives, though one that could absolutely have been foreseen. In any event, checking your quotes against market is still good practice.

SUMMARY

I realise Insurance isn't an exciting topic so the content in this chapter has likely been a great antidote for insomnia! But it's an important consideration as part of a well-rounded financial plan so one we must take seriously. When provisioned appropriately it protects from unforeseen events and supports our financial goals.

Avoiding large, unexpected bills wherever possible helps keep debt under control and allows us to stay on track with our plan. The example where I broke ribs and found care resulting in a bill for over $7,000 highlights the benefit. Travel Insurance covered this entirely for the £200 (at the time) annual premium (Winter Sports cover with Terrain Park addon to Worldwide Including US policy). Well worth it, despite what seemed a high upfront cost.

No-one wants a large, unplanned bill like this. Think of our earlier discussion, what would be many people's only option to cover such a debt? High interest credit like a credit card or loan? We've seen the impact of servicing long-term debts versus investing in our future self so know our opportunity cost is far larger than the $7,000 initial bill.

Insurance also allows us to provision for family in a worst case scenario, to leave them with a financial benefit. While money is never able to replace us it can at least help make their lives better by clearing debt like a mortgage or providing regular income to stop them falling into financial hardship.

Overall, insurance is an undeniably dull topic, some might argue most of finance can be, but it's a hugely important consideration within our financial plans. We don't want to be in a situation where we've planned and executed everything to the best of our ability, over multiple decades, then it's undone by an unforeseen event we could've insured our risk against. As we'll discuss, risk management is an important learning within the finance arena and ultimately insurance is a form of this key practice. It protects from the tail risks life can throw at us, limiting impact on our finances for a controllable monthly or annual premium we can plan for.

You should consider insurance requirements for yourself and your family, seeking financial advice from local and reputable professionals if required. This chapter explains some key insurance products as important parts of a well-rounded financial plan but other option are available. You should look to make said provision, execute against plan and review annually for changing requirements and cost effectiveness.

ACTIONS

- Refer to tab "A. Actions" in the Financial Plan template.
- Complete the actions defined in section ".: 12 :. | Are You Sure About Insurance"

13

Risk & Risk Management

"The essence of investment management is management of risk, not management of return."

[Benjamin Graham | Economist]

MY TRADING FRIENDS WILL BE surprised this comes in chapter thirteen given my often sermon like espousal of risk and risk management, but we had to work our way here! Before the investment section of your financial plan I want to ensure you understand risk and risk management principles so you might treat them both with the respect they warrant. I say this not to invoke fear, quite the contrary it's to help you manage greed.

I'll concentrate here on an overview from a long-term investing perspective as risk management for trading is a different beast entirely. I'll cover that in a brief trading introduction later.

Firstly, it's important we understand the different types of risk within markets so we can make informed portfolio decisions. Knowing them helps to identify these major risks and employ appropriate risk management techniques to mitigate them, so with this in mind let's start with some risk type overviews.

RISK TYPES: MARKET RISK

Sometimes referred to as "systematic risk", this describes the risk inherent within entire markets, asset classes or specific sectors (like Technology or Energy). It's a risk found in factors beyond our control as investors, things like geopolitical events, economic downturns or interest rate fluctuations that ultimately impact the value of our investments.

An example of market risk materialising would be a recession which leads to widespread decline in investment valuations across all instruments. During recession we typically see unemployment rise while consumer spending and corporate earnings fall. This adversely impacts share prices, market or sector wide.

The GFC market crash of 2008 or the 2000 Dot Com Bubble would be examples to investigate in charts for more detail on price movement. It's beyond the control of investors but impacts heavily on portfolio value. Without exposing oneself to different risk (like market timing) mitigation is done mainly through diversification. Spreading our portfolio geographically, by sector and by asset class can reduce the overall impact of market risk materialisation if it comes in any single market, asset class or sector. Some classes also act conversely to each other. You've maybe heard for example Gold (commodity) can hedge against equity price decline.

Market risk events can also be opportunities. Baron Rothschild, an 18th Century member of the Rothschild banking family once famously said "the time to buy is when there's blood in the streets". Those greedy when others are fearful often position strongly for future growth when markets recover. Of this notion I've heard it put better by current investor and 42Macro lead Darius Dale who says something akin to "Don't buy when there's blood in the streets, buy when you hear the sirens coming to clear it up". He's rightly highlighting it's better to look for signals you're not too early, before the metaphorical bleeding stops.

RISK TYPES: LIQUIDITY RISK

Liquidity in this context refers to the ease with which an asset can be bought or sold without significantly moving its price. Liquidity risk is the risk your trade execution (buy or sell) moves the market, your transaction essentially too large in relation to asset liquidity. This happens either because the asset itself is low liquidity, or in a highly liquid asset because your order size is very, very large.

Limit orders are "maker" orders where one defines the price they wish to buy (or sell) the instrument. This order sits on the orderbook waiting to match with a seller (or buyer) willing to sell (or buy) at your desired price. If no-one meets your price the order remains until the defined expiry period or cancellation.

Market orders are "taker" orders where one instructs their platform to buy (or sell) the asset for whatever price is available on orderbooks with the capital assigned. You'll incur "slippage" as your order eats the orderbook (limit orders) at whatever prices are offered until fully filled. In this scenario your purchase price (averaged) is unknown till after. Slippage is a form of liquidity risk materialisation. In illiquid markets slippage can be extreme with your order moving the market enough to have serious repercussions on the post fill value.

There are two risks here. Firstly, the market is so illiquid the limit price you want to sell at is never met by a buyer and you must reduce asking price (think slow housing markets). Secondly, you execute a market order and it's so illiquid your order consumes a huge range of the orderbook incurring extreme slippage.

We mitigate liquidity risk by ensuring we diversify across liquid assets with fairly active markets, avoiding concentrated positions. When we have to exit or enter large positions we should look to scale (or ladder) in or out to avoid moving price. This generally isn't a huge issue for retail investors as the capital we play with is miniscule when deployed on most instruments, in most markets. I also prefer to utilise limit orders where possible.

RISK TYPES: CREDIT RISK

This is the risk that borrowers are unable to repay their debts, also referred to as "default" or "counterparty" risk. It's fundamental in lending where a bank, for example, assumes the risk and often takes collateral as risk mitigation. In investing it generally refers to those occasions we'd be utilising debt instruments like corporate bonds, where we're the bank and assume the risk that the borrower (corporation) experiences financial difficulty or even default. It's a lesser issue when utilising government debt like US Treasuries or UK Gilts as governments from stronger economies are less likely to default, their debt is highly rated.

You may be aware of ratings agencies like Moody's, Fitch or Standard and Poor's whose function is to "rate" debt quality. Each agency uses slightly different ratings (see Fig 13.1) but in general "AAA" is considered safest. Below a certain point, usually around "BBB-" debt is considered "Junk" with far higher credit risk.

Consider an example: Imagine you've invested in a 2 year corporate bond issued by "example corp." who promise a 7% yield. You expect to receive 7% annualised return on investment, paid on the timescale set by the coupon and to receive your principal back at the end of 2 years when the bond matures. These bonds are essentially loans to "example corp." and you've assumed a credit risk. If the company continues to post profit and pay its yield then you make 7% return annually and receive your principal back on maturity. However, if the company faces financial difficulties and is unable to generate sufficient revenue to meet debt obligations it could default on bond payments and when the bonds mature you don't receive your principal back if the company is in default. In this instance credit risk has materialised and you suffered "total loss".

Our main mitigation strategy is to pick appropriately rated debt. Investment grade certainly, the higher the better. "Junk" grade exposure should be limited and where used this should be with the acceptance of potential for total loss.

Moody's	Fitch	Standard & Poors	Notes	
Aaa	AAA	AAA	Prime. Considered very low risk	Investment Grade
Aa1	AA+	AA+	High Grade Debt. Presumed relatively low risk	Investment Grade
Aa2	AA	AA	High Grade Debt. Presumed relatively low risk	Investment Grade
Aa3	AA-	AA-	High Grade Debt. Presumed relatively low risk	Investment Grade
A1	A+	A+	Upper Medium Grade Debt. Risk is increasing.	Investment Grade
A2	A	A	Upper Medium Grade Debt. Risk is increasing.	Investment Grade
A3	A-	A-	Upper Medium Grade Debt. Risk is increasing.	Investment Grade
Baa1	BBB+	BBB+	Low Medium Grade Debt. The lowest level considered "Investment Grade", further increased risk.	Investment Grade
Baa2	BBB+	BBB+	Low Medium Grade Debt. The lowest level considered "Investment Grade", further increased risk.	Investment Grade
Baa3	BBB-	BBB-	Low Medium Grade Debt. The lowest level considered "Investment Grade", further increased risk.	Investment Grade
Ba1	BB+	BB+	Non Investment Grade Debt. Considered Speculative	Non Investment Grade ("Junk")
Ba2	BB	BB	Non Investment Grade Debt. Considered Speculative	Non Investment Grade ("Junk")
Ba3	BB-	BB-	Non Investment Grade Debt. Considered Speculative	Non Investment Grade ("Junk")
B1	B+	B+	Highly Speculative, High Risk Debt.	Non Investment Grade ("Junk")
B2	B	B	Highly Speculative, High Risk Debt.	Non Investment Grade ("Junk")
B3	B-	B-	Highly Speculative, High Risk Debt.	Non Investment Grade ("Junk")
Caa1	CCC	CCC+	Carries Substantial Risk. Extreme Speculation	Non Investment Grade ("Junk")
Caa2	-	CCC	Carries Substantial Risk. Extreme Speculation	Non Investment Grade ("Junk")
Caa3	-	CCC-	Debt Default is considered imminent with little to no prospect for recovery. Assume Total Loss.	Non Investment Grade ("Junk")
Ca	CC	CC	Debt Default is considered imminent with little to no prospect for recovery. Assume Total Loss.	Non Investment Grade ("Junk")
C	C	C	Debt Default is considered imminent with little to no prospect for recovery. Assume Total Loss.	Non Investment Grade ("Junk")
-	D	D	Confirmed as being in Default. Assume Total Loss	Non Investment Grade ("Junk")

Fig 13.1 | Debt Ratings

RISK TYPES: INFLATION RISK

We discussed real rate of return (RoR) earlier so this specific risk you'll hopefully recognise. Inflation has an adverse impact on spending power over time and if the rate of inflation is higher than the rate of return on investments, real returns could be diminished or even negative. This is inflation risk.

A previous example applies: if inflation is 2% and your portfolio returns 6% the RoR is 4% (6% - 2%) and spending power increased. But if inflation is 10% and your portfolio returns 6% then your RoR is -4% (6%-10%) and spending power decreased. From an investing perspective we look to ensure we return more than inflation year on year but there will likely be periods where it becomes difficult (like in 2022).

To mitigate we can consider assets that historically outpace inflation like equities or real estate and diversification of assets across markets is also important. We can consider inflation hedging strategies like commodities (often Gold is used for this) or Treasury Inflation Protected Securities (TIPS). I find the less one messes with their core portfolio the better though, as we'll cover in a few risks time!

RISK TYPES: INTEREST RATE RISK

Sometimes referred to as "duration risk" this refers to the potential for fixed income investment valuations, like bonds or gilts, to fluctuate due to changes in interest rates. When rates rise bond prices generally fall and vice versa which affects the market value and income potential of existing fixed income investments. If for example we purchase a 10 year bond with a 3% coupon but rates later increase to 6%, the value of our bond can decrease. As new bonds with higher yield become available, demand for older and lower yield bonds like ours falls. Who wants a 10 year fix paying less than a 2 year? This doesn't present great risk if you plan to hold to maturity, but if you needed to sell to raise capital you may suffer a loss, getting less back than originally invested plus any coupon return already paid.

Though not considered interest rate risk in the traditional sense I think it's also worth saying rates impact equities portfolios too, just the inverse of fixed income. Historically equities perform well into rising rates, they tend not to like rate reduction cycles and drawdown comes once rates peak. Data suggests our interest rate risk on equities materialises in the period after rates roll over into eventual rate lows.

We mitigate interest rate risk by diversification across rate sensitive instruments and by staggering fixed income investments across maturity timelines. We can also consider adjustable rate securities or the use of interest rate derivatives like swaps but these are more complex and not suitable for amateur investors. We should also always stay informed about economic indicators that influence interest rates, not just for our investments but as we've discussed for overall financial health.

RISK TYPES: POLITICAL & REGULATORY RISK

By now my view on politicians is pretty clear. Here's another reason, the risk they introduce to our investments through policies, regulatory change, political instability or just plain stupidity (UK "Mini Budget" anyone?). These actions can affect business within their regulatory framework and our investments.

Consider for example you invest in a green energy company that benefits from government subsidies or incentives and these play a significant part in their growth. When a new government is elected they change or revoke these incentives impacting revenue of the company, leading to loss of share value and investor capital.

Or imagine you were an investor in the cryptocurrency XRP in 2020 when the US SEC sued its creator, Ripple Labs, for allegedly selling unregistered securities. This unexpected regulatory issue dumped the price of XRP, a freely tradable asset on a free and open market, more than 70% in 2 weeks. This case was brought under hugely questionable circumstances and the SEC ultimately lost in 2023. It had a hugely negative impact on XRP investors during the period, those the SEC are supposed to protect.

Political and regulatory risk is something we need to be mindful of, though we rarely have any control over it. Our main mitigation is diversification across our portfolio, particularly geographically. If all of our investments fall within the same political and regulatory jurisdiction our risk is "concentrated". By investing across jurisdictions, asset classes and sectors we can minimise potential impacts of political and regulatory change as they potentially only impact fractions of our portfolio.

RISK TYPES: CURRENCY RISK

Also known as "exchange rate risk" this one's straightforward. If you invest in foreign markets like US equities when based in the UK then fluctuations in exchange rates (£ v $ in this example) can influence investment value in your local currency.

For example, let's say you purchase 10 shares of Tesla (NASDAQ: Ticker TSLA) for $101 while the £ to $ exchange rate is $1.18 in January 2023. Your book cost is £855.93 ((10 x $101) / $1.18). Come February 2023 TSLA has surged to $217 for a 113% gain, projecting you'll return £1,823 (£855.93 + 113%). The £ though has made a run against the $, up to $1.27. When you repatriate your investment the value is £1,708.66 ((10 x $217) / $1.27), not £1,823.

Fluctuating exchange rates mean you make a lower overall return than expected in this example, which shows currency risk materialising. It also works the other way: had the £ weakened against the $ instead, to say $1.09, you'd have enjoyed a higher overall return of £1,990.83 (10 x $217) / $1.09).

There are mitigations, like using currency hedged instruments or sticking to local markets, but for a global investor who wants to utilise individual equities it's complicated. For fund investors a GBP (or your local currency) hedged fund is the easiest option as it's managed for you within the fund.

RISK TYPES: VOLATILITY RISK

Where an asset, sector or market exhibits price swing volatility which impacts portfolio valuation day to day. Highly volatile assets are great for intraday and short-term swing traders but can cause concern for investors who pay too much attention to daily or weekly swings in pricing. Generally if your outlook is over a long enough period (10 years or more) volatility is less of an issue as markets drift up and to the right.

The tech sector in traditional equities and the cryptocurrency market are known for their high volatility and wild price swings. As an example, look at our previous TSLA trade. TSLA is a tech stock on the US NASDAQ and those prices we used are actually accurate from the period of January 23 into February 23. A 113% move. Between February and April it declined 30% before surging a further 96% between April and August.

If you were Dollar Cost Averaging on a long-term time horizon you probably wouldn't care about the 30% pullback as you'd be significantly up overall. But if taking position at the first peak, seeing the 30% decline on your capital without the initial 113% increase, you'd likely be a little nervous! As explained though, for long-term investing this is rarely a concern, price volatility tends to be an issue for short-term traders with stocks historically trending upwards over long enough time horizons.

Mitigating volatility can be moot as it's this volatility that makes us return. But broadly speaking diversification across markets, sectors and geography works the same way here as the other risks in our list, reducing concentration to any single point of failure. One can utilise stop loss orders as well, but this is more of a trading risk management technique than investing.

RISK TYPES: MARKET TIMING RISK

"Time in the Market is better than Timing the Market", a succinct way of describing market timing risk. Attempting to time the market, to buy or sell investments at the "right time" is risky. Most can't do it with any consistency and anyone who says they sell tops and buy bottoms regularly is, in my experience, lying. As the saying goes "if you try to pick bottoms you get smelly fingers!".

Timing is a trading practice, not an investing one and even the best traders in the world don't get it right 100%. Trading "edge" (as we'll discuss later) is systematic and based on probability, including invalidation criteria to manage the risk of loss over the series. A win rate above 60% is excellent. Although I'll talk a little about trading, our focus is on long-term investing. Slow, boring and methodical to give ourselves the best opportunity to build wealth over time.

Timing market sells and buys doesn't work for most. The best mitigations against the temptation of market timing risk are diversification, patience and DCA. One can also deploy a "play" account to take calculated risk, a small amount separate from core.

RISK TYPES: BUSINESS SPECIFIC RISK

Sometimes referred to as "unsystematic risk" as it's specific to an individual company or industry. Things like changes in management structure, newly emerging competition, legal trouble or bad publicity due to failing products would be some of the examples of this risk materialising.

Our previous example of the SEC legal case brought against Ripple Labs would be an example of this risk, as well as political and regulatory risk, given the issue was limited to one single market participant. Another example would be the 2013 frozen lasagne and Bolognese storm, products found containing 60%-100% horse meat, not beef. This impacted suppliers like Findus, Tesco and Aldi through manufacturing issues at their supplier, Comigel. Where affected companies were traded publicly they saw an adverse impact on their share price.

Other than our old friend diversification and making sure we're not too heavily concentrated in one company, our best mitigation tactic is performing appropriate due diligence on any companies we invest in.

RISK TYPES: EVENT RISK

Anyone who lived through the last two decades doesn't need much of an explanation of Event Risk! Simply put, sudden and unexpected events like pandemics, wars, natural disasters, terrorist attacks or corporate scandals can have a significant impact on financial markets and investments.

2001 WTC, 2008 GFC, Covid & the Ukraine invasion are easily identifiable examples of event risk. In these examples you'll also recognise a few other risks we've mentioned already, it's common for more than one risk type to apply and materialise concurrently. Fig 13.2 from Trading View shows the SPX (US S&P 500 Index) with the last three events listed and their market impact marked. You can see the event risk materialisation broadly on the market (systematic and systemic risk too!) was negative.

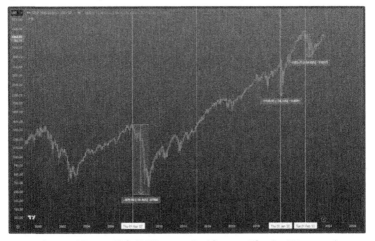

Fig 13.2 | Event Risk (GFC 2007, Covid 2020, Ukraine War 2022)

Moral questions aside, these can be opportunities for long-term investors who continue to DCA while price goes lower, lowering their cost basis. When the market recovers profit is higher. Those who these risks impact most are those in the drawdown phase of their pension or 401k, or those trying to time the market and getting it wrong. Diversification and DCA are mitigants here for builders, for those in drawdown de-risking to safer assets like fixed income or even an annuity can help mitigate.

RISK TYPES: LONGEVITY RISK

This one primarily affects retirees, those in the drawdown phase of their investment portfolio or pension. It describes the risk of outliving your savings due to increasing life expectancy, improved healthcare or as we discussed earlier underfunded retirement.

Our first mitigation for this unsurprisingly is to ensure we're building enough in the accumulation phase of our planning, which we know many aren't. We do this by planning, committing money to our future selves and tracking progress. We diversify these investments to suit our risk appetite. In the drawdown phase we can de-risk some or all of the account by moving into less risky instruments like bonds or gilts or we could even consider taking part of our fund in an annuity to guarantee a base level of income. We also need to manage lifestyle inflation in retirement as closely as before!

RISK TYPES: CONCENTRATION RISK

I've mentioned this a few times already so it shouldn't be a surprise to see it here. This refers to the risk of your portfolio being too "concentrated" in a specific asset, sector or investment type. If a significant portion of assets is concentrated in one area then adverse events affecting said area can lead to substantial losses. An example would be if your portfolio was 100% in Bitcoin (or 100% in cryptocurrency) at the end of its traditional four year cycle and standard 80%+ crash. There are many other risks in this example, but you certainly suffer from concentration risk as well!

No prizes for guessing the main mitigation for this one: diversification. Spreading investments across various markets, classes, assets, industries or geographic regions reduces the impact of negative developments in any single area.

RISK TYPES: OPERATIONAL RISK

Something many don't think about, this is the potential risk of loss resulting from inadequate processes, systems, human error or external events impacting instruments, platforms or brokers we utilise or even ourselves. It encompasses disruption in daily operations like technology failure, fraud or regulatory compliance issues or even security issues on our end (like a computer virus).

As this is specific to one area there's a crossover with concentration risk and the main mitigants are diversification of assets, proper investment review of individual companies we invest in and diligent security in our own practice.

RISK TYPES: SYSTEMIC RISK

This one has crossover with many risks already described, most similar to market risk but deserving its own distinct explanation. This is the risk an event like a financial crisis or economic downturn can destabilize the entire financial system, affecting multiple interconnected institutions, markets and classes. It's characterised by widespread market disruption leading to cascading impact on broader economies. Covid would be an excellent example of this as it impacted markets worldwide.

Mitigation for the retail investor in these scenarios is hugely difficult without exposing ourselves to other risks on our list, like market timing. Though not a popular technique, I do have a smaller percentage of my portfolio in a play fund where I regularly take profit into cash. This can help in these scenarios by at least providing capital to take advantage of any opportunities, reducing overall impact. Realistically we're at the mercy of the markets without taking different risks during materialisation (timing). We need to consider this holistically, selecting the least worst option.

RISK TYPES: DERIVATIVE RISK

I include this because you'll potentially see it listed inside KIID documents for ETF's or Funds, but it shouldn't be something retail investors need to worry too much about managing. It comes from trading instruments whose value is derived from an underlying asset, index or interest rate rather than the instrument itself. Common versions include futures and options. Derivatives are powerful tools for hedging and speculation but their intricate nature demands thorough understanding and as such they aren't suitable for inexperienced market participants.

One would mitigate this risk by not speculating with derivatives, using them only for hedging (taking opposing positions to make major fluctuations neutral, one position goes up as the other goes down for no profit or loss on the combination). Most won't need to factor this risk into thinking, they may just see it listed in Fund KIID's where the risk is managed on their behalf.

RISK TYPES: YOU RISK!

Not always on traditional lists but one I bring up with people almost every time I'm in a discussion about trading and investing strategies. We must acknowledge the biggest risk in the room can often be ourselves! Although we're undoubtedly best placed to manage our own finances, we can cause ourselves all sorts of problems when we try to get too clever or go off plan, when we succumb to fear or greed. The best way to mitigate the "You Risk" is to create a plan and stick to the plan unless it invalidates!

Market timing risk is one example where we believe we can beat the market. The data shows unequivocally this isn't the case, managed funds consistently underperform against unmanaged tracker funds. There are exceptions of course, like Fundsmith (By

Terry Smith) but overall passive funds are a historical better bet. This becomes more apparent over longer timeframes as fund managers do have decent individual years where they beat the market but numbers drop significantly as each year passes.

RISK TYPES: SUMMARY

The aim of this section is to help you understand some of the main risks from an investment perspective. We've only scratched the surface but hopefully it leaves you better placed to manage these risks in your journey.

Knowing your risk tolerance and investment goals is crucial in determining the right approach for you to manage these risks. This is generally the first thing a professional financial advisor does with new clients, some form of investor questionnaire. I think traditional investor types have become out dated but it's still a useful exercise so it's where we'll head next.

INVESTOR PROFILE: UNDERSTANDING YOU

Traditional profile categories have become a little outdated, so I've updated with my view on how they might be refreshed. One should remain cognisant these are fluid with degrees of overlap, so most investors display characteristics from multiple categories. It's unlikely to find a "Conservative" investor displaying attributes of a "Speculative" investor, but a "Growth" investor may indeed share some speculative qualities.

Don't be concerned if you can't find one you think you fit neatly into. These only exist to get you thinking about where you might fit to help inform decisions.

CONSERVATIVE INVESTORS (RISK: LOW) prioritise capital preservation and stability in portfolio value over high returns. They're risk-averse, preferring instruments like cash or cash equivalents, high-quality bonds and stable dividend-paying stocks that provide income. In the context of a retirement portfolio the closer one gets to retirement the more conservative they tend to be, reducing Risk On allocations and increasing cash instrument and fixed income allocations (Risk Off).

MODERATE INVESTORS (RISK: MODERATE) have a fairly balanced view of risk and reward, more willing to accept moderate risk for the potential of higher returns on at least some of their portfolio. Portfolios tend to be well diversified as a result with a mix of equities (stocks), bonds and sometimes even a small allocation to alternative (higher risk) asset classes like cryptocurrency. The popular 60/40 portfolios (equities/fixed income) fall into this category.

AGGRESSIVE INVESTORS (RISK: HIGH) Are much more comfortable taking higher levels of risk with more of their portfolio in exchange for potentially significant returns. They're more likely to invest in growth stocks, high-yield higher risk bonds, riskier assets like emerging market equities or more speculative asset classes like cryptocurrency.

GROWTH INVESTORS (RISK: HIGH) focus mainly on capital appreciation and long-term growth potential. This usually means higher weighting of Risk On classes like equities, with many younger growth investors allocating 80% to 100% of portfolio in this manner. They're willing to tolerate higher volatility in chosen instruments in pursuit of higher returns and tend to invest in growth oriented stocks, technology companies, cryptocurrency and industries with strong potential growth.

INCOME INVESTORS (RISK: MODERATE TO HIGH) prioritise regular income from investments, usually through selection of equities with a strong history of dividend payment, bonds with a regular coupon yield and real estate investment trusts (REITs) offering consistent payouts based on rent. Achieving a portfolio to cover an annual salary without drawdown on value is often the long-term goal so in the early years these investors dividends are reinvested automatically to capitalise on compounding.

INCOME AND GROWTH INVESTORS (RISK: MODERATE TO HIGH) are a combination of the previous two categories, aiming for balanced portfolios which provide both income and potential growth. This leads to a more diversified portfolio and selection of dividend paying equities or funds, bonds and an allocation to more growth oriented stocks like those in the technology sector.

SPECULATIVE INVESTORS (RISK: VERY HIGH) are more than willing to take significant risk with large parts of their portfolio in the hopes of achieving substantial gains, usually in shorter periods of time. Often invest in highly volatile assets and asset classes where total loss is a possibility, like early-stage startups, unproven investment types or unregulated markets like cryptocurrency. Often, these investor types are inexperienced and chasing fast return, or in a position financially where total loss is of no detriment to their overall situation.

VALUE INVESTORS (RISK: MODERATE TO HIGH) seek undervalued assets they believe to be trading below their intrinsic value. Warren Buffet and Charlie Munger built Berkshire

Hathaway as investors concentrating on value. These investors seek out equities, bonds and other investments they believe undervalued by the market, usually by focussing on the fundamentals of the company. This creates expectation these investments appreciate over time.

IMPACT/ESG INVESTORS (RISK: INSTRUMENT DEPENDENT) are a fairly new category who prioritise around instruments aligned with their ethical, social and environmental values. In recent times many of them have reduced exposure to Oil and Gas extraction companies and replaced with perceived "Green Energy" companies or funds. In general they look for companies or projects contributing positively to society and the planet. Many Investors, even when not fully Impact/ESG, will look to allocate a portion of their portfolio to ESG type instruments.

RETIREMENT INVESTORS (RISK: MODERATE): are focused on building retirement portfolios to support post work goals, usually through a mix of income and growth oriented instruments. Generally they're similar to Conservative Investors though with specific retirement goals in mind. They tend to reduce exposure to Risk On classes as they get closer to retirement to protect capital.

This completes my updated version of standard investor types. It's important to remember individuals can span categories and risk tolerance isn't fixed. Changing personal circumstances, market conditions or financial goals cause risk tolerance to increase or decrease so it's important to review at least annually to rebalance your portfolio as required.

In my experience most people who start their investing journey with the goal of building wealth fall into the "Growth Investor" category. This includes pension and investment account savers. Most don't want to get into the weeds of markets and be picking individual assets, which is higher risk in any event, they want to assign money regularly and watch it grow in the background.

"If you don't find a way to make money while you sleep, you will work until you die"

[Warren Buffet | $Billion Investor]

Assuming you're young enough to have a ten to twenty (or more) year outlook, an 80% to 100% Risk On allocation and dollar cost averaging into low fee index funds on a regular basis is a solid strategy for most. This would sit you right in the growth category. Some will think 80% to 100% Risk On is too high, with the traditional 60/40 and moderate investor profiles in mind. This is absolutely fine, we must each make our own decision about allocation and the risk we're willing to accept.

MANAGEMENT: SPLITTING FUNDS & F*CK AROUND, FIND OUT

If you're inclined to dive deeper and learn the intricacies of markets you can perhaps look to assign some (not all!) capital to learning, keeping your primary goal of risk management in mind. For example, I like markets (as you can tell!), it's been a hobby for two decades. One thing those two decades have taught me, unequivocally, is like most fund managers I **cannot** consistently beat the market. I'll have some wins, sure, but consistently I underperform trying to "time" it (remember our risk). But, I enjoy the challenge and one decent win can make it profitable over years!

So, I assign 85%-90% of my portfolio to all-world index accumulation funds (two at the moment) and consider this my "Core Portfolio". My pensions are separate, also invested in index funds and part of "Core". I do this index fund investing via my ISA and don't touch it as my time outlook is long. I just keep feeding money in and (hopefully) watch it grow. The other 10%-15% is my "Moonshot Portfolio", or "F*ck Around, Find Out Portfolio" if you prefer! This allows me a capital allocation to play with, to identify opportunities, to learn and to try to beat the market. Having these two allocations completely separate is how I manage the "me" risk. If I do something silly in the Moonshot Portfolio it doesn't affect long-term plans. If I do well there though, I rebalance proceeds into the long-term core to maintain target split. This is where I look at emerging asset classes like cryptocurrency, do all my active trading and where I pick individual stocks based on technical analysis (another hobby).

This is a common approach, one many of my peers within the financial sphere operate. It allows for a growth portfolio which over time should reflect the wider market performance but also allows for some learning and experimentation without breaking anything. This is a risk management technique you may consider.

MANAGEMENT: DOLLAR COST AVERAGING (DCA) REMINDER

I've mentioned DCA a few times. It's also a long-term risk management strategy, so let's remind ourselves what it is with an example to illustrate. DCA describes the act of regularly investing an amount into a predefined set of investments over time, regardless of market conditions. It aims to reduce the impact of market volatility (volatility risk) on the average cost (book cost) of investments and provide better long-term return than trying to "Time the Market" (market timing risk). For those paying regularly into pensions, this is DCA. The same amount is invested each pay period, buying however much of the predefined assets or funds it can with the expectation it trends up over time.

For example, let's say you invest £1,000 for 10 months into an all-world index ETF (Exchange Traded Fund):

- Month 1: Invest £1,000 at £50 per share (20 units).
- Month 2: Invest £1,000 at £45 per share (22.22 units).
- Month 3: Invest £1,000 at £55 per share (18.18 units)
  ....
- Month 10: Invest £1,000 at £40 per share (25 units).

In this example your investment is £10,000, for a total units purchased of 225.77. The average price is (£10,000/225.77) £44.31 per unit.

Alternatively, you invest the entire £10,000 upfront at the initial price of £50 per share. Here the investment is £10,000, for a total units purchased of 200. After one year, the stock rebounds from initial drawdown and reaches a price of £60:

- Dollar Cost Averaging:
  o Current Value: £60 * 225.77 units = £13,546.20
  o Total Return: £13,546.20 - £10,000 = £3,546.20
- Timing The Market:
  o Current Value: £60 * 200 units = £12,000
  o Total Return: £12,000 - £10,000 = £2,000

In this example, using DCA methodology to continue during drawdown resulted in larger returns overall, +35.46%/£1,546.20. 77% more than the +20%/£2,000. DCA helped smooth out price fluctuations, lowering average price and enabling higher return when price recovered. DCA isn't guaranteed to outperform lump sum investing in all scenarios, nothing's ever guaranteed. However, the strategy has been shown consistently to outperform timing the market over long time horizons for most people. An often overlooked benefit is it helps manage emotional stress when making single large investments by feeding in gradually for an average price. Hopefully this provides a better understanding of why DCA is such a powerful risk management strategy. It's the most efficient method for most people, as always though personal circumstances vary so you must decide what's right for you.

MANAGEMENT: DIVERSIFICATION

I won't labour this as it's a little like telling you how to suck eggs, but I've mentioned it as a key risk management practice in investing so should define briefly to avoid doubt. Diversification is the act of ensuring your portfolio is split across asset classes at the top level then sectors and geography at the second level. Generally one defines how much they want to allocate to each of the major classes something like:

- Equities: 70%, Fixed Income: 10%, Commodities: 5%, Real Estate: 5%, Cash: 5% and Cryptocurrency: 5%

This defines the target top level allocation to each asset class which can then be broken down individually within by sector and where applicable geography. For example, in equities you may want to split:

- 50% USA, 15% UK & Europe, 25% Asia and 10% Asia Emerging.
- Technology:50%, Financial Services:20%, Healthcare: 15% and Consumer Defensive: 15%.

These numbers aren't recommendations, they simply highlight diversification of a portfolio on two levels as a risk management technique. We'll get into this further in the investing chapter.

MANAGEMENT: REBALANCING A PORTFOLIO

This will make more sense after the investing chapter but it's an important risk management concept so I want to make sure we cover it. Rebalancing your portfolio to make sure you remain within target allocations is the way we manage risks associated to allocation and diversification.

This won't apply where allocated entirely to ETF's or Funds in a core portfolio as the rebalancing is done within these instruments automatically in line with the Key Investor Information Document (KIID).

If managing a portfolio of assets yourself though, rebalancing will be required. In simple terms, as valuations of assets within your portfolio change so will the percentage balance of your portfolio. If you have, for example, 80% equities, 15% fixed income and 5% cryptocurrency allocation at the start of a Bitcoin bull market, odds are (given volatility in Bitcoin) cryptocurrency allocation will grow as prices go up, so in % terms equities and fixed income shrink.

On your regular rebalance cadence (quarterly, bi-annually or annually for example) you'd rebalance this to manage risk by taking profits from cryptocurrency positions and investing into equities and fixed income to return to your target 80/15/5. When dealing with volatile instruments like cryptocurrency this is an important part of overall risk management, forcing you to redistribute within your portfolio. It also helps to manage your greed: many cryptocurrency investors hold to the top of the bubble then all the way back down when Bitcoin crashes 85%. They try to squeeze out another 10%, often having made 300%+ already. Redistribution is a mechanical method for managing this risk and forcing you not to fall victim to this type of greed.

For those who take more active roles in portfolio management, even just a small portion in a "FAFO" allocation, getting into the habit of rebalancing regularly is good risk management practice. Commonly this is done quarterly, but whatever timescale suits your needs is fine. Any lower than quarterly arguably becomes trading over investing so personally I review quarterly and my rebalance average is between bi-annually (6 months) and annually.

MANAGEMENT: SCORING

When utilising the Fund variations we'll discuss in the next chapter, risk scoring and commentary is provided for investors in the KIID to help with decision making. KIID's are available on all UK platforms where one can invest in the instrument. It outlines fund objectives, the benchmark or index it aims to track, performance history, how derivatives will be used and so on.

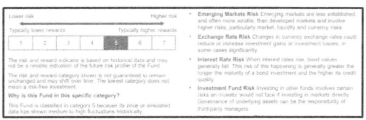

Fig 13.3| Example KIID Risk Profile Section

The risk profile and specific risks the provider thinks apply will be detailed for consideration in a format like Fig 13.3. This makes it easier for investors to identify risk levels suited to their appetite. One should always review the KIID prior to investing in any fund, they contain useful detail to help shape our decision making.

SUMMARY

This is an important chapter and one where I've had to reign in what I could have written to keep it succinct! I focus on risk primarily in my investing and trading so it's a subject I could write an entire book about in its own right. But few people would want to read **that** book! (hopefully more want to read this one!)

When trying to grow wealth through investing, understanding the risks, how they materialise and how we mitigate them through strong risk management practice is vital for our long-term success. Risk Manager first, everything else after. We've discussed the different types of risk to look out for and risk management strategies like:

- **DIVERSIFICATION:** Mentioned in almost every risk description, spreading investments across different asset classes, sectors and geography to reduce the impact of risks materialising in any single area. In general this also helps mitigate against the risk of poor performance in any single class, sector or locale.

- **REGULAR REBALANCING:** Track your target allocation versus current portfolio periodically and adjust to maintain desired asset allocation. This keeps it in line with long-term objectives and also forces you to take profit on positions doing well, helping to fight greed. I also mentioned my Core/FAFO portfolio split allowing me some funds to play without impacting the long-term. Maintaining this balance is part of my rebalancing routine.

- **RISK ASSESSMENT:** Regularly evaluate and reassess risk tolerance and financial goals. This is part of understanding what type of investor you are and what risk you're willing to take to meet your goals. Our "Investor Profile".

- **AVOIDING MARKET TIMING:** I've mentioned this so many times you should realise it's an important one! Focus on the long-term as an investor rather than attempting to time the market, which is notoriously difficult. You've no idea the number of people I have the pleasure of helping **after** they've tripped themselves up through either lack of patience or through forgetting the unequivocal truth: **the market is always right.**

- **DOLLAR-COST AVERAGING:** Invest regularly regardless of market conditions to reduce the impact of market volatility over time. Super simple, fire and forget, no management really required outside of annual rebalancing.

- **EMERGENCY FUND:** Pulling from previous conversations to add to this summary, maintain an emergency fund to cover unexpected expenses and avoid the need to liquidate investments during market downturns. Don't put yourself in a position you're forced to crystalise a loss you didn't need to, like Silicon Valley Bank!
- **STAY INFORMED:** Monitor economic conditions, market trends and changes in the investment landscape to make informed decisions. Look out for the wider economic risks we discussed, those coming from interest rates, political & regulatory changes or wider market conditions. Even if not doing much with your portfolio to mitigate market timing risk it may still present opportunities with any cash allocation while "there's blood on the streets" and you can hear the sirens.

Take risk management seriously. I cannot put it any more plainly. It's not the most exciting subject, boring many tell me (and more often than you know!) but to hark back to one of the themes of this book: risk management is something successful investors (and traders) do very well but unsuccessful investors (and traders) do poorly or not at all.

Correlation in this instance I do believe is causation. So which one do you want to be?

ACTIONS

No specific actions in the Financial Plan, all I want you to do is decide which Investor Profile you think you fall into before we move to investing detail. This will help inform your risk tolerance and assist in building your target portfolio allocation. This can change over time, so don't worry about picking the wrong one now! I think most start out as either growth or moderate investors, so take a look there to begin with.

14

Investing Demystified

"Never depend on a single income. Make an investment to create a second source."

[Warren Buffet | Multi $Billion Investor]

WE'VE REFERENCED INVESTING OFTEN IN our journey, mainly to model the impact of financial decisions against potential returns over time. In this chapter we'll dive deeper into investing itself, a subject both complex and fascinating.

I can't hope to relay full depth of investing knowledge in a single chapter, many full books are devoted to investing and themselves only scratch the surface. We can though endeavour to spark your interest with a detailed introductory overview which can be used alongside our risk discussion to start your investing journey in a safer, more informed manner.

Studies like the Global Wealth Report by Credit Suisse consistently show the stock market has driven more wealth creation than most other endeavours. Real estate, business building and entrepreneurship are all excellent pursuits and I'd never claim investing the universal "right option" for everyone. For average people with day jobs though it's the most accessible, least onerous, lowest barrier to entry way to realise the dream of becoming millionaires (or our aim of financially free).

I'll cover trading separately to highlight the difference as I find many people conflate the two to their detriment. I'm a proponent of both, enjoying their unique challenges, but I understand the different risks involved and have specific strategies to manage them. I also segregate trading from investments, as described by my Moonshot portfolio. With DCA, risk types and risk management techniques freshly in mind then let's dive into the ocean of investing, firstly by looking at available instruments.

If you're completely new to markets this instrument overview could become overwhelming, I remember this from my learning. Please, don't be deterred by perceived complexity though, time and energy are all you require and it takes different amounts for different people. Give yourself enough of both. Markets are hugely complex and capable of consuming time and capital in equal measure but we can simplify our processes to build strong, risk managed portfolios that return positive outcomes over time.

Let's start by introducing the best available simplification option for everyday people with limited time to devote to managing investments: different types of funds.

DISCLAIMER REMINDER

The information provided here isn't financial or investment advice. Investing involves risk. You must conduct your own research, consider risk tolerance and if required consult qualified financial professionals before making investment decisions. The value of investments can go down as well as up and past performance doesn't guarantee future results. Always verify information from reliable sources and tailor investment decisions to your own specific circumstances. All decisions are your own, take this accountability seriously.

FUNDS | MUTUAL FUNDS, OEICS & UNIT TRUSTS

Disclaimer behind us let's start with Mutual Funds, OEICs and Unit Trusts, broadly similar fund types with different names in different locales. In the US and Canada they tend to be known as "Mutual Funds" while the UK and Europe tend to refer to them as "Open Ended Investment Companies" (OEICs), "Unit Trusts", or simply "Funds".

Although there are some technical differences, they're all funds that pool investor money to invest in diversified portfolios of assets like equities, bonds, cash instruments and commodities. They're often managed by professional portfolio managers who buy and sell assets within target markets to maintain the target fund balance and provide capital gain. They can also be passive funds aiming to track a defined index or "benchmark" where instruments auto balance based on the benchmark.

They generally offer accumulation and income variants, defining what happens to any dividends paid by holdings. In accumulation funds all dividends are automatically reinvested and in income funds dividends are paid into investor brokerage accounts as cash. Rolling over dividends (accumulation) is beneficial due to long-term compounding effects, especially for young investors.

In the UK the KIID (Key Investor Information Document) and factsheet outline to prospective investors the aims of the fund, asset classes, how the fund is managed, the balance target or benchmark it'll track, the risk profile and geographic spread. This allows investors to select funds suiting their diversification target.

The primary differences lie in legal structures. Unit Trusts issue units to investors, while OEIC's and Mutual Funds issue shares. I personally like OEIC's (as they tend to be low fee) and utilise two within my core portfolio, both all world index trackers (accumulation).

Be aware these fund variants aren't "Exchange Traded" so not all platforms offer access. Some brokers, including most low cost or zero commission variants, only offer ETFs. Some platforms that offer these instruments charge larger than normal fees to hold them on your behalf too, so always check to avoid paying larger fees which impact heavily on portfolio growth over time. Not being exchange traded also means settlement can take a few days so plan for this when buying in or selling out.

FUNDS | EXCHANGE TRADED FUNDS (ETF):

Almost identical in concept, ETFs offer investors exposure to multiple assets and asset classes via single instruments. One can DCA with the convenience of someone managing and rebalancing on their behalf or tracking a benchmark just the same, based on KIID and factsheet definitions. There are thousands of ETFs designed to track against all manner of goals and risk appetite.

The main difference is ETFs are traded, as the name implies, on exchange like a regular equity or commodity. Prices update in real time rather than (typically) once per day, they're more liquid (settlement is generally faster), fund management fees can be low (especially passive funds) and platforms tend not to charge additional fees to hold them. We also have accumulation or income options in many ETFs. They're another cheap, simple option for anyone looking to start investing without management overhead and available on pretty much every platform/broker.

As an analogy, think of ETFs (and other funds) like a streaming service offering a collection of diverse content (assets) in one single subscription (fund). Investors access a broad range of shows (stocks, bonds, commodities) without individually purchasing each one and having to manage them as different subscriptions. They're a convenient, cost effective way to diversify investments without actively managing a portfolio.

FUNDS | HEDGE FUNDS

These are typically only open to accredited investors, not "retail" (us). They employ various strategies to generate returns and have more flexibility in terms of assets, derivatives and alternative investments. Fees are structured differently, fund managers often levy a 2% annual fee with an additional 20% of any profit made over and above declared targets (the "hurdle rate"). You often hear this called "two and twenty". I include these for completeness, but they're not of much concern for us in the retail majority.

FUNDS | MONEY MARKET FUNDS (MMF)

Cash equivalent funds investing in short-term, low-risk securities like treasury bills and commercial paper. They often aim to return close to or in excess of the central bank rate. They're highly liquid instruments used to provide stability for modest return, most often "defensively". MMFs aim to maintain a NAV (Net Asset Value) of 1 (unit of currency). NAV is calculated by dividing Total Net Assets (all assets minus any liabilities) by number of outstanding shares. If this falls below 1 the fund "broke the buck". The aim is to provide modest growth without breaking the buck.

I currently utilise a UK MMF tracking SONIA, the Sterling Overnight Index Average. It represents the average interest rate banks and financial institutions pay to borrow unsecured funds in the overnight market. This fund currently returns ~5.0% annually for minimal risk. It's an efficient place to park some "Moonshot" portfolio cash, gaining reasonable return while waiting for opportunities. MMFs tend to be "Exchange Traded" too, so they're available on most platforms.

FUNDS | REAL ESTATE INVESTMENT TRUSTS (REIT)

REITs allow Investors to gain exposure to real estate rental return without having to buy bricks and mortar property. The barrier to entry is much lower, providing a level of income through real estate owned by the fund. Commercial, residential or mixed variants exist and can be good options for those who want yield generating property exposure in their portfolio.

FUNDS SUMMARY

Funds are a diversified collection (or basket) of assets, balanced on your behalf as defined in the KIID and factsheet. Balance is managed by fund managers (active) or by tracking a benchmark (passive) making it easy for retail investors to gain market exposure in a risk managed fashion without the overhead of managing a portfolio manually. One can select a fund (or funds) to DCA monthly and those funds automate the process of buying multiple other instruments for us. We don't have to do any more. They can even contain other funds in their asset lists.

This is the simplest, lowest risk way for **anyone** to enter the market for the first time. One can pick something like an all-world index tracker, or S&P 500 tracker or FTSE Tracker. Whatever we choose the fund does the management for us (for a small fee).

My preference is to utilise all world index tracker funds and I've two in my core portfolio just now. One includes emerging markets and excludes UK, the other excludes emerging markets with a small UK allocation. This provides the diversification I desire. You may feel such trackers the way for you to take your first steps into the world of investing and many don't go any further than this very successfully (assuming they're patient).

There are other types of funds than those listed, like growth, commodity, equity, ethical, bond and so on. The general construct of these is broadly the same as described just the makeup of assets within vary to suit the goal of the fund. Ultimately I consider these variations of either the ETF or Mutual Funds/OEIC/Unit Trusts.

INVESTING FEES

Fee consideration is important when selecting platforms and funds as they can cost you significantly over time.

Most higher end platforms like Hargreaves Lansdown or Interactive Investor in the UK charge PLATFORM FEES to host your portfolio. Pension funds do the same. For some it's a percentage of portfolio value, for others a flat monthly fee. I personally utilise a platform with a fixed monthly fee for my core portfolio as it saves me thousands of pounds per year over one charging a percentage of account value. Over thirty years of compounding thousands per year is quite significant! Some platforms, like Trading 212, don't charge any platform fees.

(FUND) MANAGEMENT FEES are sometimes called the "Expense Ratio" and apply to individual Funds or ETF's. These are charged as a percentage of fund valuation. Generally these are listed in the KIID, factsheet, broker analytics platform plus during fund selection and it's common for savvy investors to filter potential funds they're considering based on these fees. Anything below 0.1% is excellent, between 0.1% and 0.2% OK. Anything higher I'd consider on a case by case basis but they're "expensive". These don't apply to individual stocks, only to funds.

Brokerages and investment platforms also charge TRADING FEES within your account(s), the price you pay for buying or selling a position. Zero commission brokers waive this, others charge flat fees per trade, some take a percentage of position size. Some platforms allow regular investing without trading fees (monthly DCA) and some offer set numbers of free trades per month depending on membership.

These fees can add up and given they're paid from account the larger the fee the larger the impact from a compound perspective. For example, a fixed monthly fee platform can potentially save between £24,000 and £50,000 in fees over 30 years. At 6% the lower £24,000 saving (£800 per year averaged for illustration purposes) equates to ~£67k opportunity cost in fees. So make sure you understand all applicable fees and charges, selecting a reputable platform that won't break the bank! There are a couple of other potential fees worthy of mention:

- **ADVISOR FEES:** If working with financial advisors who set up investments on your behalf it's not uncommon they levy perpetual fees at 1% - 3% of account value. I don't like this fee model so tend to avoid it given long-term impact. As I explained earlier though if an advisor beats the market by 6% by taking 3% it provides benefit. If you're being charged ensure it's earned on an ongoing basis. Most reputable advisors shouldn't have an issue with such stipulations.

- **INACTIVITY FEES:** Some platforms charge fees if there's no trading activity within specified periods. Personally I wouldn't use such a platform, but be aware if this is a stipulation of any you consider for you.

I dislike high street banks for investment ISA's and default company pension funds partly for fee reasons. They tend to have higher fees and offer more limited investment options. I prefer managing my ISA on a low fee platform, selecting low fee funds and trading core portfolio minimally to reduce trading fees. I utilise zero commission brokers for my moonshot portfolio so I can trade with no fees or platform fee. In 2023 this presents a tax overhead outside my ISA but regulation changes for 2024 mean we can fund multiple ISA's in the same year so will mitigate this. Pensions I prefer to move into lower cost, higher equity allocation funds but workplace providers options are limited. As discussed in the pension chapter, we shouldn't always stick with the default funds allocated, they're often sub optimal. So review what your pension's being invested into and make sure it's working optimally for you.

Many good platforms exist, so review those available within your geography to select those most suitable for you. Fee structure should be part of this consideration, no doubt.

ASSET CLASSES: INTRODUCTION

Having outlined the various funds available to us and explained how these are the easiest and most common way for retail investors to start their investing journey, let's look at the different instruments within these funds. One can of course invest in these directly too. Don't worry about information overload on first read, you can easily spend your entire investing life in low cost funds never concerning yourself with any of this lower level detail. For those who want to understand a little more though, lets dive in!

ASSET CLASSES: EQUITIES (STOCKS & SHARES)

The staple of most portfolios, directly or via funds. Equities, also known as stocks, shares or securities, are shares in publicly traded companies. Owning them means you own equity in the company so you'll be able to vote as a shareholder and if the company pays a dividend you'll be eligible on a per share basis. One can purchase full shares and with some platforms even fractional (partial) shares as well, helping those with less capital to build equity.

Equities are traded on various worldwide exchanges, the most well-known being New York, London, Frankfurt and Tokyo and they can be split further into different market sectors depending on the type of company. This is useful for portfolio diversification as different market sectors react differently to wider macro-economic conditions. Experienced investors sometimes position some or all of their portfolio based on these (projected) market conditions, attempting to protect capital or to maximise gains.

When investing in equities one should be aware of the different types available and their key attributes.

COMMON STOCKS typically come with voting rights in corporate decisions and may receive dividends when the company distributes profits. They offer potential for capital appreciation but also come with higher volatility compared to other types of equities. Stockholders are also "residual claimants" meaning they have last claim on any assets after company obligations are met.

PREFERRED STOCKS have characteristics of both stocks and bonds, offering a fixed dividend payment similar to bond interest but usually without voting rights. Shareholders have priority over common shareholders when it comes to receiving dividends and assets in the event of a company's liquidation.

GROWTH STOCKS are from companies expected to experience above average earnings growth who may not pay dividends as they reinvest profit to expand operations.

VALUE STOCKS are companies considered undervalued based on fundamental analysis. There are many different ways to value companies from simple price to earnings to much more complex methodologies. Value (and patience!) made Buffet a Billionaire.

DIVIDEND STOCKS consistently pay dividends and can provide regular income in addition to potential capital appreciation.

FOREIGN AND INTERNATIONAL STOCKS are from companies outside your home market. Investing in these offers exposure to global markets and geographic diversification.

SMALL CAP STOCKS come from smaller companies with lower market capitalisation (sometimes called "penny stocks"). These can offer higher growth potential but are also higher risk due to their smaller size and potentially lower liquidity.

MID CAP STOCKS fall between large cap and small cap in terms of market capitalisation. They offer a balance between growth potential and risk.

LARGE CAP STOCKS are from well established companies with significant market capitalisation. These are often considered more stable and less risky compared to smaller companies.

BLUE CHIP STOCKS come from large, well-established and financially stable companies with a long history of consistent performance. These are considered less volatile and associated with lower risk compared to small, less established companies.

In addition to stock types there are also generally accepted market sectors in which companies fall. These are commonly grouped into three "parent" classes: **CYCLICAL, DEFENSIVE** and **SENSITIVE**. These are further divided within.

CYCLICAL instruments are sensitive to business cycles, including their highs and lows. It splits into four sub-categories:

- **BASIC MATERIALS:** Companies like building materials, chemicals, paper, commodity exploration and commodity processing (Oil, Gas or Gold for example).
- **CONSUMER CYCLICAL:** Companies like retail, automotive (including parts), construction (residential) and entertainment.

- **FINANCIAL SERVICES:** Companies like banks, savings & loan, asset management, credit, brokerage and insurance.
- **REAL ESTATE:** Companies like property management, mortgage and REIT companies (not the REITs themselves).

DEFENSIVE instruments are non-cyclical, meaning things generally always "required" by consumers regardless of market conditions and not so sensitive to business cycles. It splits into three sub-categories:

- **CONSUMER DEFENSIVE:** Companies selling "living" items (like grocery stores), manufacture of food and drink, personal products, household products, packaging, tobacco, education and services.
- **HEALTH:** Companies like pharma, bio, medical research, healthcare, home healthcare, long-term care and medical equipment.
- **UTILITIES:** Companies supplying gas, electricity and water.

SENSITIVE instruments are similar to cyclical in that they're sensitive to business cycles, but not quite as correlated. It splits into four sub-categories:

- **COMMUNICATIONS:** Companies like fixed line or wireless networks, internet services, internet related companies and software companies.
- **ENERGY:** Companies that produce oil or gas, oil field services & equipment, pipelines, coal mines and nuclear.
- **INDUSTRIALS:** Companies that manufacture machinery, hand held tools, aerospace, defence and logistics.
- **TECHNOLOGY:** Companies supplying computing equipment, OS and software, technology consulting, data storage, networking equipment, semiconductors and components.

SECTORS EXAMPLE

To help understand how we use this information, imagine for example technology companies like Apple (AAPL) or Microsoft (MSFT) as something investors want to sell (some of) in a recession event, for perhaps consumer defensive companies like Walmart (WMT) or healthcare companies like Johnson & Johnson (JNJ). Why? In recession discretionary consumer electronics spending would be assumed to reduce as consumer spending power reduces. But everyone needs to eat or use medicine regardless of economic conditions. Those sectors are still impacted, but potentially less.

Fig 14.1 is an example from the 2008 GFC. Top is Apple Inc. (AAPL) and bottom Walmart (WMT). You can see when Apple had its initial drawdown of 42%, Walmart actually went up 4.6%. In the subsequent event Apple dropped 50% (having recovered much of its initial drawdown) versus Walmart which lost 21.34%. I'm not suggesting 21% drawdown is desirable, but it's better than 50% drawdown! In any event the actual drawdown on Walmart over the full period was 1.77% (Dec 2007 to Feb 2009), over which time Apple lost 57% value. This is defensive positioning.

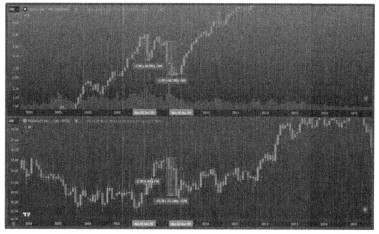

Fig 14.1 | Example from 2008 GFC (from Trading View)

Retail investors tend to be unsuccessful when trying to position equities portfolios this way. This is market timing risk and "you" risk. This example is to illustrate sector relationships only. Equity types and sectors are useful to know and can help shape decision making, but the reality for most retail investors is they can do more harm than good messing too much with core allocations.

ASSET CLASSES: FIXED INCOME (BONDS, T-BILLS & GILTS)

The Ying to equities Yang. The duo of fixed income instruments and equities have long been staples in traditional portfolios like the moderate 60/40 portfolio or growth 80/20. The smaller number is fixed income allocation and is viewed as a hedge against equity volatility. The expectation is these asset classes move (mostly) counter to each other, so if equities draw down then fixed income should grow, hedging some of the losses. As we saw in the early 2020's this isn't universally the case in high rate, high debt, high inflation, expansionary monetary policy times! Some might say "high" policymakers too! Nevertheless, these portfolio constructs are still popular.

There are various fixed income instruments, ranging from lower risk/lower return government bonds (like US Treasuries or UK Gilts) to riskier corporate bonds, all the way down to extreme risk junk bonds. These instruments are debt, where investors provide loans and assume risks similar to those a bank would when providing loans to the public. In return the investor gets a "fixed income" by way of the coupon interest and their principal is paid back on maturity, in both cases assuming normal operation of the borrowing entity. Governments rarely default making those safer but generally lower return. Corporate debt can offer higher return but companies also present higher default (credit) risk for those potential returns. Fig 14.2 shows standard debt ratings. Potential quality is top to bottom: high to low and associated risk is top to bottom: low to high.

Moody's	Fitch	Standard & Poors	Notes	
Aaa	AAA	AAA	Prime. Considered very low risk	Investment Grade
Aa1	AA+	AA+	High Grade Debt. Presumed relatively low risk	
Aa2	AA	AA		
Aa3	AA-	AA-		
A1	A+	A+	Upper Medium Grade Debt. Risk is increasing.	
A2	A	A		
A3	A-	A-		
Baa1	BBB+	BBB+	Low Medium Grade Debt. The lowest level considered "Investment Grade", further increased risk.	
Baa2	BBB+	BBB+		
Baa3	BBB-	BBB-		
Ba1	BB+	BB+	Non Investment Grade Debt. Considered Speculative	Non Investment Grade ("Junk")
Ba2	BB	BB		
Ba3	BB-	BB-		
B1	B+	B+	Highly Speculative, High Risk Debt.	
B2	B	B		
B3	B-	B-		
Caa1	CCC	CCC+	Carries Substantial Risk. Extreme Speculation	
Caa2	-	CCC		
Caa3	-	CCC-	Debt Default is considered imminent with little to no prospect for recovery. Assume Total Loss.	
Ca	CC	CC		
C	C	C		
-	D	D	Confirmed as being In Default. Assume Total Loss	

Fig 14.2 | Debt Rating Agencies Example

Investment grade fixed income instruments are generally less risk than equity but offer lower potential return as a result. Active bonds can be traded, the bond market one of the largest and most liquid in the world, but when selling a bond before maturity you should be aware of interest rate risk. If rates have risen then newly issued bonds will likely offer higher yield than yours, reducing its value. In this instance you may suffer a capital loss from selling.

Fixed income instruments are often utilised in portfolios to provide income generation (coupon yield), to preserve capital as part of risk management strategy or in certain circumstances as a hedge. For example, retirees drawing down from their portfolio often move more into bonds trying to protect capital value.

There are many ways one can define fixed income market sectors. We could use simple "Investment Grade" and "Non-Investment Grade (Junk)" categories shown in Fig 14.2, or use the individual ratings for each instrument. My preference though, throughout my investing life, utilises four categories.

GOVERNMENT (LOW RISK) uses instruments like T-Bills, Bonds or Gilts to provide capital to (highly rated) governments in exchange for fixed return over set periods. They carry low (near zero) risk. If the UK or US Government stopped paying debts the whole system would implode and we'd have much larger problems than investment loss! They're lower return as a result of lower risk.

CORPORATE (MEDIUM RISK) uses anything down to around A+/A1 corporate debt, generally from blue chip, high market cap and well established companies. These operate in the same way, set return over a set period. As they're a little more risky they usually offer slightly higher yield.

HIGH RISK CORPORATE is the remainder of "Investment Grade" corporate bonds down to BBB-/Baa3. It's a broad category and I don't ever feel the need to utilise it. From a risk perspective I prefer equities to these as the potential return is higher for similar risk. They operate the same, set return over a set period with potentially higher return for the higher risk they present.

JUNK (ULTRA-HIGH RISK) is everything BB+/Ba1 and below, the "Non-Investment Grade" category. They offer much higher risk for the potential of higher return, but remember if companies fail your principal is lost. You essentially risk 100% capital often for ~10% potential return. That Risk:Reward is 10:1. For comparison, the risk on a UK Gilt, though notionally similar at 100% capital risk, has a far lower probability of materialising for only marginally lower yield.

Fixed income instruments are certainly useful for many reasons, especially when looking to be defensive about a portfolio. Interest rate risk, market risk and regulatory risk (among others) still apply, but the likelihood of materialisation reduces in these lower risk instruments. Fixed income can generally be considered "defensive" posture.

ASSET CLASSES: REAL ESTATE

Most people understand property, either investors want ongoing yield from rental return or capital growth from the asset, sometimes both. Owning physical property though comes with overhead and risk. Some people navigate this well, building successful businesses. Others struggle. But many are unaware exposure to property and rental income is available without physical bricks and mortar, other instruments are available directly inside investment portfolios.

DIRECT OWNERSHIP of brick and mortar property is an option, either fully capitalised or more commonly via leverage (mortgage) with the aim of using rent to cover debt service. This carries obligations as a landlord and the associated risks of dealing with tenants (like non-payment, legal costs, rising interest rates or non-occupancy). Many build successful businesses around this model but it's not for everyone. The barrier to entry in terms of money, time and energy required is high.

REAL ESTATE INVESTMENT TRUSTS (REITs) have a lower barrier to entry as they allow investors via brokerage accounts or investment platforms to buy equity in a trust which pools investor money to buy property. Investors benefit from their share in the rental yields and capital appreciation. This provides property exposure without purchase, maintenance or management of the property or its tenants. It can be useful where property is part of a diversification strategy without the management overhead or risk.

REAL ESTATE FUNDS are similar to REITs, pooled funds investing in a wide range of real estate sectors. You can find funds that traverse all sectors or specific funds that only invest in, for example, residential property or commercial property.

REAL ESTATE ETFS are similar, presenting different real estate benchmark options. As with real estate funds these may contain a wide range of sectors or be specific to a few like commercial or agricultural.

REAL ESTATE CROWDFUNDING is a relatively new option listed for completeness but with caveats. It isn't be my cup of tea given the counterparty risk involved. In essence there are online platforms which facilitate the crowdsourcing of real estate investment through a pooled model similar to funds but without the fund management company. It seems ultra-high risk to me, so of absolutely no interest, but you may like the idea.

There are options then to add property exposure to a portfolio without buying physical property. I personally carry less than 3% property via a REIT inside my pension, but this is just personal preference. There's nothing wrong with property exposure it's just not my taste. You may feel differently thus the options listed give you some ideas other than traditional property ownership.

Real estate market sectors provide further options to consider. Many REITs, funds and ETFs will allocate across these sectors to differing degrees, some specialise from a subset to a single sector. If choosing exposure to property through any fund route you should be aware what sectors are utilised and ensure they meet with your requirements as an investor. The main sectors are:

- **RESIDENTIAL:** Single family homes, multi-family property (duplexes), flats/apartments/condos.
- **COMMERCIAL & RETAIL:** Offices & office buildings, shops & shopping centres, consumer services (like hairdressers and laundromats).
- **INDUSTRIAL:** Manufacture, distribution and warehouse.
- **HEALTHCARE:** Medical facilities, end of life care & hospices, nursing homes and assisted living.
- **HOSPITALITY & TOURISM:** Short-term rentals, hotels, resorts and vacation lodging.
- **AGRICULTURAL:** Farmland, agricultural properties and agribusiness.
- **DEVELOPMENT:** New projects like residential estates, commercial builds and development land.
- **INTERNATIONAL:** Any of these categories purchased outside your home country.
- **LAND:** Purchase of raw land, for any of the above purposes.

Each instrument and market sector has its own risk and return characteristics with most retail investors defaulting to residential or commercial as they're familiar. As always, risk tolerance and market expertise plays a part in reviewing your options as investing in things we know nothing about is dangerous. International property or healthcare may not suit everyone for example. As with any investing, diversification across sectors and instruments can help mitigate risk and enhance overall portfolio performance but try not to spread too thin within any asset class or the portfolio as a whole. Real estate is worth consideration but exposure will depend on personal preference.

Many investment professionals recommend an allocation of 5%-15% as adequate for property. I don't feel the need for this exposure personally as my expertise lies in other areas, so I'm less than 3%, but this is simply my own view. If you feel you'd like exposure to property then 5%-15% guidelines give you an idea of general thinking.

ASSET CLASSES: COMMODITIES

Raw materials like gold, silver or crude oil and primary agricultural products like wheat, coffee or sugar are traded directly (in physical form) or through derivatives. Commodities are essential in the production processes for the goods and services we consume on a daily basis so provide investors with a diverse range of industries and sectors in which to speculate on raw materials.

Commodities can help with portfolio diversification as well as provide exposure to global economic trends (commodities are part of the worldwide supply chain). However this exposure comes with risk. Commodities are historically volatile, heavily influenced by things like global supply and demand dynamics (think timber prices post Covid), geopolitical events (think natural gas prices post Russia invading Ukraine) and changes in global economic conditions (think the oil crash from $150 to below $40 per barrel pre and post 2008 GFC).

They're useful instruments for investors and their volatility makes them popular with traders, but they should be used with appropriate risk management because of this volatility. Consider the chart in Fig 14.3: on top is the NASDAQ (equities) index and bottom crude oil (commodity). NASDAQ trends up and to the right over time as the companies making up the index continue to grow. However crude has been more "horizontal".

Yes, it returned 477% over the period, but look at the volatility versus the NASDAQ as it gradually climbed nearly 7000% over the same period with limited major drawdown events. A volatile commodity like crude is probably not one you'd want to be invested in for the long-term. Even gold, the least volatile (in my view) of popular commodities "only" returned 700% since 1999.

I certainly think there's a place for gold and other commodities in well balanced portfolios, but not on a large allocation basis. Conventional wisdom says 5%-10% allocation range. Precious metals like gold and silver are the most common commodity additions, some buying the metals themselves through merchants who store the gold or silver securely for a small fee. Some even store bullion at home or in their bank. There are also ETFs and funds providing exposure for those who want to allocate.

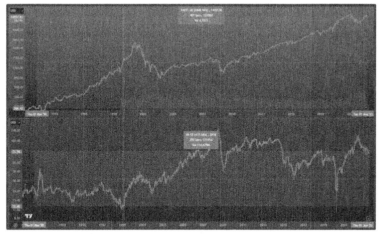

Fig 14.3 | NASDAQ v Crude Oil 1990 – 2023 (from Trading View)

Personally I don't allocate specifically in my core portfolio to commodities, though I get ~2% via a fund in my pension. Again this is personal choice. I trade them over shorter timeframes where opportunities present using technical analysis but prefer equities in my core. I accept this risk in line with longer term goals and with equities diversified across market, sector and geography.

Commodities fall broadly into the following categories (or market sectors) including some examples:

ENERGY:

- **CRUDE OIL:** Used in industry globally it's a key driver of global economic activity and macro-economic conditions. For example, rising oil prices impact shipping rates, increased shipping rates increase the cost of imported products and rising prices on products brings inflationary market pressure.
- **NATURAL GAS:** Used in heat and electricity generation residentially and within industrial processes. Again, price increase has wider knock on impacts on macro-economic conditions and it contributes to inflation.

PRECIOUS METALS:

- **GOLD:** Long considered the "safe haven" asset, investors allocate as a hedge during inflationary or rate fluctuation periods that impact equities. Also used in the manufacture of consumer goods like jewellery and electronics.

- **SILVER:** Next most popular precious metal and also used in the manufacture of many consumer items like jewellery and electronics. It additionally has industrial applications.
- **COPPER:** Used in construction (like pipes and cabling), consumer electronics and in many manufacturing contexts.
- **PLATINUM/PALLADIUM:** Multiple industrial applications and used in consumer items like cars (catalytic converters).
- **OTHERS:** Many other precious metals are available to investors, most of which find their application in either consumer luxuries, consumer electronics or industrial goods/processing. These include Ruthenium, Rhodium and Lithium (used in battery creation).

AGRICULTURAL:

- **SOYBEANS:** Used in animal feed and food products with some industrial applications.
- **COTTON:** Used in clothes manufacture with other textiles.
- **CORN:** Used in animal feed, food products and biofuels.
- **WHEAT:** Used in baking and general food products.
- **SUGAR:** Used in production of food and drink.
- **COFFEE:** It's coffee, we drink it. "Go Juice"!
- **COCOA:** Used in confectionary products like chocolate.
- **ORANGE JUICE:** Another consumer drink.
- **LUMBER:** Used in the building/construction industry.
- **PALM OIL:** Used in cosmetics as well as confectionary and other foods (like margarine).

LIVESTOCK:

- **LIVE CATTLE:** Typically traded as futures contracts.
- **LEAN HOGS:** Similarly tend to trade as futures contracts.
- **PORK BELLY:** Used to be widely traded but not as a distinct contract these days.

Sometimes agricultural and livestock commodities are grouped together and referenced as "Soft" commodities. Essentially anything "grown or reared". And water has become more popular in the last 10 years, made so by "big short" investor Michael Burry. We have options for how we invest in all of these commodities, the most common being:

- **EXCHANGE TRADED FUNDS:** Many "one stop" ETFs have an allocation specifically to commodities as outlined in the KIID. There also exist ETFs specifically for commodity investing, either in specific groupings (like precious metals) or individual commodities like gold or silver. There also exist ETFs tracking commodity indexes as their benchmark providing wider exposure. In the world of ETFs one can find almost anything to suit their desires and it's the easiest way for investors like ourselves to gain exposure.

- **FUTURES CONTRACTS:** Derivatives offering investors the ability to speculate on a commodity price in future. Some providers offer perpetual futures contracts, others are time bound. I don't want to discuss options in too much detail in this book as they're complex instruments not really intended for the retail (us) demographic.

- **MUTUAL FUNDS AND OEIC/TRUSTS:** Some Mutual Funds (North America) and OEIC/Trusts (UK and Europe) specifically offer exposure to diversified portfolios of commodities. These can be another simple option for retail investors should your platform support their purchase, just watch out for the fees.

- **PHYSICAL OWNERSHIP:** The purchase of the commodities. More straightforward for things like gold and silver through bullion merchants, stored either by them for a small fee or in self-custody. Many retail investors take this approach. Self-custody of precious metals and other commodities obviously isn't a convenient approach for many. Not only are you limited by storage space, you could struggle to insure any stored at home for reasonable cost. Also, it wouldn't be particularly nice storing wheat, lumber or worse still live cattle at home!

These are the main instruments, types and sectors in commodities. Investing in these can provide diversification and exposes investors to global economic trends. But it's important to be wary of the volatility in commodity markets and allocate appropriately if you wish to hold. As before 5%-10% is "normal".

ASSET CLASSES: CRYPTOCURRENCY

This is where my traditional markets colleagues get twitchy! My background is in Financial Services IT, primarily in development (both infrastructure and application). I'm a tech guy and a coder so naturally I was curious as crypto developed. Having spent years now within the market I'm a fan of the class, for specific purposes.

This is **not** a universal position! Many traditional marketeers are hugely negative about cryptocurrency, citing many different reasons, some legitimate, some misunderstanding and some just downright false (personal bias). As with everything in finance, personal due diligence is key before putting any capital at risk.

The most common "reason" is: crypto is for scammers and criminals perpetrating fraud or laundering money. Scams are certainly rife as are fraudsters and the technology is undoubtedly used by some for criminal purpose. But this is true of traditional financial systems too! My experience working in fraud prevention technology at a major bank confirms this for me. The most widely used currency in fraud, criminal enterprise and money laundering is the US $, unsurprisingly given it's the world reserve currency. Fraud, money laundering and criminality can and does occur with **any** medium of exchange, so while I acknowledge the issue I find it hypocritical as a reason not to utilise crypto. By the same logic we should ban all fiat money too, rather than aim to improve controls around these nefarious practices.

Further, the premise of the technology is that **all** transactions be written to (mostly) public blockchains, completely traceable, in perpetuity, for all time. Tracking funds wallet to wallet via public ledger is a fundamental requirement. It doesn't mean scam victims always get funds back, they don't always in traditional finance either, but it means we can track the money over long periods, as evidenced by high profile convictions like Ilya Lichtenstein (investor) and Heather Morgan (entrepreneur, journalist, and rapper) who were caught years after their 2016 hack of Bitfinex.

I've concerns, sure. I think KYC (Know Your Customer) and other security and regulatory measures from traditional finance are net positive for adoption and fully expect more regulation like this in the sector as it matures. I both support this and think it's needed. But I acknowledge the emerging nature of the asset and don't expect perfection from the outset.

Another common complaint is "there's no intrinsic value". Equities have companies, products and profit for example. This is true to an extent if assuming apples to apples, but projects aren't like traditional companies. In many cases the token itself **is** the product, providing utility on the network like ETH (Ethereum) or XRP (Ripple Labs). Say a mother in South America wants to send money to her son living in Australia. This could take days, even weeks if traditional payment corridors don't exist. It introduces exchange rate risk while the cost for currency conversion and cross border services is typically significant. Or, she can convert into XRP **in seconds**, send around the world **in seconds** and the recipient can convert to their local currency **in seconds**. All for fractions of pennies. One can utilise the network to send money worldwide 24x7, with no third party (bank), for next to nothing, near instantaneously. This is an example of the value proposition and arguably why traditional finance has such issue. Mighty hard to compete with this on legacy technology......

Where I absolutely agree is the huge amount of dogsh*t, excuse the language, in crypto. Projects created with zero utility, zero purpose and zero point. In an immature market driven by narrative and hype people lose money on these through greed. It's like penny stocks on steroids where the greed on the part of those gambling, taking outlandish risk, creates a breeding ground for scams. You or I could create a crypto on Ethereum or Solana in about an hour. I'm an accountability advocate though, so if someone drops $50k into "Cumrocket" or "dogecat" because it was hyped by shills and it goes to zero, is it anyone else's fault? Criminals exist and as I've said we must live in reality, not fantasy. In reality we can avoid our exposure to these situations by controlling our own actions, by managing our own fear and greed.

Without going on too much of a rant about the volume of useless projects, let me just agree it's a problem detracting from those offering true innovation, disruption and evolution. For example I think Bitcoin does everything gold can do but better (only ~10% of gold is used in manufacturing, the other 90% is speculative, it's major use case by a distance) and Ethereum is revolutionary as a platform for building innovative, next gen products and services. Unlike some of my traditional market peers I'm not in favour of throwing the baby out with the bathwater. I prefer to find ways to manage risk, allowing for safer navigation of this market. Cryptocurrency is more than a decade old and though it presents higher risk I think there's a place for it in portfolio allocation when risk is managed appropriately. My personal guide is 5%-10% maximum. I know others believe more which is fine, it's personal choice. More represents too much risk for my taste.

I do want to note "currency" in the class name is a misnomer. Bitcoin maximalists argue otherwise, it's "perfect money" in their view, but having worked in finance my entire life I simply don't see a world where goods and services are priced in Bitcoin. My view is cryptocurrency evolves into a commodity type market, store of value and potentially facilitates conversion between fiat currencies for instant cross border transfer and trade given speed and cost versus current nostro/vostro mechanisms.

Enough background for now, this isn't the place for a full retort of the bad press crypto receives, another complete book in its own right! I want to concentrate on my view of its use case for investors and how we manage risk in a well-rounded portfolio. I'll start with some general pointers on safety.

SELF-CUSTODY: Always self-custody cryptocurrency holdings outside of active trades, preferably in cold wallets (offline hardware, not software wallets). "Not your keys, not your crypto". As a young, largely unregulated market we see events like FTX collapse or BlockFi. People mistakenly treat exchanges or service providers like traditional banks, which they most certainly aren't. Move funds to your own wallets and self-custody to avoid counterparty risk. This is actually one of the great strengths of crypto, but one must think about it in entirely different terms to traditional banking. It's easy to assume, like in traditional finance, money is safer in the bank than in self-custody, but bank safety comes from regulation and built in protection in traditional finance. **None** of this exists in crypto, so be your own bank!

WALLET DAPPS: Never hook your primary wallets up to dApps (decentralised Applications). While part of the ecosystem and they serve some purpose, connecting them to your wallet instigates smart contracts or approves additional permissions. These can lead to exploit. By all means play with dApps, but do so through wallets other than your primaries (software wallets are free) with only small amounts held in them. Limit your risk.

BROKERS: Pick reputable brokers, but never trust them! I know many claim there's no such thing in crypto but some are more reputable (and thus less risky) than others. Never put all eggs in one broker basket, spread the risk around if possible.

SECURITY: Use authenticator based 2FA (like RSA or google authenticator), anti-phishing codes, withdrawal whitelists and never click links in emails to exchanges or wallets (same as traditional banking). Always go direct. Never answer social media messages from anyone claiming to be "support" and never, for the love of all things sane, give anyone your seed phrases. Anyone who even asks for them is 100% trying to scam you!

NYETCOINS: A name given to me by a close financial friend, don't gamble on "Nyetcoins": new projects or low cap "shitcoins". It's easy for anyone to set up a crypto project and rug pull once money has flowed in. You wouldn't put your net worth in a penny stock, so don't here!

DON'T BE A DUMBASS: Theres no such thing as free internet money. A random stranger on the internet offering you some is as legit as the African prince who mails us asking if we could help him move $10 million by sending $10k first. If someone asks you to send a Bitcoin and they'll send two back, that's a (fairly obvious) scam. It still amazes me how many fall for this.

DON'T DEGEN: Stick to spot buys and sells if you aren't experienced in trading. Crypto exchanges offer high leverage and perpetual contract trading which causes a lot of inexperienced, greedy and impatient traders to lose money. Leverage and futures trading is for experienced traders with well tested, well defined, rules based strategies inclusive of strict risk management. Don't get sucked in by the promise of huge returns, there's no so such thing as get rich quick and if you get greedy you likely get "rekt" even quicker. I've seen it so many times.

Really, just be sensible about risk exposure to projects, counterparties and your expectation of return. Using my moonshot portfolio (~5% - 10% of overall portfolio) is plenty for me. It allows me to benefit from the volatility of crypto and if it grows quickly I'll rebalance back to ~5% to de-risk. If I lose it all there's minimal impact on my modelling for long-term growth.

A 2024 Bitwise report suggested 5% is sensible for most traditional portfolios, providing confluence for my long-term approach. I don't believe cryptocurrency a mature enough market for large allocation personally and I worry when I speak to people who are "all in". I find no respect paid to risk there. Having a small allocation though allows me to utilise shorter cycles (~4 years) for mid-term positions and shorter term trading opportunities.

Being a fledgling market how do I define sectors within and use them to manage risk? There aren't universally accepted definitions though many differing views exist. My own personal designation and the one I use when speaking with people about their cryptocurrency exposure is below. You'll notice I consider the start point as "Medium" risk, there's no low risk here.

MEDIUM RISK DIGITAL:

- **BITCOIN:** The longest established, most traded, OG digital asset. While I regard all cryptocurrency as "High Risk" compared to equities, within the class Bitcoin is the lowest risk asset (relatively). It has over a decade of history, is making its way onto corporate balance sheets, has spot ETFs approved in traditional markets (making it available in regulated accounts) and is gaining popularity in institutional investing.
- **LARGE CAP PROJECTS WITH HISTORY:** Ethereum and the other top 30 projects by market cap, excluding stablecoins,

with established project teams or actual companies behind them and history longer than a single crypto cycle. Longevity (relatively) has been proven and although unlikely to return huge yield, from a risk perspective less likely for total loss.

- **STABLECOINS:** Coins pegged to fiat currency 1:1 and long established. Mainly USDT (Tether) and USDC. Excludes any stablecoins created as part of new projects, based on recent history (LUNA and the collapse of its algorithmic stablecoin).

ADVENTUROUS DIGITAL:

- **LARGE CAP PROJECTS WITH NO HISTORY:** Coins in the top 30 by market cap but with no history over cycles. Appeared and gained popularity quickly but have no track record that could alleviate risk concern. Higher risk for higher potential returns.
- **MID CAP PROJECTS WITH HISTORY:** Tokens outside the top 30 but with history over multiple cycles, enough to give confidence in survival and legitimacy. Unlikely to return huge numbers but represent potentially undervalued projects with limited total loss risk.

HIGH RISK DIGITAL (NYETCOINS!):

- **MID CAP PROJECTS WITH NO HISTORY:** Projects outside the top 30 with no history, essentially appeared and gained large enough market cap not to be considered "small", but with no history to alleviate concern over total loss risk.
- **SMALL CAP PROJECTS WITH HISTORY:** New projects with limited market cap but limited history of a cycle. Potential for large return but also total loss, so high risk.

VERY HIGH RISK DIGITAL (SHITCOINS):

- **SMALL CAP PROJECTS WITH NO HISTORY:** New projects with no history. The home of the rug pull! Some of these could return massive profits, if timed correctly, many will result in total loss, many are scams. Super high risk, more likely to go to zero than return a profit. You're gambling.

Of these, I primarily focus on Medium Risk Digital and Adventurous Digital. I keep a small allocation for the lower categories but I accept these could result in total loss so exposure is limited in both concurrency and frequency. I rarely have more than 5 positions concurrently in these and generally only at certain times within the overall cycle.

There'll be plenty who disagree with my categorisation and allocation rules, I accept this. I'm only laying out my personal process, everyone must develop their own. I manage risk first, make profit second. So be it if I don't make the sums many claim to make (remember wealth is quiet). I won't shill degen dreams of becoming a fast crypto millionaire as I won't encourage reckless resource use, our goal is long-term sustainable financial security.

How you decide to proceed is up to you, but my view is a small 5%-10% risk managed allocation that's rebalanced regularly allows exposure to the cryptocurrency market in a way minimally impacting long-term modelling from an investment return perspective.

ASSET CLASSES: CASH & CASH EQUIVALENTS

Highly liquid assets either in actual cash or convertible into cash quickly with minimal risk of capital loss. These are generally used over short time periods to provide safety, stability and easy access to liquidity. When utilising these assets, look for the highest liquid yield possible (highest interest rate or return on capital) to combat the effects of inflation risk.

CASH is the easiest example, physical currency including coins and paper held in pocket or bank accounts. This is the most liquid option but generally also suffers most from buying power shrinkage as cash account rates are generally lower than inflation. I try to avoid these, keeping only enough on hand for expenses. Any savings are invested or in savings specific accounts with higher returns.

SAVINGS ACCOUNTS are bank accounts offering higher rates than current or checking accounts but with instant/easy access. Some limit the number of withdrawals by period (3 per year) or by reducing rate if you withdraw in more than a set number of transactions. These would include cash ISAs in the UK and general savings accounts offered by most banks. Again RoR on these can be negative so one always needs to be careful with how much of our portfolio is held in cash.

CERTIFICATES OF DEPOSIT can be referred to as CD's and are offered with fixed terms and interest rates. They provide higher rates than regular savings accounts but have penalties for early withdrawal should you need access. The premise is similar to fixed income where you provide capital for a set period in return for set yield. Like Bonds and T-Bills these are optimal where you know you won't need access during lockup periods. If you know you will it makes more sense to utilise savings accounts or money market funds (where platform fees aren't too expensive) instead.

MONEY MARKET ACCOUNTS or MMA's are bank accounts offering competitive rates but for higher minimum balance requirements than ordinary accounts. Offered primarily by "wealth" providers like Coutts in the UK.

MONEY MARKET FUNDS or MMF's invest in low-risk, short-term debt securities to maintain stable return. They often track something like SONIA (Sterling Overnight Index Average), the rate banks lend to each other linked to base rate. We covered these in funds earlier. I like these as a safe haven for cash and utilise for cash in my Moonshot portfolio awaiting opportunity.

TREASURY BILLS are technically fixed income assets as they're short-term debt securities issued by the U.S. Treasury. However, you can utilise T-Bills for periods from a few days right up to a year so they can be utilised as a short-term cash equivalents. Return on these is linked to central bank base rate so one must account for interest rate risk. Ensure RoR meets your needs, accounting for inflation.

COMMERCIAL PAPER like short term corporate bonds are technically fixed income instruments, short-term debt issued by corporations to meet short-term funding needs. It's typically unsecured and considered low-risk so can be a good option, their duration meaning they can be utilised as cash equivalents. I'd always consider the company issuing the debt and stick to those rated as investment grade as a minimum, preferably high investment grade as outlined in the fixed income section. Again, ensure RoR meets your needs and account for inflation.

SHORT-TERM BONDS are again technically fixed income but these bonds can have short maturities of a year or less so could be considered a cash equivalent at a push. If conditions change and rates go up, selling may invoke a capital loss (interest rate risk) so it's best to only utilise these or T-Bills/Commercial Paper when you know you'll hold to maturity. These tend to offer slightly higher yields than paper and T-Bills but you must ensure any corporate debt meets your risk parameters. If utilising these as a risk management strategy versus risk assets (like equities or crypto) you don't want to introduce higher risk for lower reward.

Cash and cash equivalent investments are widely used. They're useful to retail investors to gain return on cash waiting for investment and for preserving capital in changing market conditions. In reality there's no "allocation" specifically required for these they're more useful for cash you have waiting to gain higher yield. Moving in and out of investments is a dangerous game (market timing risk) so it's important to define your use cases. To give you an idea mine are twofold:

- **SAVINGS FOR A KNOWN EVENT:** For example saving for a holiday, home improvements or school fees. You know the timeframe and know you won't need the money in the interim for any other purpose. Can be useful in these circumstances without adding market or currency risk.

- **PARKING CASH ALLOCATION WAITING FOR INVESTING:** In my Moonshot portfolio I keep a cash allocation aside for opportunities I'm tracking. I don't like opportunity to present and have no capital so I maintain a cash allocation by taking profits and rebalancing. Rather than have this sat not earning, I'll often add to a Money Market Fund to gain some return or hold in a higher interest savings account. Something I can liquidate within a day or two as items on my watchlist move towards my buy or sell zone. This allows me to take opportunities and to somewhat fight shrinking of spending power versus inflation.

Others may have differing reasons to utilise these instruments, these are simply mine for illustrative purposes. In terms of market sector, nothing to report. These are simply cash or cash equivalent instruments. Nice and simple.

ASSET CLASSES: DERIVATIVES

Before we go into detail I want to say: these are **expert level** instruments, not for novice or passive investors due to inherent complexity and risk. Derivatives are "synthetic" assets whose value derives from the performance of an underlying asset, index or benchmark. They're "contracts" between two parties to trade based on the price of the underlying, without any actual purchase or sale of said underlying. This allows speculation on or hedging against future price movements.

Let's say you bought a perpetual (meaning non expiring) futures contract on crude oil. Your contract tracks the price of the physical asset but you never own the asset, you own a "contract" with your futures exchange linked to the asset. If price goes up (or down) you can sell back to cash for profit or loss and the contract is fulfilled. All without ever owning the underlying asset to which the contract is linked. There are different flavours:

FUTURES are standardised contracts obligating parties to buy or sell an asset at a predetermined price on a specified future date. They're commonly used to hedge against price fluctuations or to speculate on market movements.

FORWARDS are similar to futures but non standardised, they're generally customised to suit each party. Agreements to buy or sell an asset at a specific price on a future date.

OPTIONS provide a right, with no obligation, to buy (call option) or sell (put option) an asset at a predetermined price within a specified timeframe. Options are used for hedging, speculation and income generation. If for example one purchases a call option for 30 days' time with mark price at $50, you've acquired the right to buy the actual asset at $50 in 30 days. You pay a small premium for the option. If after 30 days the price is $45 you'd be in loss buying for $50 so you let the option "expire" and lose the premium. If the price is $60 after 30 days you can call in the option, buy the asset for $50 and you're instantly in profit (the person selling the call makes the loss). Same works in reverse for puts.

SWAPS are more complex still, involving the exchange of "cash flow" based on different financial variables. Common types include interest rate swaps, currency swaps and commodity swaps. They're used to manage interest rate risk, currency risk and other exposures. You may be familiar with, for example, the credit default swaps Michael Burry (and others) utilised pre 2008 to bet against the US housing market when they realised there was a bubble likely to collapse.

CONTRACTS FOR DIFFERENCE are also known as CFDs and are agreements to exchange the difference in the value of an asset between the time the contract is opened and closed. They allow investors to speculate on price movement without owning underlying assets and involve the use of margin or leverage (credit). I want to mention here "Perpetual Futures" utilised heavily in cryptocurrency trading and "Spread Betting", a tax efficient UK derivatives trading method. While these are not exactly the same they're close enough I'll group them together for completeness. In all three the contract is perpetual and acts similarly to trading the underlying asset (though spread betting concentrates on the spread, as one would imagine, rather than actual price).

DERIVATIVE OPTIONS are options whose underlying asset is another derivative. For example, an option on a futures contract or an option on an option. This, like most derivatives, is a super complex world not for retail investors.

It should be said retail investor access to many of these is restricted in some jurisdictions, including the UK. Regulators claim this a risk based decision in the name of investor "protection". I find this condescending and would prefer they simply ensured retail investors agree to personal accountability in advance. It's hypocritical seeing betting shops on almost every corner with spread betting, one of the more complex derivatives options, allowed but others restricted for "consumer protection". I don't favour nanny state legislation.

In terms of markets, you can find derivatives for almost anything. EQUITIES, where individual stocks and market indices derivatives allow speculation on price movements of underlying assets. For example ES1 is the "mini futures" market for the S&P500 index. Hedging is also a popular use case: if a position is in profit but you're concerned the asset may enter drawdown, you can take a corresponding short position via a derivative to avoid selling. If your long position starts losing money, your derivative short position gains the same amount (assuming matching size). Your overall position value is net neutral (less fees) until you close one of the positions.

INTEREST RATE derivatives like swaps and options on interest rate futures are used by financial institutions to manage interest rate risk and create yield curves.

FOREIGN EXCHANGE (FOREX) derivatives include forwards, options and swaps. These are used to hedge against exchange rate risk or speculate on currency movement. If for example one has a "Cable" position (GBP/USD) and believes $ is going to strengthen they can take out a put (sell) option paying a premium to guarantee selling at a set level in future. This hedge allows them to exercise the option if prices fall significantly, protecting capital. Or they let it expire if Cable price goes on to exceed option price losing only the premium. It's a kind of "insurance" for traders.

CRYPTOCURRENCY options and futures (Perpetual) contracts are available on cryptocurrency exchanges, generally with ridiculous leverage options. These allow for speculative trading of underlying crypto assets and hedging of spot positions. For example if one has a spot long Bitcoin position but thinks price decline is incoming, they can open a perpetual contract short to hedge the spot position and protect capital should price decline. This is the same method as described in equities.

COMMODITIES derivatives on instruments like oil, gold and agricultural products allow investors to gain exposure to price movements without physically owning the commodities. They work in the same way as described already.

FIXED INCOME includes interest rate derivatives like bond futures which help manage interest rate risk and exposure to changes in yield curves.

Derivatives are available for pretty much any instrument in any market. They can be powerful tools for managing risk but in my experience they're utilised by retail investors speculatively, often with no risk management at all. I've witnessed many people get "rekt" by irresponsible use of leverage within derivatives markets so I advocate restraint.

I've included Derivatives as an overview to build knowledge, but when building your investment portfolio, particularly if this is a new endeavour for you, these instruments you can largely ignore. There's no need to consider them in your planning. Perhaps as you gain experience and if you find markets to be something you enjoy you may revisit, but for now you can be content you know roughly what they are without having to utilise.

ASSET CLASSES: SUMMARY

This completes our high level rundown of the main asset classes and instruments available to us as investors, alongside the market sectors or categorisations within, certainly as I see them. In reality, funds are the simplest entry point for new investors, with the least ongoing overhead. A decent all world index tracker can fulfil the needs of many, so this may be where you start investigations to find something suitable to you. At least though you'll know what goes into these funds so start off a little more informed.

GEOGRAPHIC DIVERSIFICATION

From a diversification perspective we also need to discuss geography. If we diversify a portfolio across asset classes and sectors to manage risk, it makes sense we'd do the same to some degree to manage risk (political & regulatory for example) within jurisdictions based on geography. Let's look at geographic considerations per asset class, starting with those where it's not so important:

- COMMODITIES: There's no direct link to geography. Gold is gold, oil is oil, wheat is wheat and so on. This is a true global market so we don't need to concern ourselves with geographic diversification.

- **CRYPTOCURRENCY:** Similarly, no real geographic link. There are some projects linked to companies who reside in a particular geography, like Ripple (US Based) linked to XRP, but for the most part geographic diversification isn't a consideration in the crypto market.

For some asset classes it depends on the underlying asset:

- **DERIVATIVES:** If a commodity or cryptocurrency derivative then like the underlying asset the geography doesn't overly concern us. For other types of asset, like bonds or equities, then the geography of the underlying asset is of interest. This can likely be ignored as you won't be using derivatives anyway, remember!

For **EQUITIES, FIXED INCOME, CASH & CASH EQUIVALENTS AND REAL ESTATE**, as well as the various **FUNDS** utilising them, geography is a consideration we'd want to make. It's OK to be heavier some places than others, for example most portfolios are probably quite heavily weighted US, the idea is simply to have some exposure globally, not all in a single geographic location. There are also some specific considerations based on your own locale:

CASH & CASH EQUIVALENTS: Are generally traded in local currency (though hedged versions do exist) so they're tied to the geography of the investor. For example, buying a MMF denominated in £'s means the fund is linked intrinsically to the performance of the £ and the wider UK market. As a UK based investor I'd prefer this for cash instruments so I don't introduce currency risk. If I invested in a $ based MMF, the $ gaining against the £ might mean I incur a loss even if the fund itself went up in $ valuation. I'd stick to local denomination, or worst case a local currency hedged version if available.

EQUITIES, FIXED INCOME AND REAL ESTATE: Obviously these span geographic locations and includes emerging markets alongside established markets. In general the geographic split I utilise in my own portfolio is fairly common, split into three parent groups and sub groups as follows:

- **EMEA (EUROPE, MIDDLE EAST & AFRICA):**
  - UK & Ireland
  - Mainland Europe
  - Africa
  - The Middle East

- **ASIA AND AUSTRALASIA:**
  - Japan
  - Australia
  - New Zealand
  - Asia Developed Markets
    - South Korea
    - Brunei
    - Polynesia
    - Hong Kong
    - Guam
    - New Caledonia
    - Macau
    - Singapore
    - Taiwan
  - Emerging Asia Markets (all other Asia)
- **THE AMERICAS:**
  - North America
    - USA
    - Canada
  - Latin America (South)

Diversification across geographic regions assists in mitigating risk, for example political & regulatory, currency or inflation risk. It spreads the portfolio across location specific events, economic cycles, political developments or currency fluctuations. Utilising different geography can also be a useful method of increasing or decreasing risk at different times, like tweaking allocation to emerging markets during global financial issues. Emerging markets traditionally carry higher potential return for higher risk.

Geographic diversification is part of overall risk management while managing a portfolio. If choosing to invest via any of the different fund options this is generally done for us based on the allocation strategy defined in the KIID or factsheet, so reviewing these can give you some working examples. The optimal allocation geographically, like asset classes and market sectors, will depend on your individual risk tolerance, investment goals and outlook.

One should be aware when we talk about diversification, to any of the categories in which it can be applied, the target is **not** an equal split. We would expect to weight heavier in some assets than others, some sectors than others, some locations than others. The idea of diversification is to reduce risk by having appropriate allocation to fit our risk appetite and potential return.

INVESTING PLATFORMS

Before we start choosing investments we must choose platforms to manage them and for this multiple providers will be available in your jurisdiction. Depending on the asset classes you wish to use you may need multiple platforms/providers. Popular ISA, LISA, JISA, SIPP and General Investment Account (GIA) options in the UK include Interactive Investor, Hargreaves Lansdown, Vanguard and Trading 212, but there are many to choose from. Popular cryptocurrency brokers include Kraken, Binance, Huobi and Bybit, but again there are many to choose from.

The account types discussed in our pensions chapter apply, so we won't detail again, but as a reminder one should always take advantage of their tax allowances before using GIA's: ISA, LISA, JISA, Roth IRA for example. Once maximum deposits are reached on these tax advantaged accounts move onto GIA's to avoid unnecessary capital gains or income tax exposure. At the moment cryptocurrency isn't an option outside of crypto specific brokers, which qualify as GIA's from a tax perspective. Check your local options in the order tax advantaged first, then non tax advantaged.

As I'll likely refer to them, my platforms of choice are Interactive Investor for ISA and JISA, my pensions are with Aviva and Legal & General and I use Trading 212 for GIA (and a second ISA in 2024). Kraken, Binance, Huobi and Bitrue I use for cryptocurrency. I chose Interactive Investor for two reasons: their flat monthly fee and access to OEIC funds at no additional cost. T212 I use as they don't charge trading fees and have a nice interface for trading. Cryptocurrency accounts change frequently depending on market and regulatory developments, these are simply the exchanges I use at the moment. I always self-custody outside of active trades. Pension providers are employer enforced.

I **don't** offer this as a recommendation of providers, only to highlight I utilise multiple to deliver my target diversification and explain the reasoning. Other providers may suit you better. The platform you choose can significantly impact your investment experience though, so make sure to do your due diligence here. Considerations you might make include:

- **PLATFORM FEES:** Platforms have different fee structures, as outlined earlier. Platform fees are generally either a percentage of account or flat monthly fee. My preference is flat fee as greater than £32,000 in account and I'm better off (using £11.99 monthly fee versus competitor 0.45% fee). This will be listed in the fees section of the platform website.

- **TRADING FEES:** The cost to execute trades (buys or sells) on the platform. Some are free, some offer set amounts free monthly, some charge flat fees per trade, some charge a percent of trade value. Know what they are and select a suitable cost structure based on the type of trading you'll do. Consider whether free regular investing is offered making monthly DCA free. This will be listed in the fees section of the platform website.

- **FUND FEES:** If you plan to utilise funds (not ETFs) check if fees for holding these apply. Some do levy fees (like Hargreaves Lansdown) and some don't (like Interactive Investor) at time of writing. Some, like T212 (who also offer an ISA's) don't offer Fund access. These are generally listed on T&C's or fees pages of the platform website.

- **ASSET CLASS ACCESS:** Not all platforms offer access to all assets. Some free platforms for example only offer ETFs, not Funds (OEIC). Further, some platforms (like Vanguard) only offer access to their own selection of assets and funds (not market wide) and high street banks generally only offer access to their own bespoke funds, usually for higher management fees. Make sure any platforms you're considering offer all the assets you want. You can usually check this through the platform research tools.

- **SECURITY:** Do they offer 2FA? Do they have whitelists for withdrawals and good alerting mechanisms for when something changes on your account? Do they enforce password standards and allow you to use, for example, anti-phishing phrases in all email communications so you can tell it's them? Not all platforms offer all of these, which is fine, just make sure they offer enough to meet your needs. In my view, 2FA should be an absolute minimum. If not listed on websites you can webchat, call or email to ask.

- **REGULATORY CLARITY:** Where possible (it isn't always, like crypto) make sure prospective platforms are covered by local regulatory frameworks, specifically any compensation schemes. This at least offers some protection against the provider failing. This is usually listed on websites.

- **TYPES OF ACCOUNT:** Check they offer the types of account you require. ISA, GIA, SIPP, Roth IRA for example. Whatever you need, make sure they offer it. From a Risk Management perspective I prefer to diversify across providers. My GIA and ISA are with different platforms. This allows doubling up on compensation schemes and reduces exposure to a single platform. In environments like crypto where there's no compensation scheme, I utilise multiple exchanges and self-custody to manage risk.

- **RESEARCH TOOLS:** For a long time (in my opinion at least) Hargreaves Lansdown led the way in market research tools and all round access to data, but most have caught up to offer some excellent research and analysis tools now. There's also a plethora of free sites available on the internet for researching ETFs and Funds, like trustnet. Access to research tools should be part of any modern, holistic platform so check what's on offer and if it suits your needs.

- **USER INTERFACE & MOBILE APP OFFERING:** There's really no excuse for a poor UI, but we still see many platforms who don't get this right, either in the browser or via mobile applications. Most users expect a mobile interface, many exclusively (I prefer the computer, I'm old!!) so if it's a requirement for you then ensure your prospective providers have what you require at the quality you expect on the medium you want.

- **CUSTOMER SUPPORT:** Check reviews on support experiences and what methods of contact are available (like email, phone & chat). No-one likes it but technical issues are an inevitable part of digital life. Where infrequent, not always happening during times of market volatility (I'm looking at you crypto exchanges!!) I find the most important thing is how platforms deal with issues when they occur. If they fix things promptly and without any user loss I'm generally OK. Unfortunately this isn't always the experience, so one should know support history of platforms as part of the consideration process.

- **REPUTATION:** It's always worth looking at reviews of providers to get a feel for what others think. If you can ask people you actually know, all the better, as you tend to get more honest reviews this way. Keep in mind people are more likely to leave negative feedback than positive, so you have to take online reviews with a pinch of salt. But it does give you a view.

- **ACCOUNT MINIMUMS & MAXIMUMS:** Check if minimum or maximum amounts are required to qualify for the account. Not a huge consideration, but certainly worth knowing.

- **INTEREST ON CASH BALANCES:** Different platforms provide different levels of interest on cash balances. You're better getting something for your cash, however little. Remember the power of compounding!

- **WITHDRAWAL & DEPOSIT LIMITS:** Some platforms have limits on withdrawals or deposits over certain time periods. Check the detail of those you're considering to ensure they meet your needs. Of the platforms I utilise no such limits exist (outside crypto where limits **always** exist).

- **AUTOMATION & COPYING:** Some platforms offer the ability to copy other investors or automate building portfolios based on a few simple questions. This is sometimes referred to as "copy trading" or on platforms like Trading 212 "Pies", where users create pie charts of investment diversification and regular investing automatically splits deposits over the pie. If this is of interest check if it's an option on platforms you're considering.

- **TRACKING TOOLS:** What tools are available for monitoring portfolio progress? Some platforms are better than others, some are pretty basic. At a minimum, you should easily be able to see individual positions and the profit and loss (PnL), as well as overall PnL, current value and book cost. In all honesty I record everything myself, but I know not everyone wants to do this. If not, make sure the tracking tools provide the data you need, especially for tax purposes in GIA's.

In my view these are the main things to consider, allowing you to select a platform or platforms meeting your individual requirements. Choice of investment platform should align with your financial goals, investment strategy and level of comfort with technology. You're free to move platform at any time, but be aware if instruments you invest in with your current provider aren't available on new provider it likely means selling to cash to transfer, taking you out of the market for a period and meaning you have to feed back in. This can leave you susceptible to market timing risk if trying to buy in all at once after cash is transferred.

NOTE: If transferring to a different provider always transfer using the approved process and where possible transfer assets rather than liquidate and transfer cash (this will be outlined and facilitated by the provider). During an approved transfer you generally get the option to transfer the investments themselves, better where the investments exist on both platforms. This is optimal.

For tax advantaged accounts specifically, **never** liquidate assets, withdraw cash then deposit to a new account. If you do this you'll be beholden to annual limits on the new account so may not be able to put all of your capital in. For non-tax advantaged accounts like a GIA, liquidating would be a taxable event making you liable for capital gains tax on any profit (depending on jurisdiction). So, use official transfer mechanisms where possible.

BUILDING A TARGET ALLOCATION

We've been working through the minimal knowledge required to build a target allocation for your investment goals, risk appetite and time horizon. This defines which asset classes you'll invest in, where in the world and to what percentage of overall portfolio. It'll be personal to you based on the instruments and risks we've discussed. You'll review this for ongoing relevance within your financial plan and rebalance periodically as required.

In my experience people get themselves hung up here, seeking perfection and not investing till they think they've found it. But target allocation can be tweaked and portfolios rebalanced at any time through regular reviews, so don't be fixated on "getting it right". Keep things as simple as possible and get started, it's better than hanging off and investing nothing in my view.

Those preferring the fund route who don't want to manage a portfolio manually, which in reality is most people, have less to do here. They still have a target allocation as it's how ETFs or funds are selected, but they need not be so precise. All World Index Funds for example have target allocations, generally 100% global equities, so they simply need accept the allocation defined by their selected fund. I'm an advocate of this approach for most with an outlook longer than a decade given equities historically trend upwards. Certainly for the majority of a portfolio, mine included.

If you want to manage a full portfolio yourself the main caution I'd offer is the "You" risk we discussed. Actively managing a full portfolio and beating the market over prolonged periods is something the majority of full time money managers can't even do, so the odds of you or I being able to emulate Terry Smith are extremely low! I prefer a small "Moonshot" portfolio allocation where we can dabble safely, without destroying long term plans. This decision is yours though, just consider the risks outlined.

Target allocation can be sliced whichever way individuals want but generally equities dominate most non conservative portfolios. Other asset classes generally form smaller allocations depending on investor. Here are some example allocations for illustration, to help you visualise. These are just asset class examples, level 1 of

L.T. Noelle

most target allocations. We can refine these further based on sector and geography too, as discussed:

GLOBAL EQUITIES GROWTH PORTFOLIO (RISK: VERY HIGH):

- Global Equities: 100%, Fixed Income: 0%, Real Estate: 0%, Commodities: 0%, Cash: 0%, Cryptocurrency: 0%

AGGRESSIVE GROWTH PORTFOLIO (RISK: VERY HIGH):

- Equities: 75%, Fixed Income: 0%, Real Estate: 5%, Commodities: 5%, Cash: 5%, Cryptocurrency: 10%

BALANCED PORTFOLIO (RISK: MODERATE):

- Equities: 50%, Fixed Income: 20%, Real Estate: 13%, Commodities: 10%, Cash: 5%, Cryptocurrency: 2%

TRADITIONAL 60/40 (RISK: MODERATE):

- Equities: 60%, Fixed Income: 40%, Real Estate: 0%, Commodities: 0%, Cash: 0%, Cryptocurrency: 0%

CONSERVATIVE PORTFOLIO (RISK: LOW):

- Equities: 25%, Fixed Income: 45%, Real Estate: 5%, Commodities: 3%, Cash: 20%, Cryptocurrency: 2%

INCOME FOCUSED PORTFOLIO (RISK: LOW TO MODERATE):

- Equities: 27%, Fixed Income: 55%, Real Estate: 10%, Cash: 5%, Commodities: 3%, Cryptocurrency: 0%

INFLATION HEDGE PORTFOLIO (RISK: MODERATE TO HIGH):

- Equities: 47%, Fixed Income: 3%, Real Estate: 15%, Commodities (Gold & Silver): 20%, Cash: 5%, Cryptocurrency: 10%

DIVERSIFIED PORTFOLIO (RISK: MODERATE):

- Equities: 50%, Fixed Income: 20%, Real Estate: 10%, Commodities: 10%, Cash: 5%, Cryptocurrency: 5%

TECHNOLOGY & INNOVATION PORTFOLIO (RISK: VERY HIGH):

- Equities: (Tech Sector) 40% / (Emerging Markets) 10% / (Other): 10%, Fixed Income: 5%, Real Estate: 5%, Commodities (Precious Metals Hedge): 10%, Cash: 5%, Cryptocurrency: 15%

To reiterate, these are examples of potential target allocations and notional risk. These aren't suggestions to pick from, certainly not an exhaustive list of potential configurations. I've also left out derivatives entirely as I genuinely don't think them suitable for new investors. These examples are simply meant to show how one **might** look to build portfolio allocations.

Notional risk scores I've determined by level of "Risk On" versus "Risk Off" assets and concentration within classes. For my processes I consider "Risk On" to be most equities, all commodities and all cryptocurrency. "Risk Off" I consider fixed income, real-estate, defensive equities and cash. "Risk On" tends to thrive in favourable economic conditions, "Risk Off" does better during economic uncertainty.

From a geography perspective it really is personal choice. My funds weight heavier in the US (around 60%-70%) because the US represents a huge proportion of global markets. UK and Europe is fairly small at 10%-15% with Asia and Asia Emerging allocation too. The best idea here is to review some funds or ETFs you like and see how they're split to give ideas.

Your understanding of risk and your risk tolerance, your time horizon, your knowledge of asset classes, sectors and geographies and your investing goals should now allow you to start thinking about how you want to build your portfolio. You should also be able to consider whether you want to use mainly funds or to manage yourself. And you should have an idea whether you'd like to keep a small allocation to play and learn with. If so you should know what asset classes you'll utilise in there. For example, my crypto allocation is within my Moonshot portfolio for risk reasons.

With this knowledge you'll be able to start investing if you choose to. If you feel overwhelmed by the options, remember you can always opt for the fund route, be that all-world, home country (like S&P500 in the US or FTSE in the UK) or some other configuration to suit your personality. I must confess, part of the reason I wanted to detail the available options is to show the complexity, to convince those at the beginning of their journey the funds route is generally the best place to start. You can always build from there over time.

MODELLING: PROJECTIONS & PITFALLS

I've been deliberate in using different percentage returns to make illustrative projections throughout. I don't have space in this book to provide multiple projections per example but I think absolute modelling with one percentage target can be dangerous. It can set expectation. I prefer to model with high, low and midpoint targets for projective illustrations. I then plan using minimum bound of the range as I'd rather overshoot than undershoot. As long as I'm tracking inside somewhere, it's good.

It's also valid to say projections use averages. We don't know what the future holds so averaging growth is useful for planning but we acknowledge there are ups and downs in markets. Some years outperform and others underperform. Common sense right? You'd be amazed how often I see people in the finance world use absolute projections without acknowledging potential variance and the difference it can make to outcomes.

Any projection, no matter if simple or complex, only outlines possible return. Assumed probability based on historic data. They guarantee precisely **nothing.** Projections are tools, part of our wider toolkit but built entirely on a series of assumptions, any of which can fail and impact actual results. Modelling should always be viewed through this lens. A tool used for strategic planning, risk management and scenario analysis to inform overall decision making. Creating models **does not** guarantee their projections.

They're incredibly useful tools though, used by financial professionals and amateurs successfully the world over. They shouldn't be discounted, we should just be aware of limitations which we'll discuss briefly now.

Projections are **BUILT UPON AND HIGHLY SENSITIVE TO THE ASSUMPTIONS** used as inputs into the model. Even minor variance from assumptions can lead to significantly different outcomes, especially over the longer timeframes we're talking about. When using projection models you should always monitor assumptions to adjust as required if they fail. For example, is long run inflation rate matching the variable you modelled against? Or long run average YoY return?

Relying solely on projections with no other data or risk management can lead to **OVERCONFIDENCE**, thinking models are "absolute" outcomes. Projections can't predict the future, they're a guide to how an investment portfolio might perform if the assumptions they're built on remain true. Be mindful of this.

Some models are very **COMPLEX**, requiring a strong understanding of financial concepts and the underlying mathematics they're built on. Complexity introduces potential for error, make those errors more difficult to identify and potentially lead to wide variance between reality and projection. Whilst it's true more complex models can be useful, one must understand how they're built to be able spot potential errors.

Projections are generally based on **BACKWARDS LOOKING** datasets. Think of the year on year example I've used a few times for the S&P 500. We're using this backwards looking data to attempt to model forward looking projections. Firstly, any inaccurate or incomplete data can lead to flawed projections. Secondly, life just isn't this simple! There will always be some variance between model and reality as a result.

Financial markets are influenced by a wide range of **UNPREDICTABLE FACTORS**. Models can struggle to capture these accurately. For example, think about Covid or the Russian invasion of Ukraine, further back the GFC. Models wouldn't account for this sort of drawdown in averages.

I've mentioned this already, but Investors often unconsciously input assumptions within models to align with their **BIAS** or expectation. Humans are notoriously susceptible to confirmation bias. In an investing context this leads to overly optimistic or pessimistic projections. This could be considered part of our risk awareness as discussed earlier.

Assuming models to be predictions of future outcomes gives a **FALSE SENSE OF EXPECTATION**. When people realise too late they often don't have time to remedy. This is where tracking and adjusting becomes key. Think about the example of pension provision in the UK where so many don't have enough but mostly aren't aware of this issue and won't be till it's too late.

If using third party **BLACK BOX MODELS**, one should consider the transparency of the platform. There are plenty out there but they don't all provide detail on how their projections are arrived at. Some of the more complex platforms in particular can lack transparency. This isn't for nefarious reasons, more to protect intellectual property, but while understandable this makes it challenging to understand how conclusions are made. We should be wary of not knowing the "how", especially if over reliant on the models.

Projections are a hugely powerful part of our investor toolset, we just need to understand and utilise them in an appropriate manner with their risks in mind. Something I discuss often within my financial circle is the art of thinking probabilistically about markets, of not becoming expectant of absolute outcomes then becoming paralysed by this bias. I don't mean constantly chop and change, we've already discussed the inherent risk in this. My point is, when your outlook is decades long, having a model projecting a range of returns (often referred to as "scenario analysis") provides a dataset you can track against to identify variance on the low side. This allows you to make timely adjustments, if you so choose. Realistically the risk is on variance below the pessimistic case (low bound of overall projections), as we're rarely concerned when we escape above the high bound and return more than expected! The earlier one can identify potential issues below the low bound, the less resource it takes to move back inside the range. Remember the example of Theo Doretire who through tracking realised £71 per month was the shortfall. Had he not realised this till later, that figure could have been much, much higher.

Why do I choose three models to provide my range? I like simple and three is simple. It really is that, erm, simple! I model using 4.5% (low), 6% (mid) and 8% (high), which is quite conservative but works for me. There are plenty of platforms allowing for modelling over far more outcomes than three with multiple variables included. Some even tell you how many different scenarios out of 100 you'd have hit your goals based on historic data. These are definitely useful, particularly if you like data (like me) but they can also be costly and difficult to build yourself, creating platform reliance.

In summary, one should exercise caution when using financial projections, remaining aware of their risks and limitations. We should review assumptions critically, incorporate a margin of safety and consider a range of possible outcomes from a scenario analysis perspective. When utilised appropriately they're really useful tools for managing risk and long-term investing outcomes.

SUMMARY

We've only scratched the surface of investing here but it should provide enough of an understanding to get you started. I think everyone should have exposure to markets, it's proven the best way for "normal" people to build wealth for generations so represents an excellent way for us to escape the Consumer, Debtor, Employee triad. Of course, history doesn't guarantee future results, I've been consistent in my view on this risk. But probability suggests growth over long enough timeframes.

You may decide the simplest option described is the one for you, setting up a tax efficient account like an ISA or SIPP and DCA on a weekly or monthly basis into All World Index Funds. Or this may have stoked the fire in you and you want to learn more with the aim of building a more complex portfolio. In either case you might start with funds to get going while you learn!

While there are other pursuits one can choose to build wealth, like real estate or entrepreneurship, investing presents a lower barrier to entry. You can start with as little as £1/$1. There's also a lower ongoing overhead in terms of time and energy. The potential power of long-term investing can't be overstated. I said at the outset there was no silver bullet but investing consistently over a long enough timeframe is as close to one as you're likely to ever find. Investing carries risk, the value of investments can go down as well as up, but probability is in our favour.

How can I say probability is in our favour? Well, pick **any** 25 year period in the last 100 years and cash has **never** outperformed investing. This applies to both the US S&P500 Index and the UK FTSE 100. Barclays Equity Gilt Study in 2023 found investing in UK FSTE 100 equities over any 10 year period had a 91% chance of outperforming cash in the previous 123 years. The FTSE isn't one of the strongest markets by any means. This data and others like it is why I'm comfortable saying probability is in your favour, historically we can say with some certainty that investing over cash saving gives the better opportunity for building wealth. Further, even if we underperform investing targets we're **still** more likely than not to outperform cash savings over longer periods.

And to further emphasise my confidence, as we discussed previously when looking at retirement saving: putting ~£146 per month into an Index Fund tracking the S&P 500 between 20 and 65 would make you a millionaire at 65 during **any** 45 year period in the last century.

There's been a lot of detail in this chapter which for beginners may have been overwhelming at points. My desire to give as much detail as possible in the word count we have, to help in building the knowledge we spoke of in an earlier chapter, meant I had to go into this detail. Please, don't be put off by this. If you feel it's too complicated then know your instinct is positive. One of the main risks retail investors face is themselves not paying markets enough respect by thinking markets are simple. If you're inclined away from this hubris, preferring to keep things as simple as **you** can with good risk management, this is a good instinct.

Those who read this detail and acknowledge the complexity actually have a **better chance** statistically than those who would over tinker. By just choosing a fund (or funds) to meet your requirements and setting up automatic regular investment in each you likely beat most tinkerers. This is how ~90% of my portfolio, my core allocation, operates (and ~90% of my daughters JISA too).

Something I do want to raise with respect to Global (or All World) Index funds is the notional "type" of investing. Essentially, these funds fall into the category of "momentum" investing, because the fund allocates on the basis of the size (the success, or momentum) of the assets within. If an asset, say Tesla, does better than other assets in the market it becomes a larger slice of the overall fund, meaning more of your investment is allocated towards Tesla. The "Big 7" US Tech stocks are a good example of this in practice, where they tend to make up large portions of most Global Index Funds because of their success against the market (their momentum).

As we discussed, risk exists in trying to beat the market, but I should also acknowledge the potential concentration risk involved in here too, where stronger companies, often already expensive, take higher weighting. Momentum investing tends to do well when markets are strong, like they have been since 2008, but in bearish conditions or when markets are choppy this isn't always efficient. Someone rebalancing their portfolio regularly to avoid being overweight any outperformers may do better.

There's not much one can do if prioritising the simplicity of All World Index Funds though, this is simply a risk to be aware of and accept. I still believe it an excellent option for those with little time or inclination to manage a portfolio and I'd rather see more people invest than currently do. I still believe this the most convenient option for most, even accepting this risk.

Finally, if you still have concerns but you're convinced of the potential, consider seeking the help of a qualified financial advisor or planner. I maintain my belief we each have the capability to manage our wealth journey, but seeking help if it's the difference between investing or not is obviously a better outcome. A financial professional will incur additional expense, but if it provides value then it's worth it. All I'd caution is be wary of signing up to any product where an advisor takes a perpetual fee without earning it.

ACTIONS

- Refer to tab "A. Actions" in the Financial Plan template.
- Complete the actions defined in section ".: 14 :. | Investing Demystified".

Trading 101

*"Markets can remain irrational longer than
you can remain solvent."*

[John Maynard Keynes | Economist]

OUR FOCUS HAS BEEN ON long-term investing as a means to build wealth over time, a tried and tested method giving investors (with the required patience!) a high probability of positive outcomes. Nothing is guaranteed, portfolio value can go down as well as up, but investing over long enough outlooks has historically provided high probability of positive return for fairly low effort. Automate a DCA strategy and wait long enough is all one requires.

I'm deliberately introducing trading separately because one needs to clearly understand the distinction, especially those predisposed to gambling tendencies. In my experience there are many who view trading as an alternate to investing because they prefer the "excitement". It's not. Investing and trading are two very different beasts and if either are "exciting" you're gambling. There should be no emotion involved.

I think everyone should invest what they can. It should be a constant in long-term financial plans and I believe one should focus the majority of their available capital here, compounding over time. Trading in addition, for those drawn to its perceived glamour, should be treated with caution. Risk is amplified because we're backing our ability to time the market, both on entry and exit. It needs mechanical strategies and strict risk management.

I'm realistic, as already outlined. A ~90% Core portfolio which I DCA invest into and a ~10% Moonshot portfolio where I do my trading. This is a risk management decision on my part. If I make a mess of 10% it's not going to be fatal for my long-term outlook but trading 100% of capital has larger potential implications.

Before we start, I want to introduce these housekeeping points to keep in mind throughout the detail in "Trading 101":

- Although I enjoy the challenge I respect the risk. Risk must be managed consistently and efficiently using a rules based risk management plan. One must accept they're "Risk Managers" first, "Traders" a distant second.

- Profit is an outcome of a consistent and mechanical process repeated over a series of trades. Profitability, the outcome, is the cumulative result of all trades in a series so individual trades only matter in so far as the mechanical process was followed. The aim can't be to be right every time, that's not possible, the aim is to make it OK to be wrong within the series.

- Trading shouldn't be considered a replacement for or have capital allocations larger than investing for most people. Trading allocation should be smaller in my view.

- I'll provide a brief overview to satisfy inquisitive readers because I don't like the idea of anyone going off and hurting themselves based on trading mentions made thus far. My trading thoughts and practices could fill another book in their own right, so this will not be exhaustive.

- I'm a Technical Trader, meaning I utilise technical analysis (price charts and patterns) to identify opportunities. I'm not a fundamental trader who looks at balance sheets and company performance. I do follow economic calendar events like CPI, PCE and FOMC (US), but anything I discuss is technical in nature. Be aware fundamental trading also exists but that it isn't my practice or background.

DIRECTIONALITY

Let's start with one of the major differences between investing and trading, dual directionality. Investing for most people is buying assets (like equities, funds or commodities) with the expectation of price accumulation over time. In 10 years it'll be worth more than was paid, this growth the return on investment. Long timeframes make this sensible as we know markets don't go up in a straight line. Regular investing means we're not concerned by volatility as long as price drifts upwards over our time horizon.

In trading though we generally think in far shorter timeframes, often weeks, days or even as little as minutes depending on trader. In this context if we only buy assets for growth we're limiting ourselves to one side of a market, potentially the wrong side in relation to short-term trend. In trading then we can (and do) take positions both ways, "go long" or "go short". These are likely terms you've heard, so let's explain what they are.

DIRECTIONALITY: LONG

Buying an asset with the expectation **price will rise** and you can sell for more than was paid. The difference is profit. Long positions require no leverage or margin. You can utilise it, but you can also fully purchase "spot" positions with available capital, meaning no funding fees or risk of liquidation/margin call.

Risk in a (non-leveraged) position is capped at position size (in fiat currency). For example if you buy 2 AAPL shares at £200 each, the most you can lose if AAPL went to zero is £400 (£200 x 2 shares). Most people are comfortable with the concept of long trade directionality. Buy low, sell high, profit on the difference.

DIRECTIONALITY: SHORT

Selling an asset with the expectation **price will fall** and you can buy back cheaper. The difference is profit. The technical definition is actually "selling an asset you don't own", usually borrowed from your broker, then "covering" by buying back what you borrowed to return it. As shorting involves borrowing assets it generally incurs funding fees in both spot and derivative markets.

Risk in short positions is technically infinite as you **always** need to cover to give back what you borrowed. In a long, if the asset goes to zero then 100% is the most you can lose. A short though is backing price to go down and upside is notionally unlimited, making risk **more than** 100%.

When shorts are forced to cover due to runaway price action it's known as a "short squeeze". As shorts close they must buy the asset to return and this buying puts pressure on the order book often pushing price higher and increasing the loss of covering. This is what happened in 2021 with GameStop, pushing the price of the stock up 2440% in 3 weeks! Some large funds with heavy short positions took significant losses. I'm compelled to share this risk for clarity but it doesn't preclude us from participating. We have tools available to manage risk which we'll discuss.

Shorting is often new to people, so let me give an example. Say I think crude oil is displaying "heavy" characteristics technically and I think price likely to decline. With a derivatives exchange I open a short contract (perpetual) on oil at $100. I sell a position of 10 contracts for $1,000 (10 x $100). If I'm right and oil falls in value to $80 I "buy to cover" for $800 (10 x $80). The exchange and I are now square as I fulfilled the 10 contracts but I bought for $800 having sold for $1,000. My profit is $200. If I was wrong and oil increased to $120 then it'd cost $1,200 (10 x $120) to "buy to cover" incurring a $200 loss. I haven't included funding or trade fees to avoid confusion but those are generally added on top. The longer you hold a position, the more funding fees you pay.

DERIVATIVES & LEVERAGE

Derivatives are a popular alternative to spot (buying/selling actual assets) as access to leverage is more straightforward, particularly in markets like cryptocurrency. If you're new to trading you've **no business**, **zero**, **nil**, **nadda**, **none** utilising leverage. I'm firm on this within my trading group. If you don't have rules based strategies tested on hundreds of historic iterations and deployed in live markets on a small account to prove viability, with a comprehensively documented risk plan you follow religiously, then using leverage to scale will get you rekt. Period.

You can't pick up a tennis racket and take on Nadal tomorrow. You can't jump in a go cart and beat Verstappen the next day. You can't watch a YouTube video then do heart surgery next week. Don't think you can start trading using leverage as a beginner. With this warning, let me explain leverage and how it works:

LEVERAGE allows traders to take larger positions than their account balance would otherwise allow. It magnifies potential profit and potential loss. Leverage is usually expressed as a multiplier like 10x or 50x which indicates how much larger the position can be compared to capital. 50x means if you put £100 of your own capital into a long position, the actual position size is 50x£100 = £5,000. If price moves up 1%, you return 1% on the £5,000, so £50 from your £100 capital (a 50% RoI). Sounds great until you factor the risk. If price falls by 1% you also lose 1% of the £5,000. Congratulations, you just lost 50% of your capital on a 1% move. Many degens do this with entire accounts, risking huge amounts in single trades, which is both crazy and irresponsible.

MARGIN is the amount a trader needs to set aside in their account to open and maintain a leveraged position. It's the collateral required by the broker to cover potential losses. Margin is typically expressed as a percentage of the total position size. Using the £5,000 position again, if the broker requires 10% margin, you must have £500 available in your account to cover the leverage. If not you may get margin called or if using derivatives liquidated (your entire account). Margin requirements vary by broker, by asset type and by market and change depending on market conditions. For example, perpetual contracts (derivatives) calculate margin requirements based on position and account size and you're presented with a liquidation price on order. If breached, your position is closed and (in cross margin as opposed to isolated) any money held in your entire leverage account, even if not in the actual losing trade and including other open cross positions in profit, is forfeit to cover the loss.

This covers enough for an introductory chapter. Leverage and margin are complex topics so I reiterate those new to trading who do want to learn should avoid them, sticking exclusively to spot.

TYPES OF TRADING

Next I want to introduce different types of trading. I've seen these named differently but they all mean the same things. These are the designations I use when working with people which I find well received and relatively easy to understand.

ALGORITHMIC TRADING: Automated trading carried out by complex algorithms (code) mechanically. Sometimes referred to as "quantitative trading" or "bots" it's often done on micro price moves, trades opened and closed in seconds. Generally institutional traders rather than retail (us).

SCALP TRADING: Ultra short time duration, scalpers look for minor moves in price (fractions of %) and utilise leverage to increase profit within risk tolerance. Must make super quick decisions, often little time to think, so needs to be mechanical. Takes a lot of skill and high risk tolerance.

INTRADAY TRADING: Scalp Trading can be considered one variation but there are others. For example, many intraday traders are session specific, trading Asia, London or New York sessions by opening and closing trades within these specific periods. Intraday trading (or "Day Trading") is the practice of closing trades regardless of status at the end of each trading day or session. The premise comes from non 24 hour markets (like equities) where trading has a pre and post markets only accessible to certain traders. When using very small price moves as part of intraday systems, holding after close puts you at risk should price gap up or down in the post or pre-market. This risks large loss as you can't close till next market open. Intraday traders then tend to close positions to avoid this out of hours risk.

SWING TRADING: Anything held overnight up to a month or two. Generally done on higher timeframes like 4 Hour and 1 Day rather than 15 minute to 1 minute charts popular with intraday

L.T. Noelle

and scalp traders. One gets more time to review data and make decisions with higher timeframes also meaning larger individual trade risk which reduces the requirement for leverage to meet max risk guardrails. Often trades are actually sized down instead of up to meet risk management plan maximums.

POSITION TRADING: Closest to investing, this utilises macro trades on high timeframes like 1 day, 1 week or 1 month charts, often held over months or years. In my mind anything less than 5 years outlook where a single entry is made based on a chart is position trading and anything involving DCA without a chart is investing.

Intraday and swing trading are my favoured methods (with some position when opportunities present). These work well for me. Swing positions I can hold over days so doesn't interfere with life or work, setting orders and leaving them with little management involved. Intraday I can concentrate on the New York PM session which happens outside of UK working hours so doesn't interfere during the day. I've rules based strategies and I'm a pure price action trader (just price, no indicators), sometimes using Elliot Wave on a macro scale for confluence.

Which, if any, work for you depends entirely on you. It's important in trading not to trade someone else's system or timeframes. To be successful one must spend the time identifying patterns and trends, creating and testing their own strategies and finding what timeframes and trading types work for them.

DCA INVESTING VERSUS SCALING INTO TRADE POSITIONS

A pet peeve of mine, particularly in cryptocurrency, is traders doing technical analysis then declaring they're "DCA in position" because of something they see. My feedback is always the same, if looking at technical detail to define when to buy you're not doing DCA, you're scaling into trade positions which is very different.

It may sound pedantic but there's good reason for enforcing the distinction: DCA is (traditionally) an investing technique that employs different risk management strategies, like diversification across classes, sectors and geography. It's regular investing for long time horizons. Trading using charts and Technical Analysis (TA) requires **very different** risk management and when people conflate DCA with scaling they almost universally, in my experience, employ DCA style (if any) risk management. This is a major mistake. In trading one relies on technical analysis to identify trades, DCA investing doesn't involve looking at a price chart **at all** by design.

RISK MANAGEMENT

Risk management is vital when trading because **you will be wrong, often.** This is a universal truth. No-one, no matter if they're the best trader in the world, is right 100% of the time. We're playing a game based on probabilities, not absolutes. Risk management is how we protect ourselves from being wrong, how we make it ok to be wrong and how we ensure being wrong causes minimal damage. This can be summarised as "consistency", but the process involves a lot more.

To be successful traders must have documented risk management plans they follow in all strategies. Different traders use different detail, but what's universal is good traders all have one. Mine includes:

- **MAX ACCOUNT RISK PER TRADE (MTR):** How much of my **account** I'm willing to risk per trade. Mine is 2% max but I use 1% on most strategies. Many new traders don't understand the two risks in every trade: **trade risk** is the distance between entry and stop loss in individual trades. This is always different as trades have different technical characteristics. Then **account risk** is how much of your account equates to trade risk based on position size. This is constant in every strategy, providing consistency of loss.

- **RISK LADDER TECHNIQUE:** Describes if you'll use a scaling method for risk to reduce exposure over a series of losers or a flat risk level. A common variation is 2% > 1% > 0.5%, where the first loss halves the risk, the second loss in a row halves again and it stays there till the first loss is recovered.

- **MAXIMUM MARKET RISK:** Concurrent market exposure. I use 10%. Protects against market wide events (systematic risk).

- **MAX RISK BEARING TRADES:** Max market risk / account risk per trade. 10 / 2 = 5 trades for me at 2% (10 at 1%).

- **MINIMUM RISK:REWARD FOR ENTRY:** Minimum R:R to enter trade. My personal number is 1:2.

- **TARGET RISK:REWARD:** Optimal R:R for strategy based on testing and optimisation. Different for every strategy and defined in testing.

- **MAX DAILY, WEEKLY & MONTHLY DRAWDOWN:** Allowable losses before stopping. Protects me from myself and chasing losses. If triggered, no more capital is risked in that period. My numbers are 4% (daily), 6% (weekly) and 10% (monthly).

- **MAXIMUM LEVERAGE:** I don't look at leverage as maximising profit, rather maximising permissible risk. For example, an intraday trade with 0.25% trade risk can utilise 4x leverage to size up to 1% account risk (1% / 0.25%). A swing trade with 4% trade risk enters with 25% capital to make 4% trade equal 1% account (1% / 4%). I don't believe leverage can be used any other way safely.
- **STOP LOSS MANAGEMENT:** How to move stops. Never wider, only narrower. Generally I move to break even once a key level is taken and no more. Once I make a trade risk free by moving to break even, either I hit target or I don't. Often if moving stops too much behind price you can be taken out before price continues to target. Testing shows it's optimal to move no higher than break even (including fees).
- **POSITION SIZING RULES:** How I consistently position size to ensure consistent risk, so the series is balanced. Position sizing allows me to standardise risk in every trade. This in turn makes sure R:R and win rate together are profitable over time. It's a big game of maths really!

Consistency is key. Consistency of position sizing, risk management, rules followed. When we do this as traders we make losing individual trades OK, because individual trades don't matter. What matters is the outcome over the **series of trades**. Consider the famous Bruce Lee quote:

"I fear not the man who practiced 10,000 kicks once, I fear the man who practiced one kick 10,000 times."

[Bruce Lee / Actor and Martial Artist]

The same applies to trading. If you're taking 10,000 different trades once, how do you know what's working and what isn't? How do you achieve mastery of a strategy and gain the results coming from mastery? You can't. The intention behind mechanical, rules based strategies and strictly defined risk management is to ensure we trade the same trade 10,000 times.

I could write so much on risk management for trading, It's a subject I'm passionate about as those from my groups know! I think as an introduction this is allows me to make my point: trading is about more than picking an asset and taking a position like many new traders think. It requires planning, testing, refinement, discipline and strict risk management. It requires both a strong psychology and the knowledge of how this affects you while trading. And most of all it requires consistent execution of all of the above, mechanically, leaving emotion on the sidelines.

POSITION SIZE MATHS

As I introduced this in the risk management plan it's worth going over quickly. My sizing maths is:

- $MTR (Max Trade Risk) = $Account * %MTR
- $RP (Risk Premium) = Long: $AE (Average Entry) - Stop or Short: Stop - AE (Average Entry)
- Position Size = $MTR / $RP

And an example showing this in practice would be:

- Variables: Average Entry: $10, Stop Loss: $9, Account Size: $2000, MTR: 1%, Target 1: $12
- $2000 * 1% = $20 ($MTR),
- $10 - $9 = $1 (RP)
- Position Size = 20 / 1 = 20 Units, $200 (20 x 10)
- $20 Risk (1% account), R:R 1:2, Profit Target: $40 (2% account)

This same calculation is applied to every position, meaning the sizing **always** comes out at %MTR, no trade loses any more than any other. On a 1:2 R:R it means the win rate required to make profit is +33.33% over the series. At 1:3 it's 25%. But **only** if risk is kept consistent this way!

In this example **trade risk** is 10% ((10-9)/10)*100 and the sizing maths makes **account risk** 1% as required. These are the two risks and their relationship as introduced earlier.

RISK GRID EXAMPLE

Since I introduced win rate calculation, Fig 15.1 shows an example Risk Grid from my website. Along the top is number of trades and corresponding win rate and down the left the R:R levels. The grid shows on a $10,000 example account how many wins in 10 trades are required for profitability as win rate changes. When testing a strategy against historic data we can use this detail to define whether the trade strategy idea would have been profitable or not over time.

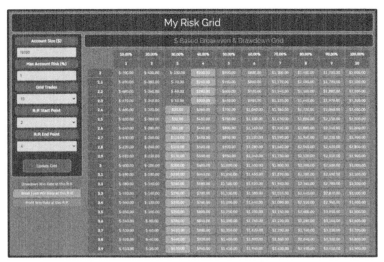

Fig 15.1 | Risk Grid example, 2R to 3.9R

STOP LOSSES

Our primary tool for implementing risk management strategy is the stop loss. This is a special kind of order that can be placed in different ways on different platforms, from actual stop loss orders to OCO (One Cancels the Other). It's an order we place saying "if price breaches this level my idea was wrong, get me out as quickly as possible, take the loss".

Taking the loss is something one must get comfortable with. Many a budding trader has been wiped out by thinking the market is wrong, moving their stop loss wider and wider till half the account is lost on paper. Markets are never wrong. Ever. So when it's clear we are, we need to cut losses quickly and the stop loss helps us do so. Some people overcomplicate stop locations, I think of them simply: I'm taking position based on a technical setup, so where's the technical setup invalidated? Wherever invalidation is, there's the stop location. And stops should always be known **before** placing a trade, they form part of the trade plan.

Fig 15.2 shows an example trade and stop loss location (black number). The marked entry area is a specific point of interest I use in my strategies. Once structure changed on the high timeframe (H4 here) this became an active area of interest for me for a short, if price came back to it and met entry conditions. As it moved back on the lower timeframe it presented the setup (you can just see the little pink triangle pointing right). Entry was midpoint of the range and stop was above the range high. Why? Because my experience tells me if price moves above range high I'm wrong, so it's where I want to get out. As it happened, it didn't, making target for a very good trade. We don't need to complicate stops any more than this. "Where am I wrong?".

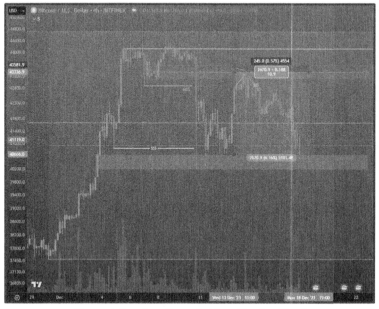

Fig 15.2 | Stop Loss Example *from Trading View)

BEING REALISTIC

When in 1-2-1's with new traders trying to help improve their technique I find one of the biggest issues is expectation. Expectation of return, of win rates and of how long it takes to become proficient. Proficiency, like in any discipline, takes time. It takes 10-18 months for most babies to learn how to walk confidently, the average 14. Trading proficiency is similar for most. Many times the issue is expectation of shorter timeframes and putting capital into trades too early as a result.

Win rate is another interesting expectation. I ask: "what win rate are you targeting?" and get answers ranging from 70% to 100%. This, my friends, is delusional. Some of the best Traders in the world get by on win rates of less than 60%, some on win rates as low as 20%! This highlights the actual reason I ask, win rate in isolation doesn't matter, win rate only matters when combined with consistent Risk:Reward ratio. A low win rate is fine if it provides high R:R consistently. But a high win rate is required if R:R is low. This can only be discovered with a solid trade strategy back tested against historic data to find the optimal levels of both.

The other expectation I find interesting is the process. People see trading shows on TV and think it all super exciting, when the reality is trading is mostly dull as a doorknob! It's analysing price data, testing on paper, planning and waiting, with the occasional execution when your rules are met. Less than 5% of my trading time is executing and executing is the highest risk bit because of me so I make it mechanical to keep me out of it! If you're interested in trading, make sure your expectations are realistic.

PSYCHOLOGY

Psychology directly influences overall success in trading. Fear and greed cloud our judgment and lead to impulsive actions, those irrational choices outside of our trading plans. Understanding our psychological tendencies is crucial for maintaining discipline and preventing emotion driven trades breaking strategy rules. Traders who master their own psychology are better equipped to handle losses gracefully, learn from mistakes and stay focused on long-term goals. As was hopefully obvious from the risk management section, in trading the person who is best at losing most often becomes the best at winning.

Journalling is a useful strategy for controlling this, where we record our market actions, what we saw, what met our setups and what didn't, how we felt when we saw these things, the decisions we made, what we could have done better and so on. Controlling ourselves is important if we have hopes of becoming successful traders and journalling is a very good method for doing this.

MECHANICAL PLANS

This is something specific to each individual trader but I can give you my views on building and testing mechanical trading strategies. Like everything I don't assume these perfect, they're just what work for me.

I always work in multiple timeframes, executing on the low timeframe and building narrative on the higher timeframe. Narrative is where I always start: what's the higher timeframe (like 1 Day or 4 hour) expectation and where are the higher timeframe points of interest where we may be presented with lower timeframe opportunities. At a very high level I want to identify what the higher timeframe probability is then trade in that direction on the lower timeframes. This is for two reasons: firstly it puts me onside as higher timeframe always takes precedent, secondly it makes it more likely to get a "runner", a trade that goes further in my favour, because I'm onside with higher timeframe structure. So, higher timeframe will define whether the direction of the trade I'm looking for is long or short. If trend is long, structure is printing long and we're low in a range, I probably want to be onside long, for example

Once I've identified narrative and I've marked the areas I want to look for entries, I'll drop to lower timeframes (15 minute down to 1 minute) to look for my entry conditions being met for the strategy I'm trading. If conditions are met I'll define my risk, calculate position size and place limit orders. Then wait. Once the trade is open the stop loss is set, as is the initial target (where I remove a partial profit). My only other management is moving stop once the first major swing in direction of trade is closed beyond. After this the trade is de-risked and I let it do its thing.

So what do I need for a mechanical strategy: Narrative (direction) and structure (builds narrative). High timeframe points of interest. Entry conditions on lower timeframe, stop location, targets to scale out and stop to breakeven level. I like to keep them fairly simple. Super complex trading strategies are hard to trade.

TESTING

Part of the process of developing mechanical plans is testing, as I've referenced a few times. This is another of the boring behind the scenes activities new traders often don't want to do but form a key part of the process. There are two types of testing, **back testing** and **forward testing**.

Back testing is the act of looking back through historical price data to identify instances of your strategy and recording the details. It helps you to understand whether an idea would've been profitable over time. You should look to find 50-100 instances of your setup and record the results. Often this testing helps you to refine the strategy, providing better potential results in live.

Forward testing is the act of trading your strategy on paper using live data as it prints but no actual capital. This happens after back testing and allows you to get used to trading the strategy live before risking money. As you might imagine, looking for instances in historic data involves some bias about what we might or might not have done as we can already see the result. Forward testing allows you to record the same detail but in instances you haven't seen the results yet. It's trading live without risking capital to make sure you can trade the right side as it prints, not just the left side historically. I like to look for 25-30 instances in forward testing to get comfortable.

Once strategy testing completes we know viability, expectation in terms of win rate and R:R and if we can trade it live or not. This all happens before capital is involved to manage risk and it's a lot of work, for every strategy you think up.

SUMMARY

I think this adequately covers a "Trading 101". I don't want to get into the weeds of trading too much here as we don't have the space. My intention is to give an introduction to trading and why it shouldn't be considered an alternative to investing. The distinction should be clear with some insight into the life of a trader. This isn't meant to dissuade you if it's something you want to try, it's simply to outline the differences and ensure you treat trading with the respect it deserves. Mastery of this art takes time and energy, for some who try to circumvent this, it takes even more money.

I'll leave you with a final quote, one of my favourites from a legendary trader I use often in my sessions. It covers one of the other things new traders struggle with: over trading.

"There is a time to go long, a time to go short and a time to go fishing"

[Jesse Livermore | Trader and Investor]

If you're interested in trading, make sure you heed this warning. We all sometimes could do with finding the time to go fishing! In terms of starting a trading account, any of the providers we've discussed already and many more are available. I use T212 in the UK and like their platform, but do your own due diligence to select one suiting your needs. Also, remember any trading account is taxable so maintain good records, including buy/sell exchange rate if trading foreign assets.

16

The Art of Self-Rescue

"No one is coming to save me; no one is coming to make life right for me; no one is coming to solve my problems. If I don't do something, nothing is going to get better."

[Nathaniel Branden | Psychologist]

AS INDIVIDUALS WE'VE MORE INCENTIVE to deliver our goals than anyone else. Other people can help but their support usually requires some mutual benefit. Where this benefit isn't present, incentive doesn't exist so action in support of our goals rarely materialises. Their influence can actually become counter to our goals in favour of theirs. This may sound a rather cold summation of human interaction and while I agree it's not a pleasant depiction, it's nonetheless highest probability. Understanding what drives people helps us to adapt our behaviours, it stops us assuming anyone else is coming to save us, let's us logically assess outside influence and strongly promotes personal accountability.

I think influence comes in two categories: conscious and unconscious. Conscious influence is where counterparty self-interest trumps everything. When at odds with our interests they'll actively and often knowingly act against us but when our interests align these people can be powerful allies. There also exists unconscious influence, where someone truly believes they're acting in our best interest but unknowingly acts against us, usually through lack of knowledge or understanding. This is true of life in general and certainly finance.

Conscious and unconscious influence surround us, they exist in every interaction, every day of our lives. When people think "influencer" they commonly associate the term with modern social media and the plethora of individuals openly calling themselves such, but influence spans human history, before spoken or written word never mind YouTube or Twitter (X). Influence then is wider than the realm of social media and if not actively managed can derail our pursuit of improved financial outcomes.

Social media influencers are an ideal example of conscious counterparty though. I hope everyone knows these individuals are paid by the products and services they promote, their aim being to part you from your resource for their own financial gain. The financial benefit derived from their influence is wholly reliant on their ability to make us spend money on the products and services they're paid to "shill". We're their revenue stream. Think logically, if companies who pay influencers didn't profit from these engagements, why would they continue to do it?

They're only one example of conscious counterparty though. Politicians, employers, consumer brands and mainstream media are a few other examples of entities who exist to promote their own interests ahead of ours. And they're very, very good at it. Consumer, Debtor, Employee!

Narrative setting within these groups is plentiful. We live in an era where perception is viewed as reality by too many people and perception is controlled by exerting influence. For those who look closely at the actions behind the words it's quickly evident the reality for most of these conscious influencers is very different to the perceptual narrative being spun.

Conscious counterparty is fairly easy to explain then. Metaphorically it's akin to old fashioned spy craft where the perception of personal relationship is cultivated to exert influence on an asset (us) for the benefit of the influencer and their agenda. Technology advance has made it easier to do on a mass scale, but the intent remains: cultivate assets (you) for influencer benefit, no matter the cost to the asset(s). We each need to be accountable for buying into these narratives and wasting our limited resource enriching these influencers rather than ourselves and our families. We must adjust behaviour by learning to identify and regulate it.

Unconscious counterparty is often more difficult to identify and even more difficult to accept as it mainly comes from those closest to us, family and friends. Their influence is without conscious intent to adversely affect our outcomes but adversely affect them they often do. Think back to the Framingham study and the impact on social groups where one member becomes obese, increasing group member obesity probability by 56%. This is an example of unconscious influence without nefarious intent.

In this chapter then I want to discuss influence and the financial risk of not managing it. I'll make the case no-one is coming to save us, especially those claiming they are. We must rescue ourselves. We won't be able to cover every individual example but we can raise awareness of the problem and make you think about the adverse influences in your own life.

START LINE HANDICAP

We've discussed this previously: while true start positions differ they don't necessarily define whether our goals can or can't be achieved. I don't downplay individual socio-economic variables, I raise this simply to say individual challenges rarely alter what's required of ourselves: personal agency, accountability and proactive planning towards future financial self.

We share in a single reality of finance, economics and markets from a **procedural** perspective and when it comes to beneficial actions within this procedural reality, those we're discussing, in my view they transcend the individual and starting point. At a fundamental level having a plan, getting debt under control, living beneath your means, improving income prospects and investing, for example, are universal. Individual approaches to "how" will differ but the "what" persists. If applied from any start point this "what" can help deliver the positive outcomes we're targeting. I've said many times my hope for readers is "better" and so although start lines will differ per person, so will finish lines where "better" is as subjective to each individual as start line.

Recognising that the principles, strategies and behaviours discussed provide a framework to overcome individual obstacles and take control of financial destiny is step one. We must ensure our mind works in what "is" not what "we'd like it to be" as a basis for sound financial decision making. So don't let your individual starting point or anyone pointing towards it negatively influence your belief. Remember Ford's quip: "whether you think you can, or you think you can't; you're right".

YOUR FAMILY DON'T WANT WHAT'S BEST FOR YOU

I'll start with the most controversial example of unconscious influence, the notion our family (and close friends) don't actually want what's "best" for us. This is an emotive subject which always elicits a defensive response when I raise it, but before you discard it as nonsense let me make my case first.

Our families and close friends care for us (hopefully!). They want to see us happy, healthy, content and free from pain or suffering. I'd hope we could agree on this point. But this is also where their unconscious influence originates, they never want to see us in pain, being uncomfortable or having to worry. Within us this instinctive desire exists to protect those we care about first and foremost and it can unwittingly become the thing adversely impacting success in our loved ones. What's "best" for us is **not** always safe, comfortable or without worry.

Success in a financial context generally means doing things differently. It means taking (controlled) risk and exposing oneself to potential discomfort, anxiety and even financial loss. It means acting in a manner counter to the "common knowledge" within our peer groups. This immediately puts us at odds with the primary objective of "protection" which is most often applied in a social norms context.

Think about the issue I described in "How did we get here", the message we received versions of during childhood to do well at school, get a good job, chase the promotions and so on. It's conventional wisdom and considered by most to be a blueprint for safety, security and happiness. The idea of working a good job for 45 years, living in a nice home with a nice car and a nice family.

This vision resonates with people and the accepted societal norm for how to achieve it is one of consumption, credit and working 45 years in a job you don't really like to pay for it, with interest. In the context of our discussion, of living without expensive debt burden and building long-term wealth for our families, I think we've adequately covered by this stage why this societal norm is actually detrimental, not beneficial.

Building real wealth, going debt free and delivering financial comfort isn't done by doing what 90% of people do. You must be different, doing what the masses don't. You must push yourself outside your comfort zone, you must take responsible risk and do many things those closest to us, our friends and family, won't understand because they do what the other 90% do. They think, incorrectly, it's how the comfortable, safe, pain free life they want for us is achieved. I've lived this paradox for two decades.

Our families and friends, thinking they know what's best for us and wanting to protect us from discomfort, pain and suffering, look at things we do differently and question the wisdom. And this is the issue: "are you sure?" from trusted advisors, those so close to you they warrant consideration, adds enough doubt to make you question yourself. They absolutely think they're advising what's best because they don't want you to be uncomfortable but unless they've gone through the process of becoming financially free and built whatever you're setting out to build, do they know what it takes? Their advice comes from a position of love and protection, but often not from one of knowledge or experience. Most of them are trapped in the Consumer, Debtor, Employee mindset and they wrongly see it as the safest place for you too.

You don't take tax advice from the postman or advice on legal matters from someone in the pub (unless they happen to be a lawyer!). If you want to improve your financial situation, why take advice from anyone who doesn't understand why you might be taking a certain course of action? I don't say this as an attack on friends and family, quite the opposite, I say it because I know how much influence they have and I want you to be aware of it. My wife, father and brother hold more influence over me than anyone. You're the one doing the work, using multiple data sources to improve your situation, to break the cycle. Maintain conviction in the face of bemusement as long as you've done the homework.

Do your due diligence, do your own calculations, do your own projections and if you deem it appropriate employ the help of a qualified financial advisor for a second opinion on specific questions tailored to your personal circumstances. But don't be talked out of taking action by anyone who knows less than you if you're sure it's the best course of action. Even if they're family who think they've your best interests at heart. This unconscious influence is generally the hardest one for most to overcome.

POLITICIANS

Difficult conversation done, let's talk about some folks I'm sure won't elicit such a sceptical response! Politicians.

> *"Only those who do not seek power are qualified to hold it."*
>
> *[Plato | Ancient Greek Philosopher]*

Politics is self-serving by design so I don't blame politicians. I could outline many instances of obvious self-interest like the hypocrisy during Covid, PPE scandals or contracts for friends and family, but I simply want to make the observation: anyone whose job is reliant on making popular decisions over good ones has incentive to make popular decisions over good ones. Show me the incentives, I'll show you the outcomes.

Fig 16.1 | The Overton Window

The Overton Window shown in Fig 16.1 outlines how politicians think. They act within a window of popularity and only push new ideas if they fall within this popular window. Ideas can move one way or the other but politicians only act once an idea has popular support. This doesn't depict left and right ideology, simply sliding scales of idea popularity and the folly of political discourse. Often the best ideas sit outside this window, so never garner political support because they don't win the votes to keep politicians in a job. Incentives in practice.

For example, we discussed earlier the unaffordability of the UK state pension. Data is clear and everyone, including politicians, knows we need a grown up conversation on its future. But even the suggestion of state pension reform is deeply unpopular with a large chunk of the electorate who are change averse and don't understand the problem, never mind the potential benefits in other solutions. So most politicians won't entertain it, preferring to perpetuate the same short-term thinking (like triple lock) that retains votes rather than engage in the difficult conversation we need to have. Pension reform falls outside the Overton Window.

My intent here is simply to highlight conscious influence from politicians. They tell us what they believe to be popular within such concepts as the Overton Window and do so whether it's the best thing for the general public or not. Often it's driven by what's best for them personally. Their incentive to keep their job (or make money from the public as many politicians do) is stronger than the incentive to do the right thing. No matter anyone's reason for entering politics, once there they become politicians. They prioritise what they can spin to get votes to keep their job. Cynical? Absolutely. Wrong? Historical evidence would suggest not.

The constant barrage of influence from politics, most of which is perception based, is rarely founded in reality. Another example can be found in how both sides in the UK claim the financial high ground. The other guys are reckless, they're not the ones to trust with the economy (because they know the economy is important to people, a "popular" topic). So who's lying, if anyone? Is one side better at balancing books than the other? To set the scene, in July 2023 UK national debt stood at £2.6 Trillion according to the ONS. I've some reservations about this figure, there seems some double counting making it higher than it ought to be, but we'll use it as the "official" figure. £2,537 Billion, £2,537,000 Million or £2,537,000,000,000. I break it down as many people have trouble conceptualising the scale of "Trillion", 12 digits after the first number. To put this into more context:

- Since year 0 there have been 2023 years with an average of 365 days = 720,188 days A.D.
- If we'd spent £1 million **more** than income **every single day** since year zero we'd be in debt to the tune of £720.2 Billion, 28% of current UK National Debt.
- The Great Pyramid of Djoser was built in Ancient Egypt in the 27th Century BC, ~2700 BC or 4,723 years ago. 4,723 x 365 = 1,727,180 days from the end of 2023.
- You can see where this is going! If you'd spent £1 Million **more** than income **every single day** since the oldest of the Great Pyramids was built, debt would be £1.73 Trillion, 68% of current UK national debt (I actually think this is closer to the correct number, double counting removed).
- You'd need to overspend by £4 million every day since the year zero (or £1 Million every 6 hours) to reach current national debt levels. This doesn't account for inflation.

This isn't total spend, it's **overspend**. How much you spend **more than income**. This may seem a strange sidebar, but it sets the scale of national debt in your mind in terms people can relate to. Remember this is national debt, not inclusive of personal debt.

Both sides use it as a political football and it's this attempted influence I want to concentrate on. I don't want to get into the debt itself, simply the influence each side attempt to yield with it and what harm is actually done to our personal finances.

So, does one side manage a budget better, like both claim? Well, the Tories have more than doubled national debt since 2010. That's not great, but as the sitting government we've no fair comparison with Labour, their opposition. Labour may well have done the same or worse if in power during this period. Fig 16.2 I think offers a fairer comparison, showing the last 53 years of budget deficit in the UK. Since 1970 in only five years has any government, Labour or Conservative, run a balanced budget. 5 / 53 (9.43%) where any government "lived within their means". Two of these years were a Thatcher Tory Government and three a Blair Labour Government. Tories have been in power (or coalition) for 25 of those years, Labour for 18, meaning Tories balanced the books ~8% of the time and Labour ~16%.

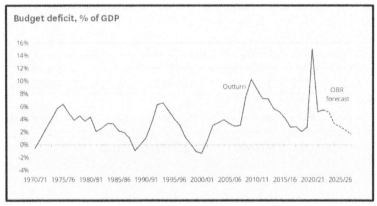

Fig 16.2 | UK Budget Deficit as % of GDP

In short, while the Tories have run more regular deficits than Labour and Labour may claim to be "better", neither have a recent history of responsible spending. Let me ask this a different way: do you think it makes much difference to financial competence if you balance your household books 8% or 16% of the time over 53 years, or do you think both would result in some financial issues?

Now, I know a national budget isn't managed in the same way as a household budget and we could debate the pros and cons of fiscal deficits all day so this point is somewhat facetious, but it's still a useful reflection on the influence I'm talking about. We could also look at how that money was spent, or rather who it went to, which would reflect more poorly on the Tories. Overall, Labour are slightly better, historically speaking, but they're both rubbish. Financially, it's like choosing whether you want to spend £45 or £52 on a single slice of chocolate cake, neither are particularly good but one is better than the other. They both spin this every which way to gain your favour to keep their jobs but both tend to adversely impact personal finance.

When they spend recklessly it invariably leads to tax rises, larger deficits, or both. We pay a higher price for poor budget management as governments continue spending like the Joneses through the self-interest of trying to retain power. They manage to convince the populace that tax rises which impact mainly those in work (mostly lower and middle classes) are required or as we've seen in 2023 just lie and tell us tax rises are tax cuts.

Politicians universally and demonstrably have self-serving expenditure issues. They spend for votes and try to resolve this with income because it's not popular to resolve expenditure issues at source and they're incentivised to do what's popular over what's right. They think if they can just "earn a little more" it'll be ok. Sound familiar? It's equally as counterproductive in politics as in personal finance. The general public being forced to give people who consistently show they can't be trusted with money more money to waste is like being forced to give an alcoholic a job in a brewery. We can, with high probability, predict the outcome.

2023 gaslighting from our Tory politicians and Prime Minister around inflation, tax cuts and wage increases are further examples of conscious influence. The narrative spun is one of the Tory Government having "halved inflation" (despite claiming they had no control over it when it was going up, conveniently!). At the same time they told us how great their tax cuts are for "putting more money in our pockets" and warned of the dangers of rapidly increasing wages.

The reality is their policies had minimal if any impact on inflation, the tax overhead for **everyone** is projected to increase over the next 5 years and wage growth has been all but static for over a **decade**. This is blatant spinning of the truth for self-interest. Conscious influence, knowingly lying to us for their own benefit not ours. I say knowingly because the only alternative is "stupidity" and that seems less likely than "dishonest".

Fiscal drag, which they're surprisingly quiet about, had minimal impact on inflation as the heavy lifting was done by BoE rate rises and reducing utility prices. But it's a stealth tax rise, meaning more people pay higher tax than ever before. In 2021/22 the UK Tax bands were frozen until 2027/28, meaning they won't move to the right with inflation and wage increases. Those already struggling will see their tax liability increase as wages rise but tax bands remain static, reducing the positive impact of rising income on families. The impact of this is estimated to be £25 Billion in additional lower and middle class taxation during a cost of living crisis.

It's estimated in 2023 alone an additional 10% of the UK workforce, around 3.2 million people, have been affected. As we move towards 2028 it will continue to suck more in as the government utilise fiscal drag to take more in tax from each of us. People are pointed towards "the rich", not realising it's impacting them and our leaders tell them how great they're doing at reducing tax while actually **increasing** it.

Finally we have the furore over the past 12 months around wage growth, the highest recorded since 2001. Politicians have tried to paint "greedy workers" a problem. Firstly, in real terms (when accounting for inflation) average UK pay is 2.7% **less** than it was in 2008. In 15 years, living standards have gone backwards, not forwards. This political narrative, perpetuated by the mainstream media is disingenuous.

Inflation being lower than wage growth at a specific point in time doesn't account for the higher periods of inflation previously. If the price of a basket of goods rises 3% YoY for 10 years as wages rise 1% YoY it means goods rise 34.4% and wages 10.5% (accounting for compounding). A delta of 23.9%. If in the 11th year wages rose 3% and inflation reduced to 2% it doesn't mean the problem of the previous decade was magically resolved. Theres still a massive delta over the period where people are significantly worse off, their spending power eroded massively. This is why many get a pay rise every year and still feel poorer, real terms wage growth versus nominal wage growth.

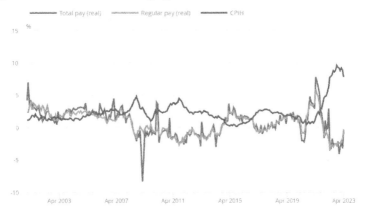

Fig 16.3 | UK Pay versus CPI (ONS Data)

Consider this chart from ONS for 2001 to 2023. You can see wage growth (blue lines) lower than inflation (red line) for much of these 22 years. Whenever the blue lines fall below zero, UK employees are getting **poorer** despite their pay rises. Politicians are trying to convince us rising wages today risks making people worse off. I'd counter this chart shows people are significantly worse off already and have been consistently so for a long, long time! They didn't seem to care about it before, so why now?

The Millennial generation is likely the first in recent history to be worse off than their parents with political waste a major factor. Cost of living is increasing with each generation as levels of taxation drift upwards and the services we receive in return are getting worse or in the case of the state pension slowly failing completely. The impact of political influence on personal finance for the lower and middle classes is net negative regardless of rosette colour, though I accept the "least worst" argument. But overall, politicians are absolutely the last people I'd trust to spend money wisely given their record.

So, politicians certainly try to exert conscious influence as these examples outline. They indirectly impact personal financial decisions and their policies directly impact financial outcomes. Their job, like social media influencers, relies on their ability to convince people up is down and all manner of other narratives suiting their own or their party agenda. We can choose to operate under the assumption politicians are selfless public servants who wouldn't lie to us. Or we can choose to operate in reality by looking at their history, across political parties. We can identify their incentives, so we can project the most likely outcomes.

CENTRAL BANKS

I want to look at central bank conscious influence through the lens of monetary debasement, asset bubbles and the Cantillon Effect. As you'll remember from our inflation discussion, debt can be reduced to an extent via monetary debasement. Consider again the example of £100k debt used to return a yield higher than both debt service and inflation. After 20 years the £100k invested has grown in real terms while the debt has shrunk in real terms, the cheap capital allowing for the leveraging of asset appreciation to profit over time. This is by central bank design (mostly).

Inflation then isn't always accidental. Asset bubbles either. Boom and bust cycles too. They're often by design, a part of the system. The Cantillon effect describes the uneven distribution of wealth from changes in inflation and money supply. Those receiving money early (banks, finance institutions, politicians and wealthy investors) benefit most by being able to buy assets at lower cost before bubbles inflate. Those receiving it later (or not at all) are worse off. Who receives the benefit later or not at all?

The general population have reduced opportunity after early beneficiaries have theirs, the worst impacted being low income individuals with no ability to purchase assets and benefit from inflation. At the same time these individuals see their already limited spending power decrease further. It's a wealth transfer, basically, from poor and middle classes to the wealthy such as we saw during Covid. Estimates are ~£700 Billion transferred from the general public, mostly middle class to wealthy investors or businesses and this will impact living standard for years to come.

I realise some will disagree with this summation and I'm more than happy to concede economics on this scale is an intricate web of variables, the interplay between any number able to produce the effects I'm describing. Differing arguments could be made. I'm also happy to concede central banks and regulators monitor this data and attempt to manage risk, with varying degrees of success.

But, none of this detracts from my overall point: conscious influence exerted by central banks is rarely in your best interests. You should **never** look towards politicians or central banks to make your life better! Certainly not to help you build wealth and clear debt because it's in their interests you take debt and continue working to support the economy they're responsible for. Be aware of their conscious influence, particularly when trying to convince you of a particular course of action, like for example CBDC's (Central Bank Digital Currency) which I'll discuss later. We operate within the constraints they impose, often trying simply to minimise adverse impacts. We **should not** rely on their actions being anything other than adverse, finding ways to get onside.

MAINSTREAM MEDIA

Journalism in a functioning society is traditionally considered vital in fostering honest public discourse and holding those in power to account. The role of news media is to provide accurate, unbiased information while maintaining independence, basically to present detail without narrative or opinion so recipients can interpret critically and decide themselves what it means.

I think it's fair to say traditional journalism of this kind is long dead. The majority of mainstream outlets today are far from objective, unbiased or in many cases even accurate. They pick sides and their editorial decisions are based on furthering their own agendas. Worse still, some outlets are bought and paid for so their reporting is designed specifically to further the agenda of sponsors, advertisers or partners and this often centres around parting their target audience from their resources. They've become no different. to paid social media shills, masquerading otherwise via a cloak of perceived mainstream credibility.

Gone are the days journalists were fiercely professional, keeping bias in check to present facts. I don't expect journalists to have no opinions, I'm not so unfair, we all have views on any range of topics. My criticism isn't having them, it's abusing their influence to promote their opinions as objective fact to benefit themselves. Not that this should surprise me using rational choice theory, as we discussed earlier.

Legacy media has given up on impartiality in favour of pushing their own or someone else's paid for agenda. I could give many recent examples where it was abundantly clear the presenter came with an agenda and used their platform to further it, generally without actual facts to back their position. The BBC interview of Elon Musk was a particular highlight of the ineptitude of modern journalists. As much fun as it is seeing these types dismantled by their interviewee, it simply confirms they can't be trusted to provide fact without personal or corporate bias.

It's obviously individual choice whether daily news is something you need. Just know the game in the context of our Consumer, Debtor, Employee triad. Distraction mainly through fear, through outrage farming, through promoting products and services helping you alleviate the very fear and outrage they stoked. Division in general. Keep us looking at each other so we're not looking at the real problems. Divide and conquer. Nothing useful while trying to find the time in your busy life to improve your financial outlook.

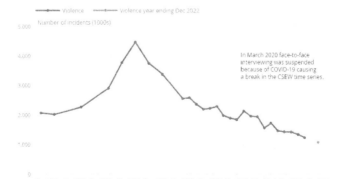

Fig 16.3 | UK Violent Crime Statistics (ONS)

Let me give a simple example. In the UK, violent crime statistics have been falling in general terms since the 1990's. We could debate whether it's actual crime number reduction or just recording of crimes that's reduced, but these are the numbers. In 1995 the rate peaked, gradually declining through 2020 (see Fig 16.3). So, violent crime rates have been steadily falling for nearly 30 years. Yet reporting on violent crime has increased (as news cycles shorten and outlets fill their timeslots) and public perception is that violent crime has increased, at odds with the data. This is also true of the US where reporting increased, violent crime stats reduced. Public perception is that it's higher than ever.

"If it bleeds, it leads". The sad reality of journalism in 2023 is fear sells. It sells more advertising, it sells more products, it sells more stories, it gets more people watching, reading or buying. Profitability for the outlets and personal gain for the journalists furthering careers trumps objectivity. There's limited incentive in objectivity, the incentive is to push the public in the direction the outlet or sponsors want. We must understand these incentives and protect ourselves from becoming caught up in the narrative spun for us. Never trust, always verify. Think critically about the data being presented and when it smells, look for the bull.

SOCIAL MEDIA

I'm not going down this rabbit hole again, I'll just remind you any "influencer" who possesses no demonstrable expertise, verified consistently in their content, is likely nothing but a paid shill who'll sell anything for enough money whether they use it or not.

I've no issue when businesses with social media presences make money. There are some I happily I pay to consume their content and these include channels who do paid sponsor promotions. The difference between these and the bloodsucking charlatans in my experience is they're upfront about it. They give examples of where they actually use the products and services they promote along with clear and unbiased opinion which includes positives **and** negatives. The products and services are within the sector they operate (like trading platforms for investing channels) and they have clear knowledge and expertise of the subject matter.

Plenty of experts provide excellent services for a small fee or even free content infinitely better than you find on mainstream networks. The trick is to find these amongst the pretenders. This is, after all, the age of pretence!

EMPLOYERS

We covered this in detail earlier. Corporate culture and all of the effort spent in buying your loyalty is conscious influence fuelled by self-interest. Making you loyal makes you less likely to push for market value for your skillset and allows employers to reduce their resource costs year on year in real terms at your expense. I'd hope you've been thinking of this one through this chapter given we covered it in detail earlier.

INFLUENCE SUMMARY

Many examples of conscious and unconscious influence exist in our individual lives. This chapter introduces some larger and more nefarious incarnations but the issue isn't limited to these. It's obvious to most people influence exists but in my experience we don't always pay enough attention or think critically about the messages given, allowing our resource to be consumed by those exerting it. We must consciously manage this in our financial lives so we protect our resource for delivery of **our** goals.

LIFE ISN'T FAIR

I want to discuss the reliance on the concept of fairness, something I've observed increasingly as I've aged. The expectation of fair can quickly derail the pursuit of the able mind. We've discussed this in a few different guises already, from blaming others to making excuses. It can be summarised in something else we've discussed: taking on the world based on how things are, not how we'd like them to be. An expectation of fairness puts one at a disadvantage.

"Life is not fair, it never was, isn't now and it won't ever be. Don't fall into the trap of feeling like you're a victim. You are not"

[Matthew McConaughey | Actor]

If you're of the mindset your outcomes are entirely as a result of someone holding you back, then you're only correct in so far as it's you and your mindset, you're the "someone". Get after it. Accountability is a more useful approach than victimhood.

One of my favourite phrases in this regard is "good things come to those who wait". Utter nonsense. Those waiting for their perceived turn instead of making it happen themselves through planning, skill building, hard work and determination are missing out to those getting after it. Be assertive and make it happen, don't wait for or expect someone else to hand anything to you and don't feel bad about trying to deliver your goals for the benefit of you and your family

It's a frustrating issue more prevalent in younger generations, though as with all things not universally. I've had the absolute pleasure of working with youngsters who know what they want and aren't afraid of putting in the work to get it. They take accountability and go after their goals. But they appear, subjectively at least, in the minority. At the risk of sounding like an old man howling at the moon: I've encountered more who expect reward for taking part than who grab the bull by the horns.

This can manifest in a couple of ways. There's a self-harming manifestation where the expectation of fairness and "everyone gets their turn" is a quiet, patient type of person who does their bit but never seems to get ahead because they're waiting their turn. Waiting for someone else to come and help them. Maybe they try a couple of things but they don't work out the way they want so they decide it's not their time and retreat back to waiting.

These are the folks I feel for as more often than not they're capable of doing it themselves they just don't know they have the agency. Life convinced them they're bad people for pushing for what they want, they're taking someone else's spot. Competence and work rate are high, they're not coasters. I've known a few in this category and my instinct was to help them to help themselves, some with success and others not. It's a hugely difficult mindset to change, leaving these super capable people millimetres from what they want but unable to reach out and grab it because they're holding themselves back.

If this is you, please stop waiting. You're more than capable, believe in yourself and step forward, one small step (or chip!) at a time. This doesn't mean be loud or obnoxious, I'm an introvert as you know, this means be competent, build skill, build knowledge and build a reputation as someone who delivers. Make sure you, not someone else, gets the credit for what you deliver and put aside any fear of failure. Ask the question about progress, test the market if you don't get the answer you want. The bottom line is if you give it your all and fail, your no worse off than you are **right now.** All upside, limited downside, Risk:Reward in your favour!

The second way this manifests is the polar opposite. Entitlement. People who think they "deserve" whatever they want. It should be handed to them based on nothing more than existing. Not through hard work, displaying competence or building and developing skill and expertise. "I exist, therefore I deserve and the world should give it to me or they're holding me back". These types are loud and obnoxious, generally. With all the respect it deserves: F*ck off. When you get there, F*ck off some more and when you get back, f*ck off again.

I apologise, but I'm Scottish so we've done well to get this far without me using profanity as verb, adjective and noun! This is one I feel rather strongly about!

I inherited a team once including some apprentice software engineers. Kids essentially who left school and hadn't gone to University but were successful in finding apprentice roles in a massive industry (financial services IT). Two 16-19 and one a little older (who was an absolute pleasure to work with and I'd still do anything for them going on a decade later).

The team was 4th line, the furthest along the technical career path where a hire from open market would require a degree and 5 years' experience. An apprenticeship was a decade advancement on a career in software development, an opportunity you'd hope would keep apprentices on their game. Imagine how hard it was then to keep a straight face when one of them asked for a meeting after 6 months to declare they'd "be better suited to the graduate scheme than the apprentice scheme" and it "wasn't fair" they were excluded from a graduate pathway. They felt "disadvantaged".

There's one pre-requisite for being on a graduate scheme, which his pretty darn self-explanatory. You need to be a bloody graduate! Our friend was adamant they deserved to be on the scheme and it was a form of prejudice they weren't allowed to join. The content there was "more suited to their ability". No accountability, someone else's fault, couldn't see the opportunity already given and didn't want to do the work required to take it. Despite having a 10 year advantage they think they're a victim. Pretty much "bingo" in all the things we've been discussing!

In summary, the first group expect fair and wait lifetimes for it to materialise when they're more than capable of going and delivering what they want themselves. The latter have such a warped view of what fair is through ingrained entitlement they'll never find it because they'll **always** think they're a victim even when in a position of absolute privilege. Mindset is a dangerous thing.

The best way to avoid either of these categories, or just the fair trap in general, is to acknowledge the reality of life. It isn't now, nor was it ever, nor will it ever be "fair". Don't wait for your financial future to materialise expecting fair, take accountability and work for it knowing fair is a myth and you're in charge of your outcome. Remember, no-one ever became a millionaire by accident and though that isn't our universal goal, the sentiment remains.

ATTRIBUTION BIAS: THE "LUCK" PARADOX

Attribution bias is a psychological phenomenon that leads to people attributing the success of others to chance external factors like "luck", rather than recognise the internal factors displayed by the individual to achieve their outcomes. Things like planning, knowledge, hard work, skill and determination. Have you, or anyone you've been in conversation with ever said: "They're so lucky", or similar, to describe another's success while overlooking the competence displayed and energy expended to get to where they are? Don't worry, it's common.

When seeing others succeed it's easy to simplify the complex combination of internal factors as "luck". People do so as a pseudo excuse, because it makes the outcome easier to explain in the absence of their own commitment to those same internal factors. They never consider outcomes earned, it needs no accountability on their part if it wasn't earned. They don't believe luck is, in most cases, the intersection of knowledge, planning and hard work.

This tendency to over-emphasise the significance of luck, downplaying what it actually involved on the part of the individual is a damaging form of "copium" and serves no useful purpose. It leads to resentment, envy and usually the complete dismissal of the struggle individuals went through to achieve their success. These mindsets form part of our earlier discussions on making excuses and believing we're being held back by some unseen hand.

I've been on the receiving end of this, from a member of my extended family no less. I'm sure others think similar I just don't know about it, but in this example they were shameless enough, or stupid enough, to say it directly. In conversation I was told I was "lucky" to have what I did, the inference being financially.

The irony is we were sat in the house she'd been given for free, for the kids she'd had young having never worked since leaving high school, on furniture bought on credit, watching a huge new TV, also bought on credit. The literal definition of things you can't afford with money you don't have trying to impress people you (clearly) don't like. Someone putting in zero effort but envious of family who earned some outcomes she felt she didn't have the opportunity to. Luck, not the additional education, experience (in my case starting a consulting company while at university to pay for it), planning or effort. Nope, we were just "lucky".

The truth is it's much easier to resent what others achieve and attribute it to luck superficially because it absolves the individual of any accountability for their personal outcomes. They believe success is determined by external factors beyond ones control, not by anything they have the agency to progress. "There's no point trying because I'm not that lucky".

Nonsense. So, if you suffer from this kind of thinking then you need to get rid right quick. No-one is accountable for, or in control of your outcomes or how you go about trying to achieve them other than you. This is how successful people think. If you want to be successful, you need to think like successful people and they don't see themselves as victims of luck, they see themselves as the output of their process. They don't believe they're being held down by anyone and even if they did, they'd double down on energy rather than collapse like a house of cards.

> *"I'm a great believer in luck, and I find the harder I work, the more I have of it."*
>
> *[Thomas Jefferson | US Founding Father]*

More than twenty years after this event I still see the "luck paradox" in daily life. Through invisible financial decisions and execution of our financial plan we're on track to meet our long-term goals, many are already delivered given time spent. We cleared the mortgage at 36 (35) and don't have any other debt, meaning we can invest for the future as we've been discussing and we have options when opportunities present.

My wife has a difficult vocation as a teacher, generally under appreciated by society. Having watched what she's put into it over the years physically, emotionally and financially (many teachers spend their own money on school supplies for their kids) when it was obviously starting to take a toll we had to look at whether it was worth it, from a health and happiness perspective. We did the maths and calculated if I were to work for an additional two years beyond planned (early) retirement then we could absorb her dropping to two days per week for the next eighteen years. I like what I do for the most part, but even if I didn't two years added to my working life is a tiny price to pay for 18 years of my wife's health and happiness.

Having the ability to make this choice was something earned through long-term financial management and the sacrifices we'd made. Most didn't see these and wouldn't make them themselves anyway. It was fully costed for our future selves and the books, with a few assumptions made as always, balanced.

Just as twenty years earlier, my wife being able to drop to two days per week has been viewed by some as "lucky". People want to know "why" because it's "not normal". Having had so much practice over the years I'm quite numb to it, especially as I know how few people are willing to make the choices and sacrifices we have over the years to be able to make these decisions now. We can't control the lack of accountability other people have for their own outcomes. We made difficult choices most clearly weren't willing to (or knew they could) make because we looked at the long-term outcome over short-term gratification. Our ability to make these decisions now is the outcome of our historic choices, just as those who think us lucky are enjoying the outcome of theirs.

In the same expanse of time we've deliberately bought and paid for two houses, a starter and a final, those people who think we're lucky have had five or six. In the same expanse of time we've had three cars each, both reasonably priced pre-owned standard (5 Ford and 1 Kia) vehicles, they've had six or seven cars each, often luxury brands, sometimes new and sometimes leased. That's just two simple examples I've already shown costed out over a lifetime.

Thankfully, those close enough to us whose opinions we value, our unconscious influence, know the reality of our situation and never ask these questions or make the lucky assertion.

I've no issue with people making their own decisions and no interest in telling anyone else how they should or shouldn't live. I'm simply pointing out all decisions have consequences and in financial terms you can't have your debt burdened consumer cake and eat it. For those of us who said no to the cake while you were feasting on it, you shouldn't be surprised twenty years later when we can buy the bakery. You certainly shouldn't consider it lucky!

It's just two sets of people living out the differing consequences of their historic choices. We're not angry we didn't get to drive luxury cars while we worked toward having no mortgage. We're not angry we didn't move house a lot. Because we understand these are mutually exclusive outcomes, you can't have it all. This is our payoff, our delayed gratification driven by balance. If your payoff is instant, that's your choice and it's fine, but understand the implications.

Either you live by short-term decisions inside the Consumer, Debtor, Employee triad, or like us you opt out of the system through the choices you make over the long-term. As I've said throughout this book, no-one is accountable for your decisions other than you, so don't pass off the achievement of others as "luck". Find out how hard they worked to get lucky, in the words of Jefferson. Ask yourself "what did they do that I'm not to get where they got, what do I need to do to get there". See these people as an opportunity to learn. What knowledge did they add, what work did they do, what process did they follow. Mostly you'll find the attributes you require absolutely within your gift, you just have to be willing to reach out and grab them, then put the work in.

So while you pursue your goals, never dismiss someone else's achievement as luck. That's a weak mindset, an excuse that doesn't help you move forward. Instead of asking them "why", ask them "how". You'll get a much more useful answer, one you can use to rescue yourself!

Then when you find yourself on the other side, once you deliver the goals you're setting out: never, I really mean this, apologise to anyone for being different financially, for having a plan they didn't and for executing your plan. The position you carve out for yourself may seem like privilege to those who haven't paid attention to the sacrifices, the work and the decisions you made to get there, but you'll know. Be proud of it, don't ever let anyone make you feel bad about it and certainly don't feel like you ever need to apologise for having the wherewithal to think strategically over long timeframes, taking a different path to their social norms.

SUMMARY

This chapter is a little varied but it covers some important psychological aspects of your journey. We've reiterated the importance of accountability for individual outcomes and that our outcomes are the sum of the choices we make in the process of arriving there. No-one else can make those decisions for us and when we look for excuses, for others to blame, it's self-defeating. Accountability means treating everything, even getting it wrong, as an opportunity to learn. Own it and use it as fuel to better yourself ensuring you never make the mistake again.

Further, we all need to be aware of the influence exerted upon us. This can come unconsciously via those we're closest to, friends and family who perhaps don't understand our goals and think they're doing the best thing for us. It can also come from sources consciously exerting negative influence for their own benefit, usually trying to part you from the very resource we're focussed on improving.

Whatever the source, being aware of and managing influence is vital for long-term financial improvement. It requires treating every interaction with healthy scepticism, a critical mind and an openness to what the other side of the trade is. What are the counterparty incentives and what do they say about likely outcomes? Retain agency, think about your decisions and ensure you haven't been unduly influenced by anyone into thinking something is good for you when data objectively says otherwise.

We discussed the pitfalls of expecting fairness, specifically in finance. This is never the case, especially if one is waiting "their turn". It's counterproductive to delivering your financial goals as success is an active endeavour not a passive one. This is true of most goals in life, even those not specifically financial. The promotion at work, the new job, finding a partner: the concept of fairness, while noble, doesn't help deliver them. This isn't a call to treat others unfairly, I think character and competence are the only two attributes that matter in people, it's a warning not to expect fairness from others.

We discussed making decisions based on how things really are, not how we'd like them to be. This is something people who manage to build wealth do well, they acknowledge working hard and waiting your turn is as counterproductive as feeling entitled and complaining it should be your turn without earning it. We need to use the agency we have to define how we'll deliver our goals, then go out and put the time into executing the plan.

Finally we discussed the luck paradox from both sides. Don't assume those with success have simply been lucky. Use them as examples, find out what it took, what they had to do, what did they learn, what decisions did they have to make and use the knowledge to inform your own journey. Attributing success to luck isn't an accountable behaviour, it's an incarnation of "can't" because you aren't accepting it was achieved you're assuming it was given and in doing so relinquishing your personal agency.

On the flip side, when you're the one who achieved your goals and others assign luck to you, shake it off, know what you had to do, know the decisions you made most others wouldn't and never apologise to anyone for it.

17.

What's in a Schedule?

"We are what we repeatedly do. Excellence, then, is not an act, but a habit."

[Aristotle | Philosopher]

I WANT TO QUICKLY DISCUSS this simple technique for managing time and energy, our other two base resources. I'm conscious our focus has been predominantly on money. This is inferred in previous chapters via discipline and planning but it's something people struggle with so I want to cover it specifically: having a schedule can help, especially in the early stages of your journey.

A schedule helps us create an environment where we can succeed, where we can be consistent in spending time and energy to our benefit. It removes the temptation to make excuses and reduces the impact of our often default setting that let's time drift without holding ourselves to account for it. I said I wanted this to be a holistic view of how one goes about escaping the system and this is a procedural foundation of successful outcomes.

As we've discussed, the key to improving finances over time is consistency. Consistency of process, effort and mindset. There'll be days you turn up and put in the work but don't feel you achieved much, we've all had bad days where we feel we never stop but look back and don't achieve anything. The key though is turning up and doing the work. Every good day was built on the foundations of one of those bad days we turned up ready for.

Often you'll have a run of crappy days then in the first hour of the next it all comes together and you jump forward 10 paces. As Aristotle described, excellence comes from habit, so we create an environment to build habit. I'm an advocate of building a clear schedule and holding yourself accountable for sticking to it to achieve this. I know, it's hardly rocket science, but the most impactful things rarely are! Successful individuals appreciate there's no quick fix and that the impact of compounding marginal gains over time adds up. This is another of those little actions, one of our "little chips" in Andy's Shawshank wall.

I'm a huge fan of marginal gains theory, employing it in my own practices. For those familiar, you'll have seen the fingerprints throughout the book. I've built the content trying to facilitate incremental improvements across a range of topics in your personal finances with the sum of these small gains combined to make a much larger difference.

Marginal gains theory, for those unfamiliar, was born in sport. Its origins are in the hugely successful British Cycling and Team Sky racing teams of Sir Dave Brailsford with the general idea that significant improvement can be made in any discipline by making a series of small, incremental efficiency and optimisation changes across all aspects of the entire process. It promotes the idea that looking for one large change (the silver bullet I've described) is less impactful than the sum of the series of smaller changes which lead to substantial progress.

Marginal gains theory has been employed widely with great success outside of cycling, within industry, business and scientific fields. When it comes to financial improvement at a personal and family level I genuinely believe it provides similar benefits, the "compound interest" for our processes working just like it does with our invested money. Small amounts consistently. It's certainly benefitted me and is why I advocate our "one chip at a time", "shortened feedback loops" and "no silver bullet" mentality.

The purpose of this book is finance, but this can be applied more broadly. The scheduling of financial tasks to deliver on your goals and utilise your time, money and energy won't take up every spare hour you find in a day. You'll likely have a job to work around. You need time to recharge, time for family, time to take care of yourself physically and mentally and so on. So when I talk about scheduling as an overarching principal I don't mean singularly from a financial perspective. But all of my financial requirements are certainly planned in my wider schedule.

I aim to time block activities I need to fit into a week to deliver my goals, financial or otherwise. It removes the need to think about "when" or "what" I should be doing and allows delivery to become habitual. I just turn up where I should, when I should and do what I should be doing. This breeds consistency, consistency breeds success.

If you know what you're supposed to be doing in any time block you're less likely to context switch. Context switching (jumping between multiple things) destroys productivity.

If you know what you're supposed to be doing in any time block you're less inclined **not** to do the work. When it's in your mind, it's not real, when it's written down you become accountable for it.

If you have time blocks assigned to complete specific activities, like 3 hours per week for learning or an hour per night to manage investments, it becomes habitual. You're more likely to do it.

I think most can relate to the following example. Families try to plan meals and schedule the weekly shop to make sure they have the ingredients. This keeps food costs consistent and you can budget on them. But think about post vacation week when you missed your scheduled shop. Maybe you've a few extra days off work and you're still in vacation mode. You don't have food to make meals so you head to the shop on Monday to pick up stuff for Monday, maybe a takeaway on Tuesday then back to the shop for more food for Wednesday night.

The outcome from a cost and calories perspective? You spend more and eat a poor diet. It gives us the excuse to throw whatever we want in the cart when "just popping in" and we come home with things we wanted but didn't need. The same logic applies to everything we do. It's been shown in countless studies: scheduled routine maximises productivity and focus, leading to better performance. One such example is the 2014 "Scheduling Software and Time Management Study" conducted by the University of Warwick's Department of Economics. It recorded a 13% increase in sales performance and 9% decrease in absenteeism in travel agent branches included in the study versus those not.

American boxer Joe Louis has the longest reign of any champion in history at 25 consecutive title defences from 1937 through 1949. He famously said of this notion:

A champion doesn't become a champion in the ring, he's merely recognized in the ring. His 'becoming' happens during his daily routine."

[Joe Louis | Heavyweight Champion]

This is an excellent summary. Many people see the result and think "they were lucky" as we discussed earlier. They don't see or appreciate what went on behind the scenes to achieve success. What went on behind the scenes is driven by the schedule which defines the time one commits to expend energy on their goals.

There are many ways you can define a schedule. I have three views: daily, weekly and monthly which I've included in the template (D. Schedule Creator) if you wish to use it. My Daily schedule covers everything from when I wake to going to bed. For example: going for a walk/run, eating windows, gym sessions, checking markets, identifying trade setups, writing, working and coaching. Everything I do in a day. My daily and weekly schedules are in one Monday through Sunday calendar repeating every week. I add new slots as needed. My monthly schedule is a list of tasks I only do once per month with the day and week allocated, so I can slide those into the weekly view.

This allows me to execute without thinking "what should I do today". I turn up where and when I need to and start the time block I've defined as providing me the most value. I don't have to prioritise on the fly and I can happily ignore anything not delivering the benefit I want. On most days at least.

There'll always be days with unforeseen issues or emergencies and our schedule needs to be changed at short notice. The key is these are exceptions. We don't step back from structuring our lives because there might be exceptions, we plan for the rule and deal with the exceptions as they come. These are genuine exceptions I'm talking about too, not "missing the game". I mean things like "my wife got stuck at work so I need to pick up my daughter" or "dad fell off a ladder, again, he needs help" type deviations.

How you choose to structure your schedule is within your gift, but I'd advocate having at least a full week (seven days) mapped out to start, so you can follow for a while and refine as you see what works and what doesn't. This doesn't have to be mapped to low level task either, time blocking is enough detail. For example "18:00-20:00: Write Book, 20:00-21:00: Look for trade setups for next day". This kind of level, just a block of time you know the activity, not the specific details. The main thing is to use the schedule to focus your time and energy (money if required) into specific blocks you consistently turn up for and work on delivering your goals. The schedule is just what ensures you turn up.

I also advocate **not** viewing weekends as "free days". It's generally when we have most time and while it's important to spend time with family and do things outside our financial plan, don't wipe out entire weekends and achieve nothing towards your goals. It's not how successful folks do it!

Estate & Tax Planning

"In levying taxes and in shearing sheep it is well to stop when you get down to the skin."
[Austin O'Malley | 19th Century Writer]

THE FINAL SECTIONS OF OUR financial plan are estate and tax planning. Although we can reasonably define some skeleton detail within these, both areas are best finalised in conjunction with relevant experts given the moving regulatory parts. You'll also need a lawyer/solicitor for the Will and Power of Attorney.

In estate planning we're looking at the optimal inheritance of assets for our beneficiaries. In tax planning we're looking for the most efficient and legal method of reducing tax liability in our jurisdiction. Both are complex endeavours with often changing regulatory guardrails, documentation requirements and penalties for getting it wrong. These penalties can be severe, so professional help is worthwhile to manage this risk. Remember though, you remain fully accountable to your local authorities.

Having made the case for professional advice and with the acknowledgement I utilise outside expertise myself, we can look at some of the considerations you might make.

ESTATE PLANNING: A SKELETON FRAMEWORK

Estate planning is specific to individuals as you might expect, as every individual has a unique estate. Your estate is all assets and liabilities including property, belongings, financial holdings and debt. These are distributed to beneficiaries in line with your will or in the absence of one, applicable local law. The financial plan we've built concentrates on accumulation of this estate, this section pertains to distribution of the estate you build **after** your death.

Distribution should align with your circumstances, inheritance goals and the beneficiaries you wish to provide for. You should periodically revisit your estate plan to keep it up to date in light of changes in assets, general circumstances and regulation but it doesn't need review quarterly. Generally I do mine annually.

Your estate plan should firstly record your **BENEFICIARIES** and share of estate if not uniform. You can also declare specific items you wish each to have. This should be recorded in a notarised Will as well. You should update beneficiary declarations on financial accounts, insurance policies and retirement plans to include those identified. Most instruments have individual declarations so you should ensure these all align with your wishes.

POWER OF ATTORNEY allows you to define individuals to make financial or healthcare decisions on your behalf, if you become unable to do so. Consider both financial and healthcare PoA to ensure cover and be mindful they do **not** need to be the same person. If you feel different individuals provide different value you can define separately. These provisions should also be made in legally notarised documents with a lawyer.

We discussed **LIFE INSURANCE** in the insurance chapter so you should have this provision there already. I'm adding here as a reminder and because it forms part of your estate planning too.

TRUSTS can help in estate planning for IHT purposes and asset transfer. We've a number of options in the UK and while we'll cover common ones, trust regulation is complex so selecting to suit your circumstances really needs expert advice from financial and legal professionals.

BARE TRUSTS (or simple trusts) give beneficiaries the right to income and capital from the trust at the age of maturity (normally 18). Prior to this the assets are held by trustees. We could utilise **LIFE INTEREST TRUSTS** to provide income for beneficiaries for the duration of their lives. After their death, assets pass to other beneficiaries (specified in the trust deed). We may also utilise **CHARITABLE TRUSTS** to provide tax benefits for the settlor of the estate (to reduce liability). These must be used only for charitable purposes though or they could fall foul of the law.

A **DISCRETIONARY TRUST** gives trustees the discretion (as you might imagine!) over how assets (income and capital) are distributed among named beneficiaries. Their flexibility can be useful for IHT purposes and to protect assets by shielding them from creditors. We can use a **MIXED TRUST** which combines some elements of this discretionary trust with the life interest trust to provide a "best of both" option too.

One more commonly used for IHT planning is the **NIL-RATE BAND DISCRETIONARY TRUST**. This allows married couples and civil partners to protect the nil-rate band (currently £325k) of the first partner passing away. Generally, if one of the couple die their assets transfer to the surviving partner exempt from IHT, but that partner retains only their nil-rate band allowance later. By setting up the trust the first partner can have assets, up to their nil-rate band, placed in trust rather than transfer to the surviving partner. Other beneficiaries like children can be named, including the surviving partner. When the surviving partner passes away, the portion of the first partners assets held in trust are not subject to IHT and the second partner still retains their full nil-band rate too.

Trusts are powerful options for estate planning and certainly something you should consider, but as said this should be done in conjunction with financial and legal professionals to ensure you remain on the right side of local laws.

We mentioned it a lot in trusts so let's look at **ESTATE TAXES**. UK inheritance tax (IHT) is currently 40% of estate value above £325k (2023). If leaving primary residence to children or grandchildren and the overall estate is less than £2 Million you get an additional £175,000 residence nil-rate-band. With house prices rising this is becoming a problem for ordinary families so finding legal ways to reduce liability is helpful. **GIFTING**, **EXEMPTIONS** and the aforementioned **TRUSTS** can be investigated for this purpose.

GIFTING is an option often unused due to concerns over the 7 year rule. If you die within 7 years of giving the gift then IHT will be due. In the first 3 years this is the standard 40%, but between years 3 and 7 this works on a sliding scale known as "taper relief", currently 32%, 24%, 16%, 8% and 0% (for 3-4, 4-5, 5 -6, 6-7 and 7+ years respectively). I don't think this is a reason to avoid gifting, particularly as we have tax free gifting allowances of £3,000 per year anyway, which we can roll forward for one year (to total £6,000). Theres no tax liability on this annual exemption. We can also give £5,000 to children, £2,500 to grandkids and £1,000 to anyone getting married. All tax free in addition to the £3,000. Many people build inheritance lump sums unaware they're able to give these gifts, save on IHT later and see the benefit while alive.

I also want to mention **GIFTS OUT OF EXCESS INCOME** here. Technically this is part of **GIFTING** but it's an often unknown allowance. On top of the gifting allowances mentioned, if you have "excess income" from any source (including pension, dividends and property) you're allowed to regularly gift this **tax free** as long as it doesn't impact your standard of living. It has to be regular and come from income and you must record it for beneficiaries to claim as part of estate settlement, but it's another way you can give your children regular excess income (like pension) completely tax free as inheritance **before** your death, again not subject to lump sum inheritance tax. Few people utilise this, but if you're saving a lump sum using excess income that'll be subject to inheritance tax later, this presents a perfectly legal way to reduce the tax burden with the added benefit of being alive to see your children spend it, like I mentioned in gifting allowances above.

I've mentioned a few times, but a **LEGALLY NOTARISED WILL** should be part of your estate planning too. This is a legal document outlining how assets should be distributed after death. It outlines your estate, beneficiaries discussed earlier and specific split of assets. This allows you to propose items like artwork or jewellery go to specific beneficiaries. You can also appoint an executor to manage your estate to avoid infighting (we've all seen Judge Judy!). This is a legal document so needs to be formulated and notarised by a legal professional, which usually carries a nominal charge of a few hundred pounds. You may have both a living will (crossover with Medical PoA) and a last will and testament.

These are the common items one would consider in the estate plan but there are others you may consider depending on personal circumstances. This is not exhaustive, which is why an estate planning specialist would add value, but it gives further ideas:

GUARDIANSHIP FOR MINOR CHILDREN: Those with kids may wish to designate guardians in their will to care for them if both parents pass away. Planning this allows you to discuss with potential guardians, explain how you'll leave funding and how you want it to be spent to the benefit of the children. It also provides an opportunity to discuss with family members you won't define as guardians so you can explain your choice to avoid confusion. This may be an awkward conversation but it shouldn't be avoided.

Consider your preference for **FUNERAL AND BURIAL ARRANGEMENTS.** What do you want? My own plan is simple: I'll be dead so I don't care, do what you want with my corpse. Set it on fire, throw it in a hole, leave my bum pointed out the earth for a bike stand, whatever floats your boat it makes no difference to me! I don't want a religious ceremony but in my view it's for those I leave behind, not me, so my loved ones should do whatever they need to allow them to move on, I'll cover the bill from this plan (within reason!). As well as documenting this in your plan it's pertinent to discuss with loved ones in advance. It's morbid but it helps to share verbally so there's no miscommunication.

FINANCIAL ACCOUNTS AND PASSWORDS: not together in plain text. You should have records of financial accounts and platforms so beneficiaries know what you have and where. It's estimated up to £15 Billion (gov.co.uk and entitledto.co.uk) lies unclaimed because people don't leave adequate records for their loved ones. From bank accounts to investments to pensions to life insurance policies. To avoid your family losing the assets you've worked hard for you should have detailed records. Having a list of locations in your plan (and Will) then recording account details like usernames and passwords (encrypted) in a safe, safety deposit box or some other such (offline) secure repository will save time and help avoid forfeiture of the inheritance you built. After death your beneficiaries can't use these to transfer assets, they must go through the legal process, but it will help to outline what's actually there and most importantly, where.

DIGITAL ASSETS AND PASSWORDS is a separate section given the added complexity of dealing with self-custodial wallets and digital asset exchanges, if you have such assets. As there are no middle men in self-custody you need to leave instructions on how to access assets and liquidate them via an exchange. If they're on an exchange (firstly, why! Self-custody) you need to provide details. Don't leave account details together with passwords and never leave seed phrases online (cold storage like a safe or safety deposit box). If you utilise two factor authentication (you should) then detail where it's configured and if possible have a second device configured in case primary is lost. As this is an emerging market, dealing with the legalities of death are likely to be difficult so the easier you can make it for loved ones to access your digital assets without putting your assets at risk, the better. You should have a portfolio with records of what you have and where, so they know where to look too. A simple spreadsheet can achieve this.

DEBTS AND LIABILITIES: The money map we built can act as an accurate accounting if updated. It allows beneficiaries to see liabilities in your estate. This includes loans mortgages, credit card balances and any other outstanding debt they likely need to clear. You can define, if you wish, how you'd like these debts to be settled utilising the assets in your estate.

You've heard stories of spinsters leaving their estate to their cats! Hopefully you won't be so extreme but if you wish to support charitable causes through **CHARITABLE GIVING** you can include these in your plan and will, avoiding any contention between beneficiaries and charities later. As with all estate planning, clarity of wishes can avoid issues, even if they don't satisfy everyone involved! You should consider establishing charitable trusts or foundations if you have substantial assets to donate.

From a tax efficiency perspective, hopefully it's clear why seeking expertise in this area can be of benefit. There's a lot we can do ourselves but if your estate is larger than £500,000 as an individual (£1 million as a couple, both at time of writing) then accounting for this and finding legal ways to remedy the IHT overhead is useful for our loved ones. A reputable advisor can provide benefit tenfold or more their fee. Whatever the tax implications in your locale, knowing these and actively planning for them provides optimal outcomes for those we leave behind.

TAX PLANNING: A SKELETON FRAMEWORK

Tax planning is also an important aspect of managing your finances efficiently as the potential compounding effects of tax inefficiency over time combined with tax inefficient drawdown in retirement can cost six figures plus in unnecessary liability.

INCOME TAX

In the UK most income tax is deducted from salary through PAYE. Individuals outside PAYE complete self-service tax returns with HMRC to calculate their dues. This is similar in most jurisdictions, either automatic collection via salary or declared via self-service. For those with multiple income streams you likely need to do both. You can legally reduce liability in most jurisdictions too, which is where a tax expert with local regulatory knowledge adds value. In the UK for example this includes:

- Fully utilising tax allowances (like tax free allowance, starter rate for savings and capital gains).
- Assigning larger amounts to pensions (income tax free).
- Fully utilising marriage or civil partnership allowances.
- Ensuring dividends come from tax advantaged accounts like ISA's.
- Ensuring you receive any tax credits you're entitled to.

You should understand **PERSONAL ALLOWANCES,** the levels up to which you pay no income tax on various activities and instruments. In the UK your tax free allowance is currently £12,570 on income. Earnings below this incur 0% income tax. You should also be aware of personal allowances on interest earned and capital gains (outside of tax advantaged accounts). For example the starter rate for savings if you earn less than £12,570 is £5,000 in interest. Basic rate tax payers pay 0% on £1,000 of cash interest earned, higher rate tax payers on £500. Capital gains allowances on non-tax advantaged accounts is £3,000 in 24/25, inside tax advantaged accounts like ISA's it's tax free.

Let's use the example couple we used during our pension discussion for consistency, but their income is from any source (property, small business, part time job) rather than pension:

- £12,570 income each (tax free allowance) = £25,140
- £2,500 each in interest payments (from perhaps an offshore bond) = £5,000
- £12,000 from ISA savings (6% on £200,000 saved meaning principal remains) = £12,000
- £1,000 each in high interest savings accounts (for £20,000 capital at the moment) = £2,000

That's £44,140 in household income liable for no income tax by legally utilising allowances they already have. For comparison, if they each earned half as income, £22,070, their net would be £19,220 (2024) for £38,440. £5,700 worse off (annually).

You should be aware of local **INCOME TAX BANDS** so you can optimise income, deductions and asset building. This is particularly useful for identifying potential pension savings to reduce tax liability and build retirement accounts. In England, Wales and N.I current (23/24) bands are: Basic rate £12,571 to £50,270: 20%, Higher rate £50,271 to £125,140: 40% and Additional rate over £125,140: 45%. In Scotland these are higher: Scottish starter rate £12,571 to £14,732: 19%, Basic rate £14,733 to £25,688: 20%, Intermediate rate £25,689 to £43,662: 21%, Higher rate £43,663 to £74,999: 42%, (new in 2024) Advanced rate £75,000 to £125,140: 45% and Top rate above £125,140: 47%.

You should also regularly check your tax code is correct. HMRC publish details of these, with most people 1257L (signifying the £12,570 nil band allowance, S in front for "Scotland"). To avoid overpaying check regularly and contact HMRC if you think its incorrect. I've had to do this twice and they've been great, acknowledging a data mistake on correcting. It usually changes instantly with notification sent to employer.

Make use of **PENSION CONTRIBUTIONS** to reduce income tax liability and maximise pension investments while working. In 23/24 the UK Government increased annual pension allowances from £40,000 to £60,000 (or up to 100% of annual earnings if lower than £60,000). The lifetime allowance, formerly £1,073,100, was removed (gone completely in 24/25). For many this provides additional options to use pensions for tax benefit. For example, if you fall foul of the new Scottish "Advanced" tax rate then adding to pensions to remain below threshold is now worth 45% tax savings on earnings above £75,000. I keep talking about incentives, there's a rather large one. The same applies to all tax brackets though, contributing anything above £43,663 saves 42% tax on this delta too, for example.

As a reminder, if you're in pension drawdown then understand how to take advantage of any **TAX-FREE LUMP SUM**. In the UK we're permitted to take up to 25% tax free, either over time in retirement (DC) or in one lump sum at the outset (DC and DB).

Understanding your allowances, tax bands and efficiencies you can make for building future-self can have profound effects on outcomes over time. Tax is a complex subject though, so a local tax expert or accountant may be something you wish to consider and as always, remember the liability for any mistakes rests with you.

INVESTMENTS & CAPITAL GAINS

As we've discussed, **INVESTMENT ACCOUNTS** like ISA's, IRA's, Roth IRA's and pensions offer tax advantages, reducing overall tax liability (some income, some capital gains). Utilising these can positively impact on building wealth, so where possible make the most of these allowances. Adding more to pensions to save income tax when flirting with tax bands as discussed above for example.

CAPITAL GAINS TAX is paid on profit made on assets (capital) if not inside tax advantaged accounts. Anything you sell for more than you paid is a taxable event incurring a capital gain and a tax liability. Many people don't realise this includes sales of belongings like technology, cars, art or clothing if profit is made. Each individual has annual **CAPITAL GAINS ALLOWANCES**, though in recent years these have reduced dramatically. In the UK the limit reduced from £12,000 to £6,000 in 2023 and drops again to £3,000 in 2024. In other jurisdictions this varies, sometimes based on the length of time you hold an asset (over 1 year commonly). Ensure you're aware of local regulation and utilise allowances to reduce your liability.

Many people aren't aware **CAPITAL LOSSES**, up to certain limits and for maximum time periods, can be used to offset capital gains liability. In the UK for example you can carry capital losses for up to 4 years to offset against future capital gains. So, make sure you record capital losses and declare these via self-service to allow you to utilise where available in reducing capital gains tax liability.

Where possible then, utilise tax advantaged accounts before general investment accounts, understand capital gains allowances and minimise wherever permissible by offsetting losses.

TAX CREDITS & BENEFITS

Check if you (and any partner) are eligible for and **TAX CREDITS OR BENEFITS** like Working Tax Credit or Child Benefit/Child Tax Credit. Those with children or who are on lower incomes often don't realise they have these rights and no-one is going to chase them down! Be aware though if one member of the household earns £60,000 or more and the other claims Child Benefit the higher earner must declare via self-service tax return and pay a portion back in tax. If they earn more than £80,000 the entire child benefit will be paid back in taxes, so it's not worth the hassle. The UK government raised this to £60,000 to £80,000 in 2024 with further changes planned to move from individual to household totals in future. These changes are positive and should mean more people are eligible for the benefit so do check.

UNIVERSAL CREDIT replaced several other benefits and has been widely (and rightly) criticised in the UK. If eligible though you should understand limits and allowances to ensure you're getting help you're entitled to. Broadly speaking you're eligible if aged 18 or over, under State Pension age, not in full time education or training and don't have savings over £16,000. Entitlements range from ~£292 monthly for single individuals under 25 to ~£578 for couples over 25 (you must claim jointly).

These systems should not be abused by those who could otherwise find gainful employment, but many who could benefit from them, even in employment, are unaware. If you're in a low income or single income household, check to see what help could be available here as you move towards "better" financial health.

STAMP DUTY & PROPERTY TAXES

In the UK there's **STAMP DUTY LAND TAX** when buying or selling property, so we should be aware of thresholds. Breaching them can add significant sums to the purchase or sale, even on primary residence. Current these are £250,000 for residential properties, £425,000 for first-time buyers (buying a residential property worth £625,000 or less) and £150,000 for non-residential land

and properties. The levy is 5% of the value between £250,000 and £925,000, 10% from there to £1.5 million & 12% above.

If you live in a jurisdiction where **PROPERTY TAXES** are levied on value, be aware of the rate applicable and any exemptions or credits you can utilise to reduce liability. In the US for example property taxes average around 1.1% but they're local assessments so vary between states, municipalities and for different valuations. They fund public services like schools and infrastructure. There are legal exemptions, like primary residence (or "homestead"), senior citizens, veterans or in some states agricultural. Renewable energy incentives have also become popular.

Whatever your jurisdiction, understand the liability and any allowances or exemptions that could be applied. As always, no tax man is going to tell you what you're entitled to save, only what you're required to pay, so you must identify these for yourself.

SELF EMPLOYED BUSINESS EXPENSES

Legitimate **BUSINESS EXPENSES** can be used to reduce taxable income when running your own company, sole trader or limited. Understanding what you can and can't claim is necessary and can be a tricky delineation. For example if you do business from home you can claim a portion of heat and electric bills to cover the room you work in and write this off against profit to reduce tax liability. Business travel (actually used to carry out business) can also be claimed but miles covered on personal business, even in a company car, can't. It's particularly useful to utilise the services of a credible accountant for this review. If self-employed or running your own business, certainly retain all receipts and record anything that could legitimately be claimed as a business expense.

TIMELINES

Ensure you understand tax completion timelines and ensure you submit and pay any liability by due dates. Penalty charges levied for non-completion, inaccurate completion or late completion increase overall liability. You want to avoid this, for obvious reasons. Taxes are a necessary expense and though no-one likes paying them they're a net good. Make sure you declare honestly and pay what you're due. Utilising permissible strategies to minimise liability is perfectly legal, but you should **never** evade paying tax or be (knowingly) dishonest in your submissions. This is illegal as well as morally wrong. Pay what you're due, always.

In the UK filings for the past financial year must be completed (online) by the following January (31st) with payment due by the same date. For paper filing it's October following the April 5th tax year end. You can generally update filings for the current and previous financial year if you spot an error, but after 2 years they're normally locked without contacting HMRC.

EXPERTS

Consulting with qualified tax advisors or accountants to ensure you're making the most of available tax planning opportunities while staying compliant with tax laws can be hugely beneficial over long time periods. Many people don't like the fees experts levy against their services but remember if saving you more than you're paying, legally, their advice is worth it. If not perhaps it's time to consider the requirement.

Tax planning should align with your overall financial goals and you should stay as informed as you can about regulation changes impacting your financial strategy. All items discussed can change year to year, another benefit of professional advice being experts must stay up to date with changes so can pass on their knowledge.

SUMMARY

We've only scratched the surface of tax liability, concentrating on the income side without considering expenditure. Many people don't realise how much of their income goes towards tax or how, in many cases, we're taxed multiple times, including on the first tax already applied. Consider UK fuel and Alcohol duty (~53p per litre and 13.4%) applied to the price **before** VAT, with VAT then charged on duty as well product (so taxed on the tax).

Utilising legally permissible options to reduce overall tax liability means we reduce the impact on our families over time. Through lack of knowledge of their local tax system many lower and middle earners end up paying more tax than most people far wealthier than them. As should hopefully be apparent by now, the delta between how much wealthy people actually pay and the continual squeezing of the low and middle class is my main gripe with taxation policy based on income, the view income equals wealth. It's become a continual transfer of actual wealth from the working classes to the wealthy via taxation.

I find it frustrating when talking to people about increasing levels of income tax that many are in favour of increased taxation without thinking about the consequences for those actually affected because they've been blinded by the big foam fingers pointing at those they want to be affected, but rarely are.

For individuals, limiting tax liability via understanding the rules and acting within them helps long-term financial goals. Tax evasion is illegal, tax avoidance through legal means, the utilisation of allowances and strategies to reduce liability, is not. Politicians like to vilify utilisation of legal means, claiming moral high ground. The reality is most of them, their families and friends employ the same strategies, they just don't think they're for you. If enough of us learn how the system works and utilise it the same way they do, maybe we'd have no option but to look at taxing actual wealth instead of the fake vision we're sold as income.

Estate planning may not be a key consideration right now depending on age. Those younger and without significant assets may not feel this necessary yet. You should at least have something outlining beneficiaries registered with your pension scheme if you're of working age and paying into one (which you should be). Although unlikely, life happens, so outlining your wishes in the event of your death is also something you can do at any time. Let's face it, your wishes are unlikely to change often outside of large life events (like children or marriage).

For those with assets starting to think about inheritance you should already have beneficiary statements complete and records of assets and liabilities, you should also have a notarised Will. If not these are the first things to remedy. Once you do, look into options in your jurisdiction and if required employ the services of a reputable estate planner. It may be advantageous, for example, for you to use gifts from excess income sooner, rather than later.

Estate and tax planning aren't the "sexiest" parts of a financial plan, but as a holistic plan for your financial future they're an important piece of the puzzle. One should treat these as seriously as any other section. We don't want to do the hard work building and realise our loved ones get less at the end of that hard work.

ACTIONS:

- Refer to tab "A. Actions" in the Financial Plan template.
- Complete the actions defined in section ".: 18 :. | Estate & Tax Planning"

Embrace Discomfort & Prioritise Value

"Too often, we enjoy the comfort of opinion,
without the discomfort of thought"

[John F Kennedy | US President]

AS WE APPROACH THE END of our journey I wanted to include this short discussion on mastering discomfort and concentrating on value. I intentionally left this until the closing stages as for many new to finance and personal money management there may be a feeling of discomfort setting in at this stage.

I've intimated I want this book to encourage you to take action for the financial betterment of yourself and your family, to help you escape the trappings of everyday societal norms and begin to build for future you. Taking action personally is the only way those benefits can be realised. To quote a previous chapter, no-one else is coming to save you, so I don't want you to be discouraged by any discomfort at this stage. Quite the opposite, I want you to embrace it as a necessary part of the process.

Discomfort can be an easy excuse we use in trying to justify not pushing forward with something new or something we're trying to improve in. "I can't" or "It's too hard". No-one ever finished anything without starting and the voice in all of our heads telling us we can't do it needs muted. If we don't try, it'll definitely be right. If we do try it might just be wrong.

We'll never get rid of this voice entirely but we can develop the ability to use it when beneficial and quieten it when not. This is how we embrace discomfort when adopting something new, turning the uncomfortable into the comfortable. This bookends nicely with our early conversation on controlling fear and greed because discomfort comes from fear, from lack of knowledge and experience. Learning and doing is how we gain knowledge and experience so we must not deprive ourselves of it through the feeling of discomfort.

So if you're feeling overwhelmed by anything we've discussed, from getting to grips with investing or sorting out your cash flow to looking at your expenditure honestly or understanding tax regulation, that's absolutely fine. This is a journey and one reading this book and others like it won't be the end of. Embrace any discomfort you're feeling at the moment, know you can overcome it through experience and allow yourself to gain experience through doing. Think about when you learned to swim, or ride a bike, or drive a car. Proficiency is built through conquering discomfort.

It sounds simple, but I know it's not quite so easy in practice! So, let's look at some things that help embrace the uncomfortable.

No surprise, **PREPARATION AND EDUCATION** is the first building block just as it was one of the first issues discussed in this book. Knowledge is a sure fire way to boost your confidence in any arena. Look at my previous examples of learning to swim, ride a bike or drive. Even look at your job and how much better you are at it five years after you start. The same applies to finance. Learn as much as you can and don't be afraid to fail (more on this in a minute!).

You can't go from zero to expert in 5 minutes, so set **REALISTIC EXPECTATIONS**. Understand financial improvement is a process measured often in years and decades, not days and weeks. Recognise discomfort is a natural part of growth and don't expect yourself to be perfect or entirely at ease from the beginning. Accept the learning curve, treating mistakes as opportunities to learn not opportunities to beat yourself up or quit. In my trading circle unrealistic expectation is a huge part of what drives the huge (90%+) dropout rate, so I think it's a good example here.

BE POSITIVE. Paraphrasing Henry Ford, don't talk yourself out of the uncomfortable, talk yourself into it. Know your strengths and weaknesses and focus on what you **can** do rather than what you **think** you **can't**. Don't let the person holding you back be you through negative attitude.

"You either win, or you learn". One of my favourite trading quotes of all time and the mindset I advocate, understand making mistakes is part of the **LEARNING PROCESS** and rather than dwelling on perceived failures, see them as valuable experiences leading to future improvement. Certainly don't use them as excuses to quit, convincing yourself you can't do it and proving yourself right in one fell swoop!

Next. something else we spoke about earlier: the importance of being able to tick things off and being able to see progress. Achieving these smaller milestones can boost your confidence and motivate you to keep moving forward, so "Value Slicing" into SMALLER, MANAGEABLE GOALS is an excellent technique for keeping positive feedback loops, any feedback loop, constant.

Don't hesitate to reach out and SEEK GUIDANCE from mentors, colleagues or friends who have experience in the field or faced similar challenges. Again as we've discussed successful people can be role models so ask them "how and why" rather than ask those who aren't successful. Often people are happy to share experience, all you have to do is ask. When someone has gone through the process themselves they're generally open to sharing their guidance and reassurance because they know how hard it was.

It's so easy to make negative assumptions, which we touched on in our chat around making excuses. CHALLENGE NEGATIVE ASSUMPTIONS WITH DATA, always. A data driven approach takes the subjectivity out of many situations and allows you to make objective decisions based on rational thought not irrational fear. One of the primary tenets of this book has been to move people from making unconscious financial decisions to making conscious ones and we do this best with data.

DO NOT DEMAND PERFECTION, PURSUE EXPERIENCE AND GROWTH. Understand improvement takes time and you will make mistakes, perfect doesn't exist. Your outcomes are the result of your process, the result of your growth, not the only measure. Remember, most wealth is lost in the second and third generation not because they don't understand wealth but because they don't understand what it took to build it. The process, the learning, the growth yields and retains the results. Results without growth often leads to negative outcomes, just look at the number of lottery winners who go broke......

I raised this earlier when talking specifically about education and learning, but the same applies in an overall context. We should INVEST IN OURSELVES. Adequate sleep, exercise and a balanced diet take care of your physical and mental well-being which can help you better cope with the discomfort of finding yourself in a new world of finance you didn't know existed. I firmly believe success is a holistic venture. Invest in yourself also covers learning (buying books for example!) and actual investment in assets for your future-self. This one is important, one of the major mindset shifts this book has taken aim at. Prioritising future-self **is** investing in you, just be aware this can be done in more ways than just buying assets. Education, physical and mental wellbeing, sleep, diet are all aspects of investing in yourself too.

You must learn to **ACCEPT AND SHAKE OFF CRITICISM.** Recognise not everyone will respond positively to your new venture or ideas, particularly as we've discussed those who don't understand them or the reasons why you might take a particular approach outside "the norm". By now you know "the norm" is broken and those successful from a financial perspective operate outside of it. This is your benchmark, not those who operate inside. Think "the Matrix" and be prepared for rejection and criticism from all the agents who think the system is paramount without being adversely impacted.

Said many times but keeping here for completeness, **OBSERVE AND LEARN FROM THOSE WHO SUCCEED FINANCIALLY.** Model their behaviours, strategies and mindset and learn what they did to get to where you want to be. Often times, it's not complicated, just different.

Something I find immensely helpful in general and from a trading perspective is **KEEPING A JOURNAL** to refer back to. It helps refine process, helps identify mistakes, record areas I need to improve and in general keeps me grounded even when things are going well. What you journal is personal to you, but from the perspective of making the uncomfortable comfortable keeping a journal of what that is and what you're doing to overcome it can certainly help maintain a psychological level.

Lastly but importantly: **GIVE YOURSELF CREDIT.** It's easy to beat ourselves up when things don't go well, always looking at the negatives. In many people, myself included, this is far easier than acknowledging positives. To turn the uncomfortable comfortable in financial endeavours one should celebrate their achievements, no matter how small they seem. Recognise effort and success along the way as a means to keep you motivated to move forward. Reading this book to this stage, for example, is an achievement. Not only because of my verbosity, but because it can be a dry subject with plenty of technical subject matter that's hard to get through. But if this subject matter were easy, everyone would be rich. We know that's not the case, so give yourself the credit for getting through it!

These are just a few of the things you can develop into your routines to help to make discomfort while implementing financial change in your life more comfortable over time, as you gain valuable knowledge and experience. This forms part of your escape from the Consumer, Debtor, Employee triad.

The final thing I want to raise in this message is a reiteration of something we discussed earlier, the prioritisation of value in the actions you take. I hope you've found this book valuable and it's lit the fire of action underneath you as intended. As you define what these actions look like for you at an individual level, doing your own research and due diligence of course, prioritise them based on the value they provide you. We discussed this earlier in detail so I offer this here as a reminder that we should put value at the heart of the actions we take. And this isn't always financial value, it can be value in building and maintaining relationships or in defining a new method by which you'll ensure continuous learning.

When prioritising though, remember it's easy to get caught up trying to do everything at once, which can be counterproductive. Prioritise highest value items and concentrate on those first. Financial examples could be found in reducing your interest liability by targeting certain debt first or by prioritising pension contributions based on pension modelling, for example. Whatever you decide, know the value of each item on your backlog, make it data driven and prioritise using that value. Make time a factor in this decision. If you have 3 items for example, item A delivers the highest value but takes 6 months and items B and C deliver similar value but will take 3 months each, then you may wish to consider B or C first based on value and time.

This is all I really wanted to discuss here, I did promise a short discussion! No specific actions, just a message after going through some heavy content chapters: any feelings of discomfort are normal and when embarking on changing your financial outlook it's both OK and something you should get used to. The rewards of progressing can far outweigh the discomfort you need to overcome and turning the uncomfortable into the comfortable is a skill worth developing in and of itself, for all things not just finance.

Review & Execute Your Plan

"That which is measured improves. That which is measured and reported improves exponentially."

[Karl Pearson | Mathematician]

WE ARRIVE THEN AT THE end of your financial plan creation with a little chat about execution, tracking and review. I'll keep this short before a final supplementary chapter and closing!

TIMESCALES & WHAT TO DO

We'll start with the easy bit, setting up a review schedule. How often should we review our overall plan and what are we looking to achieve when we do so? Review cadence is personal, whatever fits your circumstances best. Personally I like quarterly with a larger annual review looking at regulatory and income changes.

QUARTERLY REVIEWS are on a shorter feedback loop allowing adjustment if required without waiting too long. This includes:

- Ensuring goals unchanged in last 3 months (no unforeseen events like change in employment, health or family issues).
- Ensuring I've done what I needed to do in the last 3 months to stay on track. If I missed anything what do I need to do in the next 3 months to remedy.
- Have there been any market changes I wish to take advantage of? For example, if a recession declared or is on the horizon do I want to do anything with my moonshot positions to free capital to take advantage of opportunities. Or can I utilise any other capital I have with low risk (like holiday savings) for a short period to take advantage.
- Have any new risks presented in the past 3 months I need to take action to mitigate before they materialise as issues?

- Is my tax planning on track for last quarter or do I need to make adjustments?
- Is my money map where I would expect it to be or am I over/under spending?
- Do I need to do any portfolio rebalancing?
- If you have debt liabilities, you may wish to track whether your plan is on track or if you've incurred additional debt/interest (changes in interest rates for example).

ANNUAL REVIEWS on a longer timeframe let me review the macro aspects of my plan and any changes outside my control like pay increases, tax assessment submission and regulatory changes. Having these inflection points four times per year on a quarterly basis, with one being a full annual review works well for me. I also have other review cycles on shorter timeframes for trading, weekly and monthly, but that's a different discussion.

Ultimately, pick a frequency you'll **stick to**, allowing the balance of short-term and long-term feedback. You don't want to be in a situation where your feedback loop is so long you can't make adjustments in a meaningful timeframe when your goals fall off track. But equally you don't want to be reviewing so frequently that you get annoyed doing it so stop or make so many changes they actually knock you off track. There's a balance and it comes with time and experience. You can always adjust this as required, so start with something like quarterly and change as necessary.

UPDATES

It took me a while to realise it's beneficial to have previous data to refer back to. It's tempting to simply update the sections in your plan and save it with the same name but this becomes troublesome to track decisions over time, even with track changes switched on.

I now prefer to save a new copy every quarter with the date of review as a filename prefix. I then always have a copy which allows me to look back at previous quarterly versions of the plan to see specifically what I changed and why. I recommend this for record keeping purposes. The second thing I'd add through this experience is the recording of "why" in your plan, even if it's just a rough note. There's nothing quite so frustrating in this endeavour, especially as we get older, than trying to remember why we made a 2% adjustment to pension contributions 3 years ago in Q3!!

To assist with this I've added a "B. Audit Log" sheet within the planner file allowing you to record date, plan version, section, change made and why. As you save this file as a new version every quarter these audit logs (if you maintain them) will move with each new version and you can refer to this sheet at any time to see all of the changes made in the past, to what specific sections and why you made them. This data is invaluable to me, hopefully you understand the benefit in maintaining it as well!

THE HARD PART - EXECUTION

What you need to execute your plan is going to be individual to your plan. I know I sound like a broken record in saying personal finance is personal to individual circumstances but it's absolutely true. Having gone through the detail you've hopefully built a skeleton plan for yourself, to your specific circumstances. Your goals and the actions required to deliver them should be clear to you now, having done the work to put them together as part of this journey. You should also have some of the knowledge required from the technical discussions to start executing on these actions, or worst case know what you want to investigate more within the detail to do your own due diligence and allow you to progress.

So, it's over to you my friend. You hopefully have some new insights into personal finance and escaping the system. You have a plan with a destination and a roadmap you've defined to get you and your family there and you know many of the societal, personal and influential pitfalls fighting against you as you try.

My message, having come this far, is simply to keep going. Don't let the work you've done here go to waste. Don't let this be a book you put down without taking beneficial action, letting the rubber band snap back. Don't let those who don't understand what you're doing talk you out of aiming for financial betterment or worse those who do understand influence you out of it. Take the action you've defined, inspect what you expect by constantly reviewing the output of those actions and your plan, become a builder of assets, not a consumer of liabilities.

Step away from societal views of "normal", safe in the knowledge normal fails 90% or more people who subscribe to it. Break the wheel for the betterment of yourself and your family, opting out of the Consumer, Debtor, Employee triad forever.

ACTIONS

- Refer to tab "A. Actions" in the Financial Plan template.
- Complete the actions defined in section ".: 20 :. | Review & Execute Financial Plans"

CBDC: Supplementary Thoughts

"The danger of an unelected official is that he's never thrown out of office and his temptations are to think he's above the law, not accountable to the people."

[Michael Bloomberg | Businessman & Politician]

I SWITHERED WHETHER I SHOULD include this supplementary chapter but in the context of changing financial landscapes the rising volume of Central Bank Digital Currency discussion concerns me. It's something one should be aware of when trying to improve financial outcomes for the long term so I want to offer some views and explain why I'm watching the progress of these very closely.

WHAT'S A CBDC?

First, let me explain what CBDC's are for those who maybe aren't aware. A Central Bank Digital Currency is a digital form of fiat currency issued and regulated by a central bank like the Fed, Bank of England or ECB. Unlike traditional physical currencies, CBDC exists in electronic or digital form only, there's no corresponding cash and coin. The central bank has the sole authority to issue and manage the currency, extending into the digital realm in a way never seen before.

Some are confused by this as our currency is already viewed as "digital", with the rise in internet banking, banking apps, electronic transfers and so on. But this is simply an electronic representation of the movement of traditional fiat currency, not a digital implementation of it. The major difference is CBDC's leverage blockchain or distributed ledger technology to ensure secure and transparent transactions. Yes, just like cryptocurrency (remember, cryptocurrency is bad though, according to policymakers pursuing CBDC).

It can take two general forms: retail CBDC's accessible to the general public for everyday transactions and wholesale CBDC's designed for financial institutions and interbank transactions (in some ways similar to nostro/vostro but without the overhead of parked funds around the world).

The motivations espoused by CBDC proponents, like the UK's Rishi Sunak, often include enhancing payment efficiency, reducing the reliance on physical cash, addressing issues related to financial inclusion, safety (always has to be there!) and staying ahead in the evolving landscape of digital currencies. CBDC would also provide the central bank with direct and digital tools for implementing monetary policy, monitoring transactions, and influencing the money supply.

The introduction of CBDC's raises a number of issues related to privacy, cybersecurity and the overall structure of the financial system though and it's these issues which give me concern. I don't worry about the technology, as will likely be obvious from some of my other commentary my concerns centre around the people who will control it. Governments and central banks worldwide are actively exploring CBDC initiatives with some countries like Brazil and China already in advanced stages of development or pilot programs. The Bank of England, US Fed and ECB are all actively pursuing this technology so we should certainly all be aware of it.

UNELECTED OFFICIALS

Now that I've explained what CBDC's are, why do they have me concerned enough to add this short chapter? I've a few concerns to raise, though I'll say openly that in general anything politicians and the ruling class try to sell me in the name of "convenience, safety and security" has me concerned right off the bat!

One of my primary concerns is the potential concentration of power in the hands of unelected officials within central banks. In traditional monetary systems elected representatives and policymakers together impact the economy but with CBDC's unelected officials gain more influence, raising questions about democratic accountability and oversight. Decisions regarding interest rates, money supply and other monetary policy can already be made by small groups without public input but some accountability remains through the intersection of policy and politics.

I come from a technology background within financial services and one of the fundamental security principles (historically termed segregation of duties) is that no singular individual could implement change unilaterally. In CBDC's it's a risk. I hear "but they wouldn't do that, that's not the plan" a lot. It's "not the intended use case". Ask any technology auditor anywhere in the world and they'll tell you it's not what they say they "**won't**" do, it's what they "**can**" do. In this scenario these small unelected groups would be able to do any number of things unilaterally without public oversight, which leads me to my next concern.

PROGRAMMATIC MONEY

So, we have the danger of unelected officials and smaller groups with the ability to make unilateral changes to the money we all need to survive, but in practice what does this mean? This is where I believe the major risks for Consumer, Debtor, Employees reside. Programmatic money means the use of smart contracts which enable predefined rules to be embedded within our financial transactions. This is another advent of the cryptocurrency world (remember, the one these same folks want to tell you is bad).

The functionality is in many ways revolutionary as it removes the requirement for a "middle man" like a bank or financial institution where counterparty trust issues were traditionally resolved. The trust is defined within the smart contract itself and this can be entered into by both sides without paying the middle man (the bank). Sounds great, where's the downside?

Well, one aspect of programmatic money at a central bank level could, for example, be an expiry date. Your money could be given a time limit in which you must spend it or it ceases to exist, you lose it. This can't be done with traditional fiat money because people would simply withdraw notes from the bank and trade them among each other for goods and services. But if we live in a system where debt is required to drive the workforce and debt requires consumerism, as I've been at pains to highlight is our current society, then wouldn't it be a useful thing to be able to give people expiry dates on their money to force them to FOMO spend for the betterment of those who have, not those who have not? Wouldn't it be useful to deprecate cash and coin, moving entirely to CBDC only so people have no choice to withdraw cash to trade among themselves? Why are we seeing so many countries move in this cashless direction, removing hard currency, I wonder?

Another form of programmatic money could be savings limits, where it's simple to impose an upper limit on how much any single individual can have at any time without a permit or licence to hold more. Again, this has been talked about and sounds reasonable from a wealth redistribution perspective if that were the goal. But we live in a society currently where even the elected officials are constantly caught helping their friends and family enrich themselves, so in a scenario where one needs a licence to own more of the money that can be given an expiry date, who might we surmise unelected officials, answering to no-one, might give those licences to? And given the wealth inequality we currently see when the public at least has someone to hold to account, how do you think it might go if said power was out of the public hands entirely as control shifts to those unelected?

Programmatic money also means the ability to limit what one can do with their money. Those unelected officials could pick the winners and losers, who we can spend our own money with and who we can't. Consider the trucker strikes in Canada where those attempting to support had their bank transfers blocked. They still had the option to send crypto payments (despite Canadian authorities trying to block this too) but in a CBDC world those unelected officials get to choose programmatically who is whitelisted and who is blacklisted. What if their family member or friend sets up a new company in competition with your family business and all of a sudden it becomes programmatically impossible to pay your business because you find yourself on a blacklist? "Cancelled" financially with no explanation. People are up in arms about the "de-banking" issues of today, consider this on steroids. "But we wouldn't use it for that". Yes, but you **could**.

Programmatic money is without doubt a technological advance and one with great power as can be seen in the cryptocurrency world. This has been utilised in DeFi (Decentralised Finance) for years proving the use case. The difference, where the risks present, is moving this programmatic potential from being decentralised where a market can dictate winners and losers based on performance, to a centralised version in the hands of unelected bureaucrats who have to answer to no-one. Human history doesn't have a great track record of such power existing and as we heard from Lord Acton earlier "absolute power corrupts absolutely".

Many CBDC proponents would label me a crazy conspiracist for raising these risks because in 2023 that's how we debate, people don't discuss the content of a thesis anymore they discredit the speaker through straw man and subterfuge. So let me say again clearly, I'm not saying this **will** happen, I'm saying it would be made **possible**. For me to embrace CBDC as a net positive I would have to be persuaded these risks could be mitigated to a satisfactory level. To me, privacy and personal freedom are important for the meritocracy approach I prefer. This leads me to...

PRIVACY

Another of my concerns, linked to both unelected officials and programmatic money, is privacy. I think "If you've nothing to hide" rhetoric is both stupid and ignorant of human history.

Firstly, "if you've nothing to hide" presumes nefarious action on the part of the person (or people) who want to retain privacy. Secondly, what someone may want to keep private is completely subjective, no-one gets to be the arbiter of another person's fear, anxiety or insecurity. This Orwellian, 1984 "thought police" line of questioning is tyrannical at best, idiotic at worst. Look at the rise in cancel culture over the past decade, people looking back in history and holding others to the standards of today, standards that have changed significantly (mostly for the better). How would one even know what to hide today given time shifts all goalposts?

Let's continue to use Orwell as an example. With current monetary systems if I purchase one of his books on my Visa debit card then the seller, the remittance company for Visa, my bank and I are involved in the conversation. For the government or the authorities to know I've bought "Animal Farm" (to find out some animals are more equal than others) they must have just cause and convince a judge to allow them to view my financial records to ascertain I've bought it. Animal Farm could be construed as a book with political opinion at odds with our ruling class you see.

With CBDC's, they have access to the detail the second I buy the book from the retailer. No need for just cause or warrant, they have all the date and can then maintain their lists of those who may be opposed to their ideology (whatever it is at the time). Before you know it a knock at the door and an interview with "the thought police" ensues. An extreme example? Yes, of course, I am deliberately making the point extreme. But as I said earlier it's not what "would" be done, it's what "**can**" be done. Human history is littered with evil and as much as we like to think we're highly evolved we're simply animals, mammalians specifically, capable of the most horrific things. We saw during Covid just how divisive things became when an awful lot of people were willing to let those who didn't want vaccinations die if they needed medical treatment, mainstream news personalities even calling for it.

Fear and greed will never go away, I've described how they have existed in perpetuity already. They've been leveraged to do unspeakable things throughout human history, they still are today and even in the west, which likes to consider itself civilised, we saw just how vitriolic things can become when people can be made to perceive their "safety" being infringed by the free will of another. An awful lot of people were willing to give up the freedoms they purport to enjoy for perceived safety while simultaneously willing to throw an awful lot of other people to the wolves who were of no threat to them at all, just for thinking differently. So, this point really concerns me. Freedom of thought is as important as freedom of speech.

INFLATION

The last thing I want to mention is inflationary pressure. Unchecked issuance of digital currency would have similar inflationary impact to fiat currency. If the supply increases rapidly without corresponding economic growth it erodes purchasing power and negatively impact consumers, savers and investors.

This risk obviously exists with standard, non CBDC based fiat too, as we discussed at length. The change here is in the shift of power and lack of public oversight. In my mind this is less of an issue than those I've raised already but still worthy of inclusion.

SUMMARY

I think this covers enough of my concerns to act as a cautionary tale for you, the reader, to stay updated on CBDC developments and question the potential risks. I'm a fan of the technology, given most of it was built in cryptocurrency, but make no mistake CBDC's will **not** be cryptocurrency. They will be centralised implementations of fiat currency with additional benefits to the issuers but significant risks to us, the general public.

I'll certainly be watching developments closely and though we're unable, really, to do anything about their inevitability we must in my view look upon them with some scepticism. Remember don't trust, always verify and it doesn't matter what any individual or group say's they'll do, only what they **can** do. Identify their incentives, project the outcomes. For CBDC's I have concerns about those outcomes by looking at the incentives, who controls them and human history in general (including very recent). I introduce this here to raise these points only for your awareness and consideration.

Summary and Closing

"The most valuable of all talents is that of never using two words when one will do."

[Thomas Jefferson | US Founding Father]

AS I REACH THE END of the content I planned to write, I find myself with the stark realisation I'm cursed with verbosity! I've always enjoyed writing and in my professional life have something of a reputation for the style in which I compose even a simple email, which is to say I don't now nor have I ever seemed to possess the talent which Jefferson describes above.

I went into this well over a year ago thinking 50,000 to 80,000 words for a standard, subject based non-fiction book would be plenty for what I wanted to say, so as I reach the end of the final edit at 133,095 (down from 157,754 in the first draft having had to cut some!) it seems I've managed to use almost exactly two words for every one anticipated, per the Jefferson's quirky quote. I need to work on the talent he ascribes, it would seem! Or write more books!

Never-the-less I want to thank you for sticking with me, for taking the time to work your way through this content and I hope, above all else, you've found it both informative and enjoyable in the context in which it was intended: passing on what I've learned in finance for over 20 years, professionally and personally, to help you and your family thrive.

We covered some technical detail for your financial plan mixed with some of my own personal observations about society and how I think it impacts on our financial goals. While I realise, like most things finance, these external factors will present in different ways based on personal circumstance, hopefully you recognise at the very least the risks and understand why I've raised them.

I hope you've found value here. I hope you now have a financial plan draft you can use to build your financial future. I hope you've been entertained at least a little along the way in what is a dry subject and I hope my observations haven't been too crazy! I won't wish you luck in delivering your financial plan, obviously, but I will wish you well and hope you can use it to deliver the "better" financial outcomes we've discussed throughout.

Ultimately my goal was trying to help as many people as possible in writing this down for my daughter (and hopefully her children and children's children later in life). If she's the one currently reading, you are and will always be the most valuable outcome of my life. I'm proud of you, more so than even 132,000+ words could describe and I hope you find this useful in remaining outside Consumer, Debtor, Employee like you were raised.

The detail I've shared represents the knowledge and practice serving me well for two decades. Every attempt has been made to ensure accuracy of technical information and supporting data, but seldom is anything perfect so I make no such claim. So, don't take my word alone, do your due diligence and if you find a better way, use it. Some technical detail is binary, some my interpretation and some, particularly social and psychological, my observations about our relationship with money and personal finance.

Some may disagree, they may have their own interpretation or method for a particular subject matter and that's OK. As I've said throughout I make no claim to have "the one secret", I've simply shared what I think, what I do and what worked for me. There are many ways to achieve positive outcomes and like I say to those I help in their trading journey "don't get caught up in right and wrong as you'll experience both, sometimes at the same time! All that matters is your process provides an upward sloping equity curve over the long-term". The same applies here. The outcomes can be more objectively measured long-term, so whatever you find works for you, go with that.

Thanks for your time, it has been a pleasure. Let me finish with the same Scottish greeting for health and prosperity that opened the book:

"Lang may yer lum reek!"

And if you didn't Google it then, here's the literal translation for you now, so it makes more sense!

"Long may your chimney smoke!"

Printed in Great Britain
by Amazon

48456415R00198